The Western Australian Jurist

Volume 12

Wokeshevism:

Critical Theories and the Tyrant Left

Augusto Zimmermann

(Editor-in-Chief)

and

Joshua Forrester

(Editor)

Connor Court Publishing

Published by Connor Court Publishing Pty Ltd

Copyright © Augusto Zimmermann and Joshua Forrester 2023 (as editors)

ALL RIGHTS RESERVED. This book contains material protected under International and Federal Copyright Laws and Treaties. Any unauthorised reprint or use of this material is prohibited. No part of this book may be reproduced or transmitted in any form or by any means, electronic or mechanical, including photocopying, recording, or by any information storage and retrieval system without express written permission from the publisher.

PO Box 7257
Redland Bay QLD 4165
sales@connorcourt.com
www.connorcourt.com

ISBN: 9781922815293

Cover design by Maria Giordano

Front cover picture: Flag of gay and trans pride in solidarity with Black Lives Matter, 2 June 2020, Emercado2020, Creative Commons.

The Western Australian Jurist

Editor-in-Chief

Professor Augusto Zimmermann, Sheridan Institute of Higher Education, Australia

Editor

Joshua Forrester, Sheridan Institute of Higher Education, Australia

International Editorial Advisory Board

Emeritus Professor William Wagner, Western Michigan University, USA

Emeritus Professor Jeffrey Goldsworthy, Monash University, Australia

Emeritus Professor Gabriël A. Moens, The University of Queensland, Australia

Professor Luigi Lacchè, Università di Macerata, Italy

Professor Thomas Crofts, The University of Sydney, Australia

Professor Nicholas Aroney, The University of Queensland, Australia

Professor James Allan, The University of Queensland, Australia

Professor Gábor Hamza, Eötvös Loránd University, Hungary

Professor Ermanno Calzolaio, Università di Macerata, Italy

Professor Paulo Emilio Vauthier Borges de Macedo, State University of Rio de Janeiro, Brazil

Neville Rochow SC, The University of Adelaide, Australia

Dr Grzegorz Jan Blicharz, Jagiellonian University, Poland

Professor Steven Alan Samson, Liberty University, USA

Contents

Introduction	17
Augusto Zimmermann and Joshua Forrester	
1 Wokery and High Court 'Otherness'	31
James Allan	
2 The Origins and Impact of Neo-Marxist Ideology and Cancel Culture on the Academy	49
Kevin Donnelly	
3 Freedom of Speech in the Woke Era: The Swastika Ban, Critical Race Theory and State Neutrality	71
Anthony Gray	
4 Critical Theory, Wokeshevism, and The Chasm of Incoherence	115
Peter Kurti	
5 The Genesis of Critical Theory and Cancel Culture	147
Michael McMahon	
6 Vilification Laws: Tools for Tyranny	179
Alexander Millard and John Steenhof	
7 Being Awake to Woke	205
Gabriel A Moens	
8 Cultural Vandalism: Lust to Rule, Road to Ruin	221
Steven Alan Samson	
9 *"Get On Your Marx, Statue Topplers!"* The Links Between Marxism, Racism and Genocide	269
Augusto Zimmermann	
10 Natural Law, God, and Human Dignity	315
Robert P George	
11 Psychological Harm and the Prohibition of 'Conversion Therapy'	339
Andrew Kulikovsky	

12 A Cross-Cultural Analysis of Women, Religion and the Law 377
Laurie Stewart
Book Review: Heart of Wokeness: A Review of *Cynical Theories* 437
and *Counter Wokecraft*
Joshua Forrester

THE EDITORS

Augusto Zimmermann LLB (Hons), LLM *cum laude*, PhD (Monash), DipEd, CIArb is Professor and Head of Law at Sheridan Institute of Higher Education in Perth, Western Australia. He is also the Founder and President of the Western Australian Legal Theory Association ('WALTA'), the Founder and Editor-in-Chief of *The Western Australian Jurist* law journal, an Elected Fellow at the International Academy for the Study of the Jurisprudence of the Family, and a former Vice-President of the Australasian Society of Legal Philosophy. From 2012 to 2017 Professor Zimmermann served as a Law Reform Commissioner with the Law Reform Commission of Western Australia. Professor Zimmermann was also the Murdoch University Law School's Associate Dean for Research (2009-2012). While working at that university, he was awarded the 2012 Vice Chancellor's Award for Excellence in Research, and two Law School Dean's Research Awards, in 2010 and 2011. He served on numerous academic bodies at Murdoch, including: the Research Degree and Scholarships Committee; the Vice Chancellor's Awards and Citations Committee; the Academic Council's Freedom of Speech in Policies and Procedures Advisory Group; and the Academic Staff Promotions Advisory Committee. In January 2015, Professor Zimmermann was invited by the Tasmanian Chief Justice to address the 'Opening of the Legal Year' in that state. He is the author/co-author/editor/co-editor of numerous academic articles and books, including *Christian Foundations of the Common Law* (3 Volumes, Connor Court Publishing, 2018); *No Offence Intended: Why 18C is Wrong* (Connor Court Publishing, 2016); *Global Perspectives on Subsidiarity* (Springer, 2014); and *Western Legal Theory: History, Concepts and Perspectives* (LexisNexis, 2013).

Joshua Forrester is a lecturer at the Sheridan Institute of Higher Education and the Editor of *The Western Australian Jurist*. He graduated with First Class Honours in Politics and International Studies from Murdoch University in 1999. He then graduated with First Class Honours in Law from the University of Western

Australia in 2003. Joshua practiced in commercial litigation and has taught a number of law units. In 2008, he was awarded a Vice-Chancellor's Commendation for Teaching at the University of Notre Dame Australia. Joshua is the lead author of articles appearing in the *University of Western Australia Law Review* and *The Western Australian Jurist*. He is also the lead author of *No Offence Intended: Why 18C is Wrong*, which is listed as one of *The Spectator*'s best books of 2016. A solely-authored chapter of his appears in *Freedom of Religion or Belief: Creating the Constitutional Space for Fundamental Freedoms*, published by Edward Elgar Publishing. His shorter works have appeared in *The Conversation*, *Policy*, and *Quadrant*. Joshua has appeared before various parliamentary inquiries, including the Parliamentary Joint Committee on Human Rights inquiry into s 18C of the *Racial Discrimination Act 1975* (Cth), and the Joint Standing Committee on Foreign Affairs, Defence and Trade Human Rights Sub-Committee inquiry into freedom of religion and belief.

CONTRIBUTORS

James Allan is the Garrick Professor of Law at the University of Queensland. He has degrees from Queen's University, the London School of Economics and the University of Hong Kong. Before arriving in Australia in February of 2005, he spent 11 years teaching law in New Zealand at the University of Otago and before that lectured law in Hong Kong. Professor Allan has had sabbaticals at the Cornell Law School, at the Dalhousie Law School in Canada as the Bertha Wilson Visiting Professor in Human Rights, and at the University of San Diego School of Law. His main areas of interest are legal and moral philosophy, constitutional law and bills of rights. He has published widely in these areas, including in all the top English language legal philosophy journals in the US, the UK, Canada and Australia, much the same being true of constitutional law journals as well. He writes regularly for *The Spectator Australia, Quadrant and The Australian.* His latest book has just come out. *The Age of Foolishness: A Doubter's Guide to Constitutionalism in a Modern Democracy* (Academica Press, 2022).

Kevin Donnelly AM is a Senior Fellow at the PM Glynn Institute at the Australian Catholic University. His PhD thesis (La Trobe University 1994) was entitled: "The New Orthodoxy in English Teaching: A Critique". Kevin is one of Australia's leading conservative education authors and cultural critics. Books include: *Dumbing Down, How Political Correctness is Destroying Australia, The Culture of Freedom, A Politically Correct Dictionary and Guide, Cancel Culture and the Left's Long March, Christianity Matters In These Troubles Times and The Dictionary Of Woke.* Kevin also writes for the daily print media and the London based *The Conservative Woman.* Since first warning about the destructive impact of neo-Marxist inspired critical theory and political correctness in the mid-90s Dr Donnelly has staunchly defended Western Civilisation, Judeo-Christianity and a liberal view of education committed to the pursuit of rationality, truth and wisdom. Kevin taught for 18 years in Victorian government and non-government secondary schools. During that time he was a member of state and national curriculum bodies, including the Victorian Board of Studies, the Year 12 English Panel of Examiners, the Commonwealth funded Discovering Democracy Programme and the Inquiry into the Australian Certificate of Education. In 2014 Kevin was appointed to co-chair a review of the Australian National Curriculum and in 2016 he received an Order of Australia for services to education. Kevin's website is kevindonnelly.com.au.

Robert P George is McCormick Professor of Jurisprudence and Director of the James Madison Program in American Ideals and Institutions at Princeton University. He is also frequently a Visiting Professor at Harvard Law School. In addition to his academic service, Professor George has served as Chairman of the U.S. Commission on International Religious Freedom. He has also served on the President's Council on Bioethics, as a presidential appointee to the United States Commission on Civil Rights, and as the U.S. member of UNESCO's World Commission on the Ethics of Scientific Knowledge and Technology. He is a former Judicial Fellow at the Supreme Court of the United States, where he received the Justice Tom C Clark Award. He serves on the boards of the Templeton Religion Trust, the Lynde and Harry Bradley Foundation, the Ethics and Public Policy Center, the Becket Fund for Religious Liberty, the National Center on Sexual Exploitation, and the Center for Individual Rights, among others. Professor George is author of *Making Men Moral: Civil Liberties and Public Morality* (Oxford University Press, 1993), *In Defense of Natural Law* (Oxford University Press, 1999), *The Clash of Orthodoxies* (ISI, 2001) and *Conscience and Its Enemies* (ISI, 2013). He is co-author of *Conjugal Union: What Marriage Is* (Cambridge University Press, 2014), *Embryo: A Defense of Human Life* (2nd edition, Doubleday, 2011), *Body-Self Dualism in Contemporary Ethics and Politics* (Cambridge University Press, 2008), and *What is Marriage?* (Encounter, 2012). He is editor of several volumes, including *Natural Law Theory: Contemporary Essays* (Oxford University Press, 1992), *The Autonomy of Law: Essays on Legal Positivism* (Oxford University Press, 1996), *Natural Law, Liberalism, and Morality* (Oxford University Press, 1996), and *Great Cases in Constitutional Law* (Princeton University Press, 2000), and co-editor of the *Cambridge Companion to Natural Law* (Cambridge University Press, 2017). Professor George's articles and review essays have appeared in the *Harvard Law Review*, the *Yale Law Journal*, the *Columbia Law Review*, the *University of Chicago Law Review*, the *Review of Politics*, the *Review of Metaphysics*, and the *American Journal of Jurisprudence*. He has also written for the *New York Times*, the *Wall Street Journal*, the *Washington Post*, *First Things*, the *Boston Review*, and the *Times Literary Supplement*. A graduate of Swarthmore College, Professor George holds MTS and JD degrees from Harvard University and the degrees of DPhil, BCL, DCL, and DLitt from Oxford University. He holds twenty-two honorary degrees, including doctorates of law, letters, ethics, science, divinity, humane letters, civil law, law and moral values, humanities, and juridical science. He is a recipient of the United States Presidential Citizens Medal, the Honorific Medal for the Defense of Human Rights of the Republic of Poland, the Bradley Prize for Intellectual and Civic Achievement, the Philip Merrill Award of the American Council of Trustees and Alumni, the Paul Bator Award of the Federalist Society for Law and Public Policy, the Sidney Hook Award of the National Association of Scholars, a Silver Gavel Award of the American Bar Association, the Charles Fried Award of the Harvard Law School Federalist Society, the Irving Kristol Award of the American Enterprise Institute, and Princeton University's President's Award for Distinguished Teaching.

Anthony Gray is a Professor of Law and Associate Head – Research at the School of Law and Justice at the University of Southern Queensland. He has published more than 130 sole-authored refereed articles, and has authored numerous research monographs, including 'Evolution from Strict Liability to Fault in Law of Torts' (Hart, 2021), 'Freedom of Speech in Practice: Controversial Applications of Law and Theory' (Lexington, 2019), and 'Freedom of Speech in the West: Comparison and Critique' (Lexington, 2019). He specialises in constitutional law and human rights, including freedom of speech. He is a former Director at the Queensland Law Society, and former consultant with Engineering Education Australia.

Andrew S Kulikovsky LLB, BAppSc (Hons), MA is the author of numerous academic articles and the book entitled *Creation, Fall, Restoration: A Biblical Theology of Creation* (Mentor Press, 2009), which provides a case for the authority of Scripture in all areas it discusses, in particular in the area of origins. Andrew is a PhD candidate at Charles Sturt University in the areas of public policy and theology, specifically in the application of Thomas Sowell's *A Conflict of Visions*.

Peter Kurti is Director of the Culture, Prosperity & Civil Society program at the Centre of Independent Studies ('CIS'), in Sydney. He is also Adjunct Associate Professor in the School of Law at the University of Notre Dame Australia, and Adjunct Research Fellow at the Australian Centre for Christianity and Culture at Charles Sturt University. He has written extensively about issues of religion, liberty, and civil society in Australia, and appears frequently as a commentator on television and radio. He is the author of *The Tyranny of Tolerance: Threats to Religious Liberty in Australia; Euthanasia: Seven Questions About Voluntary Assisted Dying*; and *Sacred & Profane: Faith and Belief in a Secular Society*, published by Connor Court Publishing. He is a Fellow of the Royal Society of Arts, and an ordained minister in the Anglican Church of Australia.

Fr Michael McMahon OMI holds a BA (Hons) in Philosophy from the University College Dublin, and a MA in Psychoanalysis from Deakin University. He is specialised in EMDR and trauma therapy. Presently lecturing in Literature, English and Religious Education at Mazenod and St Brigid's Colleges Lesmurdie, Fr Michael worked for over 40 years as a psychotherapist and family therapist in Brisbane, Melbourne and Perth. He has trained counsellors and therapists in Papua New Guinea, Brisbane and Perth.

Alexander Millard is a solicitor at the Human Rights Law Alliance ('HRLA'). He graduated with First Class Honours in International and Global Studies from the University of Sydney in 2014, his honours thesis exploring the institutional development of the European Union.

He then graduated with a Juris Doctor in Law from the University of Sydney in 2018. After several years at a private consultancy, Alexander joined the legal team at HRLA to work for the protection of religious freedom rights of Christians and other religious groups in Australia.

Gabriël A Moens AM is Emeritus Professor of Law, The University of Queensland. He served as Pro Vice Chancellor, Dean and Professor of Law, Murdoch University. He also served as Head, Graduate School of Law, The University of Notre Dame Australia; Garrick Professor of Law, The University of Queensland; and Professor of Law, Curtin University. In 1999, Professor Moens received the Australian Award for University Teaching in Law and Legal Studies. In 2003, the Prime Minister of Australia awarded him the Australian Centenary Medal for services to education. He was named the "International Alumnus of the Year" by the Pritzker Law School of Northwestern University, Chicago in 2019. In June 2019 he was appointed a Member of the Order of Australia (AM) for services to the law and higher education. Professor Moens is a *Membre Titulaire*, International Academy of Comparative Law, Paris; a Fellow of the Australian Institute of Management (WA); a Fellow of the College of Law; a Fellow of the Australian Academy of Law, and a Fellow of the Australian Centre for International Commercial Arbitration (ACICA). He is author/co-author/editor/co-editor of *Enduring Ideas*, Connor Court Publishing 2020; *The Himalaya Clause*, Connor Court Publishing, 2020; *Law of International Business in Australasia* (2nd ed), The Federation Press, 2019; *The Constitution of the Commonwealth of Australia Annotated* (9th ed, LexisNexis Butterworths, 2016); *Arbitration and Dispute Resolution in the Resources Sector: An Australian Perspective* (Springer, 2015); *Jurisprudence of Liberty* (2nd ed, LexisNexis, 2011); *Commercial Law of the European Union* (Springer, 2010); and *International Trade and Business: Law, Policy and Ethics* (Routledge/Cavendish, 2nd ed, 2006). His debut novel *A Twisted Choice*, a thriller exploring the origins of Covid-19, was published in 2020 by Boolarong Press. A short story, entitled 'The Greedy Prospector', appeared in an anthology of short stories, *The Outback*, in 2021.

Steven Alan Samson is a retired Professor of Government and former Department Chairman with the Helms School of Government at Liberty University who also has taught history, geography, and humanities since 1977. His research and writing focus on the European and American intellectual, cultural, and constitutional traditions, giving particular attention to the influence of Christianity and its ideological challengers. Dr Samson holds the BA and MA degrees in political science from the University of Colorado and the PhD from the University of Oregon. He is a member of the Philadelphia Society, the Academy of Philosophy and Letters. He was also a board member of University Professors for Academic Order and a Salvatori Fellow with the Heritage Foundation. A resident of Washington State, he pursues research and educational projects, occasionally gives guest lectures, and writes for such publications as The Market for Ideas, Townhall Finance, and Review of Social and Economic Issues.

John Steenhof is the principal lawyer at the Human Rights Law Alliance ('HRLA'). HRLA is an independent, not-for-profit Australian law firm that specialises in protecting the religious freedoms of Australians. John graduated from the University of Otago in 2000 with degrees in law and science and has over twenty years commercial practice experience that includes starting his own successful firm in Western Australia. In 2019 John started HRLA and since then has been regularly acting for clients in religious freedom cases, advising Christians and religious groups on how to preserve their legal rights to act in accordance with their beliefs. John also appears at numerous parliamentary committee review hearings, advocating at Federal and State level for laws that protect fundamental religious freedoms.

Laurie Anne Stewart earned her Juris Doctor degree from Chapman University School of Law in Orange, California; her MA in Christian Apologetics from the Talbot School of Theology (Biola University) in La Mirada, CA; and her BA from California State University Fullerton. Laurie is licensed to practice law in California and in Iowa. Trained in conflict coaching, mediation, and arbitration, Laurie assists parties in negotiating to resolve disputes. In Iowa, she served as President for Iowa Association of Mediators and on the Council for the ADR section of the Iowa State Bar Association. Laurie had the privilege of serving on the Iowa Supreme Court Family Law Task Force ADR Work Group. As a trial attorney, Laurie has represented plaintiffs and defendants in a wide variety of civil matters, including defending religious liberty and traditional family values. In 2006, she received the C William Carlson award from Pacific Justice Institute for her "exceptional level of integrity and commitment." In California, Laurie has served on the board of Women in Apologetics, the Orange County chapter of the Federalist Society, Orange County Women's Lawyers, and Marketplace Women of Orange County. She currently serves on the board of Ratio Christi, Peacemaker Ministries, and Intelligent Faith. Laurie is also an Adjunct Professor at Trinity Law School.

Introduction
Wokeshevism: Critical Theories and the Tyrant Left

AUGUSTO ZIMMERMANN* AND JOSHUA FORRESTER**

I INTRODUCTION

We live in revolutionary times. While this revolution has been brewing for some time, the death of George Floyd on 25 May 2020 catalysed it. In the aftermath of his death, many rioted and cities burned. Statues fell, not just of Confederate leaders like Robert E Lee and Jefferson Davis, but also Union leaders like US Grant and Abraham Lincoln and American Founders like George Washington and Thomas Jefferson.[1] Books like Robin DiAngelo's *White Fragility* and Ibram X Kendi's *How to Be an Antiracist* became bestsellers. Corporations dedicated themselves to social justice and racial justice.

---

[1] See, eg, '4 charged after statue toppled at Montgomery's Robert E Lee High School', *WSFA 12 News* (Web Article, 3 June 2020); Mark Katkov, 'Protestors Topple Jefferson Davis Statue in Richmond, Va', *NPR* (Web Article, 11 June 2020); Marty Johnson, 'Protestors tear down statues of Ulysses S Grant, national anthem lyricist Francis Scott Key', *The Hill* (Web Article, 20 June 2020); Mike Baker, 'Protestors in Portland Topple Statues of Lincoln and Roosevelt', *New York Times* (Web Article, 12 October 2020); David Williams, 'Protestors tore down a George Washington statue and set a fire on its head', *CNN* (Web Article, 19 June 2020); 'Thomas Jefferson statue toppled in Portland, Oregon' *CBS News* (Web Article, 15 June 2020).

---

* Head of Law, Sheridan Institute of Higher Education.
** Lecturer, Sheridan Institute of Higher Education.

A new, more extreme brand of leftist thought has caught fire, consuming the old brand of left-liberalism. In an article for *Tablet Magazine*,[2] Bari Weiss observes:

> No one has yet decided on the name for the force that has come to unseat liberalism. Some say it's 'Social Justice.' The author Rod Dreher has called it 'therapeutic totalitarianism.' The writer Wesley Yang refers to it as 'the successor ideology' – as in, the successor to liberalism.
>
> At some point, it will have a formal name, one that properly describes its mixture of postmodernism, postcolonialism, identity politics, neo-Marxism, critical race theory, intersectionality, and the therapeutic mentality.

We call it 'Wokeshevism'.

II WOKESHEVISM

> The defeat of communism in the USSR… by no means assures its defeat in the world. Indeed, the release of the West from its conflict with the East emancipates utopian communism at home from the suspicion of… affinity with an external enemy. The struggle for the preservation of western civilization has entered a new – and perhaps far more deadly and dangerous – phase.[3]

The end of the Cold War was the cause for celebration and hope in the

---

[2] Bari Weiss, 'Stop Being Shocked', *Tablet Magazine* (Web Article, 15 October 2020).
[3] Harry V Jaffa, 'The Long Arm of Socialism', *The Claremont Review of Books* (Web Article, 27 April 2016).

West and around the world. In the fight against liberalism and communism, liberalism had prevailed. The above quote is from a speech Harry V Jaffa gave in 1991 and, at the time, could be considered alarmist. Not anymore. The war was only half-won. An opponent only gives up when they know they are beaten. The adherents of economic Marxism knew that they were beaten, but there were other forms of Marxism out there...

The term 'Wokeshevism' is a portmanteau of 'woke' and 'Bolshevism'.[4] The term 'woke' is relatively new, but what does it mean? Helen Pluckrose and James Lindsay observe that the woke worldview:

> [Stems] from a very peculiar view of the world – one that even speaks its own language in a way. Within the English-speaking world, they speak English, but they use everyday words differently from the rest of us. When they speak of 'racism', for example, they are not referring to prejudice on the grounds of race, but rather to, as they define it, a racialized system that permeates all interactions in society yet is largely invisible except to those who experience it or who have been trained in the proper 'critical' methods that train them to see it. (These are the people sometimes referred to as being 'woke', meaning awakened, to it.)[5]

Pluckrose and Lindsay continue:

> They are obsessed with power, language, knowledge, and the relationships between them. They interpret the world through a

---

[4] The earliest record of the use of this term that we can find is Frank Pinelander, 'Bokhari: Activism Not Journalism - CNN Pressures Brands to Join Facebook Ad Boycott', *Disqus* (Comment, 1 July, 2020).
[5] Helen Pluckrose and James Lindsay, *Cynical Theories: How Activist Scholarship Made Everything about Race, Gender, and Indentity – and Why This Harms Everyone* (Swift Press, 2020) 15.

lens that detects power dynamics in every interaction, utterance, and cultural artefact – even when they aren't obvious or *real*. This is a worldview that centres social and cultural grievances and aims to make everything a zero-sum political struggle revolving around identity markers like race, sex, gender, sexuality, and many others.[6]

Charles Pincourt and James Lindsay note that:

> Woke is a term given both to a worldview and to the people who are initiated, and adhere, to that worldview. The worldview is known under several pseudonyms: the Critical Perspective, Social Justice, and the Critical Social Justice ... perspective.[7]

Lindsay notes:

> The term 'Woke' refers to being 'awakened' or 'woke up' to the alleged realities of 'systemic power dynamics' that order society. These alleged power dynamics are said to create what sociologists call 'stratifications' in society, like kinds of upper and lower classes, depending on who has 'privilege' and who is 'oppressed' by various power dynamics like systemic racism (or white supremacy), systemic sexism (or patriarchy or misogyny), cis-heteronormativity, and so on. A certain unreality attends these arguments too, as these power dynamics are often described using dense technical jargon and making use of words in ways that seem at least slightly distorted from their original intended meanings. The Marxian flavour of this analysis – which sees them as structural and sites of necessary conflict – is also

---

[6] Ibid 15-16 (emphasis in original).
[7] Charles Pincourt and James Lindsay, *Counter Wokecraft: A Field Manual for Combatting the Woke in the University and Beyond* (Independently published, 2021). The term 'Critical Social Justice' is perhaps the closest fit for the 'formal name' noted by Bari Weiss, at least in terms of its intellectual worldview: see Weiss (n 2). As we note below, 'Wokeshevism' encompasses the zeal with which this worldview is imposed on all parts of society.

obvious but hard to pin down.[8]

Bolshevism is 'the political theory and practice of the Bolshevik Party which, under Lenin, came to power during the Russian Revolution of 1917.'[9] According to Richard Pipes, Bolsheviks embraced a philosophy of '"merciless" violence ... that strove for the destruction of every actual and potential opponent'.[10] They displayed 'a philosophical inability to deal with opinions different from their own except by abuse and repression'.[11] For these reasons, Pipes adds, 'they should be regarded not as utopians but as fanatics'.[12]

Bolsheviks rejected objective morality as a form of 'bourgeois oppression'.[13] For Bolsheviks, 'all moral questions were ultimately subordinated to the Revolution's needs'.[14] They identified themselves 'as a moral as well as political vanguard, whose messianic sense of leadership demanded that its members prove their worthiness to belong to that elite'.[15] Orlando Figes notes:

> Bolsheviks were expected ... to be involved in the daily practice of its rituals – its oaths and songs, ceremonies, cults, and codes of conduct – just as the believers of organized religion performed their belief when they attended church. But the Party's doctrines

---

[8] James Lindsay, 'Forward' in Charles Pincourt and James Lindsay, *Counter Wokecraft: A Field Manual for Combatting the Woke in the University and Beyond* (Independently published, 2021).
[9] 'Bolshevism', *Oxford Reference* (Web Page).
[10] Richard Pipes, 'Did the Russian Revolution Have to Happen?' (1994) 63(2) *The American Scholar* 215, 226.
[11] Ibid
[12] Ibid.
[13] Orlando Figes, *The Whisperers: Private Life in Stalin's Russia* (Penguin Books, 2007) 33.
[14] Augusto Zimmermann, *Western Legal Theory* (LexisNexis Butterworths, 2013) 203. It should be noted that this paragraph is based on material previously published in this work at 203.
[15] Figes (n 13) 33.

were to be taken as articles of faith by all its followers. Its collective judgement was to be accepted as Justice. Accused of crimes by the leadership, the Party member was expected to repent, to go down on his knees before the Party and welcome its verdict against him. To defend oneself was to add another crime: dissent from the will of the Party.[16]

'Wokeshevism' thus denotes the woke's revolutionary zeal to impose their worldview on all parts of society, and to crush any dissent.

III CRITICAL THEORIES

I do not, frankly, think that the [academic left] have superior ideas. Rather, they have something that may be more important for having an impact on the way things are actually done. They have more energy and enthusiasm, not to say fanaticism and intolerance. In the long run these may be more effective in changing universities than rigorous arguments.[17]

The above quote was taken from an article that John Searle wrote in 1993. His statement has proven prophetic. However, it has especial

---

[16] Ibid 34. This may explain why so many Bolsheviks surrendered to their fate in the purges under Joseph Stalin in the 1930s, even when they were innocent of the crimes of which they stood accused: at 33.

[17] John R Searle, 'Is There a Crisis in American Higher Education?' (1993) 46(4) *Bulletin of the American Academy of Arts and Sciences* 24, 41. Searle spoke of a conflict between 'traditionalists' and 'challengers' in the teaching of the humanities. At 24-25, Searle noted that the 'challengers' were:
[A]uthors from a variety of points of view: Marxists, feminists, deconstructionists, and people active in ethnic studies and gay studies, as well as many former 1960s-style student radicals who are now middle-aged university professors. Most of these opponents... in spite of their diversity, are of the left-wing political persuasion, and they tend to write in tones of moral outrage - the outrage of those who are exposing vast and nameless oppressive conspiracies - which we have come to expect from the academic left since the 1960s.

poignancy for the legal academy, for it is here that key theories driving Wokeshevism were nurtured. Drawing on Critical Theory,[18] Critical Legal Studies gave rise to Critical Race Theory ('CRT'),[19] which is now perhaps the most influential of the 'critical theories'.[20] As one of CRT's founders, Angela Harris, observes:

> [CRT] has exploded from a narrow sub-specialty of jurisprudence chiefly of interest to academic lawyers into a literature read in departments of education, cultural studies, English, sociology, comparative literature, political science, history, and anthropology around the country.

Given its role in Wokeshevism's creation, it is incumbent on the legal academy to play a role in combatting it. This volume of *The Western Australian Jurist* is intended to help with this task.

IV THE TYRANT LEFT

What do we mean by the 'tyrant left'? Here, it is useful to distinguish between the 'tyrant left' and the 'free left'. Both the tyrant left and the free left adopt left-wing political positions. However, the distinguishing characteristic of those in the free left is their commitment to fundamental freedoms, especially freedom of expression. They are willing to engage in debate, and are prepared to adopt a 'live and let

---

[18] Jay M Feinman, 'The Failure of Legal Education and the Promise of Critical Legal Studies' (1985) 6 *Cardozo Law Review* 739, 757.
[19] Brian H Bix, *Jurisprudence: Theory and Context* (Sweet & Maxwell, 7th ed, 2015) 238.
[20] Angela Harris, 'Foreword' in Richard Delgado and Jean Stefancic, *Critical Race Theory: An Introduction* (New York University Press, 3rd ed, 2017) xvi.

live' position to those with whom they disagree.

The tyrant left, however, is distinguished by its disdain for fundamental freedoms, especially freedom of expression. (In our view, the disdain for freedom of expression is one of the 'tyrant tells'.) Hence, they have no hesitation using any of all of the tools of 'cancel culture': ostracising, deplatforming, sacking, or encouraging others to do these things. Further, they support laws (such as "hate speech" laws) to prohibit speech they don't like. Finally, the tyrant left is totalitarian: there can be no 'live and let live'. Everyone in society must accept their views or be punished by society, the state, or both.

The tyrant left has had other iterations, such as Bolshevism and Maoism. Wokeshevism is but the latest one.

Wokeshevists no doubt think they are serving good by fighting oppression wherever it is found (which, apparently, is everywhere). However, this brings to mind the following quote from CS Lewis:

> Of all tyrannies, a tyranny exercised for the good of its victims may be the most oppressive. It may be better to live under robber barons than under omnipotent moral busybodies. The robber baron's cruelty may sometimes sleep, his cupidity may at some point be satiated; but those who torment us for our own good will torment us without end, for they do so with the approval of their own conscience.[21]

We also question whether Wokeshevism actually serves good. All manner of state and societal measures are justified to fight "oppressors". There appears to be no limiting principle to Wokeshevist actions, apart

---

[21] CS Lewis, *God in the Dock: Essays on Theology and Ethics* (William B Eerdmans Publishing Company, 1970) 292.

from (maybe) 'defer to those more oppressed than you'. This leads to what has been described as 'Oppression Olympics': a competition to see who is more oppressed.[22] Pluckrose and Lindsay note that contests over who is more oppressed create a 'caste system of social justice'.[23]

To recall what Bari Weiss said earlier in this introduction, left liberalism is being subsumed by the ideology that we have called Wokshevism. We hope this volume of *The Western Australian Jurist* is useful to those who value liberty, including those on the free left.

V AN OVERVIEW OF THIS VOLUME

This volume of *The Western Australian Jurist* is split into three sections. The first section deals with the topic of Wokeshevism. The second section contains general articles. The third section contains a book review.

Here is an overview of the chapters in the first section:

- Professor James Allan remarks that he is spoiled for choice when writing about Wokeshevism. However, he settles on discussing the High Court of Australia's decision in *Love v The Commonwealth*,[24] which he describes as 'wokeness on steroids'. (We note that since Professor Allan wrote his chapter, the Coalition government under Prime Minister Scott Morrison sought to overturn *Love*. However, the new Labor government under Prime Minister Anthony Albanese

---
[22] See the discussion in Joshua Forrester, Lorraine Finlay and Augusto Zimmermann, *No Offence Intended: Why 18C is Wrong* (Connor Court, 2016) 232-238.
[23] Pluckrose and Lindsay (n 63) 128-131.
[24] [2020] HCA 3; (2020) 270 CLR 152 ('*Love*').

dropped the case.)²⁵

- Dr Kevin Donnelly AM covers the impact of Critical Theory and cancel culture on higher education. Moves to 'decolonise' the curriculum have undermined the search for wisdom and truth that once characterised a liberal education. Fortunately, Dr Donnelly notes signs of resistance to this trend.

- Professor Anthony Gray examines the use of postmodern CRT to justify restrictions on freedom of speech. Noting that all sides of politics should support freedom of speech (but are not doing so), he calls for strong speech to defend it.

- Peter Kurti argues that Critical Theory significantly influences public discourse in Australia, and that it threatens liberal traditions of tolerance and liberty. He examines the flaws in Critical Theory, and provides principles to guide responses to critics who condemn Australia as systemically racist, misogynistic, homophobic, and colonial.

- Michael McMahon traces the intellectual origins of 'Cancel Culture', noting the influence of Sigmund Freud, Friedrich Nietzsche, Karl Marx, Antonio Gramsci, Michel Foucault and the Frankfurt School. He uses the concept of 'vision' to determine what drives Critical Theory and Cancel Culture, and evaluates the latter's effects on society.

- Alex Millard and John Steenhof examine the influence of Critical Theory on certain Australian vilification laws. They argue that these laws are strongly connected to core principles of Critical

---

[25] Paul Karp, 'Labor drops Coalition bid to overturn high court ruling that Indigenous Australians can't be aliens', *The Guardian* (Web Article, 28 July 2022).

Theory. However, these principles are antithetical to a healthy democracy and a free exchange of ideas. Hence, vilification laws risk suppressing debate and eroding Australian democracy.

- Professor Gabriël Moens AM discusses two interrelated aspects of Wokeshevism, the Black Lives Matter ('BLM') Movement and CRT, in the context of the destruction of monuments and statues. He notes that the BLM Movement aims to eradicate endemic racism, and that CRT argues that non-white people experience systemic discrimination. However, both the BLM Movement and CRT reintroduce race as a defining characteristic to divide society.

- Professor Steven Samson considers the state of Western civilization in light of the decline of its Christian faith. Now that cultural revolutionaries have come to claim Western civilization, whether it endures depends on the mettle of those who inherited it.

- Professor Augusto Zimmermann[26] examines the influence of Marx on Adolf Hitler and the Nazis. He argues that Marxism prepares the ideological mindset for state-sanctioned extermination of people on a massive scale. He notes the obvious similarities between Marxist class-warfare that destroys people because of social class, and Nazi race-warfare that destroys people because of ethnicity.

Here is an overview of the chapters in the second section:

- Andrew Kulikovsky examines the assumptions and claims supporting legislation banning 'conversion therapy' in certain Australian jurisdictions. He argues that these assumptions and claims are without foundation, and those supporting such bans

---

[26] Please excuse us for referring to ourselves in the third person when describing our respective contributions to this volume.

have become increasingly intolerant and authoritarian.

- Professor Robert P George addresses questions of natural law, the natural law theory of human dignity and of human rights, the role that ideas and beliefs about God and the divine will play in natural rights, and whether natural law theories are fundamentally concerned with rules or with virtues. He also addresses distinctions between new natural law theory and other natural law theories, and between new natural law theory and utilitarian and Kantian theories.

- Laurie Stewart compares four major worldviews and their impact on laws regarding the treatment of women. These worldviews are Islam, Hinduism, Atheism, and Christianity. She argues that Christianity is the only worldview that offers the best hope for recognising the value, dignity, worth and equality of women.

In the book review section, Joshua Forrester returns to the subject of Wokeshevism by reviewing *Cynical Theories: How Activist Scholarship Made Everything about Race, Gender, and Indentity – and Why This Harms Everyone*, and *Counter Wokecraft: A Field Manual for Combatting the Woke in the University and Beyond*.

VI LOOKING AHEAD

The topic for the next volume of *The Western Australian Jurist* is, simply, *Against Tyranny*. Exploring this topic may well provide an opportunity to revisit the topic of this volume, as well as that of the last volume (*Fundamental Rights in the Age of Covid-19*).

As we said earlier, the legal academy has a role to play in combatting Wokeshevism. We hope this volume of *The Western Australian Jurist* will help identify issues with it as well as ways to combat it peaceably. As Forrester notes in his book review, this fight 'will take place in workplaces, classrooms, boardrooms, bureaucracies, and in all forms of media, arts, and entertainment.' Our opponents are determined, but they are far from unbeatable. Let's get to work.

1

Wokery and High Court 'Otherness'

JAMES ALLAN*

ABSTRACT

In this article the author explains why he was spoilt for choice when asked by this review to write an article on the tendency towards wokery in today's Australian law schools, amongst the lawyerly caste more generally in this country, and across so many (and much) of our key institutions. Cancel culture limits on free speech, the emergence of a sort of 'Oppression Olympics' whereby self-declared victim groups compete to feel the most victimised, the wider rise of an illiberal identity politics, the list of potential topics goes on and on and are noted by the author. He then settles on illustrating the woke credentials of our High Court of Australia in the recent Love case. Indeed, the author concludes, depressingly, that this case was an instance of wokeness on steroids that emanated from our top court.

I FIRST CONSIDERATIONS

It is not often in today's legal academy that one is asked to write a paper on the theme of 'Wokeshevism: Critical Theories and the Tyrant Left'. Actually, nothing like it had ever happened to me before. Yes, yes, yes whole forests are daily felled to provide the paper to write

---

* Garrick Professor of Law, University of Queensland.

law review articles on the many intellectual delights of the preening social justice brigades. With little effort one can find myriad articles that might easily be classed as detailing the travails of some self-declared "victim of oppression" group or other – and this despite the fact that life in today's West is plainly the best time (in material and life opportunity terms) for anyone, ever, to have been alive – a point doubly true for women and for minority groups in the West (as compared to minorities anywhere else on the planet, ever).[1]

Or one can find all the social justice type articles advocating judicial activism and 'living tree' constitutional interpretation avenues and approaches in order to cure the perceived lapses or failings of the democratically elected Parliament. Or one can also find that portion of the legal literature aimed at supercharging 'corporate social responsibility', for some like me this being a route to allow woke, *uber* progressive and virtue-signalling corporate managers and boards to ignore shareholders' concerns about better company performance and higher stock prices in favour of almost universally left-leaning political concerns, concerns that when I went through Canadian law school in the mid-1980s would have been considered far outside the legitimate and proper remit of CEOs, HR departments (then just 'personnel departments') and boards and probably a breach of the 'best interests of the owner-shareholders' duty or 'shareholder primacy' rule.

And those examples are just off the top of my head and without even venturing into the countless peer-reviewed law articles that touch on transgenderism, feminism, critical race theory, refugees, and anti-

---

[1] Matthew Ridley, *The Rational Optimist: How Prosperity Evolves* (Harper Perennial, 2010); Matthew Ridley, 'Cheer up!', *Readers Digest* (Web Article, 6 April 2020).

colonialism. Or that support further legislative changes that promote diversity concerns, that favour "hate speech" type inroads on free speech, that look a lot like the wailing and gnashing of teeth about the supposed rise of populism, or that amount to calls for the winding back of the presumption of innocence when it comes to certain disfavoured groups (the reader here being invited to fill in the blanks of today's most obvious disfavoured groups).

In that sort of academic world, the one in which Australia's legal academics today inhabit, the reader will quickly appreciate why the invitation to write an article for the theme of this special issue, 'Wokeshevism', came as such a surprise. And was so welcome. As I said, nothing like it had ever happened to me before; and it was difficult to get out of my head the thought of how delightful the eventual release of this special issue was going to be. I could imagine the pleasure of watching the *Guardian*-reading left-wing academics fulminating in rage. Possibly my getting married and seeing the birth of my first-born would score higher in the pleasurable stakes. But only possibly.

II THE PARADOX OF CHOICE

Of course, the invitation to prepare this article also brought with it the paradox of choice.[2] This is the problem that occurs when one has too much choice, too many choices, over great abundance and experiences a sort of cognitive overload, finding it difficult to make a decision. All sorts of possible topics for my paper ran through my head, amongst

---

[2] Barry Schwartz, *The Paradox of Choice: Why More is Less* (Harper Perennial, 2005); Daniel Kahneman, *Thinking Fast and Slow* (Farrar, Straus and Giroux, 2011).

them potential pieces on the woke, cancel-culture universities; or maybe I would write something on the 'Oppression Olympics', on how supposed victim groups in the world of identity politics seemingly form a sort of informal, "laid-down by no one" league table or ordinal ranking of "victimhood" – do transgender former males competing in women's sports win out against lesbian female athletes now unable to compete, or do they lose? Do radical Muslim terrorists rank higher up the victim hierarchy or do homosexuals who would fare rather badly should the ideology of the terrorists prevail? That, I thought, might work as a pretty good topic. It was certainly a catchy title.

Then again, the philosopher in me wondered if I should go big ticket and talk about why I thought wokeness was like a sort of new religion for the secular age. This would relate to a claim I had recently made in a chapter of the book *Forgotten Freedom No More: Protecting Religious Liberty in Australia*.[3] There, as an atheist myself, I had not only admitted the often over-looked good that the religious worldview inspires. I had also speculated about the need most people have to believe in something in transcendent terms, as of higher value, perhaps in almost timeless terms. Here is what I wrote:

> Here's another factor that gets little attention. In the absence of a Christian (or other mainstream religious) worldview, how many people are likely to be content or able to function at all with what looks to be a corollary of atheism, namely a fairly bleak picture of a meaningless world where a human 'is of no greater importance to the universe than that of an oyster' (to quote Mr Hume again)? Your Bertrand Russells and your David

---

[3] James Allan, 'A Humean Take on Religious Freedom' in Robert Forsyth and Peter Kurti (eds), *Forgotten Freedom No More: Protecting Religious Liberty in Australia* (Connor Court, 2020) 133.

Humes, yes. But one suspects the vast preponderance of people who forswear the religious mindset with one hand will, with the other, have a deep need to welcome it back into their lives in some different guise. They might substitute worship of the planet, of Gaia, and instil that with some deeper significance – though truth be told, why some tiny dot of a planet in an obscure, far-flung galaxy in an ever-expanding universe should warrant that sort of souped-up, steroid-enhanced level of concern (absent a benevolent, theistic God) is not wholly clear. As a subset of that they might re-direct the religious impulse towards, say, lowering carbon dioxide emissions, again with a near religious impulse. Or they might infuse vegetarianism with this redirected spiritual vigour. The possibilities are many. And more than one commentator has suggested that most (perhaps almost all) non-believers will not actually jettison Christianity or Judaism or Islam for some bleak Bertrand Russell-like atheism, but rather for some version or other of these modern day types of Paganism. It won't exactly be a return to the Roman Republic before Christ; but there will be parallels – possibly including the tendency to live in the here and now, gratifying what you can as soon as you can. And if there be any truth in that, then the cost-benefit analysis of whether a widespread belief in a benevolent, theistic God be an overall plus or minus must include the consequences of that sort of redirected Paganistic zeal as well.[4]

As I said there, the possibilities of redirected religious zeal are many, and so maybe a big picture philosophical speculation on how a sort of woke, virtue-signalling fervour in favour of an ill-defined 'equity' and 'diversity' and general commitment to 'wokeness'– ramped up to whatever degree of transcendence the particular adherent prefers – has replaced traditional Christian beliefs might make a good article for

---

[4]   Ibid 136-137.

this special issue. I was tempted.

I was also tempted by a variant of that sort of article. Maybe I might do a review article type piece on the book *Cynical Theories* by Helen Pluckrose and James Lindsay.[5] That book tries to explain the thinking behind a whole range of currently popular theories about race, colonialism, queerness, gender, disabilities, and the so on. If nothing else the book is quite eye-opening. The gist of the authors' claims is that all these theories are operating from a similar mindset or position, one heavily influenced by Michel Foucault and Jacques Derrida, and behind them perhaps Friedrich Nietzsche.

The basic premises of all these theories – the ones we might lump together under such headings as 'wokeness' or 'wokeshevism' – is that they all seem to assert that everything (not only gender but sex itself, race, even disability) is socially constructed. The nature-nurture divide or question becomes a one-horse race.[6] And the corollary of that is that everything is about, by, and for power. It is power all the way down that undergirds all these theories about race, colonialism, queerness, gender, disabilities, and so on. And from that bleak, austere starting position readers might think that no normative conclusions would follow. Wrong. In fact, these so-called cynical theories lying at the heart of cancel culture and of wokeness are heavily normative. Here it gets speculative but it seems, as far as one can tell, that the

---

[5] Helen Pluckrose and James Lindsay, *Cynical Theories: How Universities Made Everything About Race, Gender and Identity – And Why This Harms Everyone* (Swift Press, 2020).

[6] Which to my way of thinking means that for such adherents of these Cynical Theories, *inter alia*, that evolutionary thinking and theories about humans flowing from a general belief in evolution have to be rejected out of hand as does thinking about humans as in any way like animals. It is scientifically illiterate in other words, though such Cynical Theories may well be strong enough politically to silence and cow real life scientists.

normativity comes from a sort of deep-seated passion for equality. Or maybe, as an American friend suggested to me, it is more like a powerful resentment of anything that is less than perfect equality.⁷ Or think of it this way. The core motivating principle of these theories, in basic terms, is that everything in society – absolutely everything – has been constructed to favour the powerful (or "privileged") over the weak (or "oppressed"). As a result, it all should be deconstructed or torn down. In terms of being founded on reductionist first principles these sort of theories put Marxism to shame. Moreover, no matter how charitable your reading might be, it is hard to see them as anything other than nihilistic theories. The classical liberal assumptions that most of us bring to the table – that individuals are real; that some aspects of human nature are hard-wired into us by millions of years of evolution; that race is sort of real in some half-baked sense, even if the classifications are scientific nonsense and pretty much arbitrary; that racism is a real, actual feature of the world that involves an intentional act or state of mind; and so on – all get thrown out the window if you adopt the worldview of these cynical theories. Everything, all of it, is socially constructed and about power we are to believe. As I said, I was tempted to do my invited article along those sort of lines as well.

III CONSTITUTIONALISING IDENTITY POLITICS

However, I resisted both those temptations and more besides. In the end, what with this being a law review and all and my not wanting to write a book-length diatribe, I opted to write on the wokeness of our top court in the case of *Love v Commonwealth of Australia*.⁸ In fact,

---

⁷ An unattainable goal, as even a minute's thought would confirm.
⁸ [2020] HCA 3, (2020)n279 CLR 152 ('*Love*').

what follows is a revised, updated and tarted-up amalgam of a talk I gave in 2020[9] and of a blog post I wrote after that.[10] In the spirit of this special issue's theme, let me here give readers a trigger warning. The rest of this article is very critical of the High Court. If you are part of the lawyerly caste that dislikes stinging criticism of some of our top judges – that feels the judiciary should be above all but the most modest criticisms – then do not read any further. You will be triggered, traumatised and feel the judiciary has been traduced. Everyone else is welcome to proceed.

To start, let me make plain that in my view this *Love* case is one of the best examples of what is often characterised as judicial activism that you will ever come across.[11] Readers might also benefit from being reminded that of the four Justices in the *Love* majority, three were appointed by the Coalition – these three being, at the time of the *Love* decision, the then most recent three appointees to the High Court in fact. All three were appointed by the former Liberal Attorney-General George Brandis. All three were in the woke, judicial activist majority in *Love*.

Here's my quick summary of the *Love* case: It was a case on the question of deporting plaintiffs who were born outside Australia, who are foreign citizens and who have not been naturalised or made Australian citizens, but who claim to be Aborigines. In a 4-3 decision the case effectively constitutionalised identity politics. In a weird sort of way it elevated the common law – judge-made law

---

[9] Samuel Griffiths Society, 'Zoom Discussion with Prof James Allan (14 May2020)' (YouTube, 21 May 2020).
[10] James Allan, '"Otherness" and Identity Politics in Constitutional Law', *IACL-AIDC Blog* (Blog Post, 21 January 2021) <https://blog-iacl-aidc.org/cili/2021/1/26/otherness-and-identity-politics-in-constitutional-law>.
[11] I make that point again and again in my talk found at (n 9).

to be clear – above the Constitution itself. It introduced a race-based limit on the Parliament's power. It looked very much to be a clear case of outcome-oriented judging, meaning you start with the conclusion you want and then struggle to find rationales to get you there. Amusingly or depressingly, depending on your cast of mind, the *Love* case more or less ignored or abandoned the established heads of powers interpretive methods – the ones that to my mind have unfortunately been used by Australia's top court to deliver the most pro-centre federalism case law in the world.[12] Worse, it did so out of the blue in a case where no Australian State actually benefitted from that abandonment of established federalism orthodoxy. Given the tools with which the judges had to work – remember, Australia has no national bill of rights – this case was a stunning example of raw judicial activism. It no doubt temporarily brought the task of constitutional interpretation to the widespread attention of the voting public. And I would argue that the case directly influenced the next two judicial appointments to the High Court, such was the wider reaction to this case, including to its patent wokeness (the theme of this special issue).

In providing this survey of *Love* I could be forgiven for taking the reader through some of the key concepts that drove the thinking of the judges who were in the four-person majority. Here we would open up the constitutional law textbooks and delve into the meaning of such arcane legal concepts – and I am not making this up I assure

---

[12] For a full argument to that effect see James Allan and Nicholas Aroney, 'An Uncommon Court: How the High Court of Australia has undermined Australian Federalism' (2008) 30(2) *Sydney Law Review* 245.

you – but concepts such as 'otherness';[13] or 'deeper truths';[14] or, when it comes to Australia, of a 'connection [that] is spiritual and metaphysical'[15] – all these "core legal precepts" and more then being combined together, as in some form of holistic alternative medicine brew, to claim that judge-made law now recognises 'that Indigenous peoples can and do possess certain rights and duties that are not possessed by, and *cannot be possessed by* non-Indigenous peoples of Australia.'[16] And that was just Justice Gordon.

Consider too Justice Nettle who talks of how 'different considerations apply ... to ... a person of Aboriginal descent'.[17] (Now of course one wonders why different considerations would apply in a liberal democracy committed to the rule of law and to formal equality, as opposed to one committed to the sort of identity politics poison that the British author Douglas Murray skewers in his book *The Madness of Crowds*.)[18] Still, different considerations for persons of Aboriginal descent apparently apply because that is what this judge says. If you are sceptical about that, Justice Nettle goes on to re-educate you by noting that the Commonwealth's claims to the contrary 'intuitively ... appear at odds with the growing recognition of Aboriginal peoples as "the original inhabitants of Australia"'[19] and of their 'essentially spiritual connection with "country"'.[20]

---

[13] *Love* [2020] HCA 3; (2020) 270 CLR 152, 262 [296], 292 [333], 275 [343] (Gordon J). I will say that again, 'otherness', because in my 31 years of teaching law in universities around the world I have *never* encountered a case where a judge had decided a case where this notion of 'otherness' was a core part of the ratio.

[14] Ibid 260 [289], 274 [340] (Gordon J).

[15] Ibid 260-262 [290] (Gordon J).

[16] Ibid 279 [357] (Gordon J) (emphasis in original).

[17] Ibid 298 [262] (Nettle J).

[18] Douglas Murray, *The Madness of Crowds* (Bloomsbury Continuum, 2019).

[19] *Love* [2020] HCA 3; (2020) 270 CLR 152, 248-249 [263] (Nettle J).

[20] Ibid 256-257 [276] (Nettle J).

So our top judges, all unelected and assigned the job of *interpreting* our Constitution not *drafting* it, now appear to decide key constitutional law cases based on intuitions that provide them with some sort of ineffable expertise as far as discerning 'growing recognitions' is concerned – by whom we are not told. To be frank, I would have thought that if you were looking for the group of people least likely to have their fingers on the pulse of what the community does and does not recognise, you would be hard pressed to do better than choose a cocooned committee of ex-barrister top judges who are genuflected before day in and day out. But I defer to Justice Nettle here.

These top unelected judges, continues Justice Nettle, are also able to discern 'essential spiritual connections with "country"'. (And let me note too that Justice Nettle put 'country' in scare quotes. Not country, but "country". One wonders if that in itself is an indicia of membership in 'Club Woke'.) The key takeaway here, though, is that we have yet more crucial constitutional law concepts being thrown into the mix; we have now got 'essential spiritual connections with "country"' joining 'otherness' and 'deeper truths' as things that a committee of unelected ex-lawyers happen to have extra special expertise about, and which they are able to use to remove decision-making power away from the elected Parliament. By contrast, my personal view is that all issues related to identity ought to be left to the elected legislature, not to four of seven top judges, not least because that was the clear intention of those who framed and ratified our Constitution (though it is also the more democratic choice, and the one that excludes the judiciary from dealing in jiggery-pokery-wokery).

And yet there is more. Justice Edelman, in his judgment, talks of 'essential meaning[s]',[21] 'metaphysical construct[s]',[22] 'powerful personal attachment[s] to land'[23] and then, remarkably, says 'To treat differences as though they were alike is not equality. It is denial of community. Any tolerant view of community must recognise that community is based on difference.'[24]

I have no idea of what that actually means, but neither it, nor any of the other political ramblings, have anything to do with the judges' assigned task, which is to interpret a written constitution. Moreover, if you want to talk about formal equality of the sort that underlies the rule of law, then treating those claiming Aboriginal ancestry the same as you treat everyone else is not 'denial of community'. It is how any decent jurisdiction committed to liberal democracy acts – because of course Justice Edelman's political ramblings about community could justify any group getting special treatment. Does affording the Boers special treatment in the 1970s get a tick because you do not want to indulge in (and I quote) 'denial of that community' or because 'community is based on difference'? Let me blunt, all this Gordon/Nettle/Edelman prattle is just about the worst sort of mumbo jumbo ever used in a constitutional law judgment. And believe me, there is some amazingly tough competition for the prize of worst judicial mumbo jumbo![25]

That, then, is an initial indication to readers of some of the lunatic,

---

[21] *Love* [2020] HCA 3; (2020) 270 CLR 152, 287-289 [392]-[395], 290-294 [399]-[404], 298-299 [415], 301 [422], 303 [427], 308 [437], 320-321 [467] (Edelman J).
[22] Ibid 308 [438] (Edelman J).
[23] Ibid 312 [447] (Edelman J).
[24] Ibid 315 [453] (Edelman J).
[25] Just staying in Australia, see my 'The Three "R"s of Recent Australian Judicial Activism: *Roach, Rowe* and (No)'Riginalism' (2012) 36(2) *Melbourne University Law Review* 743.

post-modernist, steeped-in-identity-politics, blatantly activism-enhancing comments – let us use the terminology of this special issue and call it 'wallowing in wokeness' – of these three Australian High Court judges, all appointed by the right-of-centre Liberal Party I say again.

IV CONSTITUTIONAL (MIS)INTERPRETATION

To put those mumbo jumbo judicial comments in context, allow me briefly to provide a more orthodox account of the *Love* case. Let me do that even though in many ways the most important criticism of it is the one I have just taken you through in highly expedited fashion – namely, that supposed interpreters of our written constitution (one of the world's oldest and most successful) decided to trade in their jobs as interpreters of legal text for the far more invigorating job of identity politics professors. (My view is that if we must wallow in identity enhanced protections and wokery then it ought to be done by the branch that is accountable to the people, the elected legislature, where its practitioners are accountable to the people and can be voted out of their jobs.)

This more orthodox account forces us to delve into federalism judicial review of legislation. In my native Canada there is a two-list system of federalism and the approach to federalism interpretation is very different to that in Australia. In Canada the approach came out of the Privy Council in London in the 19th century; it is still orthodoxy today; and the test centres on what is known as a law's 'pith and substance'.[26]

---

[26] There is a good summary of the doctrine in *Reference re Firearms Act (Can)* [2000] 1 SCR 783.

You as a judge take a contested law and ask yourself what is that law's 'pith and substance'; what is its essential character; what does it in substance relate to. If you decide that some contested statute, in substance, relates to X (one of the heads of powers on one of the lists), but incidentally and less substantively touches on Y and Z (from the other heads of powers list), then the challenged law is *intra vires* the legislative competence of the X list, the one that contains head of power X.

Or put differently, Canada in effect has a two-step process: 1) What is the pith and substance of the impugned law? 2) Take that essential character, that pith and substance, and ask which head of power it most fully falls under. Does it fall under list one (s 91 in Canada, the powers of Ottawa) or list two (s 92, the Provinces' listed powers)?

Now compare that to Australia's approach to federalism judicial review of legislation, sometimes labelled (not least by my colleague Nicholas Aroney)[27] 'interpretive literalism'. How does it work in Australia,[28] which copied the US form of federalism and opted for a one-list system (so only the powers of the centre are listed and everything not listed goes to the States)? Well, you look at the s 51 heads of powers and read them 'as widely and liberally as the words used permit'.[29] And then you ask if the contested statute can fit under any of the s 51 heads of powers, read in this wide and liberal way. If

---

[27] Nicholas Aroney, 'Reasonable disagreement, democracy, and the judicial safeguards of federalism' (2008) 27(1) *University of Queensland Law Journal* 129.
[28] To be clear I am talking about the post-1920 interpretive approach that flowed from the *Engineers Case*.
[29] That is the characterisation of my colleague Nicholas Aroney. But it is the clear effect of *Amalgamated Society of Engineers v Adelaide Steamship Co Ltd* (1920) 28 CLR 129 and *New South Wales v Commonwealth (Work Choices)* (2006) 229 CLR 1, inter alia.

so, this is a matter for the Commonwealth. If not, it is for the States.

Now it is pretty obvious that the Australian approach to federalism judicial review is remarkably friendly to the centre. It is why Australia has what is probably the world's most pro-centre federalism jurisprudence.[30] I will skip over whether that is a good thing or a bad thing – most Australians in my 16 years' experience teaching law here clearly are centralists and think it a good thing; most Canadians and Americans (and Swiss and Germans, and me too) are not centralists and think it a bad thing. I do think it is fair to comment, though, that none of the framers or ratifiers of Australia's Constitution over 120 years ago would ever have imagined that Australian States would be the emasculated mendicants that they are today, thanks in large part to the High Court of Australia.

I bring up that bit of comparative federalism and the differing approaches to federalist interpretation because in theory the *Love* case was a federalism heads of power case. So one would assume the top judges here in Australia would be playing the interpretive literalism game. One would assume what we would see is something along the lines of the same-sex marriage case, *Commonwealth v Australian Capital Territory*,[31] where the 'marriage' head of power was read in a wide and liberal way so that it included marriages between persons of the same sex. Had it not done that in that same-sex marriage case, had it read the head of power more narrowly, or in line with the framers' intended meaning, then odds are the power would not have rested with the centre. It would have gone to the States, or in this case to the ACT. But that is not the *uber* pro-centre

---

[30] Allan and Aroney (n 12).
[31] [2013] HCA 55; (2013) 250 CLR 441.

Australian way. That is not our orthodox approach to federalism judicial review, like it or lump it.

Yet when we turn to *Love* we see the majority implicitly reject federalism heads of power orthodoxy with nary a mention. Worse, this *Love* decision is a completely bizarre case to break away from orthodoxy because no State or Territory gets to benefit from the limit on the centre's power. One would have expected the majority to look at the head of power in play, s 51(xix) 'aliens', and then read that in a broad, liberal, extremely-friendly-to-the-Commonwealth manner. As they always have done, which is why our States are mendicants and why we have the world's worst vertical fiscal imbalance, etcetera. Hence using anything remotely coming close to that orthodox approach to federalism judicial review and it looks like a sure thing that the Commonwealth legislation regulating deportation will stand and Mr Love and the other foreign citizens claiming to be Aborigines will be deported. As readers will know, however, that was not the result.

The majority's outcome is doubly unusual, weird almost, because with federalism judicial review – unlike with rights-related judicial review of the sort you see in Canada and the United States under a justiciable bill of rights – the judicial task is premised on the judges having to choose between two elected legislatures, central or State. Judges "doing federalism" act as umpires between two democratically elected legislatures.[32] If legislature X does not have the power to do what the statute is doing then legislature Y does. And vice versa.

But in the *Love* case we are talking about a statutory power to deport non-

---

[32] For my full argument to that effect, and a response to Adrienne Stone, see: James Allan, 'Not in for a Pound – In for a Penny? Must a Majoritarian Democrat Treat All Constitutional Judicial Review as Equally Egregious?' (2010) 21 *King's Law Journal* 233.

citizens. There was never any chance at all that if the Commonwealth could not deport Mr Love then one of the States could do it. No. In effect the High Court majority judges took this power away from all elected legislatures. They turned a heads of power federalism case into a sort of rights-related judicial review case – the sort of case you see under bills of rights where it is held that no elected body can do what the statute purports to do. And that is almost never the scenario with federalism judicial review, to say nothing of the fact that Australia is a country with no national bill of rights. Or put differently yet again, the implication in *Love* is that there is a sort of judicialised identity politics, bastardised race-based exception to s 51(xix) – some sort of judicially created limit on Parliament's sovereignty, some sort of constitutionally implied limit, that has nothing at all to do with federalism and no obvious connection to anything in the actual Constitution.

V FINAL CONSIDERATIONS

So, how did *Love* happen when on its face the case is a federalism judicial review case? How did the majority judges transmogrify it into a bastardised rights-related case that then afforded them – those same judges – the power to say no elected legislature could do this? How did this striking example of judicial activism happen? Well, it happened with a hefty dose of 'otherness', 'deeper truths', 'different considerations for persons of Aboriginal descent', the keen application of 'intuitions', discerning 'essential spiritual connections' and 'metaphysical constructs' – the list of dry, arcane constitutional concepts continuing on in that vein.

Put more bluntly, if that is even possible, it came because four of our top judges (three of them appointed by a right-of-centre Liberal Coalition government, I repeat yet again with dismay) were infected by woke thinking. Even after being forced to sit in on one of the post-modernist grievance politics type classes now so common in Australia's universities no one (top judges included) has a glimmer, of a smidgen, of a hint, of an idea, of what 'otherness' is – or what 'otherness' means. Nor do any of us actually believe that our top unelected judges are able to discern 'essential spiritual connections'. Do they get special training on this once they are appointed to the High Court? Do they read up on Arthur Conan Doyle's essays on spiritualism? Does any reader honestly think that a committee of unelected ex-lawyers happens to have extra special expertise about any of this mumbo jumbo, enough to legitimately use it to invalidate a law passed by the democratically elected Parliament?

Or is this just an instance of wokeness on steroids having emanated from our top court? To ask is to answer, alas.

2

The Origins and Impact of Neo-Marxist Ideology and Cancel Culture on the Academy

KEVIN DONNELLY AM*

ABSTRACT

Such is the destructive impact of neo-Marxist inspired critical theory and its recent offspring cancel culture that tertiary institutions no longer embody a commitment to objectivity, wisdom and truth exemplified by a liberal education within the Western tradition. Cultural-left critics argue Western civilisation is riven with inequality and injustice and that the academic disciplines, instead of having any inherent meaning or worth, are simply social constructs designed to enforce the hegemony of the capitalist ruling class. Studying literature no longer involves an appreciation of the moral and aesthetic qualities of those literary works that have stood the test of time and history no longer involves a chronological narrative based on the evolution and development of Western civilisation. While cultural-left ideology has become the new orthodoxy as a result of the left's long march through the institutions there are signs of a counter movement gradually emerging. Indicators include the campaign to defend academic freedom and freedom of speech, establishment of professional organisation like the Heterodox Academy and prominent academics entering the public square and arguing the case for objectivity, impartiality and truth.

---

* Senior Fellow, PM Glynn Institute, Australian Catholic University.

I INTRODUCTION

WB Yeats in his poem *The Second Coming* writes 'the best lack all conviction, while the worst are full of passionate intensity'. While written soon after the First World War and the 1916 Easter Uprising in Ireland the same can be said for the times we are now living in. Such is the dominance of neo-Marxist ideology, cancel culture and the global movement to decolonise the curriculum that the very institutions, beliefs and cultural norms that underpin Western civilisation and explain its longevity and success are consistently condemned and vilified. At the same time those in the best position within the academy to defend what is most valuable and worth holding on to are either complicit or lack the courage to speak put.

II DECOLONISING THE TERTIARY CURRICULUM

> For those who would 'decolonize' our curricula, then, the curriculum is that which power and privilege have decided should be taught because it is in the interests of the powerful and privileged to teach it. These decisions are usually believed not to be intentional but implicit, accepted by the hegemon as justifiable, right, and natural. To summarize this view, when it comes to 'decolonizing the curriculum,' the curriculum is an ideological project devised by the powerful in society – meaning mostly straight, white, Western men with a 'Eurocentric' bent on things like science, reason, and rationality, among other proven epistemological and pedagogical frameworks.[1]

One of the most recent manifestations of neo-Marxist inspired critical

---

[1] James Lindsay, 'Decolonising the Curriculum' (2020) 33 *Academic Questions* 448, 450.

theory involves attempts to decolonise the tertiary curriculum. In the United Kingdom, America, Europe and Australia academics are being pressured to decolonise the curriculum on the basis, according to Dr Omid Tofighian at the University of Sydney, that the traditional curriculum is guilty of enforcing European supremacism and what he describes as 'whiteness'. Whiteness is defined as a curriculum that enforces 'different forms of domination and marginalisation — such as racism, sexism, classism, historical injustice and prejudice based on religion'.[2]

When rejecting the idea of hosting a centre for the study of Western civilisation funded by the Ramsay Centre 100 academics at the same university argue in a similar vein. In an open letter the statement is made that any centre funded by Ramsay would be guilty of offering 'a narrow, masculinist, Anglocentric view of "the West"'.[3] Such is the pervasive nature of the movement to decolonise the curriculum that even science is not immune. In the United Kingdom academics at the University of Sheffield condemn Western science as 'inherently white, since the discipline developed from the European scientific Enlightenment... science is both a fundamental contributor to European imperialism and major beneficiary of its injustices'.[4]

Students at the University of London are also intent on radical reshaping the curriculum by erasing whiteness, defined as 'an ideology which says people racialised as white are morally and intellectually superior

---

[2] Omid Tofighian, 'To Tackle Extremism in Schools We Must Challenge the White Curriculum', *The Conversation* (Web Article, 5 October 2015).
[3] Jordan Baker. '"We do not consent": Sydney Uni academics divided over new Ramsay proposal', *The Sydney Morning Herald* (Web Article, 22 September 2019).
[4] Frane Babarovic et al, 'Applying a decolonial framework to teaching and research in ecology and evolution' (Web Page, October 2020) [1.1]

to people categorised and racialised in other ways. It underpinned the development of European science, modernity and Enlightenment thinking'.[5] Instead of seeing anything beneficial or worthwhile in the works of Denis Diderot, Adam Smith, David Hume or Immanuel Kant such thinkers are condemned as promoting 'the knowledge and moral standpoint of wealthy, white, cisgendered, able-bodied men'.[6]

The global movement to decolonise the curriculum is simply the most recent manifestation of neo-Marxist inspired critical theory associated with the cultural-left's long march through universities and the dominance of a rainbow alliance of theories ranging from deconstructionism and postmodernism to radical gender, sexuality, feminist and postcolonial theories. While often in disagreement, what all hold in common is the belief there is nothing inherently worthwhile about the search for wisdom and truth associated with a liberal education as knowledge is a social construct enforcing the power and hegemony of the ruling class. Concepts like rationality and reason are condemned as Eurocentric and exploitive and TS Eliot's belief a university education should involve 'the preservation of learning, for the pursuit of truth, and in so far as men are capable of it, the attainment of wisdom'[7] long since forgotten.

III THE IMPACT OF THE FRANKFURT SCHOOL AND THE

---

[5] 'Why is my curriculum white?' collective, '8 Reasons the Curriculum is White' (Web Article, 23 March 2015).
[7] Ibid.
[7] TS Eliot, *Notes towards the Definition of Culture* (Faber and Faber, 1948) 123.

RISE OF CRITICAL THEORY

In detailing the origins of the campaign to decolonise the curriculum it is important to note the impact of the Frankfurt School established in Germany during the late 1920s. Such is the emancipatory and liberating nature of the Frankfurt School that the Italian political philosopher Augusto Del Noce writes:

> Their revolutionary stance is a radical affirmation of the transition 'from the reign of necessity to the reign of freedom', understood in the strongest sense. Thus, the disappearance of authority must be viewed as the end point of progressive thought, which, in fact, presents itself as a process of liberation from authority, theological or human, transcendent or empirical (where the theological authority continues to be viewed as a reflection of human authority).[8]

Central to the Frankfurt School is the belief classical Marxism is insufficient in furthering the cause of the working class and that the focus of the revolution should shift from economic considerations to what is now known as the culture wars. Closely associated with the Frankfurt school is the emergence of critical theory, defined as an emancipatory and liberating ideology dedicated to radically reshaping Western capitalist society in its image. The Australian academic Wanda Skowronska details the rationale underpinning critical theory as follows:

> Critical theory did not aim to tear down the economic base of western society as, with the force of history, it was inevitably going to collapse anyway. It aimed rather at tearing down the

---

[8] Augusto Del Noce, *The Crisis of Modernity* (McGill-Queen's University Press, 2014) 218.

cultural superstructure which supposedly reflected the powerful controllers of the economic system and this would enable the collapse of western civilisation.⁹

In order to overthrow capitalism and to bring about the socialist utopia those championing critical theory argue that, instead of taking to the streets and storming the barricades, a more effective strategy is to infiltrate and take control of those institutions, including universities and schools, that are complicit in enforcing what the Italian Marxist Antonio Gramsci describes as cultural hegemony. Roger Kiska, in detailing the origins of the cultural-left's long march through the institutions, describes cultural hegemony as a situation where 'the ruling class, the bourgeoise, used cultural institutions to maintain power. They use ideology, rather than violence or economic force, to propagate their own values by creating the capitalist *zeitgeist*'.¹⁰

Louis Althusser's concept of the ideological state apparatus argues the same case. While capitalism maintains dominance by employing violence equally, if not more effective, is the way citizens are conditioned to believe all is well even though they are exploited and oppressed.¹¹ As argued by the Australian Education Union, a commitment to meritocracy where students are ranked in terms of performance based on academic studies disguises the reality that such a system favours the sons and daughters of the ruling elites.¹² Women

---

⁹ Wanda Skowronska, '1960s Psychologists: Beguiling Ideologues and Smiling Assassins' in Thomas V Gourlay and Daniel Matthys (eds), *1968:Culture and Counterculture* (Wipf and Stock Publishers, 2020) 144.
¹⁰ Roger Kiska, 'Antonio Gramsci's long march through history' (2019) 29(3) *Religion & Liberty* 7, 7.
¹¹ Louis Althusser, 'Ideology and Ideological State Apparatuses' (Web Article, 3 November 2021).
¹² Australian Education Union, *Australian Education Union Policy Curriculum (as adopted at the 1993 AEU Annual Conference)*.

who are happily married and who define themselves as wives and mothers are equally deluded as, whether they know it or not, they are the unconscious victims of a patriarchal society riven with structural sexism and heteronormativity.[13]

IV THE '60S AND '70S CULTURAL REVOLUTION AND THE EMERGENCE OF THEORY

As noted by Roger Kimball,[14] as result of the '60s and '70s cultural revolution epitomised by the music festival Woodstock, the hippy movement, Vietnam moratoriums and a youth drug culture critical theory morphed into a series of cultural-left ideologies and movements ranging from postmodernism to radical gender and sexuality theories. According to Kimball, 'after fantasies of overt political revolution failed, many student radicals urged their followers to undertake the long march through the institutions'.[15] He notes the influence of Antonio Gramsci plus the German student radical Rudi Dutschke when explaining the emergence of the phrase based on the strategy of overthrowing capitalism by infiltrating and taking control of the institutions central to the continued existence of Western societies. As noted by Allan Bloom[16] the impact of the counter cultural, youth movement on American campuses was especially significant represented by sit-ins, demonstrations against the war in Vietnam and antipathy towards a liberal/arts curriculum. A time when student radicals at Stanford University demonstrated chanting 'hey-hey, ho-

---

[13] Kate Millet, *Sexual Politics* (University of Illinois Press, 2000).
[14] Roger Kimball, *The Long March* (Encounter Books, 2000) 3-35.
[15] Ibid 14.
[16] Allan Bloom, *The Closing of the American Mind* (Simon and Shuster, 1987).

ho, Western Civ has got to go!'.[17]

At the same time the counter-culture movement erupted across the Western world, universities, experienced an epistemological revolution caused by the emergence of postmodernism and deconstructionism associated with a number of European, neo-Marxist academics including Jacques Derrida, Roland Barthes and Michel Foucault. The impact of such theories cannot be overestimated, as together they had the effect of questioning and undermining once accepted absolutes about the nature of language and knowledge and how best to evaluate truth claims and achieve a more credible and realistic understanding of human nature and the world in which we exist and struggle to find meaning. Richard Tarnes describes postmodernism as the belief:

> [T]hat human knowledge is subjectively determined by a multitude of factors; that objective essences, or things-in-themselves, are neither accessible nor positable… The critical search for truth is constrained to be tolerant of ambiguity and pluralism, and its outcome will necessarily be knowledge that is relative and fallible rather than absolute or certain.[18]

Whether the argument that words have no agreed meaning as they involve an endless play of signifiers, how we relate to and understand the world is both subjective and relative, or the argument that knowledge is a social construct employed to subjugate and oppress the "other", the reality is what constitutes a university education has been radically reshaped. Foucault's work has been especially influential leading, to Helen Pluckrose and James Lindsay to write: 'Postmodernism is

---

[17] Robert Curry, 'Hey, Hey, Ho, Ho, Western Civ Has Got to Go', *Intellectual Takeout* (Web Article, 11 June 2019).

[18] Richard Tarnas, *The Passion of the Western Mind* (Random House, 2011) 395-396.

characterized politically by its intense focus on power as the guiding and structuring force of society, a focus which is co-dependent on the denial of objective knowledge'.[19]

Such has been the impact of critical theory and cultural-left ideology on the academy that universities across the West have long since abandoned any commitment to a liberal education within the tradition of Thomas Aquinas, Cardinal Newman and TS Eliot that can be traced to medieval England and Europe and the early Roman and Greek philosophers and sophists. A liberal education, in the words of the Australian academic Brian Crittenden, centred on 'a systematic and sustained introduction to those public forms of meaning in which the standards of human excellence in the intellectual, moral and aesthetic domains are expressed and critically investigated'.[20]

The way literature and a study of English have been radically redefined as a result of the cultural-left's long march illustrates how dominant neo-Marxist inspired critical theory has become. Studying literature no longer involves a study of the moral and aesthetic importance of those works that have stood the test of time and that have something insightful and profound to say about human nature and what DH Lawrence terms 'the relation between man and his circumambient universe, at the living moment'.[21] Instead, what are now defined as texts, including graffiti, SMS messaging, popular magazines, and posters, are deconstructed in terms of victimhood and identity politics. One example relates to the decision by the University of Leicester to replace teaching medieval

---

[19] Helen Pluckrose and James Lindsay, *Cynical Critical Theories* (Pitchstone Publishing, 2020).
[20] Brian Crittenden, *Cultural Pluralism and Common Curriculum* (Melbourne University Press, 1982) 88.
[21] DH Lawrence, 'Morality and the Novel' in *Selected Literary Criticism* (Heinemann Educational Books, 1956) 108-113.

literary works including *The Canterbury Tales, Beowulf* and *Le Morte D'Arthur* with what is described as 'a chronological literary history, a selection of modules on race, ethnicity, sexuality and diversity, a decolonised curriculum, and new employability modules'.[22] Even great literary works like Shakespeare's *Othello* and *Hamlet*, when they are included, are analysed and critiqued in terms of the new trinity involving gender, ethnicity and class.

The Australian Association for the Teaching of English ('AATE') is a strong advocate of cultural left theory. In books endorsed by the AATE, including Ian Reid's *The Making of Literature*[23] and *Jack Thomson's Reconstructing Literature Teaching*,[24] teachers are told they must replace the idea of teaching the literary canon with radically new approaches represented by postmodernism, deconstructionism and gender and postcolonial theories. As argued by Anne Cranny-Francis:

> It is essential that this focus on 'feelings' be deconstructed and exposed not only for its essentially repressive and conservatizing nature – these feelings are valued when aroused by readings which construct or enact dominant discourses (bourgeois, patriarchal, ethnocentric) – but also for its potentially devastating effect on those whose background (class, ethnicity, gender) does not promote the inculcation of these 'feelings'.[25]

The AATE, in addition to advocating a neo-Marxist inspired approach

---

[22] Craig Simpson, 'Chaucer to be scrapped as university decolonises', *The Telegraph* (Web Article, 20 January 2021).
[23] Ian Reid, *The Making of Literature* (AATE, 1984).
[24] Jack Thompsonm, *Reconstructing Literature Teaching* (Melbourne/Vic: AATE, 1992).
[25] Anne Cranny-Francis, 'The Value of Genre' (1999) 99 *English in Australia* 27, 44.

to literature, also champions an approach to teaching English based on the concept of critical literacy. Drawing largely on the writings of the Brazilian Marxist Paulo Freire and books including *Pedagogy of the Oppressed*[26] and *Education: The Practice of Freedom*[27] the argument is put that learning to read and write, similar to critical theory, must be a liberating and emancipatory experience that leads to overthrowing an elitist, capitalist society. Central to Freire is the argument that learning a language is intensely political and that traditional approaches to learning breed passivity instead of empowering individuals to take personal responsibility to act and to change the world. Freire argues 'Our traditional curriculum, disconnected from life, centred on words emptied of the reality they are meant to represent, lacking in concrete reality, could never develop critical consciousness'.[28]

The impact of neo-Marxist inspired critical theory and cultural-left ideology has also had a profound impact on history as a subject both within schools and universities. In the Australian context, as detailed by Stuart Macintyre and Anna Clark in *The History Wars*, the emphasis is no longer on a chronological view of history focusing on the evolution of Australia's development as a nation within the context of Western civilisation. Partly reflecting the cultural revolution of the late 60s and early 70s, Macintyre and Clark argue centre-left academics adopted an approach described as 'history from below'; a situation where the emphasis shifted 'from those who exercised power to those who resisted it'.[29] As a result, the authors argue history as a

---

[26] Paulo Freire, *Pedagogy of the Oppressed* (Penguin Books, 1972).
[27] Paulo Freire, *Education: The Practice of Freedom* (Writers and Readers Publishing Cooperative, 1974).
[28] Ibid 37.
[29] Stuart Macintyre and Anna Clark, *The History Wars* (Melbourne University Press, 2003) 41.

discipline shifted from the 'exclusiveness of traditional approaches'[30] to include long ignored and forgotten victims including women, gays, Aborigines and various ethnic and racial groups.

Evidence proving the effectiveness of the cultural-left's long march through the universities can be found in a number of surveys of Australian tertiary institutions carried out by the Melbourne-based *Institute of Public Affairs*. In a 2021 *Parliamentary Research Brief* involving 10 of the major universities the authors conclude '[t]he humanities as they are taught in Australian universities have rejected the intellectual and cultural heritage of Western Civilisation'.[31] After reviewing 1,181 humanities subjects the authors write 'the three of the most common themes are in order: (1) Identity Politics (572 subjects), (2) Critical Race Theory (380 Subjects) and (3) Gender (306 subjects)'.[32]

The results of the 2021 IPA survey are mirrored by an earlier research showing how Australian history is taught in our universities. The 2014 study involved reviewing 739 history subjects offered by 24 tertiary institutions and concludes: 'Undergraduate history degrees in Australia fail to teach fundamental aspects of Australia's history and how Australian liberal democracy came to be'.[33] Instead of encountering a substantial and chronological narrative dealing with Australia's founding and evolution as a Western, liberal democracy, students experience a range of 'more specialised, disconnected, thematically

---

[30] Ibid 173.
[31] Institute for Public Affairs, *The Humanities Dehumanised: How The Humanities Are Taught in Australia's Universities in 2021* (Parliamentary Research Brief, 16 January 2021).
[32] Ibid.
[33] Chris Berg, 'The End of History in Australian Universities', *Institute of Public Affairs* (Web Article, 1 August 2015).

based subjects on narrow issues such as imperialism, film studies, and ethnic and gender perspectives'.[34]

Such is the pervasive nature of political correctness and cultural-left ideology across Australian universities that a number of academics including Pierre Ryckmans,[35] John Carroll,[36] Merv Bendle[37] and Jennifer Oriel[38] all argue the academy no longer champions a liberal education based on Matthew Arnold's idea of the 'the best which has been thought and said in the world'.[39] Instead, as argued by Oriel:

> The free world stands on the shoulders of giants, but university leaders have so diminished freedom that the miseducated are leading the uneducated into a realm of darkness. The highest purpose of the university, to cultivate the flourishing of high culture and bequeath its bounty to future generations, is all but lost. Academics who benefitted from classical education watched universities transformed from sites of higher learning into revolutionary colleges during the late 1960s. Politics replaced the pursuit of truth, beauty and harmony as the raison d'être of higher education. Today, the university is a hollow man stripped of purpose and devoid of substance.[40]

Further evidence of the success of the cultural-left's long march through the academy is the percentage of university academics defined as left-

---

[34] Ibid 7.
[35] Pierre Ryckmans, 'The View from the Bridge: Aspects of Culture', *The 1996 Boyer Lectures*. (Australian Broadcasting Corporation, 1996) ch 1..
[36] John Carroll, 'How I became a political conservative', *Quadrant Online* (Web Article, 9 May 2015).
[37] Merv Bendle, 'The Suicide of the West', *Quadrant Online* (Web Article, 17 October 2016).
[38] Jennifer Oriel, 'Universities' in Kevin Donnelly (ed), *Cancel Culture and the Left's Long March* (Wilkinson Publishing, 2021).
[39] Matthew Arnold, *Culture & Anarchy* (Cambridge University Press, 1960) 6.
[40] Oriel (n 38) 51.

of-centre as opposed to being conservatively minded. In relation to American campuses the authors of a study published on the *Heterodox Academy* blog site investigating the political persuasions of academics, students and administrators concludes 'The data for three campus constituencies unequivocally show that liberals[41] are considerably overrepresented on university and college campuses'.[42] As argued by Kimball (the author of *Tenured Radicals*) such has been the success of the Cultural-left's long march that 'senior professors (are) safely ensconced at Yale and Stanford, at Princeton and Harvard, Duke, the University of California, and other premier institutions, where they chair departments, sit on promotion and tenure committees, and busy themselves developing and implementing radical curricular changes for their own and other institutions'.[43]

A British study titled 'Lackademia Why Do Academics Lean Left?' and undertaken by the *Adam Smith Institute* reaches a similar conclusion about the prevalence of left-of-centre ideology when it concludes '[i]ndividuals with left-wing and liberal views are overrepresented in British academia. Those with right-wing and conservative views are correspondingly underrepresented'.[44] Of interest is that one of the indicators employed to identify political allegiance used by the British study relates to the voting habits of academics. Drawing on a study by the sociologist AH Halsey the authors note that in the 2015 election

---

[41] Within the American context, 'liberals' refer to those identifying with left-of-centre politics.
[42] Sam Abrams and Amna Khalid, 'Are Colleges and Universities Too Liberal? What the Research Says about the Political Composition of Campuses and Campus Climate', *Heterodox: The Blog* (Blog Post, 21 October 2020).
[43] Roger Kimball, 'Tenured Radicals: a postscript' (1991) 9(5) *The New Criterion*.
[44] Noah Carl, 'Lackademia Why Do Academics Lean Left?', *The Adam Smith Institute* (Briefing Paper, 2 March 2017) 1, 16.

out of the academics surveyed 11 voted conservative, 46 Labour, 9 Liberal Democrat/Liberal Social Democratic Party, 22 voted Greens and 12 Other. The *Adam Smith Institute* paper also notes in relation to the 2015 national election while 50% of the public voted for right wing or conservative parties the figure for those academics was less than 12%.[45]

V NEO-MARXIST INSPIRED CRITICAL THEORY AND CANCEL CULTURE – A CRITIQUE

The dangers and flaws inherent in neo-Marxist inspired political correctness and cancel culture are manifest. While there is no doubt Western civilisation is far from perfect and guilty of a range of sins including imperialism and slavery, the subjugation of women and other vulnerable groups including LGBTIQ+ people, and the worst excesses of capitalism especially during the industrial revolution, the reality is all civilisations are guilty of crimes against humanity. Often ignored by cultural-left activists, for example, is the Islamic slave trade centred on the Mediterranean between the 16th and 18th centuries and the way women were and still are oppressed in many tribal societies. The unique strength and benefit of Western civilisation is that over time it has been capable of rectifying inequalities and the sins of the past. As argued by Arthur M Schlesinger Jr, '[t]he crimes committed by the West have produced their own antidotes. They have produced great movements to end slavery, to raise the status of women, to abolish torture, to combat racism, to defend freedom of inquiry and expression, to advance personal liberty and human rights'.[46] It should

---

[45] Ibid 4.
[46] Arthur M Schlesinger Jr, *The Disuniting of America* (WW Norton, 1992) 127.

not surprise according to the *The Human Freedom Index* Western societies dominate the top 20 places measuring freedom in terms of: legal protection, security and safety, religion, freedom of association, expression and movement.[47]

If civilisations are measured by scientific, technological and medical innovations and advances then it is clear the West also achieves a very high ranking. Inventions like the steam engine, railways, the mechanised printing press, the internal combustion engine, jet aircraft, and silicon chips and computers are all products of Western skill and ingenuity. Medical advances such as understanding how infections and diseases are spread, the importance of hygiene, antibiotics like penicillin, open heart surgery, and impregnating human embryos outside the womb demonstrate a superiority not matched by other civilisations. Central to the West's progress is the scientific method based on empiricism, rationality and reason that has allowed it to evolve from what Karl Popper describes as a 'tribal or closed society' to an 'open society'– a society aiming at 'humaneness and reasonableness, at equality and freedom' by setting free 'the critical powers of man'.[48] Epochal events like the Enlightenment that stress the importance of objectivity and truth clearly differentiate Western civilisation from less civilised ones where superstition, prejudice and witchcraft prevail. As argued by Larry Siedentop in *Inventing the Individual*,[49] Western civilisation is also unique given the vital importance of Judeo-Christianity in championing a form of liberalism based on the belief, as we are all made in the image of God, 'There is neither Jew nor Greek, there is

---

[47] Cato Institute and Fraser Institute, *The Human Freedom Index* (Report, 18 August 2015).
[48] K Popper, *The Open Society and its Enemies* (Routledge, 2011) xxxv.
[49] Larry Siedentop, *Inventing the Individual The Origins of Western Liberalism* (Penguin Books, 2015).

neither slave nor free, there is neither male nor female; for you are all one in Christ Jesus'.[50] Understandably, the *American Declaration of Independence* describes the 'unalienable rights' of life, liberty and the pursuits of happiness as 'endowed by their creator'. Also significant is that the Preamble to the *Australian Constitution* includes the words 'Humbly relying on the blessing of almighty God'.

When noting the rise of political correctness during the '80s and '90s the American nongendered feminist Camille Paglia argues what began as a justifiable campaign for increased liberty and freedom has morphed into an existential danger to free speech and academic freedom. Paglia writes the media and universities 'are currently patrolled by well-meaning but ruthless thought police, as dogmatic in their views as agents of the Spanish Inquisition. We are plunged once again into an ethical chaos where intolerance masquerades as tolerance and where individual liberty is crushed by the tyranny of the group'.[51] Denial of academic freedom and restricting free and open debate represent one of the most dangerous aspects of the cultural-left's long march. Whether pressuring the historian Geoffrey Blainey to leave the University of Melbourne for questioning the rate of Asian immigration, no-platforming speakers like the feminist Germaine Greer for questioning transgenderism, or sacking academics like James Cook University's Peter Ridd for questioning the impact of man-made global warming on the Great Barrier Reef, academic freedom has been lost. Such obvious cases of intolerance are in addition to cultural-left academics dominating research grants, peer reviewed publications, and ongoing tenured positions.

---

[50] Galatians 3:28.
[51] Camille Paglia, *Free Woman Free Men – Sex, Gender, Feminism* (Pantheon Books, 2017) ix.

If a liberal view of education embraces what TS Eliot describes as the pursuit of wisdom and truth based on rationality, reason and the belief it is possible to more closely approximate the truth of things, then theories like postmodernism and poststructuralism advocate the opposite. Activists argue knowledge is a social construct based on power relationships, that how we define ourselves and relate to the world is relative and subjective and that words can have no agreed meaning as they constitute an endless play of signifiers. Such is the restrictive and dogmatic nature of radical theory and political correctness that Roger Scruton compares today's universities with the dystopian world of George Orwell's 1984. Scruton writes such is the destructive nature of political correctness that it has led to:

> The humourless and relentless political policing of language, so as to prevent heretical thoughts from arising, the violence done to traditional categories of thought and natural ways of describing things, the obliteration of memory and assiduous policing of the past – all these things, so disturbingly described in *Nineteen Eighty Four*, are now routinely to be observed on university campuses on both sides of the Atlantic.[52]

The denial of academic freedom and the imposition of cultural-left group think and language control strikes at the very heart of what universities should be committed to and dedicated to uphold. Even more concerning is the fact that if rationality and reason are no longer viable, as they are deemed to be hegemonic constructs imposed by capitalist elites and Western imperialism, then the only alternative is epistemological suicide and violence. As argued by Dinesh D'Souza:

> Although most au courant disciples think of themselves as

---
[52] Roger Scruton, *Conservatism* (Profile Books, 2017) 122.

progressive activists, or at least on the progressive side of history, their philosophy releases relativist and nihilist forces that culminate in coercive ideologies. This is the paradox of the relativist authoritarian. Anarchy, whether social or intellectual, has a tendency to lead to tyranny, as Tocqueville observed long ago.[53]

VI CONCLUSION – THE WAY AHEAD

While it is clear critical theory and its various off shoots including postmodernism and postcolonial theory have become the new orthodoxy, it is important to note there are some academics and institutions willing to join the battle of ideas and argue the case for a more balanced and impartial view of education and the role of universities. In America the *Heterodox Academy* formed in 2015 and with approximately 1,400 members is committed to promoting 'open inquiry, viewpoint diversity, and constructive disagreement in institutions of higher learning'.[54] In Australia the establishment of centres funded by the late Paul Ramsay[55] dedicated to the study of Western civilisation at the Australian Catholic University, the University of Queensland and Wollongong University also suggests not all academics are averse to a liberal education. While not universities, the Institute of Public Affairs and the Perth-based Mannkal Economic Education Foundation are also committed to promoting academic freedom and open debate within the Western tradition. In England the Adam Smith Institute serves a similar purpose by offering a critique of cultural-left ideology and political correctness.

---

[53] Dinesh D'Souza, *Illiberal Education* (Vintage Books, 1992) 190.
[54] The Heterodox Academy's website is https://heterodoxacademy.org/.
[55] Details about the Ramsay bequest and the programs funded by the Ramsay Centre can be found at https://www.ramsaycentre.org/.

Such are the concerns about academic freedom and the impact of cultural-left group think that the Australian government initiated an inquiry chaired by the Hon Robert French to investigate the issue. As a result of the 2019 inquiry universities are expected to adopt a code to ensure a 'culture of free speech and academic freedom is strongly embedded in institutions across the Australian higher education sector'.[56] While not directly affecting what is taught, the code does present a safeguard against academics being punished for not conforming to the prevailing politically correct ethos. Also positive is an open letter published on the Harper's magazine website by some 153 authors and academics criticising what is described as 'an intolerance of opposing views, a vogue for public shaming and ostracism, and the tendency to dissolve complex policy issues in a blinding moral certainty.'[57]

Across the Anglosphere the presence of leading conservative academics and public intellectuals including Douglas Murray and the late Roger Scruton in England, Canada's Jordan Peterson and in America Dinesh D'Souza along with Helen Pluckrose and James Lindsay prove that not all academics have forsaken robust and balanced intellectual research and debate. In Australia the sinologist Pierre Ryckmans and more lately the University of Sydney's Salvatore Babones also are involved in the battle of ideas based on the need for diversity and contestation. The emerging digital technologies are also a positive sign proven by the popularity of *YouTube* videos by Jordan Peterson and Australia's ex-Deputy Prime Minister John Anderson. Both engage hundreds

---

[56] See details about the French inquiry at https://www.dese.gov.au/higher-education-reviews-and-consultations/independent-review-adoption-model-code-freedom-speech-and-academic-freedom.

[57] 'A Letter on Justice and Open Debate', *Harper's Magazine* (Web Page, 7 July 2020).

of thousands of viewers from around the globe enlightening them about contemporary issues including the need for academic freedom, intellectual honesty and the strengths and weaknesses of Western civilisation.

3
Freedom of Speech in the Woke Era: Critical Race Theory and State Neutrality

ANTHONY GRAY*

ABSTRACT

This chapter advocates for freedom of speech against the kind of post-modern critical race theory that is said to justify serious restrictions on speech relating to race. A liberal democratic society is fundamentally premised on freedom of speech. This should be a neutral political principle, espoused by all sides of politics. And yet, politicians of all political persuasions are being seduced by the woke shutdown, de-platforming vibe. This is undemocratic and those who cherish democratic, free speech principles must fight back with strong speech.

I INTRODUCTION

There have been further recent steps around Australia to impose bans on speech that many would find distasteful and hurtful. Recently, Victoria passed legislation to criminalise the intentional display of

---

* Professor of Law and Associate Head-Research, School of Law and Justice, University of Southern Queensland.

the Nazi symbol in public.[1] New South Wales and Queensland are considering similar measures. It is understandable that many associate the swastika with the hateful and murderous Nazi regime, under which many suffered, and which was responsible for the murder of six million Jewish people, and others. However, the history of the swastika is complex, as will be shown. An unspoken assumption behind many moves to 'ban' particular things, including speech on particular matters, or the display of particular symbols or signs, is that by banning them, it will stop individuals from believing particular things, or doing particular things. However, that assumption needs to be seriously assessed and proven, rather than simply espoused. The so-called 'woke era' can be seen as part of the postmodern movement of the past 30 years, in particular, and one of its manifestations, critical race theory. This theory is particularly important to some scholars in terms of their justification for banning particular kinds of speech, including speech relating in some way to race. This article will defend freedom of speech against the kind of post-modern critical race theory that is said to justify serious restrictions on speech relating to race. I will use, for the purposes of discussion, the proposed swastika ban as an exemplar of calls to ban speech. It will not consider the constitutionality of this type of law, as I have done this in other work.[2]

Prior to so doing, one acknowledgment is considered necessary. I believe it is necessary to place on the record that I am not a Nazi, or a Nazi sympathiser. Of course, racism is abhorrent in all its forms, and the murder of six million people is disgraceful, and must never

---

[1] Summary Offences Amendment (Nazi Symbol Prohibition) Act 2022 (Vic). It includes defences where the display is for genuine academic, artistic, religious or scientific purposes, genuine cultural or educational purposes, or to express opposition to fascism or Nazism.
[2] Anthony Gray 'Racial Vilification and Freedom of Speech in Australia and Elsewhere' (2012) 41(2) *Common Law World Review* 167.

be forgotten. I have visited the Auschwitz death camp on numerous occasions. More than 75 years after it was closed, it still impacts all those who attend it. I doubt that many would forget the experience of having visited it. The mad, murderous regime that it reflects remains hard to fathom. But it stands as a testament to the result when extreme racism and hatred, combined with other factors, forms into a disastrous mix. We must try to continue to learn these lessons and to ward as far as possible against the rise of this kind of ideology. I am sure that those who wish to ban the swastika and other offensive symbols are equally motivated by the desire to ward against the rise of this kind of ideology.

One other preliminary point is that, at least in current times, defence of freedom of speech has come to be associated with the 'right' of politics, in so far as words such as 'left' or 'right' retain a political meaning any more. It is not clear why defence of freedom of speech should be seen as allied with the views of the political left or the political right, or somewhere in between. This is because the idea of freedom of speech is that it is a freedom that everyone enjoys, regardless of their political views. It is against censorship of speech because of viewpoint or content. It is, at least facially, neutral.[3] I am aware that there are some who argue that it is not in fact neutral because the 'system' is loaded in favour of 'privileged' speakers.[4] I will consider this in more detail below.

Somewhat ironically in the current context, where freedom of speech has come to be associated with the political 'right', on many occasions when freedom of speech has been argued, it has in fact involved

---

[3] Larry Alexander, 'Is Freedom of Expression a Universal Right?' (2013) 50 *San Diego Law Review* 707, 709.
[4] For example, Neil Gotanda claims that a theory of race colour-blindness is really 'a disguised form of racial privileging': Neil Gotanda, 'Failure of the Color-Blind Vision: Race, Ethnicity and the California Civil Rights Initiative (1996) 23 *Hastings Constitutional Law Quarterly* 1135, 1139.

dissenters on the 'left 'of politics, including communist and socialist party members and/or sympathisers.[5] The state has sought to prosecute them for their beliefs, and they have raised freedom of speech issues. Thus, it is somewhat puzzling to me that belief in freedom of speech has come to be associated with the political 'right', and I do not know when it was that defence of free speech ceased to be associated with the 'left', and came to be associated with the 'right', or why. My view is that the essence of freedom of speech is, and should be, neutral as to politics. It is just as valuable to, and should be defended equally by, those on the political 'right', 'left' or anywhere on the spectrum. Equally, and somewhat relatedly, freedom of speech has historically assisted minorities in their causes; ironically now, it is some minority groups in society who call for significant restrictions on speech. As Strossen points out

> Just as free speech has always been the strongest weapon to advance equal rights causes, censorship has always been the strongest weapon to thwart them ... (those who wish to curb hate speech) contend that racial and other minorities, including women, are relatively disempowered and marginalised. I agree. However, it is precisely for that reason that censorship is not a solution. To the contrary, the government is likely to wield this

---

[5] In the United States, classically *Schenck v United States* 249 US 47 (1919); *Debs v United States* 249 US 211 (1919) and *De Jonge v Oregon* 299 US 353 (1937); *Dennis v United States* 341 US 494 (1951); *Barenblatt v United States* 360 US 109 (1959) and *Scales v United States* 367 US 203 (1961), and in Australia *Burns v Ransley* (1949) 79 CLR 101 and *R v Sharkey* (1949) 79 CLR 121 (convictions for sedition for those who expressed support for communist Russia upheld, though freedom of speech was not considered as a possible defence). The implied constitutional freedom of political communication would only be recognised in Australia in 1992: *Australian Capital Television Pty Ltd v Commonwealth* (1922) 177 CLR 106. Further, as Augusto Zimmermann and Lorraine Finlay have pointed out, 'the oppressed people of countries with official Marxist ideologies have never achieved any reasonable form of free speech': 'A Forgotten Freedom: Protecting Freedom of Speech in an Age of Political Correctness' (2014) 14 *Macquarie Law Journal* 185, 189.

tool ... to the particular disadvantage of already disempowered groups. Laws that censor ... hate speech are inevitably enforced disproportionately against speech by, and on behalf of, groups that lack political power ... including ... members of the very minority groups who are the law's intended beneficiaries.[6]

In this context, it is something of a mystery as to why freedom of speech has come to be associated with any particular political view, but most especially why it has come to be favoured by the 'right', and disfavoured by (at least some on) the 'left', when its essence is neutrality as to political view.

II FREEDOM OF SPEECH – BRIEF HISTORY AND THEORETICAL BASIS

Freedom of speech would take some time to be established in the common law tradition.[7] It was a serious offence to commit treason, which included 'imagining' the death of the monarch.[8] It was extended to include criticism of members of the royal family. The law recognised a system of 'prior restraint', under which anyone who sought to publish anything first required the consent of a government official or church

---

[6] Nadine Strossen 'Freedom of Speech and Equality: Do We Have to Choose?' (2016) 25 *Journal of Law and Policy* 185, 214.
[7] See for more detail Anthony Gray *Freedom of Speech in the Western World* (Lexington Books, 2019) ch 1.
[8] *Statute of Treasons 1352* (Eng).

officer.[9] In 1606 the court recognised an offence of seditious libel.[10] This included publishing criticism of the government or public office. Truth was no defence. Inevitably it was used to discourage dissent. It is notable that the offence was created by the Court of Star Chamber, notorious for its secretive, inquisitorial processes. That Chamber was abolished in 1641, and unsurprisingly, following its abolition, the volume of publications about the government, including criticism, increased dramatically. This was during and after the English Civil War and in the years leading up to the Glorious Revolution, when political discussion would obviously have been vociferous.

These censorious times reflect a society about which Thomas Hobbes wrote. At this time, it was thought that individuals were somewhat primitive, and prone to violence and unrest. It is understandable that there was a felt need for strong government, able to put down rebellion or rebellious talk, which was seen to threaten the established system of government. Obviously, government itself in England during these times was somewhat shaky, with tension between the monarchy and parliament, disagreement about the respective roles of each, tension over who was entitled to be crowned the monarch,

---

[9] In 1643, a Board of Licensors was established to consider whether works should be published; this was continued by the *Publishing Act 1662* (Eng). This system would finally lapse in 1694. Sir William Blackstone claimed that freedom of speech was adequately secured by the demise of the system of prior restraint: 'the liberty of the press is indeed essential to the nature of a free state, but this consists in laying on previous restraints upon publications; and not in freedom from censure for criminal matter when published. Every free man has an undoubted right to lay what sentiments he pleases before the public; to forbid this is to destroy the freedom of the press; but if he publishes what is improper, mischievous or illegal, he must take the consequences of his own temerity ... to punish ... any dangerous or offensive writings which (are) ... of a pernicious tendency is necessary for the preservation of peace and good order': *Commentaries on the Laws of England 1765-1769* (Clarendon Press, 1769) 152.

[10] *De Libellis Famosis* (1606) 5 Co Rep 125a; 77 ER 250.

and republican sentiment. In this volatile climate, an attempt to stifle dissent is understandable, if not defensible.[11]

In any event, over time the system would stabilise. The Glorious Revolution would establish the supremacy of parliament over the monarch. Different theories of government emerged, including that of John Locke and his social contract theory, emphasising the parliamentarian as representative of the people. In such an environment, albeit slowly, the importance of freedom of speech was recognised.[12]

Philip Hamburger notes an important change in view occurred in the early part of the 18th century. His quote also reflects that, at one time, government censorship seems to have been connected with politics of the 'right':

---

[11] An example appears in the judgment of Holt CJ in *R v Tutchin* (1704) KB 424, 424-425; 90 ER 1133, 1133-1134: 'but this is a very strange doctrine, to say, it is not a libel, reflecting on the government ... if men should not be called to account for possessing the people with an ill opinion of the government no government can subsist; for it is very necessary to every government, that the people should have a good opinion of it. And nothing can be worse to any government than to endeavour to procure animosities as to the management of it. This has been always looked upon as a crime, and no government can be safe unless it be punished'.

[12] James Fitzjames Stephen *A History of the Criminal Law of England* (Macmillan, 1904) 299-300: 'two different views may be taken of the relation between rulers and their subjects. If the ruler is regarded as the superior of the subject, as being by the nature of his position presumably wise and good, the rightful ruler and guide of the whole population, it must necessarily follow that it is wrong to censure him openly, that even if he is mistaken, his mistakes should be pointed out with the utmost respect, and that whether mistaken or not no censure should be cast upon him likely or designed to diminish his authority. If on the other hand the ruler is regarded as the agent and servant, and the subject of the wise and good master who is obliged to delegate his power to the so-called ruler because being a multitude he cannot use it himself, it is obvious that this sentiment must be reversed. Every member of the public who censures the ruler for the time being exercises in his own person the right which belongs to the whole of which he forms a part ... to those who hold this view fully and carry it out to all its consequences there can be no such offence as sedition'.

In 1710 the idea of vigorous criticism of authority was as disturbing to most Tories as it may have been congenial to a small number of radical Whigs. Among Tories, Grub Street's pamphlet and newspaper onslaught elicited deep ideological as well as practical concern. Committed to a vision of hierarchical society established by divine authority and therefore unimprovable, unchanging and uniform, Tory ideologues in the excited atmosphere of 1710 perceived no alternative to the received religious and political establishment except complete moral and social disintegration. In church and state, according to extreme Tories, the slightest dissent posed a danger, and printed criticism of the government was no exception. In their second administration under Anne, as in their first, the Tories prosecuted printers and publishers for seditious libel, relying, where need arose, upon the judges to interpret the law in a way that would not be prejudicial to the requirements of the government ... by 1720 many men began to realize that ministers and factions, with all their petty squabbles and scurrilous printed attacks on one another, would come and go, but the English Establishment, a Protestant parliamentary monarchy, would be secure in spite of all the liberties taken by the press. Accordingly, although the Whig government continued to prosecute printers for seditious libel after 1714, it did so without expecting to bring the press to complete submission.[13]

By the mid-19th century, United Kingdom courts were reflecting the importance of free speech.[14]

Traditionally, Australian law recognised freedom of speech as a fundamental common law right, in the sense that it existed, to the

---

[13] Philip Hamburger 'The Development of the Law of Seditious Libel and the Control of the Press' (1985) 37 *Stanford Law Review* 661, 748, 752.
[14] *Wason v Walter* (1868) LR 4 QB 73, 93 (Cockburn CJ).

extent that parliament did not abrogate it.[15] Parliament has done so. A notorious example is the successful prosecution of individuals for merely expressing pro-communist views.[16] In the early 1990s the High Court discerned an implied freedom of political communication as a result of Australia's system of representative government.[17] Notwithstanding this freedom, the Commonwealth[18] and the states[19] have introduced anti-vilification legislation, including vilification on the basis of race. These provisions are typically framed around inciting hatred towards, serious contempt for or ridicule of a person. In some cases, a criminal offence exists, usually where intent and/or recklessness exists.[20] The constitutionality of such measures, having regard to the implied freedom, has not yet been tested.[21]

Together with Locke and John Milton, the leading philosophical support for freedom of speech is typically sourced in the writings of John Stuart Mill. Mill espoused various rationales for freedom of speech, including the search for truth:

> The peculiar evil of silencing the expression of an opinion is that

---

[15] *Lange v Australian Broadcasting Corporation* (1997) 189 CLR 520, 564 (all members of the Court).
[16] *R v Sharkey* (1949) 79 CLR 121; *Burns v Ransley* (1949) 79 CLR 1.
[17] *Australian Capital Television Pty Ltd v Commonwealth* (1992) 177 CLR 106; *Nationwide News Pty Ltd v Wills* (1992) 177 CLR 1.
[18] *Racial Discrimination Act 1975* (Cth) s 18C.
[19] *Anti-Discrimination Act 1977* (NSW) s 20C and *Racial and Religious Tolerance Act 2001* (Vic) s 7; *Anti-Discrimination Act 1991* (Qld) s 124A; *Anti-Discrimination Act 1998* (Tas) s 19; *Discrimination Act 1991* (ACT) s 67A.
[20] *Crimes Act 1900* (NSW) s 93Z; *Racial and Religious Tolerance Act 2001* (Vic) s 24; *Anti-Discrimination Act 1991* (Qld) s 131A; *Criminal Code Compilation Act 1913* (WA) ss 80A-80D; *Racial Vilification Act 1996* (SA) s 4; *Criminal Code 2002* (ACT) s 750. Notably, s 80B and s 80D of the Western Australian legislation do not require either intent or recklessness in order for a person to commit a criminal offence.
[21] Anthony Gray 'Racial Vilification and Freedom of Speech in Australia and Elsewhere' (2012) 41(2) *Common Law World Review* 167.

it is robbing the human race, posterity, as well as the existing generation, those who dissent from the opinion; still more than those who hold it. If the opinion is right, they are deprived of the opportunity of exchanging error for truth; if wrong, they lose, what is almost as great a benefit, a clearer perception and livelier impression of truth, produced by its collision with error ... we can never be sure that the opinion we are endeavouring to stifle is a false opinion, and if we were sure, stifling it would be an evil still.[22]

He also lauds freedom of speech on the basis of the role it plays in aiding an individual's development. He notes:

> The only way in which a human being can make some approach to knowing the whole of a subject is by hearing what can be said about it by persons of every variety of opinion, and studying all modes in which it can be looked at by every character of mind. No wise (person) ever acquired (their) wisdom in any mode but this; nor is it in the nature of human intellect to become wise in any other manner.[23]

Mill's defence of freedom of speech was not absolute. His 'harm principle' was an identified limit – a person's freedom to speak ended when its exercise caused another 'harm'. Mill did not elaborate on this principle, and he did not consider its possible application to the regulation of so-called 'hate speech'.[24]

Later, scholars would attempt to justify freedom of speech with

---

[22] John Stuart Mill, *Utilitarianism, On Liberty, Considerations on Representative Government*, ed Geraint Williams (Everyman's Library, 1910) 83.

[23] Ibid 84.

[24] It has been considered difficult to apply in the context of hate speech: Anthony D'Amato, 'Harmful Speech and the Culture of Indeterminacy' (1991) 32 *William and Mary Law Review* 329, 337: 'whether harm occurred just by the utterance itself can be nothing better than a random guess'.

rationales such as the 'marketplace of ideas' notion, that an environment in which ideas openly competed with one another would most likely lead a society closer to truth.[25] Any number of historical examples from a range of fields would demonstrate that what was once thought to be unassailable truth turned out to be palpably false. It is argued that censorship actually hurts minorities disproportionately compared with majority groups.[26] It is said that censorship will not drive unpopular or unpalatable ideas away; rather it will put them underground, where they might fester.[27]

It has also been asserted that freedom of speech is necessary for, and to the extent of, a healthy functioning democratic, representative government in which individuals have access to a range of views and opinions in order to make an informed judgment about the government they wish to represent them, and to assess a government's performance in office.[28]

In sum, freedom of speech fits within a liberalist view of the legal system, where individual personal liberty is maximised, and the role of government and government regulation minimised.[29] An individual exists before society does, and has free will and autonomy,

---

[25] *Abrams v United States* 259 US 616, 630 (1919) (Holmes J, dissenting).
[26] Larry Alexander *Is There a Right to Freedom of Expression?* (Cambridge University Press, 2005) 192-193.
[27] Ibid 193.
[28] Alexander Meiklejohn, *Political Freedom: The Constitutional Powers of the People* (Oxford University Press, 1980); *Australian Capital Television Pty Ltd v Commonwealth* (1992) 177 CLR 106; *Nationwide News v Wills* (1992) 177 CLR 1. A view of free speech as the 'lifeblood' of democracy was denounced as a 'merely rhetorical flourish': Bill Swannie, 'Are racial vilification laws supported by free speech arguments?' (2018) 44(1) *Monash University Law Review* 71, 77.
[29] John Locke, *The Second Treatise of Government* (1689) 4-11; *West Virginia Board of Education v Barnette* 319 US 624, 639-640 (1943) (Jackson J, for Stone, Robert, Reed and Rutledge JJ, Black, Douglas and Murphy JJ concurring).

compatible with the rights of other individuals.[30] Liberalism makes a sharp distinction between the private and public spheres. The former substantially pre-dates the latter. Regulation is typically targeted at the latter. Liberalism would not typically favour the regulation of hate speech. Toni Massaro identifies that this is because liberalism assumes that individuals are strong with individual powers of self-identification and resilience, and because they judge that, at least typically, any injury caused by nasty speech is not at a level that would justify the intervention of the state, unless it was likely to cause an imminent breach of the peace.[31]

I will now articulate how subsequent intellectual movements, including post-modernism and its critical race theory, have come to challenge the liberal view of free speech.

III POSTMODERNISM, CRITICAL RACE THEORY AND FREE SPEECH

A *Postmodernism*

One way of interpreting postmodernism is to articulate modernism. As one scholar puts it:

> The modern period spanned the mid-Enlightenment to the 1960s and early 1970s. It was characterized by the power of reason, and the inherent dignity and uniqueness of individuals as ends in themselves. A basic tenet of modernism held that the faculty of reason could operate as a neutral court of appeal to weed out

---

[30] Stephen Feldman, 'Postmodern Free Expression: A Philosophical Rationale for the Digital Age' (2017) 100 *Marquette Law Review* 1123, 1125.
[31] Toni Massaro, 'Equality and Freedom of Expression: The Hate Speech Dilemma' (1991) 32 *William and Mary Law Review* 211, 229-230.

beliefs and practices based on superstition and blind tradition.[32]

This view of the political and legal system has been challenged. Postmodern theory has a very different view of the political and legal system, and begins from different premises. According to postmodern theory, there is no 'truth'.[33] It can be seen how this potentially conflicts with the traditions of liberalism, and rationales for freedom of speech. Freedom of speech is lauded as a means of discovering, or bringing society closer to, truth. However, this rationale falls away if, in fact, there is no truth. Feldman says that the original rationales for freedom of speech 'no longer fit in our postmodern ... society'.[34] Delgado claims the traditionalist view of freedom of speech rationales is 'passing into history. Replacing it is a much more nuanced, sceptical and realistic view of what speech can do'.[35]

Postmodernists believe that there is no innate self, that each person's

---

[32] Douglas E Litowitz, *Postmodern Philosophy and Law* (University Press of Kansas, 1997) 7.
[33] Calvin Massey, 'The Constitution in a Postmodern Age' (2007) 64 *Washington and Lee Law Review* 165, 171: 'a central postmodern claim is that there can be no such thing as a objective truth'; Stanley Fish, *Doing What Comes Naturally: Change, Rhetoric and the Practice of Theory in Literary and Legal Studies* (Duke University Press, 1989) 344.
[34] Stephen Feldman, 'Postmodern Free Expression: A Philosophical Rationale for the Digital Age' (2017) 100 *Marquette Law Review* 1123, 1148. Feldman claims that 'the concept of the classical liberal self and the three philosophical rationales for free expression assume that the absence of government regulation maximizes individual liberty. But in the digital age, this assumption is patently false': at 1161.
[35] Richard Delgado, 'First Amendment Formalism is Giving Way to First Amendment Legal Realism' (1994) 29 *Harvard Civil Law-Civil Liberties Law Review* 169, 170.

identity is socially constructed.³⁶ Race is a social construct,³⁷ not an immutable characteristic.³⁸ Presumably this social construct means that individuals cannot be held responsible for their behaviours, and the criminal law will not effectively deter or punish undesired behaviour. If an individual is 'socially constructed', this means that government regulation becomes critical in construction of 'socially desired' identity.³⁹ Of course, it is very difficult to square this idea with the fundamental principle of representative government, under which government is considered to be representative of the community it serves, rather than its master. In fact, these aspects of postmodernism seem to be more of a throwback to the bleak view of human nature espoused by Hobbes – that the state needs to shape individuals in ways thought (by some) to be socially desirable.

Postmodernists believe that existing legal structures perpetuate existing status and power and show disdain for the powerless. A pithy claim that succinctly sums up postmodernist thought here is that 'the places where the law does not go to redress harm have tended to be the places where women, children, people of colour and poor

---

[36] Calvin Massey, 'The Constitution in a Postmodern Age' (2007) 64 *Washington and Lee Law Review* 165, 174: 'the postmodern contention is that there is no coherent self that lies outside the disparate social discourses that inevitably construct us'; Stephen Feldman, 1162.

[37] Charles R Lawrence III, 'If He Hollers Let Him Go: Regulating Racist Speech on Campus' [1990] *Duke Law Journal* 431, 443; Kimberlé Crenshaw Mapping the Margins: Intersectionality, Identity Politics and Violence Against Women of Color' (1991) 43 *Stanford Law Review* 1241; Neil Gotanda 'A Critique of "Our Constitution is Color-Blind"' (1991) 44 *Stanford Law Review* 1, 23; Richard Delgado and Jean Stefancic, *Critical Race Theory: An Introduction* (New York University Press, 3rd ed, 2017) 9.

[38] Robert Hayman, The Color of Tradition: Critical Race Theory and Postmodern Constitutional Traditionalism' (1995) 30 *Harvard Civil Rights – Civil Liberties Law Review* 57, 91.

[39] Steven Gey, 'The Case Against Postmodern Censorship Theory' (1996) 145 *University of Pennsylvania Law Review* 193, 198.

people live'.[40] In the post-modern world, the distinction between the private and the public realm collapses, because the private is publicly (socially) constructed.[41]

Postmodernism would also decry another major rationale for freedom of speech – belief that it is in the marketplace of ideas that the strongest arguments will win out. A postmodernist would disagree with the assumption underlying this argument, that of fair and free access to the 'market'. A postmodernist would argue the market was 'rigged' in favour of the powerful, strong and wealthy, and that only the voices of the strong are heard in such a system. The argument is that the weak are silenced under this (broadly) laissez-faire system, such that only government intervention can bring about a system where all voices are heard. The argument would be that the government needs to intervene in this market, by muting some of the strong voices, and magnifying others, in order to ensure that all voices are heard, and the market works in a more efficient and effective manner. It would overtly favour the expression of some views over others.[42] It is argued that existing exceptions to the generally very robust protection of free speech are rooted in 'privilege':

> When powerful groups find a particular type of speech offensive, and likely to render them one-down, they pass a law to curtail it. We rarely notice these exceptions and special doctrines, however, because they are time-honoured and second nature. Of course there would be an exception for state secrets, plagiarism,

---

[40] Mari Matsuda, 'Public Response to Racist Speech: Considering the Victim's Story' (1989) 87 *Michigan Law Review* 2320, 2322.
[41] Gey (n 39) 241.
[42] Ibid 204. The United States Supreme Court has specifically rejected the suggestion that government should mute some voices so that others may be heard: *Buckley v Valeo* 424 US 1, 48-49 (1976).

false advertising and dozens of other types of speech, we say.[43]

The umbrella of postmodernism houses a range of movements, including critical legal theory. Critical legal theorists would typically criticise freedom of speech on the basis that it only permitted the voices of the strong and powerful to be heard, preserving the status quo of an unfair society.[44] They would argue that freedom of speech perpetuates existing hierarchies within society, consigning the weak and powerless to remain permanently so.[45] In their view, freedom of speech entrenches and reflects existing power structures. Critical legal theoriests would argue that "freedom of speech" is really an illusion, that individuals are not truly "free", but constrained by existing societal structures, discourse, meaning of words, their education etc.[46] Closely aligned with critical legal theory is a sub-branch known as critical race theory. Due to its importance for the immediate context of freedom of speech under discussion in this article, critical race theory, and the views of its leading adherents, warrants fuller discussion here.

---

[43] Delgado (n 35) 172. By way of respectful response, rules against plagiarism protect everyone against another person's unauthorised copying or appropriation of the work, whether the person who authored the work copied is powerful or powerless, or somewhere in between. Similarly, false advertising protects all of us as consumers, not merely the strong, wealthy or powerful.

[44] Allan Hutchinson, *Introduction to Critical Legal Studies* (Rowman & Littlefied Publishers, 1989) 3: 'offended by the hierarchical structures of domination that characterize modern society CLS people work toward a world that is more just and egalitarian ... for CLS the rule of law is a mask that lends to existing social structures the appearance of legitimacy and inevitability'.

[45] Jay Moran, 'Postmodernism's Misguided Place in Legal Scholarship: Chaos Theory, Deconstruction and Some Insights from Thomas Pynchon's Fiction' (1998) 6 *Southern California Interdisciplinary Law Journal* 155, 158-159.

[46] Stanley Fish, *There's No Such Thing as Free Speech* (Oxford University Press, 1994); Augusto Zimmermann 'The Unconstitutionality of Religious Vilification Laws in Australia: Why Religious Vilification Laws are Contrary to the Implied Freedom of Political Communication Affirmed in the Australian Constitution' [2013] 3 *Brigham Young University Law Review* 457, 470.

B *Critical Race Theory*

The late 20th century saw the development of a sub-genre within the critical legal theorists movement, focussed on race. Evolving from the idea in critical legal theory that law reflected existing power structures and privilege in society, critical race theory developed on the argument that laws reflected the privilege of a particular race, or in other words 'white privilege'. According to this viewpoint, freedom of speech was not an essential pre-condition for a healthy functioning democracy, a way in which individuals developed, or a way in which society determined or became closer to truth. Rather, it was a way in which existing power structures and privilege was perpetuated, on the basis that it was those of a particular race, and in particular 'whites', who controlled the means of communication and therefore spoke with the loudest voices, effectively silencing and drowning out the less privileged, including in particular racial minorities. This leads Delgado to claim that racism and sexism 'are embedded in the reigning paradigm' by which 'we construct and interpret reality'.[47] Race-based 'hate speech' is 'spirit murder'.[48] In this theory, 'law (is)

---

[47] Delgado (n 35) 171.
[48] Patricia Williams, 'Spirit Murdering the Messenger: The Discourse of Fingerpointing as the Law's Response to Racism' (1987) 42 *University of Miami Law Review* 127, 129-130. Williams claims that racism 'can be as difficult to prove as child abuse or rape, where the victim is forced to convince others he or she was not at fault, or that the perpetrator was not just playing around. As in rape cases, victims of racism must prove that they did not distort the circumstances, misunderstand the intent, or even enjoy it'. I must respectfully disagree with many of these comments. In criminal law, any person who accuses another of committing a crime must prove the elements of the crime at a level beyond reasonable doubt. This is as it should be. I am not aware of any defence to a rape or child abuse charge that involves questions of whether the alleged perpetrator was 'playing around', or any case in which the issue of 'enjoyment' was in any way relevant in such a context. The truth is that a rape charge typically revolves around the issue of the physical act of intercourse, and the question of consent: see for example *Criminal Code Act Consolidation Act 1913* (WA) s 325.1; *Criminal Code 1899* (Qld) s 349.

a prime instrument in the construction and reinforcement of racial subordination'.[49] I will now elaborate in some detail the work of some of the leading scholars in the critical race theory movement.

1   Mari Matsuda

A notable feature of Matsuda's work, fairly typical of critical race theorists, is the use of narrative, or personal story and anecdote. I will leave it to others to debate the extent to which use of narrative, often extensive, is appropriate or persuasive within a discussion about legal issues.[50] There is certainly conjecture about this. Regardless, in one of Matsuda's leading articles, she includes an anecdote where she claims she arrived in Perth and:

> [F]inds a proliferation of posters stating 'Asians Out or Racial War' displayed on telephone poles. She uses her best, educated inflection in speaking with clerks and cab drivers, and decides not to complain when she is overcharged.[51]

Matsuda refers to a 'structural reality of racism' in America.[52] She claims that:

> [V]arious implements of racism find their way into the hands

---

[49] Ian Haney Lopez, 'The Social Construction of Race: Some Observations on Illusion, Fabrication and Choice' (1994) 29 *Harvard Civil Rights-Civil Liberties Law Review* 1, 3.
[50] Mark Tushnet, 'The Degradation of Constitutional Discourse' (1992) 81 *Georgetown Law Journal* 251; Daniel Farber and Suzanna Sherry, 'Telling Stories Out of School: An Essay on Legal Narratives' (1993) 45 *Stanford Law Review* 807; Richard Delgado, 'On Telling Stories Out of School: A Reply to Farber and Sherry' (1993) 46 *Vanderbilt Law Review* 665.
[51] Mari Matsuda, 'Public Response to Racist Speech: Considering the Victim's Story' (1989) 87 *Michigan Law Review* 2320, 2320 (this incident apparently occurred in 1987).
[52] Ibid 2332.

of different dominant-group members. Lower and middle class white men might use violence against people of colour; while upper class whites might resort to private clubs or righteous indignation against 'diversity' and 'reverse discrimination'.

Her key argument is that what she considers to be 'racist' speech should not be protected by the First Amendment to the *United States Constitution*. In making this argument, she faces very significant hurdles in terms of precedent. The United States Supreme Court has generally very strongly protected freedom of speech in that country as an indispensable aspect of democratic self-government. It has particularly frowned upon content-based and viewpoint-based restrictions on speech.[53] It has recognised few exceptions to free speech rights, including a so-called 'fighting words' exception,[54] although the continued scope of this exception is open to doubt. In protection of free speech, the Court has invalidated an ordinance applied to stop a march involving the wearing of swastikas on armbands,[55] and one that criminalised cross-burning.[56] It did uphold a challenge an ordinance banning publications that portrayed a class of citizens of any 'race, color, creed, or religion' in a way that exposed them to contempt,

---

[53] 'If there is a bedrock principle underlying the First Amendment, it is that the government may not prohibit the expression of an idea simply because society finds the idea itself offensive or disagreeable': *Texas v Johnson* 491 US 397, 414 (1989).
[54] *Chaplinsky v New Hampshire* 315 US 568 (1942).
[55] *Skokie v National Socialist Party of America et al* 432 US 43 (1977).
[56] *Brandenburg v Ohio* 395 US 444 (1969); *RAV v Petitioner, City of St Paul* 505 US 377 (1992). In the former case, the Court limited the ability of a legislature to criminalise speech advocating force or violation of the law 'except where such advocacy is directed to inciting or producing imminent lawless action and is likely to incite or produce such action': at 447; *United States v Eichman* 496 US 310, 318-319 (1990) Brennan J (with whom Marshall, Blackmun, Scalia and Kennedy JJ concurred) noted that the First Amendment protected 'virulent ethnic and religious epithets' because governments could not prohibit the expression of idea, however distasteful, because they disagreed with it.

derision or a breach of the peace,[57] but later developments in First Amendment jurisprudence suggest this decision is no longer good law.[58]

The Court has reiterated on countless occasions that there is no such thing as a false idea. It is considered essential that all have the right to speak; the price of this is that some will say horrible and hurtful things, but we pay this price because we know the price of the alternative, government sanction of speech it happens to disfavour at any particular time, is higher and worse.[59]

Matsuda argues for reform of these free speech principles such that legislatures would be permitted to outlaw 'racist' speech. Her justification is that:

> Racist speech is best treated as a sui generis category, presenting an idea so historically untenable, so dangerous, and so tied to perpetuation of violence and degradation of the very classes of human beings who are least equipped to respond that it is properly treated as outside the realm of protected discourse.[60]

Matsuda would permit the banning of speech that was 'racist' if it met three criteria: (a) the message was one of racial inferiority, (b) it was directed against a historically oppressed group, and (c) the message was persecutorial, hateful and degrading.[61] She says that the test for

---

[57] *Beauharnais v Illinois* 343 US 250 (1952).
[58] Kent Greenawalt, 'Insults and Epithets: Are They Protected Speech?' (1990) 42 *Rutgers Law Review* 287, 304.
[59] Aryeh Neier, *Defending My Enemy: American Nazis, the Skokie Case and the Risks of Freedom* 7 (Dutton Books, 1979): 'it is dangerous to let the Nazis have their say. But it is more dangerous by far to destroy the laws that deny anyone the power to silence Jews if Jews should need to cry out to each other and to the world for succor'.
[60] Matsuda (n 51) 2357.
[61] Ibid.

whether particular material met this final requirement should be the recipient's community standard.[62] Her writing suggests she believes that the swastika would meet these requirements.[63] She justifies a legal ban on what she considers to be racist speech on the basis that it is 'wrong'.

Matsuda's argument seems to be that the 'truth' rationale for freedom of speech does not apply to what she considers to be 'racist' speech, because of the 'universal acceptance of the wrongfulness of the doctrine of racial supremacy', given her view that racist speech necessarily involves a supremacy view. Of course, I agree that the doctrine of racial supremacy is awful and wrong. But I am naturally sceptical about any claim that anything is 'universally accepted', as Mill's work teaches, and I must respectfully disagree with the claim about universal acceptance of this position. Ethnic minorities in various countries, including China and Sri Lanka, might beg to differ. Of course, persecution of a person based on race is one of the five animating factors for the *Refugee Convention*, and it would be a large claim to suggest that there is no longer any need for that part of the *Refugee Convention* based on race-based persecution, because it is no longer occurring. Regrettably, it is. But this fact surely demonstrates the folly of the universality claim.

Because of the way in which Matsuda defines racism and 'hate speech', she freely admits that:

---

[62] Ibid 2364; 'rather than looking to the neutral, objective, unknowing and ahistorical reasonable person, we should look to the victim-group members to tell us whether the harm is real harm to real people'.
[63] Ibid 2365-2366: 'there are certain symbols and regalia that in the context of history carry a clear message of racial supremacy, hatred, persecution and degradation of certain groups. The swastika ... (is) an example of a sign ... that convey(s) a powerful message to both the user and the recipient'.

Expressions of hatred, revulsion, and anger directed against historically dominant-group members by subordinated group members are not criminalised by the definition of racist hate messages used here.[64]

Matsuda claims that these expressions should not be criminalised because 'they come from an experience of oppression'.[65] Thus, ironically, she would embed what I would consider racism into our legal system, by having the law applied in different ways according to the race of the speaker. If the speaker were of a racial minority, what they said to a member of the racial majority would not amount to hate speech and therefore would not be prohibited, but the very same content expressed by a member of the racial majority to a member of a racial minority would be hate speech, according to her view. I could never accept the application of a law being dependent on the race of those involved in a given situation. To do so, ironically, would be racist (in the traditional meaning of the word, not the unusual definition Matsuda ascribes to it). Respectfully, one does not tackle racism by being racist.

She also argues that those who attempt to adopt a neutral position on certain kinds of speech she deems racist are in fact not neutral, but in complicit agreement with the relevant offensive messages. This claim appears in the following passage:

> To allow an organisation known for violence, persecution, race hatred and commitment to racial supremacy to exist openly, and to provide police protection and access to public streets and college campuses for such a group, means that the state is promoting racist speech. If not for such support, hate groups

---

[64] Ibid 2361.
[65] Ibid 2363.

would decline in efficacy. The chilling sight of avowed racists in threatening regalia marching through our neighbourhoods with full police protection is a statement of state authorization.[66]

This is not an isolated sentiment. Others who defend the right of individuals to speak are attacked by associating them with the controversial views expressed by the individual. So, for instance, the American Civil Liberties Union ('ACLU') and those who give of their time to defend human rights, including free speech, are the subject of abuse and derision. Andrea Dworkin dismisses the ACLU as the 'handmaiden of the pornographers, the Nazis and the Ku Klux Klan' for their defence of free speech in these controversial contexts.[67]

2 *Richard Delgado*

Delgado paints a bleak picture of the United States, stating it is a 'deeply ingrained' idea that a person's colour is a badge of inferiority and involves denial of opportunity.[68] He claims (without referencing any literature) that 'the psychological harms caused by racial stigmatization are often much more severe than those created by other stereotyping actions',[69] and compares the plight of racial minorities with 'persons with physical disfigurements'[70] (this is a direct quote

---

[66] Ibid 2378.
[67] Andrew Dworkin, 'The ACLU: Bait and Switch' (1989) 1 *Yale Journal of Law and Feminism* 37, 37. She also claims that 'genocidal ambitions and concrete organizing towards genocidal goals are trivialized by male lawyers who are a mostly protected and privileged group': at 39.
[68] Richard Delgado, 'Words that Wound: A Tort Action for Racial Insults, Epithets and Name-Calling' (1982) 17 *Harvard Civil Rights-Civil Liberties Law Review* 133, 135.
[69] Ibid 136.
[70] Ibid 136.

from Delgado; he used the phrase that I merely cite. I would not use these terms). His view is that the harm caused by racial insults justifies not according First Amendment speech to such expression, and conferring a civil claim on the person targeted for emotional abuse and injury. He derides the position of the ACLU, as strong defenders of free speech doctrine, as being part of a 'backwater of legal thought'.[71]

Delgado seems to share the view of Matsuda that, by curbing racially offensive speech, it will lead to a more 'peaceful and diverse' society.[72] Again, this statement is not referenced or accompanied by supporting evidence. He also defines hate speech very narrowly, as involving members of a privileged class speaking disparagingly about those of a lower class.[73] He claims, again without evidence, that university administrators 'may know, on some level, that tolerating a small degree of harassment and invective on campus confers benefits ... tolerating 'micro-aggression' keeps students of colour on edge and defensive, prevents them from feeling too secure on campus, and discourages them from making demands'. He claims university administrators might 'treat lightly' the occasional racist student, visitor or lecturer who utters a racist slur 'recognizing, perhaps unconsciously, that his transgression brings stability to the institution'.[74]

He claims that the marketplace of ideas justification for free speech is not strong, because 'the fight was not fair. Speech is expensive, not all can afford the cost of a microphone, computer or television airtime,

---

[71] Delgado (n 35) 174.
[72] Richard Delgado 'Book Review: Toward a Legal Realist View of the First Amendment' (2000) 113 *Harvard Law Review* 778, 784.
[73] Ibid 787: 'hate speech grinds down persons of lower station and power than the speaker', and hate speech 'often operates further to advantage its speakers and their class': at 789.
[74] Ibid 790.

not all have equal credibility in the eyes of the public'.[75]

Delgado shares Matsuda's position that not all racial slurs are alike. He would apparently treat very differently slurs directed at white people from those directed at African-American people. This is because the slurs directed at the latter race carry a 'dispiriting quality' and historical impact that is missing from those directed at white people. In the case of whites, slurs are often experienced 'on an individual and isolated level'.[76]

3 Charles Lawrence III

Lawrence also paints a bleak view of American society, stating that 'for over three hundred years, racist speech has been the liturgy of America's leading established religion, the religion of racism'.[77] He is dismissive of the marketplace of ideas justification for freedom of speech, on the basis that:

> [T]he American marketplace of ideas was founded with the idea of the racial inferiority of non-whites as one of its chief commodities, and ever since the market opened, racism has remained its most active item in trade ... racism is an epidemic infecting the marketplace of ideas and rendering it dysfunctional. Racism is ubiquitous. We are all racists.[78]

At times, Lawrence seems to suggest that those without direct, personal

---

[75] Ibid 791.
[76] Ibid 797.
[77] Charles R Lawrence III 'If He Hollers Let Him Go: Regulating Racist Speech on Campus' [1990] *Duke Law Journal* 431, 447.
[78] Ibid 468.

experience of racism cannot properly balance competing interests in the free speech space:

> Not everyone has known the experience of being victimized by racist, misogynist and homophobic speech, and we do not share equally the burden of the societal harm it inflicts. Often we are too quick to say we have heard the victim's cries when we have not; we are too eager to assure ourselves we have experienced the same injury, and therefore we can make the constitutional balance without danger of mismeasurement. For many of us who have fought for the rights of oppressed minorities, it is difficult to accept that – by underestimating the injury from racist speech – we too might be implicated in the vicious words we would never utter. Until we have eradicated racism and sexism and no longer share in the fruits of those forms of domination, we cannot justly strike the balance over the protest of those who are dominated.[79]

Lawrence apparently criticises civil libertarians who argue that injury to victims of racial abuse is typically minimal, and distance themselves from such activity by dismissing it as isolated and an aberration. He states that such individuals 'disclaim any responsibility for its occurrence', apparently implying that one citizen is to be held responsible for what another citizen says or does. He then refers to the unacceptable behaviour of two white university students who adorn a poster of Beethoven with particular colours, with features that these students presumably associated (stereotypically) with a particular race, after a classroom debate where there was discussion about Beethoven's ethnicity. Lawrence takes issue with colleagues who shared his outrage at the students' behaviour, but who claimed it was an isolated case of immature stupidity and a case of the rebelliousness of youth. Rather, Lawrence viewed it as the students 'imitating their

---

[79] Ibid 459.

role models in the professoriate, not rebelling against them'.[80]

He agrees with Matsuda about the government's culpability for failing to curb what he considers to be hate and/or racist speech, decrying the 'joint venture' between governments that refuse to legislate against such speech, and those uttering these views.[81] He agrees with Matsuda that hate speech needs to be regulated because it tends to silence victims.[82]

4 Neil Gotanda

One of Gotanda's leading articles attacks the liberal position of 'neutrality' towards race. A neutral view regarding race would favour the law not taking race into account in its formation or application. So, for example, it would forbid discrimination on the basis of race, whether that discrimination was against or in favour of a racial minority. It would disfavour a kind of 'identity-based' view that a person's characteristics, including race, should impact how the law applies to them.

Gotanda attacks this liberal premise as racist. He argues that it, in fact, 'fosters white racial domination' and legitimates and maintains the social, economic and political advantages that he believes white people have over other Americans.[83]

Gotanda believes that race is socially constructed. He also criticises how the dominant legal culture views race, as stable and immutable,

---
[80] Ibid 479.
[81] Ibid 446.,
[82] Charles R Lawrence III 'Crossburning and the Sound of Silence: Antisubordination Theory and the First Amendment' (1992) 37 *Villanova Law Review* 787, 792.
[83] Neil Gotanda 'A Critique of "Our Constitution is Color-Blind"' (1991) 44 *Stanford Law Review* 1, 2-3.

and reflecting what he views as a 'formal-race' concept of race, rather than his favoured view of a 'status-race' or 'culture-race' concept that he favours. Gotanda claims that:

> Subordination occurs in the very act of a white person recognising a Black person's race. Much of constitutional discourse disguises that subordination by treating racial categories as if they were stable and immutable. Finally, the treatment of racial categories as functionally objective devalues the socioeconomic and political history of those placed within them. Through this complex process of assertion, disguise, and devaluation, racial categorization ... advances white interests.[84]

He believes that discussion of race in a legal context must take place in the context of the oppression and suppression of minority races in America.[85] Gotanda claims that the attempt to make constitutional rights 'colour-blind', given his view of the social construction of rights, amounts to a denial of the distinctive culture of African-American people and would amount to 'cultural genocide'.[86]

IV CRITICAL REFLECTIONS ON CRITICAL RACE THEORY AND ATTEMPTS TO BAN RACIST SPEECH

A *Essentialism*

One of the main criticisms of critical race theory is that it involves essentialism – that it is superficial because it makes gross generalisations about those of a minority race. For example, it assumes that all those of a minority race are impoverished, powerless and silenced. It assumes

---
[84] Ibid 26.
[85] Ibid 37.
[86] Ibid 59-60.

that their life experience has been one of oppression. One example of this in the work of Matsuda is her stated view that in order to determine whether or not race-based speech should be banned, the law should ask members of the victimised group. This view apparently assumes that members of the victimised group would all answer the same way as to whether a particular statement was, or was not, hurtful and something that the law ought to proscribe. Yet, self-evidently it is just not possible to draw this kind of conclusion about a group of people.

This criticism has been made elsewhere:

> One of the chief problems with the racialist account of social power and struggle lies in the tendency to 'essentialize' the racial communities with which it represents the social world. In black racialist circles the felt necessity to articulate the stable vision of group identity and interest has underwritten a 'representational politics' in which the experience of one segment of black America is taken as the representative of the black experience in totality. As a result, Black racialism yields a flat, fixed image of racial identity, experience and interest which fails to capture the complex and changing realities of racial domination in the contemporary United States.[87]

It would clearly be simplistic and incorrect to assume the uniformity of the life experience and views of members of a racial minority. Further, this aspect of critical race theory appears at odds with other elements of postmodernist thought, which assert there is no objective truth and that individuals are social constructs. If this were true, everyone's life experience would have 'constructed' them differently, making

---

[87] Cornell West, Kimberlé Crenshaw, Neil Gotanda, Gary Peller and Kendall Thomas *Critical Race Theory: The Key Writings That Formed the Movement* (New Press, 1995) xxxi.

any assumptions about the reactions of a particular group to a given situation impossible. At this point, critical race theory approaches incoherence.[88]

Further, though critical race theorists claim the powerlessness of many in society, and control of the media by powerful white individuals, in truth social media has permitted a much broader range of messages to be circulated. If it were once true that media ownership was concentrated in the hands of a powerful few, the exponential growth of social media, permitting all a chance to express views and have them circulated widely around the world, has surely muted this concern.

B *Contradictions Within Post-Modernism*

There are many logical irregularities with a post-modern view. Firstly, post-modernists criticise existing beliefs on the basis they are not really what an individual believes, but a product of the social structures in which a person exists. It fundamentally denies that individuals are essentially free, and exercise 'free will'. Of course, the same comment could be directed to the post-modernists themselves. On this argument, surely they themselves are a 'social construct'; their views are not really the product of an independent, informed judgment, but hemmed in and constrained by their place within societal structures. On this basis, how would a post-modern view be any different to the whole range of other views that currently exist, which post-modernists criticise as being socially constructed?

Post-modernists seem to have a very benign view of government,

---

[88] See for further discussion Kenneth Nunn, 'Essentially Black: Legal Theory and the Morality of Conscious Racial Identity' (2018) 97 *Nebraska Law Review* 287.

trusting it to inculcate citizens with the "right" beliefs, beliefs which the post-modernists happen to share. But, of course, to give power to government to inculcate citizens with particular beliefs is very dangerous. What happens if a particular bloc takes the reins of government, but does not share post-modern beliefs? Would the post-modernists then deny the right of that government to engage in the kind of encouragement of "right-thinking" that they have previously lauded?[89]

C *Neutrality of the Law Regarding Race*

A hallmark of liberal thought is the neutrality of the law toward race. It is inherent in the landmark dissenting judgment of Harlan J in *Plessy v Ferguson*.[90] In a strong affirmation of the rule of law, Harlan J states that the *United States Constitution* is 'colour-blind', and there was no superior, dominant ruling class. All citizens were equal before the law, without regard to race.[91] Of course, a majority of the Court in that case adopted a 'separate but equal doctrine', but this was overturned by the Court in *Brown v Board of Education*,[92] where the court found that the policy, as administered, had the practical effect that African-American children were denied educational opportunities that were open to students of other races.[93]

This article defends the neutrality of the law toward race. It is absolutely

---

[89] These criticisms are discussed in further detail in Gey (n 39) 224-233.
[90] 163 US 537 (1896) (*'Plessy'*).
[91] Ibid 559-560.
[92] 347 US 483 (1954).
[93] *Loving v Virginia* 388 US 1, 13 (1967) (Stewart J): 'it is simply not possible for a state law to be valid under our *Constitution* which makes the criminality of an act depend upon the race of the actor'.

fundamental in a nation premised on the rule of law that the law should be applied in an objective, neutral and impartial manner to all. Identity aspects of a person, including their race, but also other things like their gender, age, sexuality, religion, political view, disability etc are simply irrelevant, and should be irrelevant, in terms of how the law applies to them. Discrimination legislation nationally and in every state and territory throughout Australia seeks to ensure equal treatment of people, and that people are not discriminated against in employment, in the provision of goods and services and in relation to accommodation on the basis of these grounds, including race. Most would laud legislation such as this. It seems wholly at odds with the equality concerns and values underpinning anti-discrimination legislation to now seek to reject legal neutrality around race.

Because I support the neutrality of the law towards race, I must respectfully, but fundamentally, disagree with the claim of Matsuda that the expression of 'race hate' by the 'majority race' should be banned if it meets her criteria, but that the expression of 'race hate' by a member of a minority race towards a member of the 'majority race' would not be prohibited. In my view, it is fundamentally mistaken, not to mention ill-advised, to apply the law differently, according to the race of the person to which it is sought to apply. It is fatally inconsistent with the rule of law. It reifies one aspect of a person's identity above all of the other things that characterise them, and seeks to discriminate positively on that basis. It seems to be the very antithesis of the 'equality' that critical race scholars claim to seek. One does not solve 'inequality', to the extent that this is perceived to be a problem, by applying the law 'unequally'. An apparently simplistic assumption that all those of the 'majority race' are favoured and privileged and powerful, and all members of 'minority races' are disfavoured and underprivileged and powerless, must be called out for what it is. It is incorrect and untruthful; it is demeaning to those of a racial minority, and is a grossly misleading view of our society. Its wildly false premises cannot be the basis for an argument that some speech be legally validated depending on the racial identity of a speaker, when the same speech made by someone of a different racial identity be legally invalidated.[94]

To reach this conclusion is not to ignore, trivialise or minimise the terrible racism and denial of human rights that has occurred in the past on racist lines, or to deny that racism continues to exist in our society. Of course, in the United States African-American people endured horrific years of slavery. After the end of the Civil War, they continued to endure blatant and endemic racism, including a denial of their most fundamental civil rights, including the right to vote. The right of African-American people to an education was blighted and crimped for many years, first by the notorious *Dred Scott* decision and then by the application of the 'separate but equal' doctrine of *Plessy*. African-American people endured years of state-imposed segregation from others in the community. Felon disenfranchisement laws, by intent or effect, have impacted on the voting rights of Africa-American people, and there are concerns that voter districting continues in an effort to disenfranchise and disempower African-American people.

In Australia, terrible atrocities were committed against Aboriginal

---

[94] Delgado and Stefancic (n 37) 27: 'critical race theorists ... hold that color blindness ... will allow us to redress only extremely egregious racial harms, ones that everyone would notice and condemn. But if racism is embedded in our thought processes and social structures as deeply as many crit(ic)s believe, then the 'ordinary business' of society – the routines, practices and institutions that we rely on to do the world's work – will keep minorities in subordinate positions. Only aggressive, color-conscious efforts to change the way things are will do much to ameliorate misery'.

and Torres Strait Islander peoples. Many of them were killed. They were dispossessed of their lands. They were originally denied the right to vote, not counted as individuals at census time, and were in some cases removed from their families by government mandate. There are multiple ongoing issues, including that some Aboriginal and Torres Strait Islander people do not believe that they have sufficient input into governance, and in particular policy issues that affect them. The mortality rate among Aboriginal and Torres Strait Islander people remains high, with life expectancy much lower than for those of other races, school attendance rates remain lower than hoped for, and domestic violence rates remain higher than the national average.

Having acknowledged this, it is submitted to be extremely dangerous for any legal system to have the application of its principles dependent on the race of individuals. It unjustifiably reifies an aspect, albeit an important aspect, of a person's identity, over and above the fundamental legal principle of the rule of law, and its promise of the equality of all people before the law. This point was made eloquently in recent times by Keane J in *Love v Commonwealth of Australia; Thomas v Commonwealth of Australia*.[95] Readers will be aware that the case essentially concerned whether a person identifying as Indigenous could be within the scope of the Commonwealth's constitutional power with respect to aliens, given that they were born overseas and had not been naturalised. In answering 'yes' in dissent, Keane J noted that

> To adopt race as a basis for differentiating between members of the people of the Commonwealth in terms of the application of laws is not a course that commends itself in terms of the exercise

---

[95] [2020] HCA 3.(2020) 270 CLR 152.

of judicial power given that justice is to be administered equally to all.[96]

Another aspect of this principle of neutrality implies the rejection of arguments made by Lawrence and others that the mere fact that legislatures or others fail to ban particular speech to which Lawrence and others object means that the legislature or other supports that speech. This is to misunderstand the concept of 'neutrality'. It presents a simplistic binary that either individuals support banning offensive speech, or in effect they support its contents. This is a falsity.[97] Neutrality means that the state takes no position as to the merits or otherwise of a particular speech. Failing to ban something cannot and should not be equated with supporting it. I am not my brother's (nor my sister's) keeper. I am not responsible for racist comments that others might make, contrary to the apparent position of Lawrence.

I must also respectfully disagree with a kind of identity politics view that it is only those with direct, personal experience of discrimination or racism that can properly balance free speech with the harm caused by racist views. Quite simply, our legal system and our society does not operate in this manner, and nor should it. It would, respectfully, be ridiculous to say that a judge could only properly assess another's

---

[96] Ibid [181]; similarly Gageler J (dissenting) rejected the suggestion of a 'race-based constitutional distinction': at [133]; compare the very different view of Charles R Lawrence III, 'Race, Multiculturalism and the Jurisprudence of Transformation' (1995) 47 *Stanford Law Review* 819, 838 denouncing 'color-blindness' in the law: 'the colorblind race baiter completes his white supremacist wizardry by blaming affirmative action itself for creating hostility, resentment and racial divisiveness'. One interpretation of this sentence is that Lawrence equates those who believe the law should be 'colorblind' with views of white supremacy. I would respectfully, fundamentally oppose this assertion.
[97] Kent Greenawalt, 'Insults and Epithets: Are They Protected Speech?' (1990) 42 *Rutgers Law Review* 287, 305: 'allowing racist rhetoric does not show support of racism'.

behaviour if they shared characteristics of the other – whether that be race, religion, gender, age or other factor. An African-American judge can of course make a judgment about the behaviour of a Caucasian person. A female judge can make a judgment about the behaviour of a male person. Acceptance of this identity politics position would reify individual characteristics of a person above all else, including the law and the rule of law. It would minimise what unites us – capacity for rational thought, empathy to others, the essence of a human being – and seek to maximise differences. It is hard to understand the benefit in so doing, but the damage to the fabric of our society that would be wrought by such a view is very clear.

D *Awareness of Racism and Racial Hatred*

Unpleasant as it is, it is considered important for society to hear the expression of racist views. In doing so, it brings our collective attention to the fact that such horrible views continue to exist in our society. By being made aware of it, the state can work to counteract it with positive government policies promoting greater understanding of different cultures, acceptance of difference among us, and hopefully an acknowledgement that the great variation in cultures, backgrounds, ethnicities, races and religion in our society is and should be seen as a source of strength. Australia is a successful multicultural nation, built on large-scale immigration from all corners of the world, together with Indigenous Australians. If governments are not aware of racism or race hatred because it has been driven underground, it is less likely to respond to these issues with appropriate policies.

E No Evidence that Laws Banning Speech Will Reduce Racism, Race-Motivated Violence or Hatred or Will 'Unsilence' Racial Minorities

Of course, all of us would like to live in a society where there is less racism, where there is less violence, including that motivated by racism, and where there is less hatred of others (on any basis, including race). We all want to live in a world where everyone is free, and feels free, to express their views on matters, and where no-one is or feels intimidated about doing so.

That said, one of the characteristics of the discipline of law is its requirement for evidence. It is easy to make claims or accusations. The law rightly requires evidence of claims in order to accept them as valid. This requirement should be applied to various claims of critical race scholars regarding the harms said to be caused by racially motivated speech.

For example, one of the claims that Delgado and Matsuda makes is that suppression of racially motivated speech is necessary because racist speech silences the targets of such speech. They claim the 'marketplace of ideas' view of free speech does not work, because those who are the targets of race-based speech tend to be silenced by the shock of hearing the racist speech.[98] However, it is not clear why only racial minorities, and not other minorities, would be affected in this way by hurtful speech, so as to justify special rules for racially-motivated speech. At a more general level too, a claim that hate speech should be banned because it silences targets has been questioned in the

---
[98] *Inquiry Into Anti-Vilification Provisions* (Parliament of Victoria, 2021) noted that vilification 'has the potential to silence the speech of others where, for example, a person engaging in the conduct has the benefit of a position of social or other authority': at 41.

literature.[99]

It is claimed that racial vilification laws seek to eliminate discrimination and hatred.[100] But how effective is it in doing so? What evidence is there that the introduction of so-called hate speech actually reduces the level of such speech in society? Victoria has had laws prohibiting racial vilification for nearly 20 years. Somewhat paradoxically, in the course of an inquiry which required the significant 'strengthening' of Victoria's anti-vilification legislation, the inquiry itself acknowledged and quoted an article authored by Katherine Gelber and Luke McNamara. They had noted in 2018 that 'there has been little or no change in the incidence of vilification in public places ... on this level, anti-vilification laws do not seem to have reduced the overall level of hate speech'.[101] The Inquiry itself noted that 'legislation alone cannot change community attitudes or prevent hate speech or vilifying conduct'.[102]

I will leave to one side the questionable recommendations of that committee to further proscribe so-called hate speech, given their acknowledgement of literature suggesting that, although that state has had anti-vilification in place for nearly 20 years, there is no evidence

---

[99] Burt Neuborne, 'Ghosts in the Attic: Idealized Pluralism, Community and Hate Speech' (1992) 27 *Harvard Civil Rights-Civil Liberties Law Review* 371, 394: 'the assertion that hate speech should be uniquely subject to censorship because it "silences" vulnerable targets is emotionally appealing, but empirically empty ... virtually every attempt at censorship is premised on an assertion that speech causes harm. A social science theory to support the claim of harm can be generated on demand'.
[100] Larissa Welmans, 'Section 18C and the Implied Freedom of Political Communication' (2019) 44 *University of Western Australia Law Review* 21, 52.
[101] *Inquiry into Anti-Vilification Protections* (Parliament of Victoria, 2021) 1. It noted it had 'heard throughout the Inquiry that religious and racial discrimination, harassment and hatred remain prevalent throughout the state': at 26. On the other hand, in 2017-2018 and in 2018-2019, only 4 official complaints were made in each year: at 109.
[102] Ibid 61.

it has done anything to reduce the kind of speech we all dislike. It is not clear to me, with respect, why the committee believed that, having failed to reduce racism or hate-related speech, an extension of anti-vilification legislation (albeit with some changes to wording, proof etc) will now achieve the desired effect. But the main point to be made here is the absolute lack of evidence that anti-vilification legislation in fact achieves its goals. When seeking to weigh up the 'costs' of such provision, in terms of their impact on free speech and the uncertainty they create, and the 'benefits' of such regulation, the dearth of evidence as to any tangible benefit, in terms of reduction of racism or hate speech (hopefully, reflecting a reduction in the number of people who have this viewpoint), is critical.

And to some extent, this lack of evidence is not surprising. Germany in the 1930s had anti-vilification legislation in place.[103] Clearly, it did nothing to stop the rise of Nazism and the persecution of Jews and others. Those intent on expressing hateful views will often not likely be familiar with the nuances of the law, with all due respect. They may not be aware that their intended speech is or may be unlawful. They may not have considered the legal consequences of expressing such views. Individuals, including particularly in the online environment, often do not think carefully before expressing views. And even if the person were aware of the legal consequences, they may relish being the subject of a legal proceeding, which might give them further opportunity

---

[103] Zimmermann and Finlay (n 5) 191: 'The Weimar Republic of the 1930s had several laws against "insulting religious communities" and these laws were fully applied to prosecute hundreds of Nazi agitators ... far from halting National Socialist ideology, these laws helped Nazis achieve broader public support and recognition, and ultimately assisted the dissemination of racist ideas'; *R v Keegstra* [1990] 3 SCR 697, 854 (McLachlin J, with whom Sopinka J agreed, dissenting).

for them to vent their hateful views, and claim a martyr status.[104] The anti-vilification legislation will not have done much, if anything, to change a person's views. It may feed a person's outsider status or sense of grievance. If it does silence a racist, it may drive them underground, to use surreptitious ways of expressing their views to others. Again, the hate speech laws will have done nothing to address the underlying problem, merely seek to address public symptoms of it.

Of course, it is a dangerous slippery slope to permit the regulation of speech on the basis it is offensive or hateful.[105] In the classic words of Kirby J in *Coleman v Power*, the *Australian Constitution* protects speech beyond the 'whispered civilities of intellectual discourse'.[106] As he observes, political discussions in Australia often involves 'insult and emotion, calumny and invective', as part of the struggle for ideas.[107] This is a critical point. It must again be made, particularly in light of argument from the bench[108] and academic writing[109] that appears to confine freedom of speech to polite, civil tones. One claims that hate speech laws do not inhibit speech provided it is 'expressed reasonably moderately'.[110] Of course, that is the point about attempts to regulate speech. No-one can be sure what 'moderate' or 'reasonably moderate' is, and it not clear that courts could or should be determining

---

[104] *R v Keegstra* [1990] 3 SCR 697, 852-853 (McLachlin J, with whom Sopinka J agreed, dissenting).
[105] Nadine Strossen 'Freedom of Speech and Equality: Do We Have to Choose?' (2016) 25 *Journal of Law and Policy* 185, 186.
[106] (2004) 220 CLR 1, 91.
[107] Zimmermann and Finlay (n 5) 188.
[108] *Chief of the Defence Force v Gaynor* [2017] FCAFC 41, [109] where the Full Court referred to the 'tone' of the person's comments in determining whether he had freedom to express them.
[109] Welmans (n 100) 58, referring to the merit of s18C of *Racial Discrimination Act 1975* (Cth) in promoting 'civilised and thoughtful political discourse which will contribute to better general education on these issues'.
[110] Swannie (n 28) 87.

the legality of speech based on whether or not it is 'moderate'. Would Socrates have been able to pass this test? Would Galileo?

F *Uncertainty Over What is Being Banned*

A further difficulty with banning symbols is that they can be interpreted in different ways. On a personal level, I attended a zoom meeting last year from my home office. Behind me was a bookcase. One of the zoom attendees questioned the display of a swastika. As it happened, this was on the spine of a book in my library collection, entitled *The Rise and Fall of the Third Reich*. Of course, by innocently publicly displaying the swastika, I was not intending to indicate support for Nazism. It was a very minor incident, but it made an important point. We cannot know what message (if any) a person intends to convey when they show a particular symbol in public. Many symbols are inherently ambiguous in nature.

For example, the swastika has a long history. It has associations with religion, including the Hindu and Buddhist faiths.[111] It is said that swastikas first appeared more than 7,000 years ago. It was used to signify good fortune and wellbeing. Unfortunately, it became associated in the 1920s with horrific ideas about racial superiority and the Nazi movement, and was adopted as the German national flag in the mid-1930s. It was banned in Germany in 1945 and remains banned in that and other European nations.

The point is that a person who displays a swastika may be intending to convey many different possible messages, or none at all. It might

---

[111] Allison Mosig, 'Hate or Civic Pride: The Speech of Symbols in the United States, Germany and Japan' (2017) 40 *Suffolk Transnational Law Review* 73, 80-81.

be intended to indicate support for the hateful and murderous Nazi ideology; it might be intended to remind those who see it of the dangers of extreme ideology, or to compare an existing movement with that movement. It might reflect a religious view. It might not be intended to express any view whatsoever. No-one can know. It is extremely dangerous for the law to presume. Through the Victorian legislation banning display of the Nazi symbol contains exceptions and defences, it is not clear how broadly these will be interpreted.

V CONCLUSION

A liberal democratic society is fundamentally premised on freedom of speech. This should be a neutral political principle, espoused by all sides of politics. Freedom of speech has often been espoused by those on the political left, together with racial and other minorities, in support of their cause. At some time, freedom of speech became associated with the political right. It is a fundamental part of Western culture and values, but has come under increasing attack by postmodernists, including critical race theorists. These theorists reject fundamental rationales for freedom of speech, denying the concept of 'truth', claiming that any marketplace of ideas is "rigged" and favours "white privilege" and claiming that freedom of speech belongs only to the powerful. Some seem to advocate racism as a supposed antidote for the racism they see, seeking the law to be applied differently to different individuals based on their colour. This is inherently racist, and fundamentally at odds with the rule of law. Further, they apparently demand that the state take sides in arguments, ignoring the fundamental premise of state neutrality, and claiming a false equivalence between not preventing something, and supporting it. It is to be regretted that some of these ideas have gained traction.

This article has documented major weaknesses with this approach to the law. It is dangerously simplistic, assuming that all members of one race are disempowered and oppressed, and that all members of another race are powerful, dominant and seek to maintain dominance over the former group. Postmodernism offers little by way of positive improvement in anything; rather it seeks to destroy what currently exists, with little idea of what should replace it. It seeks to reify aspects of a person's identity above reason, the rule of law and law itself, replacing objectivity with subjectivity. It strangely seeks to attack the idea that the law should not discriminate in terms of race, by positively advocating discrimination on the basis of race, undermining fundamental case law such as *Brown v Board of Education*, and anti-discrimination legislation. The state should be very slow to ban the expression of ideas, including unpleasant ones. It is most unlikely that banning particular speech will reduce the extent of the sentiment being banned. It may do the opposite. It is passing strange that in the inquiry that recognises that 20 years of an existing anti-vilification law has done nothing to reduce vilification, the same inquiry proposes to 'beef up' the anti-vilification law, apparently expecting a different result. History has taught us that these laws do not work to achieve their claimed purpose. Governments over-reach when they seek to ban signs and symbols, as the recent Victorian inquiry has recommended. This is because it is impossible to draw a conclusion as to what a particular sign or symbol means, if anything. It is dangerous to base any law, let alone one that abrogates freedom of speech, on an assumption as to what the person displaying it intended to convey. Politicians of all political persuasions are being seduced by the woke shutdown, de-platforming vibe. It is anathema to democracy, and those who cherish democratic, free speech principles must fight back (with strong speech). Freedom of speech is too important to fall to a false idol.

4

Critical Theory, Wokeshevism, and The Chasm of Incoherence

PETER KURTI*

ABSTRACT

Critical Theory exerts a significant intellectual hold on the formation of policy and the conduct of discourse in the Australian public sphere. In its essential form, Critical Theory holds that there are many biases and imbalances of power in society which are hidden from view by dominant cultural structures, such as use of language and the ways in which knowledge is imparted. These structures are deemed 'problematic' and need to be identified, exposed, and overturned in the name of Social Justice.

The influence of Critical Theory upon the language, culture and institutions of Australia threatens to erode our liberal traditions of tolerance and liberty. This danger is expressed in the sustained and aggressive activism, characterised by 'Wokeshevism', that has spilled out of university campuses and into our schools, businesses, defence forces, the not-for-profit sector, the churches, the medical profession, and much of the media. From there, it is directed against all the perceived injustices that, together,

---

* Director of the Culture, Prosperity and Civil Society program, Centre for Independent Studies. Associate Professor (Adjunct) University of Notre Dame, Australia.

are deemed to comprise the toxic legacy of imperialist Western civilizations.

This chapter examines the flawed foundations upon which Critical Theory rests and explains why the language used by Critical Theory activists is so perplexing. It also sets out some key principles to guide responses to critics who insist that Australia — a country we know exemplifies a liberal and tolerant society — must be condemned and branded as systemically racist, misogynistic, homophobic, and colonial.

I FIRST CONSIDERATIONS: WOKESHEVISM AND THE OCCLUSION OF TRUTH

'Ages are no more infallible than individuals,' declared the 19th-century philosopher and public intellectual, John Stuart Mill. As he explained, '[e]very age having held opinions which subsequent ages have deemed not only false but absurd; and it is certain that many opinions, now in general, will be rejected by future ages'.[1]

For Mill, unrestricted freedom of opinion and expression was the vital precondition for individual self-development because truth depended on knowledge; and knowledge was most likely to emerge when opinions collided through the free expression and exchange of ideas.[2]

Although appeal is frequently made to Mill today when freedom of speech is being defended, Mill, himself, did not view that freedom as a *right*, as such. Mill's concern was with overturning falsity and absurdity. The central concern of his most famous book, *On Liberty*,

---

[1] Quoted in Richard Reeves, *John Stuart Mill: Victorian Firebrand* (Atlantic Books, 2007) 269.
[2] John Stuart Mill, *On Liberty*, (Penguin Classics, 2006) 11.

was not constraints imposed by the state on the individual; it was *any* set of social conditions and constraints that militated against the development of truth and knowledge.³

Today, however, young Australians are among the new generation that has graduated from university and started careers armed with the conviction that progress does not develop with the free exchange of ideas.

No longer promoted by defeating falsity and absurdity in open debate, today's preferred strategy for developing knowledge is cancellation, whereby those who do not subscribe to the revolutionary agenda of Critical Theory activists are attacked and pulled down — both literally (in the case of statues,) and metaphorically (in the case of people who express unacceptable opinions).⁴ However, cancellation is just one of a number of practices bundled together under the term 'woke'. Progress is now promoted by silencing unwelcome voices, deleting unwelcome ideas, and even by eradicating undesirable brand names.

Woke is not particularly new and has been around since the early 1940s. An official in the United Mine Workers in the United States, who was quoted by a journalist, used the word to indicate the pursuit of social justice: 'Waking up is a damn sight harder than going to sleep, but we'll stay woke up longer.'⁵

Today, however, woke signifies more than simply a desire for equality between people from all backgrounds, or a commitment to end

---

³   Ibid 16, 21.
⁴   Peter Kurti, *Cancelled! How ideological cleansing threatens Australia* (Centre for Independent Studies, 2020).
⁵   See Philip Collins, 'A gag is no cure for this cancel culture', *The Times* (Web Article, 12 July 2020).

discrimination on the grounds of skin colour or gender. Woke is not just the goal; it is the means of pursuing it; 'Wokeshevism' – a neologism which evokes nicely the taint of totalitarian zealotry – describes well the absolutist ideology driving this revolutionary turmoil.

Woke campaign strategies of cancellation and eradication in Australia threaten to promote ideas about the country that are intentionally divisive and mendaciously false. This occlusion of truth is already corrupting intellectual enquiry by passing off as truth arguments and statements that are demonstrably false. One example of such a falsehood is the claim that Australia is a country built on legal slavery.[6]

The history of Australia's settlement is extremely contentious; but however it is interpreted, slavery – whether legal or illegal – certainly has no part to play in contemporary Australian society. Forms of slavery do, of course, persist in many parts of the world, including the United Kingdom.[7] Energy devoted to tearing down statues and memorials of people associated with slavery in previous centuries might better be directed at combatting contemporary slavery.

Enthusiastic about condemning the past, however, woke campaigners appear to have little optimism about, or interest in, the possibility of overturning modern slavery. They are equally resolved in their views about any number of other contemporary vexatious issues about which opinion is settled – and needs to remain so. One of the most contentious and controversial examples of this is the issue of racism.

---

[6] See, eg, Thalia Anthony and Stephen Gray, 'Was there slavery in Australia? Yes. It shouldn't even be up for debate', *The Conversation* (Web Article, 11 June 2020).

[7] See, eg, Richard Ford, '100,000 modern slaves exploited by gangs', *The Times* (Web Article, 13 July 2020).

II STRETCHING THE MEANING TO FIT THE ARGUMENT

The 'scourge' of racism is 'resurgent' in Australia, according to the Australian Human Rights Commission's Race Discrimination Commissioner, Chin Tan. In March 2021, Mr Tan declared that racism poses 'significant threats' to this country and urged the federal government to replace the existing anti-racism framework, created in 2018, with a new one that considers the actual prevalence of racism in Australia.[8]

But for many Australians, talk of resurgent racism does not accurately describe their experience of the country they know and love. This is not to say there are no racists in Australia – clearly an absurd proposition – but rather that systemic, oppressive racism is not a deeply embedded characteristic of a country that has forged one of the world's most successful multicultural societies.[9]

Yet so many critics of Australia persist in describing a society few of us readily recognise. It can feel as if those critics are depicting an entirely different country. To find the key with which to unlock this conundrum, it is important to look more closely at the language used by critics to frame their argument, and at the ideological framework underlying this use of language.

Racism originally meant a form of bigotry which held that people who belonged to different racial groups – itself now a discredited concept – had differentiating characteristics that, in turn, rendered them inferior

---

[8] Paul Karp, 'Australia urged to adopt plan to fight "resurgence of racism"', *The Guardian* (Web Article, 17 March 2021).

[9] See further, Peter Kurti, *The Tyranny of Tolerance: Threats to Religious Freedom in Australia* (Connor Court, 2017) 45-54.

or superior to other groups.

It was a definition widely accepted across the political divide and was exemplified most notably in the fervent hope expressed by Martin Luther King that the day would come 'when people will not be judged by the colour of their skin, but by the content of their character.'[10]

Even though the notion of 'race' is now discredited, King's vision appealed to a sense of common humanity in which the innate quality of human beings transcends what he considered the incidental feature of skin colour. However, when Tan used the familiar word, 'racism', he was not using it in that notable, if discredited sense to refer to prejudice, but in a new way to mean something quite different.

In this instance, he used 'racism' to identify perceived social and economic injustice, as well as imbalances of power. When he said that Australia was suffused with systemic racism, what he meant was that *all* our social interactions and institutions somehow are 'racialised'. In effect, Tan, who also thought the 'Black Lives Matter' movement highlighted the problem of racism, attempted to sweep up every problem of social injustice and deposit them in the box marked 'racism'.

Taking an old word – such as 'racism' – and attaching a new meaning to it is a key tactic used by progressive Wokeshevist warriors, who view the world through the lens of what has come to be known as 'identity politics' and claim to detect oppression and misuse of power just about everywhere. But it is a tactic that confuses the rest of us. While the words being used are familiar enough, their meaning is

---

[10] Martin Luther King Jr, 'I Have A Dream' (Speech, Washington DC, 28 August 1963).

being stretched and new meaning applied in ways that are seldom apparent – or even comprehensible.

Elasticising the language – that is, taking old words and stretching them to fit new meanings – does not just generate semantic friction between scholars of linguistics. It poses a far more serious and fundamental threat to the intelligibility of everyday, ordinary discourse. When words lose their ordinary meaning and have a veiled, political meaning drawn over them, it becomes impossible to pursue intelligible conversations about not only social, cultural, and political matters — but about *anything*. Language used in ways that manipulate the meaning of ordinary discourse threatens to precipitate a descent into incoherence and meaninglessness.

The danger we face of a descent into incoherent meaninglessness is not simply due to the faddish use of language generated in the ivory towers of our universities — although it certainly began there. Rather, the danger comes from sustained and aggressive activism that has spilled out of university campuses and into our schools, businesses, defence forces, the not-for-profit sector, the churches, the medical profession, and much of the media. From there, it is directed against all the perceived injustices that, together, are deemed to comprise the toxic legacy of imperialist Western civilizations. This activism is underpinned by a particular species of theory called Critical Theory.

So what is Critical Theory? As I wrote in an earlier work:

> In its essential form, Critical Theory holds that there are many biases and imbalances of power in society which are hidden from view by dominant cultural structures, such as use of language and the ways in which knowledge is imparted. These structures are deemed 'problematic' by Critical Theory and need

to be identified, exposed, and overturned in the name of what Theorists refer to as 'Social Justice'.

This is a narrow and doctrinaire interpretation of what most people commonly understand 'social justice' to mean. The aim of Social Justice is to correct bias and prejudice, and to redress imbalances in power. It pursues its objectives by silencing — or 'cancelling' — dissenting opinion and deleting unwelcome ideas. These practices are bundled together under the term, 'woke', because Social Justice activists believe they, alone, are 'awakened' to the realities of oppression and prejudice.[11]

III BEWARE: DANGER AHEAD!

We must not underestimate the intellectual hold Critical Theory already exerts on the formation of policy and the conduct of discourse in the Australian public sphere. In particular, the prevalence of Critical Theory, and its influence upon the language, culture, and institutions of Australia, confront us with three significant dangers:

Danger 1 — Eroding tolerance: 'unacceptable' opinions and ideas are denounced

Personal preferences, opinions, or points of view – for example, about gender, sexual orientation, race, or history – no longer belong to the private realm but have become political claims that can be enforced both by legal sanction and by social intimidation and humiliation.

This poses a great threat to the foundational freedoms of conscience and speech and, as such, represents blurring of the

---

[11] See further Kurti (n 4) 7.

boundaries between the public and private lives of individuals.

Danger 2 — Emphasising difference: discrimination is no longer bad but good

Ending discrimination against people based on gender, sexual orientation, and skin colour has been one of the most significant social, legal, and cultural changes to have occurred during the past 60 or so years.

However, Critical Theory reverses these changes and elevates incidental features of the human person, such as skin colour, above characteristics of personality and character. Critical Theory advocates discrimination and the emphasis of difference as tools of social and political reform.

Danger 3 — Inciting rage: reasonable discourse is no longer possible

Critical Theory activists are aggressive, and sometimes violent, towards people with differing opinions. Disagreement is now personalised and those who hold "unacceptable" views are targeted for attack and vilification.[12]

This can be by practices such as 'doxing' (releasing personal information such as addresses and phone numbers), de-platforming, and cancellation. Even the homes and former homes of people are attacked.[13] For Critical Theory activists,

---

[12] This happened to JK Rowling, creator of *Harry Potter*. In June 2020, she was attacked for her views about transgender identity. Her view was that gender was not determined by choice but by biology: 'I refuse to bow down to a movement that I believe is doing demonstrable harm in seeking to erode 'woman' as a political and biological class and offering cover to predators like few before it', she said. See JK Rowling, 'JK Rowling Writes about Her Reasons for Speaking out on Sex and Gender Issues' (Web Page, 10 June 2020).

[13] Wall Street Journal Editorial Board, 'The Chauvin Verdict: Guilty', *Wall Street Journal* (Web Page, 20 April 2021).

the ends always justify the means.

Critical Theory confronts Australia with all three of these dangers today; but its subversive influence — especially through its manifestation as "cancel culture" — can only be properly understood once its ideological foundations have been identified and exposed. Once that is done, it will be clear that Critical Theory activism must be understood for what it is: a political movement intent upon nothing less than the exercise of power. Australian academic Gary Marks has highlighted the danger each of us faces from this subversion:

> Citizens at home and in their workplaces are continually exposed to extremist political views. But as they are packaged in non-threatening language including social justice, equality, and progressive politics, the public is unaware that many of the issues are under-pinned by neo-Marxism, critical theory, and post-modernism. Their totalitarian agenda must be vigorously opposed by those who value Western civilization.[14]

IV HOW CRITICAL IS CRITICAL THEORY?

The term 'Critical Theory' is best thought of as an umbrella term that applies to a series of related fields of enquiry, or "studies", concerned with revealing hidden biases, prejudice, and power structures. These fields of enquiry include postcolonial theory, queer theory, gender studies, disability and fat studies, and critical race theory.

Critical Theory is the most recent form of postmodernism which is,

---

[14] Gary Marks, 'The origins of cancel culture and the left's long march', in Kevin Donnelly (ed), *Cancel Culture and the Left's Long March* (Wilkinson Publishing, 2021) 30.

itself, a wide-ranging term applying to a series of ideas that originated from the Frankfurt School, the name commonly given to the school of social theory at the Institute for Social Research, which developed in the inter-war years in Germany.

Postmodernism began its rise to prominence in the 1960s in reaction to the acknowledged failure of Marxism to overthrow capitalism and establish socialist societies in its place. It was also a reaction against the post-Second World War vision of liberal modernity that promoted concepts such as universal human rights and equality under the law for all citizens. Notoriously difficult to define with precision, postmodernism is 'a multi-faceted phenomenon encompassing vast tracts of intellectual, artistic, and cultural terrain.'[15]

Critical Theory began to emerge in the late 1990s and early 2000s and, unlike earlier forms of postmodernism, soon developed and promoted an activist agenda. Critical Theory holds that reality, and one's understanding of it, is shaped by social, cultural, and political factors. It is 'critical' to the extent that it aims 'to question the assumptions of dominant forms of thinking by challenging the power relations that are normative and assumed.'[16] But soon enough, 'challenge' gives way to revolt, with calls to overthrow all systems deemed to generate injustice and oppression.

---

[15] Helen Pluckrose and James Lindsay, *Cynical Theories: How universities made everything about race, gender, and identity* (Swift Press, 2020) 23.
[16] Elise Paradis et al, 'Critical Theory: Broadening our thinking to explore the structural factors at play in health professions education' (2020) 95(6) *Academic Medicine* 842, 843.

Postcolonial Theory: Down with the West!

Critical Theory is having an enormous impact on the education of our children through a particular manifestation known as 'Postcolonial Theory' which is informs the school curriculum. The goal of Postcolonial Theory is to expose oppressive structures imposed by the West as cultural constructs and to 'decolonise' them. Postcolonial Theory holds that 'Western' ways of knowing — as exemplified in such subjects as science, mathematics, and history — are intended to perpetuate the West's own power and influence and must therefore be devalued.

For example, the 2021 draft report of the Australian Curriculum, Assessment and Reporting Authority came under criticism for appearing to abandon Australia's heritage as a Western liberal democracy in favour of giving exclusive priority to indigenous, non-Western interpretations of the country's history.

'By all means teach Indigenous history,' said historian, Geoffrey Blainey, 'but not at the expense of classical and Western civilisations. Ancient Rome surely did at least as much as Uluru to shape the modern Australian way of thinking and living.'[17]

No longer intent upon simply describing and questioning notions of truth, knowledge, and structures of power that have been taken for granted, Critical Theory actively seeks to overturn and uproot them. As such, Critical Theory questions – and even frequently rejects – the foundations upon which contemporary modern, Western civilizations are built.

In its readiness to question all institutional arrangements and systems

---

[17] See Rebecca Urban, 'National curriculum: Christian heritage sacrificed in school shake-up', *The Australian* (Web Article, 30 April 2021).

of thought, Critical Theory has adopted a radical scepticism about the possibility of obtaining objective knowledge of truth. As political scientist Stephen Eric Bronner has remarked:

> Critical theory insists that thought must respond to the new problems and the new possibilities for liberation that arise from changing historical circumstances. Interdisciplinary and uniquely experimental in character, deeply sceptical of tradition and all absolute claims, Critical Theory [is] always concerned not merely with how things [are] but how they might be and should be.[18]

It is essential to understand that the intent of Critical Theory is not simply social reform or adjustment, but revolution. This revolutionary taint makes Critical Theory especially dangerous and heightens the importance of both understanding and resisting its agenda. In their analysis of postmodernism, Helen Pluckrose and James Lindsay identify two key principles that characterise it.

1   The **postmodern knowledge principle** is radically sceptical about the possibility of objective knowledge. Truth is held to be a representation of a cultural framework and, as such, is determined by that culture.[19] As Gary Marks has remarked:

> Since there is no such thing as objectivity, scholars are free to promote their own personal political and ideological orientations as scholarship and tailor

---

[18] Stephen Eric Bronner, *Critical Theory: A Very Short Introduction* (Oxford University Press, 2017) Kindle edition.
[19] Helen Pluckrose and James Lindsay, *Cynical Theories: How universities made everything about race, gender, and identity* (Swift Press, 2020) 32.

research findings to political agendas.[20]

2   The **postmodern political principle** holds that society is formed of systems of power and hierarchies that decide what can be known, and how, and which serve their own vested interests. This, in turn, gives rise to an ethical imperative to challenge and deconstruct all such oppressive structures.[21] As Pluckrose and Lindsay have observed:

> [Postmodernists] are obsessed with power, language, knowledge, and the relationship between them. They interpret the world through a lens that detects power dynamics in every interaction, utterance, and cultural artefact – even when they aren't obvious or real.[22]

No longer content merely to critique social and cultural structures, by the 1990s postmodernism developed a more radical approach determined to overthrow oppressive forms of power, knowledge, and language. Pluckrose and Lindsay call this activist, prescriptive form of postmodernism, 'applied postmodernism':

> For the activist-scholars of the 1980s, the suffering associated with oppression implied the existence of something that could suffer and a mechanism by which that suffering can occur. The Theorists who took elements of postmodernism and sought to apply them in specific ways were the progenitors of the applied postmodern turn and therefore of Social Justice scholarship.[23]

---

[20] Marks (n 14) 27.
[21] Pluckrose and Lindsay (n 15) 30-39.
[22] Ibid 15.
[23] Ibid 52.

Applied postmodernism asserts *with absolute certainty* that knowledge is socially constructed and that power hierarchies are oppressive. Power hierarchies must therefore be challenged by changing the language with which they are described, thus changing the knowledge. However, scepticism about the possibility of objective truth, and insistence that knowledge is legitimised by forms of linguistic discourse, give rise to a profound paradox lying at the heart of applied postmodernism.

The paradox is that, while asserting the objective truth of the proposition that knowledge is socially constructed, Critical Theory is unable to justify that the assertion is, itself, *objectively* true. Yet Theorists are undeterred, using – or misusing – whatever notion of truth best serves their purposes.

V CRITICAL THEORY AND THE ASSAULT ON TRUTH

Having denied the possibility of establishing objective truth, applied postmodernism finds itself bereft of the very philosophical category – an objective understanding of truth – upon which it needs to rely for it to have any hope of intellectual integrity. Critical Theorists assert the truth of their views while, at the same time, dismissing the attempts of anyone else to assert the truth.

Ambiguity about truth claims reveals a significant weakness in the intellectual architecture of Critical Theory and is one of the principal reasons why the prevalence of Critical Theory threatens, unless checked, to descend into incoherence. Once it becomes difficult – if not impossible – to say anything intelligible about truth, it becomes increasingly hard to say much that is intelligible about anything else.

So what do we mean by 'truth'? The idea of truth expresses a relationship between the world and what we want to say about it. Philosophers of language engage with describing the nature of that relationship and, although it is an extremely complicated area of philosophy, their responses fall, very broadly, under two headings:

Correspondence theory of truth

According to this theory, a statement is true if it corresponds with a situation and does not depend for that correspondence on the judgment of the observer. A proposition is true because it *corresponds* with – that is to say, it accurately describes – a certain situation. The correspondence account of truth is the theory that probably matches most closely the way the idea of truth functions in ordinary discourse.[24]

It is attractive because of its simplicity and because there is a broad understanding that the situation described by a proposition is objectively verifiable – that is to say, a statement either is true or it is false, and this can be verified independently of the observer. In other words, the correspondence theory of truth works by stating what is factually true.

Coherence theory of truth

A critic of the correspondence theory of truth might argue that truth depends on language and the way it is used. As such, they might adopt the coherence theory of truth which does not describe an external relation with a situation. Instead, the coherence theory of truth

---

[24] See further, 'Truth', *The Cambridge Dictionary of Philosophy* (Cambridge University Press, 1995) 812-813.

describes an *internal* relation between a set of beliefs. A judgment is true if it coheres with other judgments that are held.[25]

The truth of a proposition is determined by its coherence. In other words, what makes a fact true depends on what is believed about the fact and the extent to which it coheres with other facts that are believed to be true. Truth, understood in this way, is relative and not absolute. What is true in one culture may not be true in another culture.

This is, necessarily, a very simplified account of the two principal ways in which philosophers of language have approached the problem of truth. It is important to note that the two theories of truth are not mutually exclusive, and that one can hold to the correspondence theory of truth in some instances and to the coherence theory of truth in others.

For example, the truth of the statement, 'Today the temperature outside is 30 degrees Centigrade', might readily be accepted as true according to the correspondence theory of truth if a thermometer, the accuracy of which we can agree on, records the temperature as being 30 degrees Centigrade. In this example, the statement is considered to be objectively verifiable because it corresponds to a set of facts independently of the language used or the perspective of the speaker.

But a person who adopted the correspondence theory of truth for a statement about the outside temperature might then adopt the coherence theory of truth when arguing about an ethical statement such as, 'Abortion is always wrong.' If told that this is the moral position of the Roman Catholic Church, an advocate of abortion might argue

---

[25] See further, 'Truth', *The Cambridge Dictionary of Philosophy* (Cambridge University Press, 1995) 812-813.

that the moral truth claimed by the church does not bind those who do not accept the authority of the church. For the person adopting the coherence theory of truth, the moral statement that abortion is always wrong is true *only* if it coheres with other beliefs, but not true if it does not.

Critical Theory activists reject the correspondence theory of truth and the notion of objective truth. Yet while relying on the coherence theory of truth, they insist that the statements they make – such as that Australia is a systemically racist or misogynistic society – are *objectively true*. Theorists also reject – often with contempt – the notion that statements made by their critics can ever be true.

This assertion of radical scepticism and relativism, on the one hand, and the assertion of objective truth, on the other, is philosophically incoherent and renders the arguments of Critical Theorists a good deal less invincible than they at first appear. Critical Theorists seem to have effected this intellectual sleight of hand without being found out. How did they pull off this conjuring trick?

VI TRUTH AS 'LIVED EXPERIENCE'

Pluckrose and Lindsay argue that the trick may have been effected because of an adjustment Critical Theorists have made to the relationship between knowledge and truth, and to the way they claim to interpret knowledge.[26] Perhaps recognising the intellectual incoherence in the old formulations of their position, Critical Theorists have altered the meaning of words used, such as 'knowledge' to patch

---

[26] Helen Pluckrose and James Lindsay (n 15) 51-52.

over the gaping paradox about the nature of truth in their argument.

It is no longer enough for Critical Theorists to hold that reliable knowledge depends upon the notion of independently verifiable claims – that is to say, upon reliance on evidence and reason. Rather, knowledge is now obtained by listening to the 'lived experience' of members of marginalized groups which can be expressed in terms of purely subjective feelings and intuition. Certain favoured interpretations of marginalized people's experience are selected and anointed as authentic:

> In this way, the logical contradiction between radical relativism and dogmatic absolutism is resolved, but at the price of rending the Social Justice Theory completely unfalsifiable and indefeasible: no matter what evidence about reality [is] presented, Theory always can and always does explain it away.[27]

Critical Theory's ambiguity about truth and its equivocal use of language have enabled it to wield enormous power in the exercise of its revolutionary pursuit. When words no longer mean what we think they mean, it becomes easier for Critical Theorists and Social Justice activists to evade calls for accountability or explanation as they pursue every aspect of their deconstructionist agenda – including the deconstruction of the individual.

---

[27] Ibid 210.

VII DECONSTRUCTING THE INDIVIDUAL: CRITICAL THEORY AND INTERSECTIONALITY

Critical Theory's hostility to the individual is one of the most significant examples of its contempt for liberal modernity. Critical Theory has little time for the modern concept of the individual who attracts a universal bundle of rights and liberties in virtue of her standing as a human being. Instead, it insists a person must be viewed not as a whole, but as conglomeration of different identities, an important point noted by historian, Giles Udy:

> Critical Theory views humanity through cynical, reductive eyes. It analyses society and human relationships through the lens of power, classifying society into oppressors and oppressed. Unlike Marxism, it does so not by class alone but also by race, sexual orientation, gender identity, and so on.[28]

Furthermore, since Critical Theory also holds that these identities are social constructs that reveal – or maintain – certain forms of privilege, knowledge, and power, the identities constitutive of a person can be *de*-constructed and *re*-constructed to address these distortions. This forms the basis of what has become known as 'identity politics'.

According to Canadian philosopher Cressida Heyes: 'Identity politics starts from analyses of oppression to recommend, variously, the re-claiming, re-description, or transformation of previously stigmatised accounts of group membership.'[29]

Race, gender, sexual orientation, and disability are the most prominent

---

[28] Charles Udy, 'How Critical Race Theory Captured the Church', *Unherd* (Web Article, 21 April, 2021).

[29] Cressida Heyes, 'Identity Politics', *Stanford Encyclopedia of Philosophy* (Fall 2020).

social constructs with which identity politics is concerned, but the list of possible identities that can be manipulated and deconstructed is, quite possibly, endless. This has led Karl Zinsmeister, former Director of the *White House Domestic Policy Council* under President George W Bush, to remark that 'Identity politics is thus an aggressive marshalling of human divisions. It draws its energy from factional resentments and fractures.'[30]

Closely linked to the categories of identity is the theory of 'intersectionality', a term first coined in 1989 coined by Kimberlé Crenshaw, an American civil rights activist and Critical Race Theorist, which holds that the marginalisation experienced by an oppressed person is determined by the accumulation of identity traits, such as gender, race, or sexual orientation.[31] Intersectionality thereby reduces all analysis to examination of one or more categories, and looks for the power imbalances and biases it assumes are present.

However, in addition to being little more than a mechanism for ranking grievances, intersectionality also represents a deliberate assault on the liberal notion that basic rights, freedoms, and opportunities are universal and apply to all people regardless of identity categories, such as race or gender.

Liberalism diminished the emphasis placed on such identity categories and argued for the opening of opportunity and liberty to all individuals. The concept of 'equality under the law' extended to all individuals, regardless of incidental characteristics such as

---

[30] Karl Zinsmeister, 'The Compound Fractures of Identity Politics', *City Journal* (Web Article, Winter 2021).
[31] See further, Kimberlé Crenshaw, 'Mapping the Margins: Intersectionality, Identity Politics, and Violence against Women of Color' (1991) 43(6) *Stanford Law Review* 1241.

ethnicity or gender, simply in virtue of their status as human beings.

By contrast, intersectionality renews and enforces an emphasis on difference, and usually denounces so-called "white, Western" ways of knowing — such as the concept of 'anti-discrimination' — as tools of dominance. 'Equality under the law' is rejected precisely because it *refuses* to discriminate between people.

Instead of equality, Critical Race Theory ('CRT') substitutes the concept of 'equity', which has nothing to do with equal treatment of people *qua* human beings. Rather, the object of equity is to achieve equal outcomes for the *group* regardless of how this affects the individual; and thereby to remake society.[32]

Critical Race Theory: racial bias in medicine?

No field of human enquiry is exempt from the reach of intersectionality. A fundamental tenet of medicine is that doctors are to heal and not to harm. In times past, this tenet was expressed in the Hippocratic Oath considered to set, in general terms, the limits and scope of the practice of medicine. However, *The Economist* newspaper recently cited research into the efficacy of pulse oximeters, published in the *New England Journal of Medicine*, to argue that medical research and practice is systemically racist and sexist.

'The world is designed around white men. They share it with everyone else,' trumpeted *The Economist*. Failure 'to recognise that human beings are different from one another' leads to what the newspaper calls 'design bias' which is unforgivable, if understandable: 'In the West, which is still the source of most innovation, engineers have

---

[32] See Christopher F Rufo, 'Critical Race Fragility', *City Journal* (Web Article, 2 March 2021).

tended to be white and male. So have medical researchers. That leads to groupthink.'[33]

By running the obvious – that people and their body types are different – through the filter of intersectionality, *The Economist* used Critical Theory to attack the structure of clinical trials, medical research, and the practice of medicine in their entirety, and to argue that, far from not discriminating against people based on gender or skin colour, medicine should embrace discrimination to equalizes perceived imbalances of power.

Intersectionality thereby allows that each identity category – such as race, gender, sexual orientation, or disability – can be a focus for political activism; and since the number of possible categories can be extended without limit, the principle of intersectionality can also be applied without limit as a means for achieving "diversity". However, as James Kirkchick has observed, intersectionality is insidious and fundamentally illiberal:

> Proponents of intersectionality have elevated its categorical paradigms of all-encompassing, omnipresent 'oppression', and its attendant, identity-based hierarchies of virtue, to that of a *Weltanschauung*, a new morality to replace the basic, classical liberal principles of freedom, individual rights, and equality before the law on which Western civilisation is based.[34]

But it is a mistake to assume that the logical endpoint of intersectional analysis, as it divides people into ever smaller identity categories, is the individual. On the contrary, intersectionality leads not to individuality but to group membership. As Pluckrose and Lindsay have correctly

---

[33] 'Working in the Dark', *The Economist* (Web Article, 10 April 2021).
[34] James Kirkchick, 'How Intersectionality Makes You Stupid', *Tablet* (Web Article, 21 January 2016).

observed: 'Even if a person were a unique mix of marginalised identities, thus intersectionally a unique individual, she would be understood through each and all of those group identities. She would not be understood as an individual.'[35]

VIII FINAL CONSIDERATIONS: ON BRIDGING THE CHASM

Critical Theory may have emerged on university campuses as an intellectual fad, but it has long spilled over into wider society where it is regarded by proponents as a principal tool of Wokeshevist activism with a specific goal, something historian Giles Udy has emphasised:

> The goal of Critical Theory is to work for the liberation of the oppressed by unmasking and thus disempowering the forces which create and impose dominant ideology upon those same oppressed groups.[36]

In pursing this goal of 'liberation of the oppressed', Critical Theory poses the three key dangers identified at the outset of this chapter: erosion of tolerance; emphasis of difference; and incitement of rage. Together, these dangers combine to form a highly combustible mix which fuels the zealotry of Wokeshevism.

It is a mix that poses a grave threat not only to freedoms of speech, conscience, and association upon which a free, flourishing, and open society depends, but also to commitment to the liberal principle of tolerance of divergent and diverse points of view. As Karl Zinsmeister has observed, the dangers that stalks us point, in fact, to nothing less

---

[35] Pluckrose and Lindsay (n 15) 128.
[36] Udy (n 28).

than the death of classical liberalism.[37]

This chapter has argued that the gravity of the threat has been disguised from the unsuspecting because of the veil of language drawn across political activism. Previously unfamiliar terms that are nonetheless obscure and opaque – such as intersectionality, heteronormativity, and white privilege – have become part of a new vocabulary.

At the same time, previously *familiar* words – such as race, gender, and colonialism – have been subverted with new but equally opaque meanings. When familiar words are used in new ways to describe activist involvement, the full import of new meanings is not quickly understood. Arguments *sound* reasonable because the old, reason-based meanings of words are assumed.

But meanings have changed. Arguments are *not* reasonable; and reason, itself, has been displaced by emotion and intuition. Chaos beckons. And as words lose their common meanings, and it becomes increasingly difficult to communicate intelligently with one another, we edge ever closer to the deep and forbidding chasm of incoherence.

However, there are very good reasons for thinking this chasm can be bridged if we commit to a four-fold course of action to guide our resistance.

A *Take courage*

One of the most apparent manifestations of Critical Theory activism is cancel culture, which suppresses dissent with ruthless vindictiveness and cows into silence those who might express dissent. Cancel culture depends for its prevalence on the timidity of those it attacks. But

---

[37] Zinsmeister (n 30).

although the activists appear to dominate public debate, cancel culture is not popular.

A recent opinion poll conducted jointly in the United States – where cancel culture has been most prominent – by Harvard Centre for American Political Studies and The Harris Poll found 64 per cent of respondents regarded cancel culture as a threat to their freedom, while 36 per cent regarded it as a large problem.[38]

A similar lack of public support for cancel culture appears to be emerging in Australia, according to recent polling conducted by True North Strategy. According to that poll, 70 per cent of respondents thought cancel culture had gone too far and now threatened the spirit of larrikinism. Although many feel cowed into silence by Critical Theory activists, the research company thinks these findings are encouraging: 'If we agree what this means for politicians and the business world, we can pretty safely say they can push back harder with the weight of assurance that public opinion is behind them.'[39]

This assurance that public opinion, for the most part, does not support the destructive, cancelling campaigns waged by Wokeshevist Critical Theory activists, should encourage people to speak out against attempts made to attack, silence, and humiliate them. But it requires courage to do so: courage to withstand the ending of friendships; courage to say what others say is unsayable; and courage to have the confidence of one's own convictions.

---

[38] Julia Manchester, '64 percent view 'cancel culture' as a threat to freedom: poll', *The Hill* (Web Article, 29 March 2021). See also Matthew Impelli, 'Cancel Culture Viewed as Threat to Freedom by 64 percent of Americans', *Newsweek* (Web Article, 2 March 2021).

[39] 'New survey reveals most Australians feel cancel culture "has gone too far"', *News.com.au* (Web Article, 7 April 2021).

B *Restore reason*

It is essential to lay bare the intellectual incoherence at the heart of Critical Theory. Hostility to objective conceptions of truth, coupled with contradictory assertion of the objective truth of its own dogmas, gravely weakens the claims made by Critical Theory. This incoherence must be named and challenged – something that also requires courage because all efforts to engage rationally are likely to be rejected. As the American political commentator Paul de Quenoy has noted:

> The entire woke movement is based on emotion. The more it is challenged, the more hysterical it becomes for the simple reason that its tenets cannot withstand logic, reason, or ridicule. Therefore, it classifies logic and reason as features of oppressive 'whiteness' to be devalued, and why it is deeply suspicious of humour.[40]

However, while it is important to confront Wokeshevism, efforts to engage with it are ultimately likely to be fruitless because Theory activists reject all standards of rationality accepted by liberal modernity and employ a very different conception of truth.

Another way to put this, is to say that hope of reversing or undoing the damage done by the Wokeshevists by means of reasoned argument is almost certainly futile. However, there remains the challenge to frame reasoned arguments against Critical Theory activism, and this can help stiffen the resolve and resistance of those who neither support nor condone the antics of the Critical Theory activists, themselves.

---

[40] Paul de Quenoy, 'Fighting Cancel Culture to Win', *American Greatness* (Web Article, 20 April 2021)

C Reclaim truth

Construction of the arguments of Critical Theory activists – especially those who promote CRT – has been likened to a mousetrap: 'disagreement with their program becomes irrefutable evidence of a dissenter's 'white fragility', 'unconscious bias', ' or 'internalised white supremacy'.'[41] It is hardly surprising that many who disagree with the agenda choose to remain silent. But courage and renewed confidence in reason are essential tasks for equipping ourselves for the third key task: reclaiming truth.

Only by holding fast to an objective conception of truth whereby common agreement can be reached about the meaning of words will it be possible to do two things. First, to reject the unreasoned categories imposed in the name of 'justice' or 'diversity' or 'equity' by Critical Theory; and second, to use our own moral categories to evaluate, criticise, and refute the practical – and often disastrous – consequences of Critical Theory ideas and practices.

Far from allowing Critical Theorists to tear at the social and cultural fabric of this country, it is essential to hold fast to the objective truth that Australia remains one of the most successful and harmonious multicultural societies in the world. This has been attested to by numerous surveys, most notably the 'Mapping Social Cohesion' report published annually since 2007 by the Scanlon Foundation. These reports have been the most reliable and objective indicators of Australia's social attitudes.[42]

Speaking specifically about the need to counter the impact of CRT

---

[41] Christopher F Rufo, 'The Courage of Our Convictions', *City Journal* (Web Article, 22 April 2021).
[42] See Kurti (n 9) 46.

in schools in the United States, American commentator Christopher Rufo argues theorists must be confronted with facts about these consequences:

> Do they support public schools separating first-graders into groups of 'oppressors' and 'oppressed'? Do they support mandatory curricula teaching that 'all white people play a part in perpetuating systemic racism'? Do they support public schools instructing white parents to become 'white traitors' and advocate for 'white abolition'?[43]

Rufo's questions are just as applicable to Australia, where some schools are known to promote similar ideas about such matters as gender equity and systemic racism. For example, in Warrnambool, Victoria, male students at Brauer College were made to stand as a 'symbolic gesture of apology for the behaviours of their gender'. The principal was forced, subsequently, to offer an apology of her own when news of this 'gesture' was leaked to the media by unhappy parents.[44]

D *Never surrender!*

As the insidious influence of Critical Theory seeps throughout our society, it is essential that those who oppose it affirm the importance of reason and objective truth in discussions about the social and cultural well-being of Australia. 'There is no silver bullet' to end the culture of cancellation, warns Australian scholar Stephen Chavura; and the same

---

[43] Rufo (n 41).
[44] Sian Johnson, 'Warrnambool school sorry for making boys stand in apology for "behaviours of their gender"', *ABC News* (Web Article, 25 March 2021).

is true of the influence of Critical Theory.⁴⁵ There is no silver bullet.

As Critical Theory extends its reach through the institutions of our society, dominating public discourse and promoting falsehoods about oppression of minority groups, it threatens to divide our society by ignoring the individual person, assaulting communities, and assigning people to one or more groups of "victims". More than anything else, it is now essential that our political leaders take a firm stand on the issue and lead the nation away from this divisive and harmful ideology.

Identity politics has reared its head in the ongoing debates in Australian politics about issues such as misogyny, indigenous recognition, religion, and gender. And anyone who raises an alternative voice or puts forward a different point of view gets shouted down and humiliated.

Hence, the intervention of Prime Minister Scott Morrison in a speech delivered to a dinner in support of the United Israel Appeal on 29 April 2021, was both timely and important.⁴⁶ Morrison affirmed human dignity and individual responsibility as principal moral components of liberty and emphasised the importance of community in a healthy society. In particular, Morrison warned against what he called the 'growing tendency to commodify people through identity politics':

> We must never surrender the truth that the experience and value of every human being is unique and personal. You are more, we are more, individually, more than the things others try to identify us by, you by, in this age of identity politics. You are more than your gender, you are more than your race, you are more than

---

⁴⁵ Stephen A Chavura, 'Cancel Culture and the Left's Long March: The Way Forward' in Donnelly (ed) (n 14) 181.

⁴⁶ Geoff Chambers, 'Don't give in to identity politics, Scott Morrison urges', *The Australian* (Web Article, 30 April 2021).

your sexuality, you are more than your ethnicity, you are more than your religion, your language group, your age.[47]

His attention to the harm identity politics and cancel culture is doing to Australia is welcome, as is his determination to set an example from the top. Morrison – who has come under attack for his own religious faith – appears to think it is getting out of hand and is now beginning to make speeches about identity politics and cancel culture.

Australia's political leaders must follow Morrison's example, they must continue to mphasise the importance of the moral responsibility each of us bears as citizens, and for restoring to its central place in our society the principle of human dignity.

But this is not a task to be left to politicians alone – although strong political leadership on this issue is essential. In order that practices such as self-censorship do not become a prevailing, unconscious habit, those resisting Critical Theory need to ensure they are informed about the ideology that informs Critical Theory, and that they understand the intellectual paucity of the movement.

But above all, those resisting Critical Theory need to act with courage, and commit to the pressing task of speaking out openly and often to defeat the tyranny of Wokeshevism and defend the fundamental principles of an open and liberal Australia.

---

[47] Scott Morrison, 'Address – United Israel Appeal Dinner' (Speech, United Israel Appeal, 29 April 2021).

5

The Genesis of Critical Theory and Cancel Culture

MICHAEL McMAHON*

ABSTRACT

This article traces the genesis of Critical Theory back to the works of Freud, Nietzsche, and Marx in the nineteenth century. It will examine closely the use made of hermeneutics by those three authors and follow this legacy as it is passed down through Critical Theory to contempory Cancel Culture. The relationship between the "hermeneutics of suspicion" and the "hermeneutics of affirmation" will be highlighted, and the part played by the Frankfurt School in developing a new focus for Marxism will be explored. The theories of Gramsci, Marcuse and Faucault will be looked at look in some detail to determine their influence on the Woke Generation and Cancel Culture. The concept of Vision will be analysed in an attempt to identify the vision that drives Critical Theory and Cancel culture. Lastly an evaluation will be made of the effects that Cancel Culture makes on the life of a society.

I FIRST CONSIDERATIONS

Alan Dershowitz, the distinguished American legal scholar, in

---

* Mazenod College.

his book *Cancel Culture* declared that 'Cancel Culture is the new McCarthyism of the "Woke" Generation,' and like the old McCarthyism it ends careers, destroys legacies, breaks up families – with no semblance of due process or opportunity to disprove the often-false or exaggerated accusations.[1] As he points out, the old McCarthyism endangered constitutional rights of free speech and due process, which are the core-protectors of liberty and barriers against tyranny. The new McCarthyism – cancel culture – he writes, threatens these rights as well. Dershowitz then goes on to accuse it of being a 'child of the current woke generation,' and an 'illegitimate descendent of hard-right McCarthyism and hard-right Stalinism.'[2]

While there is a great deal of historical truth in this claim, it must be said, that the overt tenets and methods of hard-right Stalinism have been greatly softened and camouflaged by the work of Critical Theory. Few, if any, of the proponents of Critical Theory would be willing to claim a close relationship with Stalinism, but nearly all of them have been be involved in a creative dialogue with Marxism, they have also been heirs to the legacies left by Nietzsche and Freud. In this chapter I want to show firstly the origins of Critical Theory and then the decisive role that it played in the genesis and birth of Cancel Culture. I will focus firstly on the part a particular type of hermeneutics plays in Critical Theory.

---

[1] Alan Dershowitz, *Cancel Culture: The Latest Attack on Free Speech and Due Process* (Hot Books, 2020) 1-2.
[2] Ibid 3.

II THE THREE 'MASTERS OF SUSPICION' AND THE ORIGINS OF CRITICAL THEORY

Hermeneutics is the art or science of interpretation. Terry Eagleton in *After Theory* states that it is generally accepted that the German philosopher Fredrich Schleiermacher was the founding father. Schleiermacher was translating a book written by an English colonist in Australia which detailed the author's encounters with Australian Aboriginal people. Schleiermacher wrestled with the problem of how to understand and interpret the beliefs and customs of a people that seemed so alien to the European mentality. Without denying Schleiermacher the honour of being called founding father, it must be realised however that the great cultures of antiquity had sacred literature to be interpreted and re-interpreted by their priestly and royal classes, so it is only fair to say that hermeneutics has been practiced for quite a long time.[3]

There are different philosophies and methods of hermeneutics, but one form in particular has had a very defining impact on Critical Theory — it is called the 'hermeneutics of suspicion', and it first came to prominence in the late 19th century. Those who used this method saw myths, ideologies, beliefs and values as essentially falsifying consciousness and hiding the real meaning behind a deceptive subterfuge, so they employed the "hermeneutics of suspicion" to negatively interpret the real meaning of the discourse. Texts were read with scepticism so that the repressed or hidden meanings were exposed. Nowadays it could also be called reading against the grain or reading between the lines. The assumption underlying this approach is that texts, ideologies and myths may appear to be straight-forward

---

[3] Terry Eagleton, *After Theory* (Penguin Books, 2004) 23-46.

but that they are deceptive in that they contain deeper meanings and implications.[4] There were three famous, outstanding practioners of this method, and Paul Ricoeur, the French philosopher named them.[5] He called Karl Marx, Friedrich Nietzsche and Sigmund Freud the 'three masters of suspicion', believing that they each shared the same view of consciousness as false and that they used the hermeneutic to unmask the real meaning concealed behind the myths. Three short examples should illustrate the way in which each of the "masters" went about their work.

Nietzsche used a genealogical hermeneutic to demonstrate how Christian myths of salvation, redemption and transcendence could be traced back to an underlying "will- to-power", which he believed was the chief motivator in individuals and groups. Nietzsche saw the early Christians as a subservient, underprivileged people, who were dominated and persecuted by the Roman elites. Lacking the requisite power and influence, the Christians could not openly retaliate, so they repressed their resentment, and generated a new system of beliefs and values based on their actual situation. This new system emphasised the virtues of humility, submissiveness, timidity and self-denial. Thus, they gave themselves a certain power and recognition by embracing, cherishing and privileging their lowly status. Nietzsche had a very negative view of Christianity perceiving it as a religion that made a virtue out of weakness. This perception obviously influenced his hermeneutic. He also concluded that the group with the strongest "will-to-power" would be the one to establish its regime of control in society thereby ensuring its ability to declare what was the prevailing

---

[4] Richard Kearney, Transitions: Narratives in Modern Irish Culture, Ch 14 'Myth and the Critique of Ideology (Wolfhound Press, 1988) 270-277.

[5] Paul Ricoeur, *The Conflict of Interpretations: Essays in Hermeneutics* (Northwestern University Press, 1974).

ideology ie truth. Truth then was made relative depending on what particular regime held power.⁶ We will see later in this paper how Michel Foucault, the highly influential French philosopher, adopted Nietzsche's "will-to power" as one of the key fundamental principles of his method.

Freud used his psychoanalytical hermeneutic to investigate how myths could disguise and camouflage unconscious desires. He privileges the unconscious over the conscious, and in *Totem and Taboo* the origin of myth is seen as a form of compensation for prohibited experience. Religious myths were interpreted as neurosis which concealed repressed sexual desires. In his 'Obsessive Acts and Religious Practices' he holds that religious practice and the compulsive repetitive behaviour of the neurotic were essentially the same phenomenon. The study of taboo phenomenon and ritual practices in primitive cultures, was for Freud, an insight into the nature and origin of religion itself, which he assumed was a "natural" phenomenon capable of being explained away in psychological terms, and ultimately to be seen as an illusion.⁷ He saw belief in God arising through the projection of our infantile father-image. We need our god because our earthly father has failed us. Freud seemed to be unaware of the fact that even though two processes parallel each other you still cannot infer that they are identical. Evans-Prichard showed in his book *Witchcraft among the Azande* that the thought processes of those who practice magic and those who practice science are similar. Both involve concepts of cause and effect, both involve the logic of arguments from consequences, both involve consistence and coherence, but no one would draw the conclusion that they were the same.⁸

---

⁶   Kearney (n 4) 273.
⁷   Sigmund Freud, *Civilisation, Society and Religion* (Penguin, 1991) 223-228.
⁸   E F O'Doherty, *Religion and Mental Health* (Burns and Oats, 1965) ch 11.

For Marx the main dynamic in world history was the economic conflict between the working class and the wealthy business owners. The upper class unjustly exploits the lower class by profiting off the latter's labour. The lower working class (proletariat) should therefore fight their oppressors in a "class struggle". The proletarians can only be free by suppressing their adversaries with whom, by definition, they can have nothing in common. This struggle will of necessity involve violence and a large number of human beings must be eliminated if the ideal is to triumph. The ideal for Marx was a glorious vision that would see unity and equality in an earthly paradise for all of mankind. Marx used a dialectical hermeneutic of 'false consciousness' which exposed the superstructure (ideological myths, religion, art, philosophy) that concealed the exploitation and domination of the working class by the capitalist owners of the means of production (infrastructures).[9]

Marx, Nietzsche, and Freud each shared the suspicion that myth conceals the projection of false values, creating an illusion that hides its real meaning, so they use the hermeneutic to unmask what is hidden. There is a definite validity in this approach because all myths involve a conflict of interpretations and there is a genuine benefit in the purification of the myths that we live by. However, we are also entitled to ask if the critique of these myths is not itself subject to critique. Paul Ricoeur does precisely this when he looks at the Marxist rereading of history according to the model of the class struggle which champions the cause of the oppressed workers. The usual order of history is reversed and the slaves (the proletariat) become the new masters. However this ideology of liberation, of the powerless, became under Stalin an ideology which imposed a new kind of oppressive power on the proletariat. Thus the Marxist-Leninist notion of utopia

---

[9] Kearney (n 4) 273-274.

became a mere alibi for the consolidation for its repressive powers, justifying the oppression of today in the name of the liberation of tomorrow.[10] It can be argued of course that Stalin did not possess the authentic Marxian notion of blissful utopia but was driven rather by the Nietzschean "will-to-power" and ruthless domination.

Richard Kearney allows for the usefulness of the "hermeneutics of suspicion" but argues that it must be balanced by a "hermeneutics of affirmation," which can lead to the recovery of lost meanings and the creation of new ones – and the opening up of "possible worlds". Kearney goes on to say that myth, tradition and ideology can have positive functions.[11] 'Myth can be seen as a story that a society tells itself about itself in order to describe itself to itself – and to others.'[12] Kearney sees a need to continually re-evaluate and critically analyse the story, but to attempt to erase it completely can be very destructive.

A country must cherish the positive heritage of its traditions. The historical past is important, and a creative reinterpretation can generate new understandings and new possibilities. Voices that have been supressed and "erased from history" can be uncovered and as a result be incorporated into a new reading. The return of the repressed can be disconcerting but it can also be liberating and empowering.[13] Jacques Derrida, the bete noire of certain non-continental philosophers, agrees with Kearney on this point saying that 'every culture and society requires an internal critique or deconstruction as an essential part of its development. Every culture needs an element of self-interrogation and

---

[10] Richard Kearney, *Dialogues With Contempory Continental Thinkers* (Manchester University Press, 1984) 15-18, 73-75.
[11] Kearney (n 4) 271.
[12] Ibid 270, quoting Liam de Paor, *The Peoples of Ireland* (Rainbow Press, 1986).
[13] Kearney (n 4) 276.

of distance to itself, if it is to transform itself.' He will even concede that the affirmation of positive things in the heritage is important, 'Deconstruction certainly entails a moment of affirmation. Indeed I cannot conceive of a radical critique which would not be ultimately motivated by some sort of affirmation, acknowledged or not.'[14]

What legacies have been passed on from our "three masters" to Critical Theory and our modern-day exponents of cancel culture? We can say with certainty that they have acquired the "hermeneutics of suspicion" but sadly not the "hermeneutics of affirmation." The former is deployed rigorously against many facets of Western civilization, the latter is nowhere in evidence. They see themselves as engaging in a demythologizing project – a tearing down, but the impulse to deconstruct a civilization can be carried to extreme lengths. Ronald Barthes, the renowned French, literary theorist, essayist, philosopher, directly acknowledges this when he states in *Mythologies*, that the political critique of myth must be motivated by 'acts of destruction.' 'The genuine demythologizer knows not what he is for but what he is against.'[15] Some of the present-day practitioners of Critical Theory and cancel culture seem to have fully imbibed this attitude. We know that a certain schadenfreude can be had at the spectacle of well-know people being de-platformed and canceled in organized witch-hunts. but Jennifer Oriel, in her essay 'Universities', warns us of the consequences of such an approach 'silencing opposition is far easier than listening to an opponent and learning well. The act of destruction is cheap and exciting. The act of creation is exacting.'[16]

---

[14] Kearney (n 10) 73-75.
[15] Roland Barthes, *Mythologies* (Paladin Books, 1973) 157-158.
[16] Jennifer Oriel, 'Universities' in Kevin Donnelly (ed), *Cancel Culture and the Left's Long March.* See also Gary Marks, 'The Origins of Cancel Culture' in Kevin Donnelly (ed), *Cancel Culture and the Left's Long March* (Wilkinson Publishing, 2021).

Richard Kearney also adds his warning on the dangers of the unlimited use of the "hermeneutics of suspicion" in the project of deconstruction. 'The danger in all this is that myth, tradition, and custom can be so annihilated that nothing remains and we are left without purpose and direction. We may be able to free a country from the "false consciousness" of traditions, but we must also liberate it for something.'[17]

While allowing for the fact that the hermeneutics of suspicion is able to deliver valid insights and cannot be dismissed out of hand, yet it contains within itself a massive error, namely the error of reductionism. Reductionism is the fallacy of trying to explain a complex phenomenon by reducing it to one dimension. In essence it is an oversimplification. We saw it in operation when Nietzsche tried to explain the genesis of Christianity by focusing on the emotional needs of the early Christians. Freud did likewise when he assumed that religion could be explained away by psychological processes, and by his privileging of the unconscious over all other conscious factors. Marx reduced art, philosophy, religion (the superstructure) to functioning as a cover and a justification for the wealthy in the class war. The present day Neo-Marxist attacks on Western Civilization contain the same elements of reductionism. There is a prolonged assault on the historical sins and present failings of the West without any attempt to recognise its achievements and successes. The West is profiled as a ravenous, imperial, colonial, and capitalist power: its negative identity – without any dwelling on its positive attributes or its outstanding contribution to civilization.

This strategy of focusing on the negative identity has a definite affinity

---

[17] Kearney (n 4) 274.

with the methods used by the People's Republic of China's institution of thought reform through the Revolutionary Colleges. Lifton in his *Thought Reform: and the Psychology of Totalism: A Study of Brainwashing in China* gives a detailed account of the process. First came the prolonged assault on the negative identity of the person, which always contains some truth. Eventually the person will begin to see him/herself in that way, forgetting or losing sight of their positive attributes. Their former self-image, or the way they saw themselves is now drastically altered and they will begin to feel guilt and shame. The interrogator now offers hope of redemption – a rebirth through thought-reform- a new way of thinking ie Mao's way of thinking.[18]

Mao's way of thinking can undoubtedly be linked with the emergence of political correctness and its subsequent development into cancel culture. Mao dealt with political dissenters by cancelling their freedom of speech and imprisoning and killing large numbers of people. Those who could be trained in "correct thought" were given jobs that were useful to the party. Strict conformity to party rule was maintained by combining social pressure and re-education.[19] It does not involve too great an imaginative jump to see some of the same methods at work in educational establishments in America and Australia where dissenters from established doctrine are publicly denounced and sentenced to exile from the university. This phenomenon was also present in the 1950s in America when the McCarthy witch-hunt era was at its peak. Lifton recalls that when he was researching the Chinese thought-reform in Hong Kong he heard about McCarthyism back home and its 'assaults on mind and reality.' Senator Joseph McCarthy and

---

[18] See Robert Jay Lifton, *Thought Reform and the Psychology of Totalism: A Study in Brainwashing in China* (The University of North Carolina Pess, 2012) 84-86.
[19] Oriel (n 16) 56.

his followers were making wild accusations against public figures, teachers and writers. Subscribing to the wrong magazine might result in being fired from one's job. Lifton assets that thought-reform is an extreme version of the ever present human tendency to contrast one's own purity with the impurity of all else; and on that basis to justify one's claim to the ownership of reality. A tendency that is very much in evidence in the practices and pronouncements of cancel culture.[20]

Neo-Marxism in the form of cancel culture attacks many facets of Western civilization. One of its present day assaults involves the notion of 'historic collective guilt.'[21] It demands that the present generation should feel guilty for the slave trade, colonialism, and other atrocities and misdemeanours committed by the West. This goes hand-in-hand with the re-writing of history by way of destroying statues, renaming buildings and cancelling historic, public figures whose records were less than pure. We have recently seen the notion of historic collective guilt being imposed on boys at a Victorian school, who were made to stand in acknowledgement for past offences against girls.[22] This was imposed on the boys despite their not have anything to do individually or collectively with the abuse. The principal subsequently apologised for her actions,[23] but it goes to show how she had succumbed to the notion of historic collective guilt and how it had become part of her thinking.

---

[20] Robert Jay Lifton, *Losing Reality: On Cults, Cultism and the Mindset of Political and Religious Zealotry* (The New Press, 2019) 76-78.

[21] Joshua Forrester, 'Cancel Culture: Concept and Countermeasures' (Presentation, The Civilisationists, 19 May 2021).

[22] Anthony Piovesan, 'Brauer College in Warrnambool makes boys apologise on behalf of their gender to female peers at school assembly', *News.com.au* (Web Article, 26 March 2021).

[23] Chanel Zagon, 'Victorian schools says asking male students to 'apologise for their gender' in an assembly was wrong', *9 News* (Web Article, 26 March 2021).

III MARXISM RE-ORIENTATES – CRITICAL THEORY EMERGES

Terry Eagleton, in *After Theory* affirms that Western Marxists thinkers shift to culture was born partly out of political impotence and disenchantment. They saw little chance for a proletarian revolution in Western capitalist countries and were thoroughly disillusioned with National Socialism, Stalinism, state capitalism, and the culture industry which they saw as new forms of social domination. Classical Marxism was not the answer for the new prevailing conditions, and so Critical Theory was born.[24]

It was given its name and was developed by the Frankfurt school. Max Horkheimer, one of its members, defined Critical Theory as a social theory whose aim was to critique and change society as a whole. It differed from traditional theory which focused only on understanding or explaining society. Critical Theory's objective was 'to liberate human beings from the circumstances that enslave them.' Human emancipation and freedom were its key goals. Another member of the Frankfurt school, Herbert Marcuse, realized that class had outlived its usefulness as an explanatory concept and that a new strategy was needed that would engage with and change the culture that supported capitalism. So began the leftist infiltration of Western institutions, universities, schools, churches, media, business, etc – the 'long march through the institutions.'[25]

At around the same time, another important thinker, Antonio Gramsci, the Italian communist, who was imprisoned by Mussolini for many years, also came to the conclusion that culture was the key in the fight

---

[24] Eagleton (n 3) 31.
[25] Ibid.

against capitalism.[26] He too realised that the Marxist concept of class struggle was futile in bringing about change in the West. The key was cultural change. He saw that culture in the West supported capitalism, and capitalism supported a broad middle class. The ideology, the values, the beliefs of western society had to be challenged, deconstructed and changed. All the cultural institutions that supported capitalism would have to be overcome. Before communism could take hold politically and economically it had to take hold culturally.[27] Gramsci's idea was to refocus Marxism on cultural institutions, and so begin the already mentioned 'long march through the institutions' (a phrase invented by Rudi Dutschke in 1967).[28] The aim was to gradually colonise and gain control of key social institutions.[29]

Gramsci also developed Lenin's concept of hegemony which the latter had used to control society after the revolution. Hegemony means that the ruling party uses ideology, values, beliefs and practices to enshrine a world-view that is all-embracing and that leaves no room for alternative viewpoints. It was the birth of cultural politics where political change had to be cultural to be effective.[30] To paraphrase Eagleton's words, any political change that does not embed itself in people's feelings and perceptions or does not secure their consent, engage their desires and weave its way into their sense of identity will not prove enduring.[31]

---

[26] Michael Walsh, *The Devil's Pleasure Palace: The Cult of Critical Theory and the Subversion of the West*, (Encounter Books, 2017) 23, 72.
[27] Ibid 167
[28] Angela Kolling, 'Literature and Politics in Joschka Fischer's *Mein Langer Lauf Zu Mir Selbst:* A Negotiation of *Wirklichkeit* (Credibility) and *Wirksamkeit* (Efffect), Peter Marks (ed.) *Literature and Politics: Pushing the World in Certain Directions* (Cambridge Scholars Publishing, 2011) 191.
[29] Walsh (n 26) 108.
[30] Ibid 167.
[31] Eagleton (n 3) 46.

Herbert Marcuse gave what was perhaps the clearest definition of what the Marxist utopia would entail. In his dialogue with Richard Kearney, he argues that Marx did not fully realise that a purely economic resolution of the problem can never be enough, and so lacked the insight that a 'twentieth-century revolution would require a different type of human being and that such a revolution would have to aim at, and, if successful, implement, an entirely new set of personal and sexual relationships, a new morality, a new sensibility and a total reconstruction of the environment.'[32]

Marcuse had argued in *Eros and Civilization* that people should abandon traditional repressive morality in favour of sexual liberation. The aim here was not just sexual liberation but that the repressive institutions of family and marriage would be abandoned. He understood that these two institutions were supportive of the capitalist system and therefore needed to be undermined if a new unrepressed civilization was to be created.[33] Unlike Freud, he did not believe that there need exist a permanent contradiction between primary instinctual satisfaction (the pleasure principle) and repressed secondary satisfactions (the reality principle). For Marcuse the repression of **Eros** calls up the very destructive forces that repression was meant to quell, while Freud had maintained that repression was necessary for the development of civilization.[34]

---

[32] Kearney (n 10) 74.
[33] Andrew Feenberg and William Leiss (eds.), *The Essential Marcuse: Selected Writings of Philosopher and Social Critic Herbert Marcuse* (Beacon Press Books, 2007) 176-182.
[34] Sigmund Freud, *Civilization, Society and Religion*, (Penguin, 1991) 315-326.

IV MARCUSE'S IMPACT ON AMERICAN INSTITUTIONS

Marcuse was a professor at several American universities. He taught at Columbia, Harvard, Brandeis and the University of California at San Diego. He became well known in the 1960s as the official idealogue of "campus revolutions" in the USA and Europe. His effect on the humanity faculties of American Universities, their students, and certain sections of the general population, has been traced in detail by Greg Lukianoff and Jonathan Haidt in their book, *The Coddling of the American Mind*. Marcuse' lectures and publications were especially influential in the 1960s and 1970s when the American left was moving away from its focus on workers versus capital to become the "New Left" which focused civil rights, women's rights and other social movements promoting equality and social justice. The left saw themselves as progressives wanting social change and saw the right as conservative wanting to preserve the existing order. Marcuse analysed the conflict between the left and right in Marxist terms.[35]

In his 1965 essay titled 'Repressive Tolerance', Marcuse argued that tolerance and free speech is beneficial in society only when there is absolute equality in that society. If there are power differentials between groups then tolerance only benefits the already powerful enabling them to dominate institutions like media, education and politics. Indiscriminative tolerance is unfair – what is needed is a form of tolerance that discriminates. A truly "liberating tolerance" would be one that favours the weak and restrains the strong.[36] In 1960s America, the weak for Marcuse were the left – students, intellectuals, and minorities. The Right was the military-industrial complex, the

---

[35] Greg Lukianoff and Johnathan Haidt, *The Coddling of the American Mind* (Penguin, 2018) 54-77.

[36] Feenberg and Leiss (n 33) 32-55.

wealthy, and other vested interests that blocked change, and in his view 'liberating tolerance' would mean intolerance against movements from the Right, and tolerance of movements from the Left.[37]

For Marcuse when the majority in a society is being repressed, it is justifiable to use 'repression and indoctrination' to allow the 'subversive majority' to achieve the power that it deserves.[38] He goes on to argue that true democracy might require denying basic rights to people who advocate for conservative causes, or for policies he viewed as aggressive or discriminatory, and that true freedom of thought might require professors to indoctrinate their students. The ultimate goal is not equality but a reversal of power.[39]

> It should be evident by now that the exercise of civil rights by those who don't have them presupposes the withdrawal of civil rights from those who prevent their exercise, and that liberation of the Dammed of the Earth presupposes suppression not only of their old but also of their new masters.[40]

Marcuse's view of the world has had a profound impact on American universities since those words were written in 1965. His philosophy has engendered a particular mind-set among staff and students, giving rise to common-enemy identity politics with its corresponding 'cancel culture'. 'Common-enemy identity politics' should not be confused with 'common-humanity identity politics', this latter form does not denigrate or de-humanise its opponents but rather appeals to their humanity while also applying political pressure in other ways.

---

[37] Lukianoff and Haidt (n 35)
[38] Feenberg and Leiss (n 33) 32-55.
[39] Ibid.
[40] Robert Paul Wolff, Barrington Moore and Herbert Marcuse, *A Critique of Pure Tolerance* (Beacon Press, 1969), quoted in Lukianoff and Johnathan Haidt (n 35) 65.

Common-enemy identity politics on the other hand uses the Marxist dialectic to focus hostility on a particular group.[41] The Left will focus on the Right as a bastion of privilege and oppression. Its psychology will advocate an 'us-versus- them' mentality- which can easily slide into aggressive tribalism. In aggressive tribalism there is no room for dialogue between people or groups or for any attempt at mutual understanding, one's opponent must be denigrated – it is all-out confrontation, a clear win or lose situation. Saul Alinsky, the Marxist community organizer in his famous *Rules for Radicals* stated in Rule No 12: 'Pick the target, personalise it, and polarize it.'[42]

Students entering college in some American educational institutions undergo orientation programmes that will teach them to evaluate their own and others' level of privilege, recognise distinct identity groups, and see more differences between people. They will also learn to associate aggression, domination, and oppression with privileged groups. This type of training coupled with common-enemy identity politics will easily enhance the emergence of a "call-out culture," where students are credited for identifying offences by members of their community and calling-them-out. Social media undoubtedly exacerbates the cruelty and "virtue signalling" that is part of this call-out culture. It is easy to hide behind an alias and join in the chorus of shaming and denouncing as anonymity lessens the need for self-restraint and makes it easier to follow the mob.[43]

It is not surprising that a call-out culture promotes feelings of paranoia and distrust among students fearful of saying the wrong thing, liking the wrong post, or coming to the defence of someone whom they know to

---

[41] Lukianoff and Haidt (n 35) 62-65.
[42] Walsh (n 26) 85.
[43] Lukianoff and Haidt (n 35) 72-73.

be innocent, knowing that they themselves could become the victim of the mob on social media. Instead they must practice constant vigilance and self-censorship. This in its turn inevitably leads to a disintegration of college spirit and the fracture of campus life. Lukianoff and Haidt quote the experiences of students who endured the hardships of college life dominated by cancel culture. They identified four features of the culture: dogmatism, groupthink, a crusader mentality, and anti-intellectualism. These features would hardly qualify as staple diet for the intellectual freedom and the capacity for open and vigorous debate that one would expect to be at the centre of university life.[44]

V FOUCAULT'S INFLUENCE

Michel Foucault, the French, post-modernist, philosopher, has been a very influential figure in the development of cancel culture in the sense that significant elements of his theories have been incorporated into it. The first element is the notion of discourse which refers to a type of language associated with an institution (legal, medical, religious, political, economic etc). It includes also the ideas and statements which express an institution's values, meanings and ideals.[45] Foucault would argue that we are controlled to a certain extent by the discourses we employ, and an interesting example of this can be seen in the manouverings of the character Hamlet who ossilated between different discourses in the play – Renaissance discourse, Calvinist predestination discourse and the discourse of Seneca's revenge tragedies. We also know that certain historical events may not be recognised until they enter a relevant discourse. In the 1980s Professor Anita Hill claimed

---
[44] Ibid.
[45] Geoff Danaher, *Understanding Foucault* (Allen & Unwin, 2000).

that she had been sexually harassed, years earlier, by Judge Clarence Thomas, who was about to be appointed to the US Supreme Court. When asked why she hadn't reported this earlier, she said that sexual harassment didn't actually 'exist' (in a legal sense) at the time she was working for Thomas. In other words it was not recognised until it entered a legal discourse.[46]

Discourses can be elevated to positions of enormous prestiege and status under certain conditions. Foucault's notions of power, knowledge and truth are keys to understanding the ways in which may happen.[47] He perceived a complex relationship between the three. Power could be used at times to declare what truth is ("It is the victors who write history"). Possession of knowledge can create power and ideology (the cherished beliefs and ideas that the dominant group has about itself) will dictate which stories and discourses are put into circulation and which are not. The elites of the dominant groups or institutions have the ability to declare what bodies of knowledge are to be approved and circulated, consequently they have the power to enforce their version of the truth. As time passes this 'truth' is regarded as the most natural thing in the world and when this stage is reached a hegemony has been successfully established.[48] We can observe the ways in which certain universities and other institutions use this power. We see in Australia the academic censure of protest against Chinese Communist Party influence in higher education,[49] the prosecution of a well respected professor who questioned climate

---

[46] Ibid.
[47] David Couzens, *Foucault: A Critical Reader* (Basil Blackwood Ltd, 1989) 123-140.
[48] Ibid.
[49] Matthew Lesh, 'Australia's universities are failing to protect free speech', *ABC News* (Web Article, 3 October 2017).

science,⁵⁰ as well as the cancellation of speakers and publishings that were to present politically incorrect views on controversial matters such as race, climate change and transgender politics.⁵¹ We can also witness some of the phrases and words that enter and make up the cancel culture discourse eg. "systemic racism", "de-platforming", "cancelling", "I feel unsafe", "I am offended", "microaggressions", "gender fluidity", "disinvitation", are just a few examples.

Foucault was postmodern in his conviction that there were no truly grand narratives so he was deeply suspicious of global totalitarian theories which claim to offer the solution to our ills.⁵² He held that there can be no such thing as a truth independent of its regime, unless it be that of another. So that liberation in the name of "truth" can only be the substitution of another system of power for this one. The "truth" manufactured by power also turns out to be its "masks" or disguises of hence untruth.⁵³ Foucault's refusal of "truth" and "liberation" seems to be a Nietzschean one. In *Frohliche Wissenschaft*, Nietzsche declares that "there is no order of human life, or the way we are, or human nature, that one can appeal to in order to judge or evaluate between ways of life. There are only different orders imposed by men on primal chaos, following their will-to-power."⁵⁴

Since the regime is entirely identified with its imposed truth unmasking

---

50 Jennifer Oriel, 'Universities' in Kevin Donnelly (ed) *Cancel Culture and the Left's Long March* (Wilkinson, 2021) 60.
51 Glyn Davis, 'Special pleading: free speech and Australian universities', *The Conversation* (Web Article, 4 December 2018) and Hugh Breakey, 'Is "cancel culture" silencing open debate? The perils of shutting down disagreeable opinions and arguments' *ABC Religion & Ethics* (Web Article, 13 July 2020).
52 Charles Taylor, *Philosophy and the Human Sciences* (Cambridge University Press, 1992) 160-166.
53 Ibid.
54 Ibid.

can only destabilise it; it cannot bring about a new, stable, freer form. For Foucault, unmasking can only be the basis for a kind of local resistance within the regime. He speaks of rehabilitating subjugated and local knowledges against the established and dominant truth. He uses the expression 'insurrection of subjugated knowledges' and talks of resistance movements that are always local and specific.[55]

It is significant that critical theory no longer speak of a grand narrative – a utopian vision that addresses itself to the world at large. Instead it adopts the Foucauldian strategy of attacking local and specific issues – a kind of guerilla war on a wide front against many different targets – Feminism, Queer Theory, Critical Race Theory, Post-Colonial Studies, Whiteness Studies, Gender, Ethnicity, and Class.

VI WHAT VISION DRIVES CRITICAL THEORY?

Although woke/critical theory/cultural Marxist ideology no longer speak of a grand narrative and focus their attention on multiple issues, we must still ask the critical question about the motivation that lies behind their project. What is their final goal or vision when they have finished with their demythologising and deconstruction? Is there a destructive rage behind their endeavours and will they be content with destroying capitalism and emaciating Western cultural values? What type of world do they want us to inhabit? Do they still hold to some sort of Marxian utopia and if they do what sort of utopia will it be? To try and engage with these questions we must look more closely at the notion of vision. What is a vision and what are its powers? How do we go about evaluating it. Can there be a destructive vision or is it always

---

[55] Ibid.

a source of good?

In his book *A Conflict of Visions: Ideological Origins of Political Struggles*, Thomas Sowell analyses the power of visions to shape political reality. He likens visions to maps that 'guide us through a tangle of bewildering complexities, and like maps will have to leave out many details in order to let us focus on a few key items that lead to our goals.'[56] They are prior to theory in that we sense and feel how things should be before we do any systematic thinking that would lead to the construction of a theory. Marx may have started with his vision of utopia – a blissful state where people would live in equality and harmony without the irritation of restricting laws and stifling customs (the state would have withered away – it would be an earthly paradise – a return to the Garden of Eden. He then would have started to theorize on how to get there – the destruction of capitalism being a necessary first step. Visions can be very powerful as they set the agenda for both thought and action. They are both indispensable and dangerous.[57]

Visions rest ultimately on some sense of the nature of man – not simply his existing practices but his ultimate potential and ultimate limitations.[58] Sowell makes two main divisions: one he calls the constrained vision and the other the unconstrained vision.[59] The constrained vision emphasizes the weakness and limitations of human nature and consequently the need for institutions and laws to ensure justice, peace and harmony.[60] He quotes various philosophers, economists and political writers to illustrate this view. For example,

---

[56] Thomas Sowell, *A Conflict of Visions: Ideological Origins of Political Struggles* (Basic Books, 2007) 6.
[57] Ibid 3-34.
[58] Ibid 30.
[59] Ibid 31-32.
[60] Ibid 33.

Adam Smith, the economist, praises the workings of the market to appeal to the self-interest of men, while at the same time delivering benefits to the community. Smith also saw government as 'an imperfect remedy' for the deficiency of 'wisdom and virtue' in man.[61] The *Federalist Papers* note: 'Why has government been instituted at all? Because the passions of men will not conform to the dictates of reason and justice without constraint.'[62]

The American Constitution's checks and balances clearly imply that no one was to be completely trusted with power.[63] Edmund Burke, the British statesman, declared: 'We cannot change the nature of things and of men – but must act upon them as best we can,'[64] and that there is 'a radical infirmity in all human contrivances,' an infirmity inherent in the very nature of things.[65] And of course, we must add Immanuel Kant's famous dictum, 'Out of timber so crooked as that from which man is made nothing entirely straight can be built.'[66]

In contrast, the unconstrained vision of human nature saw enormous potential that could be developed. William Godwin, the moral philosopher, (anticipating Marx and Marcuse) in 1793 refers to 'men as they hereafter may be made.'[67] He was highly critical of Smith's ideas that advocated incentives and prohibitions to be used in the public forum. For Godwin the 'hope of reward' and the 'fear of punishment' were in his vision 'wrong in themselves' and 'inimical to

---

[61] Ibid 26.
[62] Ibid 27.
[63] Ibid 23.
[64] Ibid 16.
[65] Ibid 23.
[66] Isaiah Berlin, *The Crooked Timber of Humanity* (Pimlico, 2003) quoting Kant's *gesammelte Schriften* (1900) vol 8, 23.
[67] Sowell (n 56) 16.

the improvement of the mind.'[68] Instead, Godwin argued, efforts should be devoted to 'stimulate the generous and magnanimous sentiments of our nature.'[69] The unconstrained vision promotes pursuit of the highest ideals and the best solutions and it treats process cost as secondary. The French Revolution is a good example of this – defenders of the revolution will say "You cannot make omelettes without breaking eggs." In contrast the constrained vision deals in trade-offs rather than solutions, and in regard to process costs Adam Smith was quite definite: 'The peace and order of society is of more importance than even the relief of the miserable.'[70]

When Jean Jacques Rousseau said that 'man is born free' but 'Is everywhere in chains,' he expressed the essence of the unconstrained vision, in which the fundamental problem is not in nature or man, but in institutions. According to Rousseau 'men are not naturally enemies.' The opposite vision is presented in Thomas Hobbes' *Leviathan* where the power of a strong sovereign is needed to prevent the war of each against all. Life in the natural state would otherwise be 'nasty, brutal and short.'[71] Which vision contains the truth?

Aristotle would have said that the truth must lie somewhere in the middle a combination of both. Human nature is mixed and so are institutions. The paradox of human development is that we cannot develop into mature individuals without the connection with other people and society. We are social animals, and so are not self-sufficient. We need human interaction, we exist in relationships, and must have them to become free, responsible, human beings.[72] There is no such a

---

[68] Ibid 17.
[69] Ibid 18.
[70] Ibid 29.
[71] Ibid 30.
[72] Taylor (n 51) 189-192.

being as natural man running around freely – he is an abstraction – a logical fiction. But Rousseau has a point in that our development as human beings is greatly affected by the upbringing we received, and the type of society and state we live in. We know that the organisations that we work in and societies that we live in can have profoundly damaging effects on us. Elliot Jaques, the Canadian psychoanalyst, who spent a large part of his life studying organizations states that 'it is badly organized social systems that arouse psychotic anxieties and lead to their disturbing acting out and expression in working relationships.'[73]

For Jaques, organisations are formed primarily to get a job done, but if they are badly organized they will inevitably generate anxiety and stress; if well-organized they will promote mutual trust and security and consequently reduce anxiety and disturbed acting out.[74] This view was substantiated by Douglas Kirsner's in-depth study of four American Psychoanalytic Institutes. Because all the members of these institutes were trained analysts who had themselves undergone personal analysis for several years, it is reasonable to assume that they were all optimally functioning human beings, yet Kirsner found that the institutes were highly dysfunctional. Instead of operating with a culture of open, critical inquiry they behaved rather like religious sects guarding their revealed dogma.'[75] Their organization was ecclesiastical in nature with a small coterie of select individuals, 'the keepers of the flame', holding the key positions. The lack of proper organizational structure generated feelings of paranoia, suspicion and produced bitter

---

[73] Elliott Jaques, 'Why the Psychoanalytic Approach to Understanding Organizations is Dysfunctional' (1995) 48 *Human Relations* 343.
[74] Ibid.
[75] Douglas Kirsner, *Unfree Associations: Inside Psychoanalytic Institutes* (Process Press, 2000).

in-fighting over power.⁷⁶ From this analysis we could conclude that a society or state with good laws and institutions would be able to promote and encourage what is finest in human nature while at the same time restraining and curtailing its darker elements.⁷⁷

We can now ask the question where does Critical Theory and Cancel Culture stand on the question of vision? If we go back to the three 'masters of suspicion' we can see first of all that Freud's vision involved individuals gaining some liberation through the process of psychoanalysis but that did not entail any great plans for change in society. In fact in his *Civilization and its Discontents* he maintained that a certain amount of repression would have to be retained for civilization to function. His was a constrained vision. Nietzsche's vision centered on his "will-to-power," which he saw as a dark, powerful, irrational force in our human nature that could be destructive, but could also be harnessed by the individual into something good. However, with the "Death of God", Nietzsche feared that the world would fall into either nihilism or destructive totalitarianism unless the Ubermensch (the higher person) arrived with a new set of values. This is also a very constrained vision. Marx's utopian vision after the state has withered away and capitalism with its supporting superstructure destroyed, is very much an unconstrained one. But it sounds very much like Rousseau's innocent man before society put him "into chains". The trouble here is that Marx assumes that if we can destroy Capitalism and its false ideology then we will be liberated and free. He does not give us any idea of what the new ideology will be like or how society will function. He also assumes that human beings will behave and that there will be no deviancy. His assumed vision has a striking similarity to that of Zeno the Stoic, one of the first utopians, who conceived of

---

⁷⁶ Ibid.
⁷⁷ Ibid.

an anarchist society in which all rational beings live in perfect peace, equality and happiness without the benefits of institutions. No need for control, no need for a state, no need for law courts, or for any organized, institutional life.[78] This is a good example of an extreme, unconstrained vision of human nature.

We saw earlier that the Critical Theorists of the Frankfurt School and Antonio Gramsci had the liberation of people as their goal and they saw this coming about when capitalism and its ideologies were destroyed. Again like Marx there is no account of what liberation will be like when it is achieved. From our analysis of the two visions earlier we concluded that good laws and good institutions are needed to promote human flourishing, but Critical Theory and Cancel Culture give us no idea what laws or institutions we are likely to have when the deconstruction and cancelling come to an end. All we have is the assumption that Rousseau's innocent, perfect man will magically appear when the 'false' ideologies are finally demolished.

Given the attitudes and tactics of the Woke generation with their hostility, deplatforming and cancelling, it is very difficult to imagine their bearing any resemblance to Rousseau 'natural man', when utopia finally arrives, after the eclipse of western civilization. We would be more likely to end up with Hobbes' "war of each against all" and today's equivalent of life being "brutal, nasty, and short".

VII FINAL CONSIDERATIONS

We would do well to meditate on the words of Edmund Burke written in his *Reflections on the Revolution in France* concerning the Versatility of Evil. He argues that we do not always learn correctly the real lessons

---
[78] Berlin, n.66, 22.

of history because we focus on the pretexts rather than the causes. 'History consists, for the greater part, of the miseries brought upon the world by pride, ambition, avarice, revenge, lust, sedition, hypocrisy, ungoverned zeal, and all the train of disorderly appetites.'[79] These vices are the real cause of disturbance and disorder. 'Religion, morals, laws, privileges liberties, rights of men, are the pretexts. The pretexts are always found in some specious appearance of a real good.'[80] Burke goes on to say that you will not eradicate evil by wholesale changes to the pretexts:

> Wise men will apply their remedies to vices, not to names, to the causes of evil which are permanent, not to the occasional organs by which they act, and the transitory modes in which they appear. Seldom have two ages the same fashion in their pretexts and the same modes of mischief. Wickedness is a little more inventive. Whilst you are discussing fashion, the fashion is gone by. The same vice assumes a new body.[81]

Wokeism and Cancel Culture cloth themselves in the garments of anti-racism and social justice both worthy objectives in themselves, but the manner in which they promote them calls to mind Burke's distinction between causes and pretexts. With "ungoverned zeal" and not a little "pride" they adopt the methods of common-enemy identity politics to pursue their ends. It is the old Marxist dialectic at work – attack an opposite group or class – hold them up to ridicule – disempower them – cancel them. Pride also dictates that they see themselves as the "Anointed ones," the "Elect" and the sole occupants of the moral high ground- untroubled by any thoughts of humility or

---

[79] Edmund Burke, *Reflections on the Revolution in France* quoted in Connor Cruise O'Brien, *The Great Melody: A Thematic Biography of Edmund Burke* (The University of Chicago Press, 1992) 603-604.
[80] Ibid.
[81] Ibid.

self-doubt. Dershowitz claims the "Anointed" are possessed of "moral clarity" ie "The Truth", which means that there is only one correct way to see things, and that anyone who disagrees with these views is racist, morally inferior, or politically incorrect.[82] Free speech and due process are just delaying barriers to their utopia. There is no attempt at discussion, dialogue or compromise you either agree with their vision or are cast into "outer darkness" to become the benighted.[83]

The neo-Marxist inspired Cancel Culture has an aura of religious fundamentalism about it. Totally convinced of its own rectitude it combines in Dershowitz's words the 'worst elements of self-righteousness and judgementalism.'[84] Thomas Sowell describes the behaviour and attitude of elites who pursue their vision of what they deem good for country, cause or institution. Their vision (often faulty) is the driving force behind their rhetoric, actions and policy decisions.[85] In Sowell's book, *The Vision of the Anointed*, he asserts that underlying the vision is a framework of assumptions within which social and political discourse takes place in the media, academia, and in politics. Any empirical evidence that might contradict the vision is either ignored, suppressed or dismissed.[86] The vision of the anointed is not just a vision of the world and its functioning but is also a vision of themselves and of their moral role in the world. Those who believe in the vision are in a special state of grace and consequently elevated to a higher moral plane. Should you disagree with the prevailing vision you would be seen as not merely in error, but in sin.[87] Thus, we have

---

[82] Dershowitz (n 1) 8.
[83] Ibid.
[84] Ibid.
[85] Sowell (n 56) 4.
[86] Thomas Sowell, *The Vision of the Anointed: Self-Congratulations as a Basis Social Policy* (Basic Books, 1995) 186-189.
[87] Ibid. 105-116.

the sharp division into the anointed and the benighted. If you are in the ranks of the benighted then you are to be made "aware," to have your "consciousness raised," in the hope that you will "grow." Should you resist this re-education process then you will be dismissed as perverse, malignant or meanspirited, and efforts will be made to expose the "real reasons" behind your arguments and actions.[88] Albert Camus' famous statement from *The Fall* comes readily to mind to describe their attitude:

> How intoxicating to feel like God the Father and to hand out definitive testamonials of bad character and habits.[89]

Isaiah Berlin, the political philosopher, believes that some moral, social, and political values conflict. There are, he says, 'some ultimate values by which men live that cannot be reconciled or combined.' You cannot combine full liberty with full equality – 'full liberty for the wolves cannot be combined with full liberty for the sheep.'[90] Mercy and justice, knowledge and happiness can collide. Utopian solutions are unworkable because they try to combine the uncombinable. In a pluralist, liberal society hard choices have to be made, there is no avoiding compromises and trade-offs. "How much equality, how much liberty? How much justice, how much mercy?" This doesn't sit well for believers in the unconstrained vision, because they believe that no sacrifice is too great in establishing the ideal society. If blood has to be shed to create the perfect world then let it be shed. "You have to break eggs to make the splendid omelette." The danger is that once people get into the habit of breaking eggs they rarely stop – "the eggs are broken

---

[88] Sowell (n 86) chs 1, 5.
[89] Albert Camus, *The Fall* (Penguin Books, 2020).
[90] Ramin Jahanbegloo, *Conversations with Isaiah Berlin* (Haliban Publishers, 2007) 47.

but the omelette is not made."'[91] Berlin warns that 'fanatical belief in a perfect solution, even if demanded by the sincerest of idealists, the purest of heart, cannot but lead to suffering, misery, blood, and terrible repression.'[92] The Great Terror, the Great Purge, the Cultural Revolution, are compelling evidence of this. Humanity is not built for such totalitarian schemes.

We have seen that Marxist ideology strongly informs the values and practices of the Woke generation and Cancel Culture. There is no thought of reasoned debate or compromise, it is a battle between two ideologies with only one winner. Some worthy causes are espoused and supported but they are hijacked in the form of common-enemy identity politics. There is even a weaponising of the justice system to further their ideological goals. Dershowitz accurately describes the dominant facets of their modus operandi. He shows how they simplify complex issues and swiftly punish any opposing views by shaming and ostracising those who oppose them.

> It is a cancer on American democracy, meritocracy, due process, and freedom of expression ... it endangers basic liberties, miseducates students, erases history, empowers extremists, destroyes hard-earned legacies, - all without accountability and transparency ... It must be contested in the market place of ideas.[93]

Michael Walsh in his polemical *The Devil's Pleasure Palace: The Cult of Critical Theory and the Subversion of the West*, uses religious, apocalyptic, and literary discourses to depict the evil of Critical Theory. Walsh believes that gullible Americans have been seduced by the "siren song" of European theory. They have succumbed to that

---

[91] Ibid 143.
[92] Ibid 142-143.
[93] Ibid 123-124.

'hateful ideology' which tries to save humanity while despising people – its philosophical essence – 'creation is a bore annihilation is a joy.'[94]

In Milton's *Paradise Lost* Satan has been expelled from heaven and his first desire is revenge. He cannot attack heaven but he can go after "God's new toy", humanity. Walsh describes Critical Theory thus:

> In its purest form, which is to say its most malevolent form, Critical Theory is the very essence of Satanism: rebellion for the sake of rebellion against an established order that has obtained for eons, and with no greater promise for the future than destruction. We must use the word 'satanic,' which means the desire to tear down a longstanding, even elemental, order and replace it with … nothing … Like Satan, the Left must always have something to 'fight,' lest it be rendered impotent, because its driving force, as we have seen, stems not from philosophy but emotion – hatred, resentment, envy, and malcontentment.[95]

---

[94] Walsh (n 26) 141
[95] Ibid 50, 83, 193.

6

Vilification Laws: Tools for Tyranny

ALEXANDER MILLARD* AND JOHN STEENHOF**

ABSTRACT

Vilification laws share strong ties with key foundational concepts of Critical Theory. The Frankfurt School's philosophical disillusionment with revolutionary Marxism during the interwar period produced a critique that distrusted objective truth claims and encouraged social change by applied philosophy. The philosophical heritage of Critical Theory contains core principles that are antithetical to a flourishing liberal democracy and the free exchange of ideas. The arguments in support of vilification laws and the laws themselves show a strong connection to these principles. Vilification laws do not respect truth claims and encourage people to fearfully censor their own speech. If these tools continue to be used to shut down public debate the health and effectiveness of Australia's democracy will only be eroded.

I INTRODUCTION

Australian vilification laws share a strong ideological and theoretical relationship with postmodern Critical Theory. In several key ways

---

* Alexander Millard is a Solicitor with the Human Rights Law Alliance.
** John Steenhof is the Principal Lawyer with the Human Rights Law Alliance.

they are the codification of foundational aspects of this theory.

We explore the relationship between vilification laws and postmodern Critical theory in two ways.

The first is an analysis of the parliamentary debates and speeches concerning the introduction of vilification laws in New South Wales and in Victoria. The parliamentary debates concerning the introduction of the *Anti-Discrimination (Racial Vilification) Amendment Act 1989* (NSW) and the debates concerning the passage of the *Racial and Religious Tolerance Amendment Bill 2019* (Vic) show that parliamentarians use categories and ideological positions that display a strong relationship with key aspects of postmodern Critical Theory.

The second way in which we explore the relationship between vilification laws and postmodern Critical Theory is by looking at the laws themselves. In particular by looking at section 38S of the *Anti-Discrimination Act 1977* (NSW) and how the elements of vilification laws like section 38S have been interpreted and applied by the courts. It will be shown that the irrelevance of intent and actual incitement to hatred, the absence of a defence of truth and the prohibition of speech to protect a minority group are the conceptual children of key theoretical aspects of postmodern Critical Theory.

Vilification laws place civil and criminal sanctions on individuals for public speech of a particular kind. They prohibit the public expression of beliefs and ideas about other people if those beliefs and ideas relate to a protected attribute such as race or sex, and have the capacity to incite hatred and severe ridicule of the protected group.

These laws place a heavy burden on free speech because they limit the open contest of ideas in liberal democracies, regardless of whether someone is speaking truthfully or if any harm is actually caused. They are concerning because they display elements of postmodern Critical Theory that are antagonistic to a flourishing democracy. They are tools ready-made for tyranny.

This chapter does not claim that drafters of Australian vilification laws have purposively legislated in devotion to Critical Theory. As the Apostle Paul said, 'who knows a person's thoughts?'.[1] Rather, this paper seeks to show that there is a strong correlation between core foundational elements of postmodern Critical Theory and vilification laws. This relationship is concerning because it demonstrates that Australian vilification laws are not built on a foundation of objective truth, but rather seek to emancipate 'oppressed' groups from the supposed tyranny of power exerted through speech.

II CRITICAL THEORY

'Critical Theory' has become a widely used term, so that just like other such cultural monikers 'The Rule of Law' and 'Liberal Democracy', it can mean a great deal and therefore very little at all.

Key principles exist at the root of different social and political theories like postmodernism, democracy and liberalism. It is also these principles that, at their core, contain powerful and compelling aspects of theories that exert influence over society and culture.

The relationship between Australian vilification laws and postmodern Critical Theory is found in the key pillars on which postmodern Critical Theory rests.

---

[1] 1 Corinthians 2:11.

Generally, when 'critical theory' is referred to in the modern media or in popular books such as Helen Pluckrose and James Lindsay's *Cynical Theories* what is being referred to is what we might call small 'c' critical theory. It is an elastic term that refers to broadly homogenous ideologies that contain similar core ideas. This critical theory is heavily dependent on the French postmodernists and poststructuralists who were writing from the 1960s – men such as Michel Foucault, Jacques Derrida and Jean-Francois Lyotard.[2] We will treat the elements of the postmodern theory of these philosophers as the key pillars of modern 'critical theory'.

Critical Theory, with a capital 'C', is also the proper name for a school of thought developed in Weimar Germany in the interwar period by members of the 'Frankfurt School'.[3] Antecedent to the development of postmodern critical theory, the Critical Theory thinkers of the early twentieth century laid the foundation for what is now small 'c' critical theory applied today through different paradigms, such as 'critical race theory' or 'critical gender theory'.[4] It is Critical Theory applied postmodernism that has theoretical similarities with vilification laws in Australia.

Critical Theory was born out of the Frankfurt School through the philosophical efforts of theorists such as Theodor W Adorno, Max Horkheimer and Herbert Marcuse.[5] These theorists were of the Western European Marxist tradition. They were disillusioned with revolutionary Marxism and their theoretical approach was distinctive

---

[2] Helen Pluckrose and James Lindsay, *Cynical Theories* (Pitchstone, 2020) 21.
[3] Steve Buckler, 'Normative Theory' in David Marsh and Gerry Stoker (ed), *Theory and Methods in Political Science* (Palgrave Macmillan, 3rd ed, 2010) 164.
[4] Pluckrose and Lindsay (n 2) 46-51, James Bohman, 'Critical Theory', *Stanford Encyclopedia of Philosophy* (Web Page, 8 March 2005).
[5] Ben Aggar, 'Critical Theory, Poststructuralism, Postmodernism: Their Sociological Relevance' (1991) 17 *Annual Review of Sociology* 105, 107.

because it was developed in an attempt to answer what was seen as the failure of political Marxism to mobilise and change society.[6]

Though these men were dissatisfied with the efficacy of Marxism to mobilise the working classes in opposition to capital owners, they were still interested in philosophy and political theory as a normative social tool. Unlike a stereotypical ivory-tower philosopher, these thinkers were not satisfied to merely explore philosophical ideas. Their approach to knowledge and theoretical politics was purposive. It was, firstly, aimed at criticising liberal capitalism and philosophical liberalism in general. Secondly, it was normative. The paradigm that they applied to critique liberalism was also meant to supplant and 'emancipate' the 'enslaved' classes of society.[7]

The theoretical bedrock of Critical Theory is the presupposition of an ideological framework that is applied to society in order to create *change*. In a revealing early essay, Horkheimer, who is seen as foundational to the Frankfurt School's body of thought, said,

> If, however, theoretician and his specific object are seen as forming a dynamic unity with the oppressed class, so that his presentation of social contradictions is not merely an expression of the concrete historical situation but also a force within it to stimulate change, then his real function emerges.[8]

And,

> Even the classificatory judgments of specialised science have a fundamentally hypothetical character, and existential judgments are allowed, if at all, only in certain areas, namely the descriptive

---

[6] Buckler (n 3) 164; Aggar (n 5) 107.
[7] Bohman (n 4).
[8] Max Horkheimer, *Critical Theory: Selected Essays Max Horkheimer*, tr Matthew J O'Connell et al (The Continuum Publishing Company, 1975) 215.

and practical parts of the discipline. But the critical theory of society is, in its totality, the unfolding of a single existential judgment...[9]

Finally,

> However many valid analogies there may be between these different intellectual endeavors, there is nonetheless a decisive difference when it comes to the relation of subject and object and therefore to the necessity of the event being judged. The object with which the scientific specialist deals is not affected at all by his own theory ... A consciously critical attitude, however, is part of the development of society: the construing of the course of history as the necessary product of an economic mechanism simultaneously contains both a protest against this order of things, a protest generated by the order itself, and the idea of self-determination for the human race ... Every part of the theory pre-supposes the critique of the existing order and the struggle against it along lines determined by the theory itself.[10]

Critical Theory is not merely descriptive; its purpose is to change society. A particular branch of Critical Theory that has born the fruit now shaping our laws and institutions is postmodern philosophy.

III THE POSTMODERN TURN

The philosophical products of postmodernism have been given force through the application of Critical Theory as a normative framework and bear a strong relationship to the theoretical foundations of vilifications laws.

---

[9] Ibid 227.
[10] Ibid 229.

Postmodernism is deeply sceptical of the epistemological claims of scientific liberalism. Like the Frankfurt School it questions the theorist's ability to step outside of their own linguistic, cultural and sociological context in order to make any kind of objective assessment from the 'outside'.[11] In other words, the autonomous, free-thinking subject who shapes their own identity through free and independent rational choices is a myth.[12] What matters in a postmodern interpretation of the world is the 'discourse' driven narrative from which the world is being observed. Every person is just another storyteller.[13]

According to postmodern theorists like Foucault, the chosen and dominant discourse that is used to interpret the world is an expression of power.[14] The dominant discourse cannot be verified according to an outstanding standard of objective reality. Therefore, all interpretations of the world and society are competing narratives with their own value propositions. These narratives compete for dominance in order to exert power over others. The modern and ascendant 'discourse' of scientific liberalism and capitalism is therefore an expression of wilful power over others to the detriment of some groups and to the benefit of others.[15]

This theory of society elevates the importance of language to an extreme position. This is because not only are the communicated perspectives and interpretation of the world through language are important and a will to exert powerful dominance, but the words, phrases, idioms and semantic meaning of these are also an expression of power. Under this paradigm, language is no longer a vehicle for persuasion and praise,

---

[11] Aggar (n 5) 116-117.
[12] Buckler (n 3) 170.
[13] Bruce Haddock, *A History of Political Thought* (Polity Press, 2008) 255-256.
[14] Buckler (n 3) 171.
[15] Buckler (n 3) 164-165.

but the medium itself can be a tool of coercive power, depending on your socio-political outlook.

What one person may see as a normal expression of reality, another might see as a will to powerful dominance over a supressed class of people. This understanding of language and power applied from discourse is crucial to understanding the influence of postmodern Critical Theory on vilification laws in Australia.

It is not that this postmodern Critical Theory has been specifically applied to the development of vilification legislation. Rather, its traces can be seen in the way that legislators perceive the importance of language and speech and the way that these affect discrete groups of people.

Postmodern interpretations of language and power have been operationalised through normative Critical Theory approaches to society through three main 'pillars' of understanding:

> 1. Knowledge and truth are not objective – it is impossible to step outside of your own linguistic and cultural context to make objective moral truth claims, especially about social issues;
>
> 2. Language is powerful and dangerous – language is not only a means to convey meaning and argument, to persuade others to act, but is in and of itself capable of causing harm to a person;
>
> 3. All narratives and observations are expressions of power – there is no factual observation that can be made independent of a discourse that promotes the power and dominance of a social group – society and politics is a contest of different groups for dominance.[16]

---

[16] Pluckrose and Lindsay (n 2) 35-41.

IV AUSTRALIAN VILIFICATION LAW – EVIDENCE FOR THE INFLUENCE OF POSTMODERN CRITICAL THEORY

These postmodern elements are present in the parliamentary debates concerning vilification legislation in Australia. What is often argued is that certain forms of speech must be supressed or controlled to achieve safety (both physical and emotional) for vulnerable groups. This argument has evolved from a position that suppressing vilifying speech will reduce speech-induced violence to one that also asserts harm from the language and speech itself. The harm is made real by receiving the words as a vulnerable class.

Vilification laws are also seen in these debates as a means of social control and improvement. The idea being that by controlling speech society can be behaviourally improved and minority groups emancipated from oppression.

A The *Anti-Discrimination (Racial Vilification) Amendment Act 1989* (NSW)

The *Anti-Discrimination (Racial Vilification) Amendment Act 1989* (NSW) was introduced to the NSW parliament on 4 May 1989 and assented to on 17 May 1989.[17] The Act was championed by the Liberal Attorney General John Dowd and had bi-partisan support from Labor members such as Bob Carr and John Newman.[18]

In the second reading speech and following remarks made by members of the Legislative Assembly the focus of debate was on the fact that

---

[17] *Anti-Discrimination (Racial Vilification) Amendment Act 1989* (NSW).
[18] New South Wales, *Parliamentary* Debates, Legislative Assembly, 4 May 1989, 7488 (John Dowd, Attorney General); New South Wales, *Parliamentary Debates*, Legislative Assembly, 10 May 1989, 7919 (Bob Carr, Leader of the Opposition).

racist speech and speech that incited violence on racial grounds was behaviour unbefitting of the Australian public.[19] Such a speech needed to be eradicated because it could potentially incite actual violence and mistreatment of individuals and it could also be offensive to those individuals, damaging their dignity.[20]

Also present in the debate was the idea that by eradicating vilifying language and controlling language, society would be improved and moulded to be more cohesive.[21] This idea was communicated in the Legislative Council.[22] By changing the language, Australian society would be educated, and its behaviour would be changed.

Members of Parliament highlighted real violence and racist behaviour during these debates. The kinds of activities mentioned included physical attacks, racist graffiti and hateful pamphlets being distributed to the community.[23]

In these early debates concerning some of the first vilification laws introduced in Australia, there was a clear understanding that the laws were being introduced to combat public speech which offends and of which it is alleged contributes to the perpetration of violent acts in the community. The idea that language is harmful was certainly present in these debates, though it is represented as being harmful because it actually *causes* harmful events. It is also represented as being harmful because of its psychological effect on a community.

---

[19] New South Wales, *Parliamentary* Debates, Legislative Assembly, 4 May 1989, 7490-7491 (John Dowd, Attorney General).
[20] Ibid.
[21] New South Wales, *Parliamentary Debates*, Legislative Assembly, 10 May 1989, 7931 (John Dowd, Attorney General).
[22] New South Wales, *Parliamentary Debates,* Legislative Council, 10 May 1989, 7817 (Helen Sham-Ho).
[23] Ibid 7818.

The key pillars of postmodern Critical Theory are present in these parliamentary debates, particularly the power of language and discourse control. This does not mean that the proponents of the bill were motivated by Critical Theorists. However, there is a correlation between the early arguments for these laws and concepts contained within postmodern Critical Theory.

B *The Racial and Religious Tolerance Amendment Bill 2019* (Vic)

These postmodern Critical Theory ideas are also visable in more recent debates concerning the Victorian *Racial and Religious Tolerance Amendment Bill* seeking to amend the *Racial and Religious Tolerance Act 2001*.[24]

The second reading speech on the bill was delivered on 28 August 2019. The Bill sought to rename the existing Act as the *Elimination of Vilification Act*, and extend the protected attributes under it to include gender, disability, sexual orientation and sex characteristics.[25]

The second reading speech cites examples of vulgar and inappropriate speech directed towards a handful of prominent female public figures, one of whom:

> [H]as for years received daily online abuse, including rape and death threats, as well as being the target of several huge mob attacks. During the first of these 'pile-ons' she received over 2000 messages over a two-day period involving 'every kind of abuse possible'.[26]

---

[24] Racial and Religious Tolerance Amendment Bill 2019 (Vic); *Racial and Religious Tolerance Act 2001* (Vic) (*Victorian Act*).
[25] Victoria, *Parliamentary Debates*, Legislative Council, 28 August 2019, 2726 (Fiona Patten).
[26] Ibid.

Just as in the debates concerning the NSW laws discussed above, the sponsor linked public speech to the perpetration of violent acts against a group, arguing that addressing public speech must be included in the fight to reduce cases of domestic violence against women.[27]

The sponsor developed this connection between speech and violence, going beyond the relationship described in the NSW debates as being connected to hurt feelings. She identified the speech itself as a form of violence (emphasis added),

> Victoria understands family violence. We instituted a royal commission and we are implementing all of its 227 recommendations. We accept that 'we must change community attitudes towards women if we are to prevent violence from happening in the first place', to quote the Premier of Victoria. **Yet we have done little to address this type of violence against women where it is most pervasive.** Hate speech lives and breeds in social media feeds and the comments sections of news articles; it is shaming, bullying and **brutalising** via the everyday mediums that we use to communicate and consume media.
>
> Bullying in this form has led to suicide. **It causes physical, psychological and emotional harm.** It affects people's sense of self-worth and feelings of safety and belonging in the community.[28]

The sponsor further developed this point by talking of the effects of this kind of speech as inciting and itself being violence interchangeably,

> [H]ate speech that if left unchecked can embed discrimination

---

[27] Ibid.
[28] Ibid.

and prejudice; hate speech that can lead to hate crime, which does not occur in a vacuum. It is the **violent manifestation** of prejudice in the wider community.[29]

It is significant that the legal prohibition that vilification laws impose is directed towards incitement of hatred, serious contempt, ridicule and violence against another person.[30]

The sponsor has collapsed the cause and effect of the law into one. She is arguing that the speech itself, apart from a demonstrable negative effect, is violence and should be prohibited. The Victorian vilification law, like all laws with legal sanctions, must be directed toward specific behaviour. It cannot be directed only against the effect of the behaviour or behaviour that has no causal connection to a harm. However, vilification legislation actually comes as close as possible to this by sanctioning speech that has the theoretical capacity to incite an effect, without requiring evidence of actual incitement.[31] The Bill specifically inserted the words 'likely to incite' into the Act.[32]

The debates about the Bill not only display elements of critical theory in the way that they describe the importance and power of language, but also in the way that the debate was framed about protecting and emancipating a protected class of people from another class or group A council member supported the Bill out of concern for 'vulnerable and marginalised people (who) are unable to escape hatred and intolerance

---

[29] Ibid.
[30] Victoria, *Parliamentary Debates*, Legislative Council, 28 August 2019, 2726 (Fiona Patten); '*Victorian Act*' ss 7(1), 8(1).
[31] *Victorian Act* s 7-8; Racial and Religious Tolerance Amendment Bill 2019 (Vic) cl 10(2)(b); Victoria, *Parliamentary Debates*, Legislative Council, 11 September 2019, 3035 (David Davis, Leader of the Opposition); *Sunol v Collier (No 2)* [2012] NSWCA 44, [41].
[32] Racial and Religious Tolerance Amendment Bill 2019 (Vic) cl 10(2)(b).

cast towards them'.³³ Another council member also couched his support of the Bill in a discussion of marginalised groups defined by their protected attribute being verbally assaulted by another group.³⁴ The council member viewed the proposed laws as socially influential and educative, able to modify society's behaviour, as did supporters of the NSW vilification laws.³⁵ This historical support for vilification legislation reflects key elements of postmodernism. Language is powerful, language can harm, language is the assertion of power over of another class.

There exist in these debates key assumptions about harm, moral culpability for harm and how harm is caused by language that provides an effective framework for the postmodern elements discussed above to be used to push for legislative reform.

V LOOKING AT THE LAWS THEMSELVES

Vilification laws structurally display the key elements of postmodern Critical Theory.

Almost all vilification legislation in Australia uses what is known as the 'incitement' model for its legislative framework.³⁶ This incitement model was adopted in the first piece of Australian vilification legislation in New South Wales in 1989.³⁷ The wording between different State and Territory legislation is very similar, with the exception of Victoria,

---

[33] Victoria, *Parliamentary Debates*, Legislative Council, 11 September 2019, 3037 (Andy Meddick).
[34] Victoria, *Parliamentary Debates*, Legislative Council, 11 September 2019, 3038 (Samantha Ratnam).
[35] Ibid 3040.
[36] Neil Rees, Simon Rice & Dominique Allen, *Australian Anti-Discrimination & Equal Opportunity Law* (The Federation Press, 3rd ed, 2018) 682-683.
[37] Ibid 682.

though the Victorian provision has been interpreted in line with the NSW legislation.[38]

The development of modern vilification and 'hate-speech' laws that prohibit incitement can be found in international agreements on human rights such as the *Universal Declaration of Human Rights* ('UDHR') and the *International Covenant on Civil and Political Rights* ('ICCPR').

During the drafting of the UDHR, Articles 19 and 7 posed particular problems for the drafters as to how restricted free and open expression should be.[39] The final Article 19 reads as follows:

> Everyone has the rights to freedom of opinion and expression; this right includes freedom to hold opinions without interference and to seek, receive and impart information and ideas through any media and regardless of frontiers.[40]

During the drafting phase the Soviet and Czechoslovakian delegates suggested restrictive limitations that would have confined the breadth of this freedoms.[41] The suggestions were rejected by the non-communist nations.

The Soviets were not satisfied with the concept of fighting ideas with ideas and wanted to prohibit the expression of particular ideas, in this case fascism, because they thought the mere opposition of robust debate would be ineffective to prevent the rise of future destructive

---

[38] Rees, Rice and Allen (n 36) 682; *Catch the Fire Ministries Inc v Council of Victoria Inc* (2006) VSCA 284, [160].
[39] Paul Coleman, *Censored: How European "Hate Speech" Laws are Threatening Freedom of Speech* (Kairos Publications, 2nd ed, 2012) ch 1.
[40] *Universal Declaration of Human Rights*, GA Res 217A, art 19.
[41] Coleman (n 39) ch 1.

ideologies.[42] Western liberal democracies were concerned about entrenching restrictions on speech in international law where the final word on what was permissible belonged to the State.

The debate on 'hate-speech' laws continued with the ICCPR. The Soviet and communist states were successful in rejecting prohibitions on speech that only incited violence and were able to include prohibitions on the incitement of hatred in Article 20(2):

> Any advocacy of national, racial or religious hatred that constitutes incitement to discrimination, hostility, or violence shall be prohibited by law.[43]

The voting record on this adoption reveals that the 'internationalization of hate-speech prohibitions in human rights law owes its existence to a number of states where both criticisms of the prevalent totalitarian ideology as well as advocacy for democracy were strictly prohibited.'[44]

The language of incitement to hatred adopted in vilification statutes was implemented by totalitarian states that sought to eradicate any domestic opposition to communist rule.

The Australian vilification incitement model that borrows from this legal pedigree is named as such in juxtaposition to the 'causing offence' model, which is used by the federal *Racial Discrimination Act* and because the law looks to whether there is a potential for animus to be incited in persons, rather than for offence to be caused.[45]

---

[42] Ibid ch 1.
[43] Coleman (n 39) ch 2; *International Covenant on Civil and Political Rights*, GA Res 2200A, art 20(2).
[44] Jacob Mchangama, 'The Sordid Origin of Hate-Speech Laws', *Hoover Institution Policy Review* (Web Page, 1 December 2011).
[45] *Racial Discrimination Act 1975* (Cth) s 18C.

There are three differences between these models. The first concerns the effect of the conduct in question. The second concerns the perspective from which the conduct is viewed and its effect assessed. The third concern is the causal link between the conduct in question and the protected attribute of the target person.[46] The two models both have in common that they do not require evidence of actual offence or incitement, but rather an objective test is used to ascertain whether the offence is reasonably likely to occur or is capable of inciting hatred in the group receiving the public conduct.[47]

We will focus on the 'incitement' model because it is the one predominantly used in all States and Territories. The NSW Act provides a good example:[48]

> **38 S   Transgender vilification unlawful**
>
> (1) It is unlawful for a person, by a public act, to incite hatred towards, serious contempt for, or severe ridicule of –
>
> (a)   a person on the ground that the person is a transgender person, or
>
> (b)   a group of persons on the ground that the members of the group are transgender persons.
>
> (2) Nothing in this section renders unlawful –
>
> (a)   a fair report of a public act referred to in subsection (1), or
>
> (b)   a communication or the distribution or dissemination of any matter on an occasion that would be subject to a defence of absolute privilege

---

[46] Rees, Rice and Allen (n 36) 683.
[47] Rees, Rice and Allen (n 36) 697, 734.
[48] *Anti-Discrimination Act 1977* (NSW) s 38S; *Transgender (Anti-Discrimination and Other Acts Amendment) Act 1996* (NSW).

(whether under the Defamation Act 2005 or otherwise) in proceedings for defamation, or

(c) a public act, done reasonably and in good faith, for academic, artistic, scientific, research or religious purposes or for other purposes in the public interest, including discussion or debate about and expositions of any act or matter.

Vilification legislation in this form has several significant features that have been drawn out by case law:

1. It is unnecessary to prove that the respondent intended to incite hatred or serious contempt;
2. It is unnecessary to prove that anyone was actually incited to hatred or serious contempt;
3. The law is a prohibition on behaviour towards a particular group or kind of person;
4. The alleged vilifying act must have capacity to incite the impugned response in group to which the public act is directed.[49]

It is also significant that the exceptions provided in subsection 2 of the above section, which are indicative of other exceptions provided in incitement model legislation, provide no exception for statements that are truthful. The 'fair report' exception in subsection 2(a) protects public communication about events that could be vilification, like an article that reports on a public speech that contained vilifying remarks.[50] This protects a journalist, but not the public speaker. even if what they are saying is in fact true. Truth is no defence, in contrust to defamation law.[51]

---

[49] *Sunol v Collier (No 2)* [2012] NSWCA 44, [41]; *DLH v Nationwide News Pty Ltd (No 2)* [2018] NSWCATAD 217, [10]-[11].
[50] Rees, Rice and Allen (n 36) 740; *Hussein v Nationwide News Pty Ltd* [2016] NSWCATAD 139, [35]-[36].
[51] For example – see the *Defamation Act 2005* (NSW) s 26.

These features display a strong relationship to the essential elements of postmodern critical theory.

A *Knowledge and Truth are Subjective*

The first and most significant relationship is that what is objectively true is irrelevant to a test of whether vilification has taken place.

As outlined above, Critical Theory as a discipline is highly sceptical of a theorist being able to step outside of their own situation to be able to objectively assess any kind of social phenomenon by an external, objective standard.[52] What matters to the Critical Theorist is the application of the presupposed framework for analysis, with an understanding that the theorist is intellectually constrained by their own position in relation to what they are analysing.

Incitement model vilification laws display similarities to this aspect of Critical Theory in that whether what the respondent said is actually true or not, is not valued, nor relevant to ascertaining whether vilification has taken place. What matters is whether the public statement or act is likely to incite hatred for the protected person or group.

The likelihood of incitement is also dependant on the nature of the group receiving the speech.

This group could be particularly offended by certain acts or have heightened sensibilities when it comes to certain topics such that it could be provoked to hatred where another group would not.

The laws themselves are directed towards speech that has the capacity

---

[52] Aggar (n 5) 116-117.

to incite an emotion of hatred or a change in attitude towards the protected group. More than this, it is not even necessary that this incitement occurs; the speech merely must be likely to incite.[53]

Like postmodern Critical Theory, objective truth is irrelevant to vilification law. What matters is the subjective experience of a group of people and their attitude to another group of people.

B *Language is Powerful and Dangerous*

Another way in which the incitement model vilification laws are connected to postmodern Critical Theory is the way in which speech and language are treated as harmful and something to be controlled in order to effect changes in social power.

The laws seek to eradicate emotions, thoughts and actions that are deemed to be socially immoral and abhorrent because they are directed towards a group that possesses an attribute that is deemed to be privileged. Furthermore, because the speech does not need to actually produce the undesirable effects, the laws are treating the speech itself as especially dangerous and problematic – the laws are not directed towards ameliorating undesirable harms by sanctioning harm caused, but are rather directed at eradicating language and speech that challenges the social status of privileged groups.

This demonstrates a strong connection between postmodern Critical Theory in its treatment of language and speech as powerful and intimately connected to power.

---

[53] *Sunol v Collier (No 2)* [2012] NSWCA 44, [41].

C *The Purpose of Theory is to Assert Power Over Others*

Vilification laws value whether a minority group is being (theoretically) harmed by another person or group regardless of whether the dislike or contempt invoked is an objectively apposite moral response.

The fact that these laws operate in this way links them strongly to one of the key elements of critical theory, not just theoretically, but purposefully. Critical Theory's purpose is to change society by using a theoretical framework to change power relationships between groups/ classes of people.

Vilification laws are purpose focused. These laws prohibit speech that is said to have a directly harmful effect on the minority group and that is thought to encourage unsociable behaviour towards that group. The laws are directed towards a social outcome which is to protect and emancipate minority groups from oppressor groups – which is *the* key purpose of Critical Theory.

VI CURRENT EFFECTS OF VILIFICATION LAWS IN AUSTRALIA

These facets of vilification laws which are related to postmodern Critical Theory are having a negative effect on the health of free speech in Australian society.

A recent case that demonstrates the suppressive effect of Australian vilification laws is that of *Clinch v Rep*.[54] Rep is a feminist and public commentator who has been vocal in her concern about the

---

[54] *Clinch v Rep (No2)* [2020] ACAT 68.

effect that trans-activism is having on the interests and safety of biological women.[55] Clinch is a biological man who identifies as a woman, who was previously a member of the Australian armed forces and then became politically active. This case concerned a previous history of proceedings between the parties where the respondent had made a public apology to the applicant on Facebook after a mediated settlement was reached.

After Rep had posted her apology on Facebook there were a large number of comments made, some of which were critical and pejorative of the applicant and the transgender community. Clinch alleged that these comments constituted unlawful vilification by Rep.

The ACT Civil and Administrative Tribunal found that once Rep became aware of the third-party comments on her Facebook and did not remove them that she was then responsible for the comments.[56] Due to the nature of the dispute, much of the feminist content in support of Rep and which were the subject of the complaint were treating Clinch as a man who was bullying women.[57]

Underneath the arguments and the discussion of the legal issues was a fundamental disagreement between the parties about what it means to be male and female. This is irrelevant to the reasoning the eventual decision in favour of Clinch because vilification laws do not seek truth, they are only concerned with whether animus against the protected class could be incited.

This case is particularly chilling to public debate about contentious issues of significant public interest because, despite the fact that the

---
[55] Ibid [18].
[56] Ibid [41].
[57] Ibid [45].

individuals involved were going about that debate in an unsavoury manner, Rep, an individual, was held accountable for the speech of others.

This ACT Tribunal decision placed a responsibility on every person who uses social media to police public speech on their own accounts for fear of retribution by the State. This creates a strong chilling effect for free and open expression in public forums where social media is one of the key forums in which people engage in political and religious debate today.

The Human Rights Law Alliance has had experience of the weaponisation of vilification laws through assisting Queensland mother Katrina Tait.

Katrina is a professional photographer and devout Catholic who opposed 'Drag Queen Story Time' taking place in Brisbane public libraries.[58] She posted on social media the following view:

> I can't believe I have just had to sign a petition to try stop drag queen story time happening at libraries in our country. I can't believe this actually happened in Brisbane last weekend. What happened to protecting children's innocence and letting them just be kids? Why the need to have adult entertainers reading them stories? Hardly good role models with many involved in drugs and prostitution etc. Feeling scared for our children's future. Please sign and help save their innocence.[59]

A NSW LGBTQ activist saw this post and personally contacted Katrina, threatening to sue her under NSW anti-vilification law.

---

[58] Human Rights Law Alliance, 'Katrina Tait – Threatened by Activists', *Our Cases* (Web Page, 10 February 2021)..

[59] Ibid.

The activist also sent her a purported media release that would have revealed her name, her business, her previous address and her mobile phone number.

Katrina was later notified by the NSW Anti-Discrimination Board that the activist had filed a complaint. With the assistance of the Human Rights Law Alliance, Katrina was able to effectively answer the notice and the activist dropped the complaint.

Katrina's post was a benign comment that was motivated by genuine motherly concern for her children and other people's children. Vilification laws do not respect this, nor do they respect whether any of Katrina's assertion's are true or not. These are questions that should be discussed in a public forum and should be determined by assessing the facts.

The use of vilification laws by activists like the one in this case creates a chilling effect and prosecutes the key purpose of postmodern Critical Theory.

The laws attack groups and views that are set up in opposition to the chosen "oppressed" class in order to re-shape society to "emancipate" the group that is set up as marginalised. In reality the laws are being used to marginalise and silence people like Katrina and Rep because they do not share socially popular views.

VII CONCLUSION

Australian vilification laws share a strong ideological and theoretical relationship with postmodern Critical Theory.

Core elements of postmodern Critical Theory, such as the subjectivity of knowledge, the influence and power of language and the controlling use of language as an expression of power all find correlating characteristics in the debates that supported the legislation of vilification laws and in the way in which the laws operate.

These laws have proven themselves to be tyrannical tools that pay no heed to truth and the importance of open public debate for a healthy and flourishing democratic society. In practice vilification laws are not addressing actual harms. They are directed towards the suppression of speech that could be subjectively interpreted as having the capacity to incite hatred towards a protected class.

These are laws that are not designed to impose sanctions for a demonstrable wrong, as is the case with the majority of punitive laws. Vilification laws are designed to supress speech. The increased use and expansion of vilification laws will only further erode free and open debate in Australia.

7

Being Awake to Woke

GABRIËL A MOENS AM*

ABSTRACT

This article discusses two interrelated expressions of 'wokeshevism,' namely the Black Lives Matter ('BLM') Movement, and Critical Race Theory ('CRT'). It is argued that BLM and CRT facilitate the establishment of a utopian society which is free of racial discrimination. It is a society that distributes or redistributes burdens and benefits regardless of the race of the recipients. During the last couple of years, the BLM Movement has given expression to demands to eradicate endemic racism. It has done this by promoting the destruction of monuments and statues that honour alleged racists. 'Wokeshevism' has also spawned an interest in CRT, a neo-Marxist doctrine that blames privileged white people for the disadvantages of African-Americans and similarly situated people. The author of the paper argues that BLM and CRC involve the reintroduction of 'race' as a defining characteristic to divide society into groups, membership of which is determined by the racial identity of their members.

I am delighted to contribute a short piece to *Wokeshevism: Critical Theories and the Tyrant Left*. I expect that the term 'wokeshevism' will likely be embedded in even conversational English in the future. If so,

---

* Emeritus Professor of Law, University of Queensland.

this book will make a lasting contribution to the English language.

Until a few years ago, most people would not have known of the existence and meaning of the word 'woke'. However, Benjamin Butterworth, a Senior Reporter, argues that 'Once upon a time, it simply meant the past participle of "wake"' and, 'While that has rapidly changed in recent years, the modern definition of the word isn't new in the US.' But during the last five years, since its listing as a new adjective in the *Oxford English Dictionary* in June 2017, 'woke' has come to mean to be awake to sensitive social issues, especially racism.[1]

In this article, I briefly discuss two expressions of 'wokeshevism', which are based on, or inspired by, Marxism, namely the Black Lives Matter ('BLM') Movement, and the Critical Race Theory ('CRT') controversy.

I THE BLACK LIVES MATTER MOVEMENT AND HISTORICAL TRUTH

The Black Lives Matter Movement came into existence in July 2013 following George Zimmerman's acquittal in the shooting death of Trayvon Martin, an African-American teenager in February 2012. Although the Movement was responsible for many street demonstrations in the United States, it gained international exposure predominantly in the aftermath of the killing of George Floyd on 25

---

[1] Benjamin Butterworth, 'What does 'woke' mean? Origins of term, and how the meaning has changed', *inews.co.uk* (Web Article, 26 June 2021) <https://inews.co.uk/news/uk/woke-what-mean-meaning-origins-term-definition-culture-387962>.

May 2020, in Minneapolis.

The BLM Movement is a political and social movement that campaigns against claimed police brutality and advocates criminal justice reforms. It aims at eradicating endemic racial discrimination allegedly suffered by African-Americans in the United States. The BLM Movement's leaders admitted to having been trained as Marxists.[2] Although many Americans and Australians agree with the anti-discrimination message, BLM cannot hide the fact that, in its operations and ideology, it divides society, relying on 'race' in the same way that 'class' was used in Marxist proletarian ideology.

The BLM Movement has supported efforts by left-wing protesters to destroy the monuments and statues of those who allegedly contributed to racial disadvantage, rewriting 'history' in the process. This aspect of the BLM phenomenon is focused on in this article.

Most people believe that the study of history involves an accurate and objective description and evaluation of events that happened in the past. However, the BLM Movement has changed this understanding of 'history'. As is well-known, the BLM Movement depicts the history of the United States as an egregious example of exploitation, discrimination, and racism. To eradicate the continuing consequences of this culture of endemic racism, the BLM Movement seeks to rewrite history by evaluating past events in the light of its progressive understanding of equal treatment. In this context, the proponents of the BLM Movement make incessant demands to remove monuments and statues of people who are deemed to have contributed to, or profited from, racism.

---

[2] Tom Kertscher, 'Is Black Lives Matter a Marxist Movement?', *Politifact* (Web Article, 21 July 2020).

For example, in the United States, monuments to the Confederacy have been vandalised or torn down,[3] including, notably, Confederate General Robert E Lee in Richmond, Virginia.[4] Also in Richmond, a statue of discoverer of the Americas Christopher Columbus was toppled, spray-painted, set on fire, and then thrown into a lake. In the field of entertainment, HBO removed *Gone with the Wind* from its streaming service because of its depiction of slavery in the American South prior to the Civil War. Later, HBO returned to streaming *Gone with the Wind*, but with a disclaimer about the film's portrayal of slavery shown prior to the film commencing.[5] *Gone with the Wind* is perhaps the most popular and best movie ever made, an icon of American cinema.

It appears that the BLM Movement has unstoppably infected many other liberal democracies too. For example, in the United Kingdom, officials in East London removed a statue of the 18th century merchant and slave owner Robert Milligan from its place in the city's docklands.[6] And protestors in Bristol knocked down a monument erected to honour the legacy of slave trader Edward Colston.[7] The Mayor of London, Sadiq Khan, announced that more statues of colonial figures could be removed from Britain's streets. He tweeted that, 'It's a sad truth that much of our wealth was derived from the slave trade – but

---

[3] Alan Taylor, 'The Statues Brought Down Since the George Floyd Protests Began', *The Atlantic* (Web Article, 2 July 2020).
[4] 'Robert E Lee statue: Virginia removes contentious memorial as crowds cheer', *BBC News* (Web Article, 9 September 2021).
[5] 'Gone with the Wind has returned to HBO unaltered. But viewers will hear about its racist stereotyping before they watch it', *ABC News* (Web Article, 25 June 2020).
[6] 'Robert Milligan: Slave trader statue removed from outside London museum', *BBC News* (Web Article, 9 June 2020).
[7] 'Edward Colston statue: Protestors tear down slave trader monument', *BBC News* (Web Article, 8 June 2020).

this does not have to be celebrated in our public spaces.'[8] There have been calls for Oxford University to remove a statue of Cecil Rhodes, a Victorian imperialist in southern Africa who made a fortune from mines and endowed Oxford University's Rhodes scholarships. Oxford University itself recommended the removal of the statue even though Rhodes is invariably connected with the history of this University. A "Rhodes Must Fall Group" has been actively agitating for the removal of Rhodes's statues.[9]

In Australia, the privately-run *Monument Australia* website currently lists 37,106 monuments (across all themes and periods).[10] A 2017 study found that of the 520 plus memorials, statues and monuments within the CBD Melbourne, the memorial landscape mostly represents colonial landscapes, civic leadership, and patriotic and heroic achievements. Monuments, recording the achievements of men greatly outnumber those recording the achievements of women.[11]

The Australian Heritage Council, in its report *Protection of Australia's Commemorative Places and Monuments* comments:

> Colonial monuments, particularly those commemorating early explorers and administrators, are a reflection of a point in time that was almost exclusively focussed on values of settlers. They represent what was believed and understood, and what the society and government aspired to. Monuments of the

---

[8] @SadiqKhan (Twitter, 10 June 2020, 6.26am).
[9] However, due to planning and financial impediments, Oriel College decided not to start the process of removing the Rhodes statue from the College: Michael Race, 'Cecil Rhodes statue will not be removed by Oxford College', *BBC News* (Web Article, 20 May 2021).
[10] Monument Australia, <https://monumentaustralia.org.au/>.
[11] Australian Heritage Council, *Protection of Australia's Commemorative Places and Monuments* (Report, March 2018) 1.

colonial era were often large scale, solid and imposing statues memorialising values of exploration, courage, community building and innovation.[12]

The commemorative places may include a sculptural or other artistic work such as a statue, gravestone, or rock art: a plaque, fountain, seat, or bench; an archaeological relic or ruin. Monuments range in size and variety of materials. They are located both in urban and national parks, squares, and other public spaces and on private land.[13] This rich history is now under threat from the BLM Movement and those who share similar sentiments. For example:

- Monuments to Queen Victoria, Captain James Cook, and Governor Lachlan Macquarie have been desecrated in Sydney;[14]

- There have been calls for removal of the statues of John Batman (founder of the settlement of Melbourne),[15] Angus McMillan (leading settler in Gippsland),[16] Sir Thomas Mitchell (explorer and Surveyor-General of NSW),[17] and Alfred Canning (surveyor of stock routes).[18]

---

[12] Ibid 3.
[13] Ibid vii.
[14] Sam McKeith and David Barden, '"No Pride in Genocide": Historic Statues Defaced In Sydney', *Huffpost* (Web Article, 25 August 2017).
[15] John Hinchliffe, 'Call to remove statue of John Batman, "founder of Melbourne", over role in indigenous killings', *The Age* (Web Article, 26 August 2017).
[16] Kellie Lazzaro, 'Angus McMillan monument removal considered by council over his links to indigenous murders', *ABC News* (Web Article, 16 June 2020) (The shire council that was the subject of this report, the Wellington Shire Council, rejected a motion to take down the monuments to Angus McMillan: Benjamin Preiss, 'Gippsland council rejects call to tear down monuments to notorious pastoralist', *The Age* (Web Article, 16 June 2020) .
[17] Paul Daley, 'Statues are not history. Here are six in Australia that need rethinking', *The Guardian* (Web Article, 25 August 2017).
[18] Ibid.

Motivated by the BLM Movement, activists have also demanded the removal of the statue of Captain James Cook from Sydney's Hyde Park.[19] This statue, erected in 1879 bears the inscription 'Discovered this territory 1770'. A report published in the *Newcastle Morning Herald and Miners' Advocate (NSW)* on 26 February 1879, reported that the unveiling of the statue was a festive societal event:

> The ceremony was witnessed by about 60,000 people. Two hundred children sang the National Anthem. His Excellency the Governor, Sir Hercules Robinson, unveiled the statue; and; in doing so, made a speech, in which he gave a narrative of Cook's life, and characterised him as a humane, just, and God-fearing man. He added that it would be well for the youth of Australia to imitate his nobility of character.

The current anti-history sentiment is also expressed in other ways. The iconic 'Coon' cheese has been renamed 'Cheer' cheese.[20] The Coon brand name was retired in July 2021 because it arguably had racist connotations.[21] Yet, 'Coon' was the name of Edward William Coon, who patented a new cheese-ripening method.

Destruction or desecration of monuments and statues is not limited to Western countries. One only needs to mention the destruction by the Taliban of the magnificent Buddhas of Bamiyan in Afghanistan. These had been carved into the side of a cliff, almost 2,000 years ago and were destroyed in March 2001 because they depicted faces. The government deemed such depiction to be incompatible with its

---

[19] Sarah Maddison, 'Why the statues must fall', *The Sydney Morning Herald* (Web Article, 12 June 2020).
[20] 'Coon Cheese changes name to Cheer Cheese, pledging to build "a culture of acceptance"', *ABC News* (Web Article, 13 January 2021).
[21] Ibid.

version of the Islamic religion. The Taliban's return to power in August 2021 again challenges those who would like to maintain historical monuments in Afghanistan. The Taliban's fanatical destruction of the Buddhas of Bamiyan is also a reminder of the pillage of the ancient site of Palmyra in war-torn Syria by Islamic State, and the Temple of Baalshamin dedicated to the ancient God Baal.

People are also reminded of the graphically challenging television pictures of Saddam Hussein's statue in Baghdad, being toppled by an enraged and liberated crowd. This statue was erected in April 2002 in Firdos Square in Baghdad; it was destroyed on 9 April 2003. People danced on the statue of the dictator and used sledgehammers to pulverise it to pieces.

Of course, some commentators welcome the destruction or desecration of monuments and statues. For example, in an opinion piece, Professor Sarah Maddison argued that statues must fall because these statues 'do not educate, they do not inform, they do not move us closer to justice.'[22] She further contended that 'What some may have considered enlightened more than 200 years ago can be reckoned with as atrocity today.'[23] But her argument fails to consider that actions, which are considered as enlightened in our time, may be regarded as examples of barbarity in 100 years from now. No generation has a monopoly on 'enlightenment' because it is a concept that constantly develops over time. Additionally, in removing or destroying statues, people effectively distort a country's history.

How is it possible to cancel the historical heritage and culture of a country? Culture evolves over time and is inextricably intertwined

---

[22] Maddison (n 19).
[23] Ibid.

with a country's history. Nevertheless, there have been many attempts throughout the ages to rewrite history and to purge unwanted stories from the history books. These examples are as plentiful as they are objectionable.

Today's history books are replete with inaccurate accounts of the past. Often, specific events are not reported in history books; such omission is as problematic as deliberately distorting a story which does not suit the rulers of the day. For example, no Chinese textbook recounts the Tiananmen Square massacre because it reflects badly on the current Communist ruling class. Similarly, while the BLM Movement may be well-intentioned, it is ultimately a misconceived attempt to edit history.

It is difficult to assess the removal or destruction of monuments and statues. To illustrate: Saddam Hussein was clearly a modern-day despot, who was undoubtedly responsible for many atrocities. But the toppling of his statue raises an interesting question: is it justifiable to destroy his statue, but not the statue of, say, Christopher Columbus, Robert E Lee or James Cook? Is it the case that, with the passage of time, statues gain a protective veneer which hides the alleged or real crimes committed by these historical figures? At what point in time does a statue become a historical relic and a part of the history and culture of a country? These are difficult questions to answer because historical figures often have a complex history, hence, an accurate historical assessment of their contribution to history is elusive.

Bruce Charles Scales has argued that the destruction of historical property could be prevented by the adoption of what is called 'dialogical memorialisation', 'where one view of the past takes issue with another and history is seen, not as some final statement, but a contingent and contested narrative.'²⁴ Typically, 'dialogical memorialisation' involves the enlargement of a controversial monument or statue with a plaque (or counter memorial) describing the historical context which resulted in the erection of the monument. An example of 'dialogical memorialisation' is offered by the Maitland Brown Memorial (Explorer's Monument in Fremantle). In 1994 a second plaque (a counter memorial) was added acknowledging the right of indigenous people to defend their traditional lands and solemnly commemorates 'all those Aboriginal people who died during the invasion of their country'.²⁵

The Heritage Council has argued that the Explorer's Monument now stands for reconciliation, rather than division:

> The addition of the new plaque didn't edit history but added to the story. It is a striking example of how a dialogue can occur in memorialisation where one view of the past takes issue with another and history is seen, not as some final statement, but a contingent and contested narrative. 'We're actually saying that this monument is not the final truth about this event, that we can revisit this event, this question, and approach it in different ways.' Expansion could see colonial monuments turned into points of reflection and tools for education, instead of attempts to 'tidy up the past' by their removal.²⁶

Another way of facilitating reconciliation involves the dualnaming of some significant Australian landmarks and places that recognise British and European explorers. These landmarks would be given

---

[24] Bruce Charles Scales, 'Monumental errors: how Australia can fix its racist colonial statues', *The Conversation* (Web Article, 28 August 2017).
[25] Ibid.
[26] Australian Heritage Council (n 11) 17.

European and indigenous names. For example, in 1993 Uluru became the first icon in Australia to be officially dualnamed as Ayers Rock/ Uluru, later changed to Uluru/Ayers Rock.

There is a need to return history to its rightful place in the development of a mature society. Societies should learn from history, not destroy it. In an American context, this means that students should be educated about the failures of America, including, of course, the history of racial discrimination and slavery, but should also be encouraged to celebrate its glorious achievements and contributions to the maintenance of the Free World.

II CRITICAL RACE THEORY AND THE RESHAPING OF SOCIETY

A second emanation of the 'woke' culture is the teaching of CRT. Even a perfunctory review of the education and political scenes reveals the encroaching capabilities of CRT. Critical Race Theory has been taught in universities since the 1990s, but it is only during the last couple of years that this theory has started to infect the entire education system, seducing progressive politicians, and threatening to devour the institutions and way of life of liberal democracies. Critical Race Theory appeals to progressive academics, policymakers, and trendsetters because it has the capacity to reshape society. A review of the CRT literature on the Internet reveals the existence of scores of articles which describe and promote this theory.

Critical Race Theory is essentially a Marxist theory with a new veneer, involving the substitution of 'race' for 'class'. Traditional Marxism envisaged a proletarian revolution, which would result in a victory for the exploited working class.[27] As this view of mankind has proven to be wrong, Marxists are now substituting 'race' for 'class', claiming that racial discrimination is endemic in society. Critical Race Theory embraces the assumption that white hegemony and privilege are undeserved, and that non-white people are experiencing systemic discrimination.

Christopher F Rufo notes that proponents of CRT use euphemisms to describe this theory. They use terms like 'diversity', 'inclusion', and 'equity' to promote its assumed salutary nature.[28] But these apparently non-threatening words cannot mask the real objectives of the Theory's proponents.

Rufo provides an example. In a recently published paper, he stated that, 'In the name of equity, UCLA Law Professor and critical race theorist Cheryl Harris has proposed suspending private property rights, seizing land and wealth and redistributing them along racial lines.'[29] He also indicates that other proponents of CRT in the United States have suggested the creation of a permanent federal Department of Antiracism, which would have 'the power to nullify, veto, or abolish any law at any level of government and curtail the speech of political leaders and others who are deemed insufficiently antiracist.'[30]

---

[27] This theory is reminiscent of Plato's belief, expressed in *The Republic*, that society knows three classes, the artisans, the auxiliaries, and the philosopher-kings, and that there was limited social mobility between these classes. Hence, people could not readily aspire to improve their status in life: Plato, *The Republic*, translated with an Introduction by Desmond Lee (Penguin Books, 2nd rev ed, 1955) 177-195.

[28] Christopher F Rufo, 'Critical Race Theory: What It Is and How to Fight It' (2021) 50(3) *Imprimis* 1, 2.

[29] Ibid 2-3.

[30] Ibid 3.

Another word that typifies the approach taken by the promoters of CRT is 'decolonisation'. An example can be found in a paper entitled 'The potential of critical race theory in decolonizing university curricula'[31] published in the *Asia Pacific Journal of Education* in 2011. The word 'decolonizing' refers to the need to purge university curricula of the supposedly turgid and revolting Western influences, on the assumption that 'Western' knowledge and values are inherently discriminatory. The paper unapologetically states that, 'CRT is transdisciplinary and can illuminate the hegemonic and appropriating capacities of 'Western' disciplines and critique the dissonance that currently exists between indigenous and 'Western' ways of knowing.'[32]

Academic freedom and freedom of speech, in general, should ideally be unlimited and, certainly, they should not be confined to an examination of societal problems and issues which are compatible with mainstream ideas. However, CRT as an academic approach seems to be in a different category because it ostensibly manipulates the concept of 'academic freedom' for the purpose of eliminating any scholarship that is incompatible with the theory. Hence, the question must be asked whether the notion of 'academic freedom' should encompass research that is intolerant of other views and seeks to reshape society that supports, and possibly funds, this research.

The use of the word 'decolonisation' in scholarly discourse is also troubling because it intertwines research and scholarship with activism and politics. Academic research would no longer concentrate on the objective and unbiased dissemination of knowledge and discussion of ideas.

---

[31] Julie McLaughlin & Susan Whatman, 'The potential of critical race theory in decolonizing university curricula' (2011) 31(4) *Asia Pacific Journal of Education* 365.

[32] Ibid 370-1.

Those who teach and promote CRT assume that its decolonising aims are justified to compensate for past discrimination, slavery, and disenfranchisement. While it is true that, in the past, mankind routinely violated the principle of equal treatment, served the interests of advantaged members of society, and promoted flawed theories of racial superiority, CRT cannot be regarded as compensation for past discrimination. Indeed, compensation should be limited to specific identifiable instances of discrimination. If not, disadvantages would be imposed on current members of society who themselves have not contributed to discrimination and may even have used their influence to promote harmonious relationships between different groups in society. Indeed, if it were argued that living people should be held liable for discriminatory acts committed by their ancestors, then the point in time at which discriminatory acts occurred becomes irrelevant: it would no longer be necessary to make a causal connection between the act of discrimination and the transgressor.[33]

It could be argued reasonably that the most important problem posed by CRT is that the promise of the irrelevance of race in the distribution of benefits and burdens would be reversed. In such case, society would embrace the idea that race is a dividing characteristic and entitles preferred races, but not all, to benefits which are not available to others. Surely, in an Australian context, this reinstitution of the relevance of 'race', with its concomitant capacity to stereotype people, constitutes a violation of the *Racial Discrimination Act* 1975 (Cth)? If a person's race were to be taken into consideration in the distribution of benefits and the imposition of burdens, it would result in instances of racial

---

[33] See Gabriël A Moens, 'Preferential Admission Programs in Professional Schools: *Defunis*, *Bakke*, and *Grutter*' (2002) 48(3) *Loyola Law Review* 411, 443-467; Gabriël Moens, *Affirmative Action: The New Discrimination* (Centre for Independent Studies, 1985) 75-92.

segregation, and abrogation of free speech. Perhaps, it might be possible for disadvantaged, allegedly privileged, people to then rely on the contentious s 18C of the *Racial Discrimination Act* 1975 to seek relief?

On 21 June 2021, the Australian Senate voted to keep CRT out of the national school curriculum 'after the new proposed curriculum gave priority to teaching the culture, perspectives, and history of indigenous Australians across all subjects, including maths.'[34] Not unexpectedly, those who voted against the motion accused the majority of embracing a "far-right hatred" agenda.

Critical Race Theory has the capacity to promote 'race hate' in society. The message thus is that CRT subverts the proper functioning of a cohesive society, and undermines the function of universities, which according to the wise words of Cardinal John Henry Newman should be 'the education of the intellect'.[35]

III CONCLUDING REMARKS

'Wokeshevism' is a useful addition to the English language; it is a word that covers the many attempts by 'woke' people to bring about a utopian society which is completely devoid of racial discrimination. It is a society where burdens and benefits are presumably distributed, or more likely 'redistributed', regardless of the race of the recipients. However, in doing so, it reintroduces 'race' as a defining characteristic to divide society into groups, membership of which is determined by

---

[34] Rebecca Zhu, 'Australian Senate Votes to Keep Critical Race Theory Out of Classrooms', *The Epoch Times* (Web Article, 22 June 22, 2021).

[35] John Henry Cardinal Newman, *The Idea of a University* (Image, 1959) 149.

the racial identity of their members.

'Wokeshevism' manifests itself in different ways, two of which are discussed in this article. During the last couple of years, the BLM Movement has given expression to demands to eradicate endemic racism. It has done this by incessantly promoting the destruction of allegedly offensive monuments and statues of alleged racists throughout the world. In the Academy, 'wokeshevism' has also spawned an interest in CRT, a neo-Marxist doctrine that blames privileged white people for the disadvantages of African-Americans and similarly situated people.

If the Western World wants to maintain its culture and traditions, which have demonstrably contributed to the eradication of racial disadvantage, it will be necessary to be awake to the woke.

8

Cultural Vandalism: Lust to Rule, Road to Ruin

STEVEN ALAN SAMSON*

ABSTRACT

The historical dynamism and resilience of Western civilization bespeaks both the Christian faith that laid its foundations and its ability to transform the families, institutions, and cultures of the world into which it grew. As faith wanes within its realm, cultural revolutionaries vie for control over the estate and the distribution of its assets. The prospect of recovery or renewal of the West depends on the character and courage of its heirs to repent and restore a depleted heritage.

Unity and uniformity have been blended in our minds ... Here one has to remember Procrustes, the legendary Greek robber and sadist who flung his victim onto a bed. Those who were too short were stretched and hammered until they filled it; those who were too long were 'cut to size.' Procrustes is the forerunner of modern tyranny. – Erik von Kuehnelt-Leddihn[1]

I FIRST CONSIDERATIONS: BEARING WITNESS

In 2007 the political philosopher Father James Schall published a

---

[1] Erik von Kuehnelt-Leddihn, *Leftism: From de Sade and Marx to Hitler and Marcuse* (Arlington House, 1974) 19, 20.

* Professor (ret), Helms School of Government, Liberty University.

close textual analysis of a lecture given by a former college professor. Like another lecture given three decades earlier, its aftershocks reverberated for weeks if not years.

On 12 September 2006, Pope Benedict XVI addressed the assembled faculty at Regensburg, a university which, like the civilization it represents, was originally 'called forth not by itself nor from the state, but from the heart of the Church.'[2] Described as an appeal 'for freedom of conscience in religious matters and a reasoned debate,' the Regensburg Lecture was intended, in part, to recall western civilization to the centrality of that faith which had launched Europe on its historical trajectory of converting tribes into nations, spreading legal and political reform, and releasing "the genie of limitless possibility" by implementing the creation mandate (Gen 1:28) through technological innovation, economic revolution, general literacy, the rise of modern science and medicine, hospitals, public libraries, institutional liberty and self-government.[3] As Christopher Dawson noted decades earlier:

> Christianity has always been a culturally creative force. It came first into a world which was overcivilized, where the social soil was becoming exhausted and the burden of empire and law was becoming too heavy for human nature to bear. And it transformed and renewed this civilization ... by revealing the existence of a new spiritual dimension and bringing the light of hope to those

---

[2] James V Schall, *The Regensburg Lecture* (St Augustine's Press, 2007) 79.
[3] Kenneth Minogue, *Politics: A Very Short Introduction* (Oxford University Press, 1995) 48. Niall Ferguson, Tom Holland, Charles Murray, Marcello Pera, and other religious skeptics regard Christianity is essential to the West. See Jonathon van Maren, 'Grave Men Facing a Grave Faith', *Convivium* (Web Article, 25 May 2021)

who sat in darkness and in the shadow of death.[4]

Foundational to this transformation, as Father Schall wrote elsewhere, is the Gospel's Great Commission (Matt 28:20-22): 'No doubt, the inner dynamism of Christianity was to "go forth and teach all nations:"'[5]

> David Goldman, in his book, *It's Not the End of the World: It's Just the End of You*, put it this way: 'Hilaire Belloc's famous quip – "Europe is the faith, and the faith is Europe" – is precisely correct.'
>
> Europe is where Old Testament, New Testament, Greek, and Roman traditions melded with the so-called barbarians coming off of the Eurasian continent. The fusion did not happen overnight, but it did happen. Europe's unity was hammered out in thought from the Fathers of the Church to Aquinas. The Reformation was not so much an argument against this thesis, but about its origins. Luther's problem with Aristotle was a harbinger of divisions to come.[6]

At the center of this sea change lay a spiritual understanding of both God and man. Contrary to modern notions, the Christian view, as Schall observed, is that man 'is intended to a supernatural end' and 'seeks what is properly the inner life of the Godhead as his final good.'[7]

---

[4] Christopher Dawson, 'Christian Culture as a Culture of Hope' in Gerald J Russello (ed), *Christianity and European Culture: Selections from the Work of Christopher Dawson* (Catholic University of America, 1998) 49-50.
[5] James V Schall, *Remembering Belloc* (St Augustine's Press, 2013) 155.
[6] Ibid 153 (citations omitted). This Germanic contribution was marginalised through the "grand narrative" of the Great Books curriculum – what M Stanton Evans called the 'liberal history lesson' – following the First World War. See David Gress, *From Plato to NATO: The Idea of the West and Its Opponents* (Free Press, 1998); M Stanton Evans, *The Theme Is Freedom* (Regnery, 1994).
[7] Schall (n 2) 91.

The Russian sociologist Pitirim Sorokin argued that 'Christianity raises man to the highest level of sanctification, and protects him unconditionally against any use as a mere means to an end.' Yet the material superfluity of Christendom's flowering in the High Middle Ages, Renaissance, and Reformation aroused hedonism as well as a utilitarian ethic that reflected an increasingly humanistic, Sensate culture.[8]

This faith stands in marked contrast to a relativistic skepticism which marginalises its practice and asserts the primacy of will (voluntarism): an attitude that 'nothing objective exists to distinguish one view from another except power or choice.'[9] Apart from clear provisions for justice, the operation of a sovereign will – whether by one, a few, many, or a state – is apt to degenerate into despotism.[10]

Different perspectives on liturgy – the character of worship – and the place of the classical heritage engendered rifts. Pope Benedict contends that, historically, 'Biblical faith, in the Hellenistic period, encountered the best of Greek thought at a deep level,' which resulted in a mutual enrichment that culminated in an 'inner rapprochement between Biblical faith and Greek philosophical inquiry' in Scholastic philosophy. This medieval synthesis was 'countered by a call for a dehellenisation of Christianity' that arose within the Reformation and developed through a series of three stages which, he argued, led to the positivist reduction of science to 'the interplay of mathematical and

---

[8] Pitirim A Sorokin, *The Crisis of Our Age: The Social and Cultural Outlook* (Dutton, 1941) 139.
[9] Schall (n 2) 91.
[10] See Jacques Maritain, *Man and the State* (University of Chicago Press, 1951) 44-46; see also: St Augustine, *City of God*, IV, 3-4.

empirical elements' and the exclusion of 'the question of God.'[11] Man himself is then reduced to 'the outcome of accidental collocations of atoms.'[12] As Karl Marx declared: 'All that is solid melts into air, all that is holy is profaned.'[13] Indeed, all the fixed stars of the old order are falling. As Pope Benedict concluded: 'In this way ... ethics and religion lose their power to create a community and become a completely personal matter.'[14] Social atomisation invites the imposition of controls over populations rendered at once detached yet dependent, restive yet submissive.[15]

James Kurth, a Presbyterian elder, takes a different tack: 'the central and fundamental issues involved the way that the Christian believer reached a state of salvation and the roles that the priestly hierarchy and the parish community played in the process.' The Reformers were persuaded that 'the believer can achieve a greater knowledge of God ... through reading of the Holy Scriptures.'[16]

Even so, Kurth agrees that a declension has occurred. A subsequent "Protestant Deformation" takes too far the rejection of hierarchy and community in other domains of life. Although free markets and liberal democracy are valuable byproducts of the Reformation, 'the free market could not be so free, nor the liberal democracy so liberal, that

---

[11] Schall (n 2) 142. For a discussion of positivism, see 'Politics of the Mind' in Paul Valéry, *The Collected Works of Paul Valery* (Pantheon Books, 1962) vol 10, 106.
[12] Bertrand Russell, *Mysticism and Logic: Including A Free Man's Worship* (George Allen & Unwin, 1976).
[13] Karl Marx, *The Communist Manifesto*, ch 1.
[14] Schall (n 2) 143.
[15] See, eg, Christopher Dart, 'The Sixties Scoop Explained', *CBC* (Web Article).
[16] Originally a lecture at the 2001 meeting of the Philadelphia Society. James Kurth, *The American Way of Empire: How America Won a World – But Lost Her Way* (Washington Books, 2019) 58, 59.

they became anarchy.'[17] Institutions must be ordered according to some principle, such as the written contract and the written constitution. The question that confronts us today is: How may we defend these institutions – and the liberty they protect – against the siren calls of rival claimants to authority? Against the deceptive inculcation of ideologies that – like Irving Janis's groupthink[18] – coerce conformity?[19]

The historical divisions which undercut Christian unity – represented in part by the medieval Battle of the Universals – reflect an unresolved epistemological and cosmological tension that is nested within the beating heart of the West.[20] This conflict of worldviews shades into rationalism and voluntarism at the extremes.

The challenge issued by the German Pope may be likened to that of the earlier Reformer, Martin Luther. Eugen Rosenstock-Huessy, a product of the same venerable academic tradition, detected the Christian university's roots in Biblical precedent:

> Luther, the man who offered comfort to his prince, was no isolated individual like Thomas Paine; he was the rightful spokesman of the City of God, the guardian of the opened and re-opened Bible, the trusted interpreter of Holy Scripture, one of the ordained seventy interpreters of the old Church, with the power of binding and loosing, but with the authority to open and close a public discussion in matters of national interest. The German professor was always careful to keep as part of his

---

[17] Ibid 62.
[18] Irving L Janis, *Victims of Groupthink: A Psychological Study of Foreign Policy Decisions and Fiascoes* (Houghton Mifflin, 1972).
[19] These practices may be described as "an establishment of religion" in contravention of the American Constitution. Steven Alan Samson, 'Binding Leviathan: The Case for Institutional Liberty' (2021) (Mar-Apr) *The Market for Ideas* 28.
[20] On realism vs nominalism, see Larry Siedentop, *Inventing the Individual: The Origins of Western Liberalism* (Belknap Press, 2014) ch 23.

title the addition, 'Public Professor,' in order to make clear his political sovereignty ... The salvation-character of scholarship, utterly foreign to the rest of the world, is the religious key to the political building erected by the Reformation.[21]

Perhaps the closest recent parallel to the Regensburg Lecture may be found in Alexander Solzhenitsyn's 1978 Harvard Address, in which the exiled Soviet dissident diagnosed the self-inflicted wounds of a West which had, in recent centuries, turned to materialism from 'the moral heritage of Christian centuries with their great reserves of mercy and sacrifice.' The consequences of this lapse have been suicidal: 'The two so-called world wars (they were by far not on a world scale, not yet) constituted the internal self-destruction of the small progressive West which has thus prepared its own end.'[22]

In the face of mortal danger Solzhenitsyn challenged his audience: 'How is it possible to lose to such an extent the will to defend oneself?' Citing Karl Marx's assertion that 'communism is naturalized humanism,' Solzhenitsyn said he saw 'the same stones in the foundations of an eroded humanism and of any type of socialism.' Even so, the materialism of the West was no match for that of the Communist bloc:

> The interrelationship is such, moreover, that the current of materialism which is farthest to the left, and is hence the most consistent, always proves to be stronger, more attractive, and victorious. Humanism which has lost its Christian heritage cannot prevail in this competition. Thus during the past centuries

---
[21] Eugen Rosenstock-Huessy, *Out of Revolution: Autobiography of Western Man* (William Morrow, 1938) 397-399.
[22] Aleksandr Solzhenitsyn, 'A World Split Apart' (Speech, Harvard University, 8 June 1978). See also: James Burnham, *Suicide of the West: An Essay on the Meaning and Destiny of Liberalism* (John Day, 1964).

and especially in recent decades, as the process became more acute, the alignment of forces was as follows: Liberalism was inevitably pushed aside by radicalism, radicalism had to surrender to socialism, and socialism could not stand up to communism. The Communist regime in the East could endure and grow due to the enthusiastic support from an enormous number of Western intellectuals who (feeling the kinship!) refused to see communism's crimes, and when they no longer could do so, they tried to justify these crimes. The problem persists: In our Eastern countries, communism has suffered a complete ideological defeat; it is zero and less than zero. And yet Western intellectuals still look at it with considerable interest and empathy, and this is precisely what makes it so immensely difficult for the West to withstand the East.[23]

Today's West is hard-pressed to make a full-throated defense of freedom. Michael Polanyi, Paul Valéry, José Ortega y Gasset, Gilbert Keith Chesterton, Nicholas Berdyaev, Gabiel Marcel, and many others made note of this same deficiency generations earlier and attributed it to a shallow philosophical positivism that reduced man and science to strictly natural processes. These critics understood that science is

---

[23] Ibid. 'Marxism owes its remarkable power to survive every criticism to the fact that it is not a truth-directed but power-directed system of thought.': Roger Scruton, *A Political Philosophy* (Continuum, 2006) 149. On Western intellectuals who sympathised with Communism, see Paul Hollander, *Political Pilgrims Travels of Western Intellectuals to the Soviet Union, China, and Cuba* (Harper Colophon, 1983).

an offshoot of the complex Christian civilization which gave it life.[24] Once plucked from its cultural roots, science diminishes into a mere technicism that is unable to sustain the whole civilized enterprise. Scientists themselves are increasingly products of the prevailing positivism. When Ortega wrote *The Revolt of the Masses* in 1930 he described the type of man coming to predominate as 'a barbarian appearing on the stage through the trap-door, a "vertical invader."'[25] Ortega was concerned with the rise of a new primitivism, not simply C P Snow's later idea of a rift between two cultures: science and the humanities. Like Polanyi and Valéry, he believed that modern men were becoming divorced from the civilization that nurtured them.

A civilized person should be equipped, like Robinson Crusoe, to rebuild civilization. It is not simply a matter of having the right answers but knowing the right questions to ask. We struggle with a widening gap between what Erik von Kuehnelt-Leddihn called *scita* and *scienda*. *Scita* is the body of knowledge generally available to the people and their representatives. *Scienda*, however, is the knowledge necessary to make sound decisions. With the reliance – even dependency – of credulous leaders on narrow expertise, 'a new and outright humiliating fideism is being bred in the very shadow of rationality and scientism.' Formulaic thinking enjoys an advantage in the scrum of intellectual

---

[24] Marcel attributed reductionism to a 'depreciatory resentment' against the integrity of the real world. Gabriel Marcel, *Man Against Mass Society* (Gateway, 1962) 156. G K Chesterton, with typical irony, spoke up for the idea of 'science for science's sake.' Pure science is flexible; it can correct its mistakes and weaknesses. But when applied to society it is made concrete. A single moment from an ongoing process of scientific development is then preserved and turned into a social reality. G K Chesterton, 'The Inefficiency of Science' (1929) (November) *North American Review* 587, 588-589; see also Norbert Wiener, *The Human Use of Human Beings: Cybernetics and Society* (Avon, 1967).

[25] José Ortega y Gasset, *The Revolt of the Masses* (W W Norton, 1932) 87.

one-upmanship and in the interest of preserving power.

> The way to avoid a development which spells catastrophe for our freedom lies in the creation of sacrosanct domains beyond the grasp of power-hungry centralist forces, areas where the individual or limited groups can act freely, because there scita and scienda are still correlated – in the family, the small enterprise, the village, the borough, the county.[26]

The attraction that communism held in Solzhenitsyn's day – the demonstration effect of a powerful myth – is also true of present-day social justice movements. Absent from any consideration, however, is the Christian imagination that originally envisioned the West's civilizational enterprise and the powerful thrust which still carries it forward.[27]

II NEHEMIAH'S JOB: ENTRPRENEURIAL REBUILDING[28]

The economic historian David Landes described 'the Church as custodian of knowledge and school for technicians' and attributed western inventiveness – eyeglasses, mechanical clocks, printing presses – to four factors: the Judeo-Christian respect for manual labor, its subordination of nature to man, its sense of linear time, and the market of free enterprise. 'Success bred imitation and emulation.'[29]

---

[26] Erik von Kuehnelt-Leddihn, 'Scita Et Scienda: The Dwarfing of Modern Man' (1974) 3(10) *Imprimis* 1.

[27] See Vishal Mangalwadi, *The Book That Made Your World: How the Bible Created the Soul of Western* Civilization (Thomas Nelson, 2011). Christendom is the West's unacknowledged bedrock.

[28] The core of this section was published in Romania at *Profit*, 7 June 2021. The title is a hat tip to Albert Jay Nock's essay, 'Isaiah's Job'.

[29] David S Landes, *The Wealth and Poverty of Nations: Why Some Are So Rich and Some So Poor* (W W Norton, 1998) 58-59.

There resulted a great release of energy which enhanced human flourishing and brought about social changes of the sort Rosenstock-Huessy noted: the peace of the land, the free choice of a profession, philanthropy, freedom of the mind.[30] The traditional "hieratic monopoly" of Latin – a source of power to clergy and rulers alike – was broken once the Bible was translated into the vernacular languages.[31] Both literacy and liberty became widespread regardless of class and gender, placing government by consent within reach, along with challenges to traditional sources of authority. Recordkeeping flourished, as did popular literature, much of it explicitly Christian. Westerners became 'passionately curious about other peoples and societies.' Social mobility increased both vertically and laterally. As Landes exclaimed enthusiastically: '*Literate mothers matter.*'[32]

Rosenstock-Huessy similarly described the missionary calling of the West as it radiated outward from the nucleus of a loose-knit Frankish/Saxon empire through a series of clerical, then increasingly secular, revolutions – German, English, French, and Russian – that traversed the continent, then the world. It is a civilization originally fashioned out of the European wilderness and the ruins of imperial Rome.[33]

In 'The European Miracle,' the economic historian Ralph Raico draws upon the work of Peter Bauer, David Landes, Norman Cantor, Helmut Schoeck, and Harold J Berman to discern the reasons for the West's

---

[30] Rosenstock-Huessy (n 21) 30-32.
[31] A now-secularised intellectual class or clerisy has persisted. Although its roots are in the Church and monasteries, it betrays political ambitions. A century ago Julien Benda regretted the loss of a universal language: 'All humanity including the "clerks," have become laymen. All Europe, including Erasmus, has followed Luther.': Julien Benda, *The Treason of the Intellectuals (La Trahison des Clercs)*, tr Richard Aldington (W W Norton, 1969).
[32] Landes (n 29) 32, 52, 178. Italics in the original.
[33] Rosenstock-Huessy (n 21) 496.

success, noting especially its model of civil society and its relative absence of institutionalised envy:[34]

> The key to western development is to be found in the fact that, while Europe constituted a single civilization – Latin Christendom – it was at the same time radically decentralized. In contrast to other cultures – especially China, India, and the Islamic world – Europe comprised a system of divided and, hence, competing powers and jurisdictions.[35]

The West's great wellspring was a visionary and voluntary Christian missionary enterprise that began by reclaiming arable land, salvaging the remnants of its spiritual and secular antecedents, and crafting new inventions and institutions as practical embodiments of faith, hope, and charity. As Rosenstock-Huessy concluded in *Out of Revolution*, 'the unique experiment of the Western World consists in regenerating a former world.'

> No nation, no cities, yet an emperor, was the paradoxical situation a thousand years ago ... The unique experiment of the Western World consists in rebuilding a former world ... It was European civilization as a whole which was called upon to represent the idea of the ancient city-state! The civilized nations are sectors of *one* city. The concept of a universal civilization opposing a multitude of local economic units was the emperor's gift to the European tribes.[36]

---

[34] One form is redistribution of wealth; another is rent-seeking: a pay-to-play scheme that, like toll castles, enriches the gatekeeper. See Jonathan R T Hughes, *The Governmental Habit Redux* (Princeton University Press, 1991) 1-12.

[35] Ralph Raico, 'The Theory of Economic Development and the European Miracle' in Peter J Boettke (ed), *The Collapse of Development Planning* (New York University Press, 1994). See Niall Ferguson on the 'open access pattern' that arose among the elites in medieval England and Western Europe: Niall Ferguson, *The Great Degeneration: How Institutions Decay and Economies Die* (Penguin, 2013) 24-25.

[36] Rosenstock-Huessy (n 22) 488-89.

The kings of early Christendom were bound by oath to uphold the inherited body of laws that held their kingdoms together.[37] Medieval Europe was decentralised, yet a common legal order spread through most of it.[38] The condominium of church and state divided sovereignty and decentralised it with respect to territories as well as functions.[39] Civil liberty and self-government requires checks and balances to protect private initiative and free enterprise because 'every political power tends to reduce everything that is external to it, and powerful objective obstacles are needed to prevent it from succeeding.'[40] The rule of law within regimes of divided, delegated, and responsible power is an essential underpinning of Adam Smith's invisible hand and Friedrich Hayek's idea of spontaneous order.

Today's shrinking world bound by mass communication networks provokes and amplifies demands for simple authoritarian solutions to life's injustices and inconveniences. Yet we should consider: Why has a relative absence of external oversight historically prevailed where the Christian ethic of moral self-government is widely practiced? Does political, economic, and moral self-discipline require elaborate central command structures or a population force-fitted into ideological straitjackets – perhaps a Procrustean bed – that turn citizens into subjects?[41] To the contrary: Politics, the art of persuasion, flourishes best in the absence of despotism, the technology of coercion. Rather than dictate outcomes in advance, governments that respect free

---

[37] Minogue (n 3) 26-27.
[38] See Ruben Alvarado, *A Common Law: Western Civilization and the Law of Nations* (WordBridge, 1999).
[39] Joseph Lecler, *The Two Sovereignties: A Study of the Relationship Between Church and State* (Burns Oates & Washbourne, 1952) 10.
[40] Raico (n 35).
[41] See Steven Alan Samson, 'Ideological Straitjackets Turn Citizens into Subjects', *Townhall Finance* (Web Article, 28 October 2020).

inquiry, liberty of expression, and entrepreneurship have enabled innovation to flourish. As a result, the face of the world has changed within the span of an ordinary lifetime.

The West's current neglect of its moral – even more than its physical – infrastructure weakens the resilience required for nations, families, and individuals to recover from life's calamities.[42] An intrusive regulatory state that fosters dependency provokes public exasperation. Here we find parallels with the French Revolution.[43] In *Heart of Darkness*, Joseph Conrad characterised civilization as a thin veneer.[44] It is a common resource which must be renewed and defended every generation.

How each rising generation is educated is truly a matter of national security, but this does not make education the unique and specific responsibility of the state. Paradoxically, the state must depend upon virtues it is not well-equipped to instill. As the Christian political philosopher J Budziszewski puts it: 'Through *subsidiarity*, the government honors virtue and protects its teachers, but without trying to take their place.'[45] A healthy civil society nurtures a variety of institutions, including the voluntary associations described by Alexis de Tocqueville in *Democracy in America*.[46]

---

[42] Aaron Wildavsky balances anticipation (prepared and alert) and resilience (sufficient resources held in reserve). Aaron Wildavsky, 'If Regulation Is Right, Is It Also Safe?' in Tibor R Machan and M Bruce Johnson (eds), *Rights and Regulation: Ethical, Political, and Economic Issues* (Pacific Institute for Public Policy Research, 1983) xv-xvii.
[43] Thomas Molnar, *The Counter-Revolution* (Funk & Wagnalls, 1969) 6-8.
[44] Joseph Conrad, *Heart of Darkness* (Warbler Classics, 2020).
[45] J Budziszewski, *The Revenge of Conscience: Politics and the Fall of Man* (Spence, 1999) 70.
[46] Alexis de Tocqueville, *Democracy in America*, tr, ed Harvey C Mansfield and Delba Winthrop (University of Chicago Press, 2000) 489-492.

When Francis Lieber delivered his inaugural lecture at Columbia in 1859, he summarised the role of Christianity in the change from ancient to modern times:

> How else can we explain these patent facts, that modern states with liberty have a far longer existence – where is the England of antiquity counting a thousand years from her Alfred, and still free? – that liberty and wealth in modern nations have advanced together, which the ancients considered axiomatically impossible; that modern liberty may not only advance with advancing civilization and culture, but requires them; that, occasionally at least, modern states pass through periods of lawlessness without succumbing ... that the moderns have found the means of combining national vigor with the protection of individual rights; and that by international law a 'system of states,' as Europe has been called, can exist whose members are entire sovereign nations? Much of all this is owing to the spread and development of Christianity.[47]

The West – enriched by a high view of fallen human nature[48] – is now being actively and openly challenged by its progeny in favor of what Roger Scruton called a 'culture of repudiation' that mimics the fervor of the Christian faith but attacks its credibility.[49] Wayne Allen concluded:

> The twentieth century has rightly been called the 'Age of Ideology,' and it might well be the last stage of modernity in its struggle with postmodern nihilism, which will kill man's

---

[47] Francis Lieber, *Miscellaneous Writings: Reminiscences, Addresses, and Essays* (J B Lippincott, 1880) vol I, 382-83.
[48] Psalm 8:4-6; 1 Cor 6:3. Immanuel Kant referred to 'the crooked timber of humanity' out of which 'no straight thing was ever made.'
[49] 2 Tim 3:5. See: Roger Scruton, *The West and the Rest: Globalization and the Terrorist Threat* (ISI Books, 2002) 68-83.

reverence for reason entirely. Every event, each person, all actions require reconstruction in terms of the ideology if it is to maintain its status as a science (of Nature or History).[50]

One of the great ironies of the modern mindset is its subsistence on the memory and accumulated moral capital of a Christian civilization which, in its youth, built locally financed cathedrals to the glory of God.[51] Today that capital is in short supply and the old verities are nearly forgotten.[52] The past half-century's much-lamented fiscal crisis of the state, however, is not due so much to insolvency as by overextending the state beyond its competence, depleting rather than replenishing the stock from which it draws. The result – as with earlier civilizations[53] – is profligate borrowing against future diminishing returns and throwing off all constitutional restraints, impoverishing services, and intensifying compulsion. The problem is not strictly financial. It is philosophical, theological, and – as a practical consequence – demographic.[54] Even so, the culture of the West is still aided by powerful binding forces, such as belief and trust, which belong to the fiduciary life of a Western world originally shaped by the fine arts and philosophy of Greece, the architecture and law of Rome, and then bound together by the faith, morality, and prophetic

---

[50] Wayne Allen, 'The Rock of Ages,' manuscript copy of a book review of Ronald J Rychlak, *Hitler, the War and the Pope* (Our Sunday Visitor, 2000) published as 'Pius XII and the Culture Wars' (2001) (October) *Culture Wars* 42-44.
[51] See Francis A Schaeffer, *Death in the City* (Inter-Varsity Press, 1969).
[52] See Runyard Kipling, 'Gods of the Copybook Headings'..
[53] Dawson (n 4) 49-50.
[54] On the demographic decline, see Steven Alan Samson, 'The Grapes of Parnassos' (Presentation, Liberty University, 16 April 2007).

traditions of Judaism and Christianity.[55]

Near the end of a book published in 1908, *The Servile State*, Hilaire Belloc wrote: 'There is a complex knot of forces underlying any nation once Christian; a smoldering of the old fires.'[56] The default culture of the West is still recognisably – if sentimentally – Christian. The historian Willis Glover sees a 'historical continuity of modern humanism with the Christian faith' and adds: 'It would be hard to name a time when people were so consciously concerned with the problem of meaning.'[57] As the West loses the religious bond that generated its culture, careful attention should be given to reclaiming and rebuilding this moral and spiritual infrastructure.

In ancient Judea Nehemiah's job as governor was to rebuild the ancient walls of Jerusalem. Today it is the job of imaginative leaders to stand in the gap against a festering cynicism provoked by breaches of public trust and to restore the enterprising vision which inspires citizens to move mountains.

---

[55] Culture crystallises out of an original *cultus*. 'Religion' derives from *re-ligare*, to bind. Man is, Alfred Korzybski observed, a time-binder. Nicholas Berdyaev understood the weakness of Christianity's cultural byproducts when plucked from their roots. Marx and Nietzsche signified 'the end and destruction of humanism; both aroused forces which it was far from the creative mind to set in motion.' Nicholas Berdyaev, *The Fate of Man in the Modern World* (University of Michigan Press, 1935) 31; see also Marcello Pera, *Why We Should Call Ourselves Christians: The Religious Roots of Free Societies* (Encounter Books, 2011).
[56] Hilaire Belloc, *The Servile State* (Liberty Classics, 1977) 198.
[57] Willis B Glover, *Biblical Origins of Modern Secular Culture: An Essay in the Interpretation of Western History* (Mercer University Press, 1984) 15.

III MORAL INVERSION

The arc of the West's deflection from its original impetus may be discerned in Rosenstock-Huessy's observation that, although the Church was universal and the economy parochial a thousand years earlier, the balance in the ledger had so shifted from the spiritual to the mundane that, by his day, the economy was universal and the Church increasingly parochial, even marginalised, despite fervent outbursts of popular religious expression. The Church planted networks of monasteries, built great universities and cathedrals, but lost some of its missionary zeal along the way. A secularising West then divided science from faith and devolved into Vanity Fair.

The prolonged shattering of Christendom from the Reformation to the Thirty Years War – followed by Enlightenment skepticism, the French Revolution, and the Great Wars of recent memory – plunged the West into a congeries of moral crises that threaten to dissolve the religious and cultural bonds that once animated it.[58] The philosopher Michael Polanyi has described the moral inversion that resulted:

> I do not think that the discredit which the ideal of exact scientific knowledge had cast on the grounds of moral convictions would by itself have much damaged these convictions. The self-destructive tendencies of the modern mind arose only when the influence of scientific skepticism was combined with a fervor that swept modern man in the opposite direction. Only when a new passion for moral progress was fused with modern scientific skepticism did the typical state of the modern mind emerge.[59]

---

[58] Michael Polanyi, *Personal Knowledge: Towards a Post-Critical Philosophy* (Harper, 1964) 231-235.
[59] Michael Polanyi, *The Tacit Dimension* (Anchor, 1967) 57.

Michael Oakeshott agreed with Polanyi's analysis and characterised the elevation of technical over practical knowledge as 'rationalism in politics.' Technical knowledge is 'susceptible of precise formulation.'

> The Rationalist holds that the only element of *knowledge* involved in any human activity is technical knowledge. ... The sovereignty of 'reason,' for the Rationalist, means the sovereignty of technique. The heart of the matter is the preoccupation of the Rationalist with certainty.[60]

Practical knowledge, by contrast, exists only in use. The two types differ in how they are transmitted. Technical knowledge can be both taught and learned in the simplest sense. 'On the other hand, practical knowledge' – whether the artistry of a pianist, the style of a chess-player, or the judgment of a scientist – 'can neither be taught nor learned, but only imparted and acquired' through guidance and practice.[61]

Oakeshott attributed the uprooting of practical social and moral conventions to the intellectual arrogance of Rationalists – positivists, behaviorists, reductionists – who have 'no sense of the cumulation of experience, only of the readiness of experience when it has been converted into a formula: the past is significant for him only as an encumbrance.' Oakeshott referred to this as 'idolatry.'[62] Joseph Ratzinger (later Pope Benedict XVI) called it a 'mutilation of reason.'[63] What passes for 'a higher morality is merely morality reduced to a technique, to be acquired by training in an ideology rather than an

---

[60] Michael Oakeshott, *Rationalism in Politics and Other Essays* (Liberty Fund, 1991) 15-16.
[61] Ibid 15.
[62] Ibid 6.
[63] Joseph Ratzinger, *Christianity and the Crisis of Culture* (Ignatius Press, 2005) 43.

education in behavior.'[64] Much of the Rationalist's 'political activity consists in bringing the social, political, legal, and institutional inheritance of his society before the tribunal of his intellect.'[65] The Enlightenment's 'republic of letters' set the precedent.[66]

Oakeshott's colleague, Kenneth Minogue, regarded Marxism as a brilliant 'vulgarization of long-standing religious/philosophical themes.'[67] It is a template for the newer ideologies that promise liberation from oppression. All such ideologies borrow their power and persuasion from a resemblance, however vague and distorted, to the Gospel message of deliverance from sin and death. All substitute the strong arm of man for 'the power of God for salvation to everyone who believes' (Rom 1:16). This makes Marxism perhaps the perfect solvent for undermining the moral and practical foundations of a self-governing civil society. Minogue offers a three-part recipe for concocting a new ideology: first, a revelation that 'the past is a history of the oppression of some abstract class of person;' second, 'the duty of the present is thus to mobilize the oppressed class in the *struggle* against the oppressive system;' and, third, 'the aim of this struggle is to attain a fully just society, a process generally called liberation.'[68]

So effective is this formula that it has captured the imagination and devotion of elite opinion leaders and much of the German-modeled

---

[64] Oakeshott (n 60) 6, 40.
[65] Ibid. 8. Jacques Ellul concluded that the ambitious intellectual 'can no longer be anything but materialist.' Jacques Ellul, *The Presence of the Kingdom* (Seabury, 1967) 111.
[66] Molnar (n 43) 6-8.
[67] Scruton (n 23) 149.
[68] Minogue (n 3) 103. Italics in original. See also Kenneth Minogue, *Alien Powers: The Pure Theory of Ideology* (St Martin's Press, 1985).

administrative apparatus established by early Progressive reformers.[69] This new republic of letters – a politically-influential clerisy – displays a missionary zeal to correct historical injustices and imbalances while remaining self-interestedly secure in the perquisites and privileges of power and social status. Universities and media channel Herbert Marcuse's "repressive tolerance" as they determinedly purge views, values, and speakers that run contrary to the new orthodoxies. 'When social justice meets political correctness, the old liberal idea that relations between individuals are a purely personal matter is overridden. There is a right thing to do, and the state will make sure it is done.'[70]

The cutting edge of this cultural revolution today takes many forms and assumes many identities, among which are cancel culture, intersectionality, and wokeness.[71] Cancel culture is a non-judicial form of ostracism for which a 'liberating tolerance ... would mean intolerance against movements from the Right, and toleration of movements from the Left.'[72] Intersectionality is the convergence of multiple group identities embodying different shadings of privilege or oppression. Wokeness refers to a state of awareness of the pervasive reach of an oppressive system.

---

[69] Thomas C Leonard, *Illiberal Reformers: Race, Eugenics & American Economics in the Progressive Era* (Princeton University Press, 2016) ix-xiv, 10-16, 187-191.
[70] Kenneth Minogue, *The Servile Mind: How Democracy Erodes the Moral Life* (Encounter, 2010).
[71] Just as politics is downstream from culture, according to Andrew Breitbart, the cultural revolution spawns its own "radical chic," groupies, and "groupthink." See Tom Wolfe, *Radical Chic & Mau-Mauing the Flak Catchers* (Bantam, 1971). Compassion for victims, however, has Biblical roots.
[72] Robert Paul Wolff, Barrington Moore Jr and Herbert Marcuse, *A Critique of Pure Tolerance* (Beacon, 1969) 109.

IV A LONG MARCH INTO THE INSTITUTIONS

The appearance of speech codes, language police, and other sectarian expressions of identity politics on campus, in the media, at public facilities, and on the streets represents the leading edge of a decades-long subversion of the defensive and reproductive systems of western civilization.[73] An earlier phase of this 'long march through the institutions' was inspired by the strategic vision of the early Italian Communist leader, Antonio Gramsci.

> Power, in Gramsci's observation, is exercised by privileged groups or classes in two ways: through domination, force, or coercion; and through something called 'hegemony,' which means the ideological supremacy of a system of values that supports the class or group interests of the predominant classes or groups ...[74]

Gramsci believed that it is necessary first to delegitimise the dominant belief systems of the predominant groups and to create a 'counter-hegemony' (ie, a new system of values for subordinate groups) before the marginalised can be empowered.[75]

Here we come to an irony. The hegemony Gramsci wished to vanquish a century ago is shifting leftward, raising a paradoxical question: What happens when the system itself is run by people who adhere to a

---

[73] Erik von Kuehnelt-Leddihn developed the concepts of identitarianism and uniformitarianism – two expressions of a mass society – in *Liberty or Equality* (Caxton Printers, 1952) and *Leftism: From de Sade and Marx to Hitler and Marcuse* (Arlington House Publishers, 1974).

[74] John Fonte, 'Why There Is a Culture War' [2000] (December) *Policy Review*. See Steven Alan Samson, 'A Strategy of Subversion' (2020) (Mar-Apr) *The Market for Ideas* 22.

[75] Ibid. See also Dante Germino, *Antonio Gramsci: Architect of a New Politics* (Louisiana State University Press, 1990) 30.

woke ideology or counter-hegemony? Fifty years ago campus radicals warned against being "co-opted" by the system. Today, they have co-opted much of that same system, making the West vulnerable to an internal takeover through Ortega's vertical trapdoor. As Tom Flanagan describes it:

> Wokeism is clearly on the march and in some areas appears ascendant, having permeated nearly all levels and institutions of society – including where it might be least expected, like the US military. Among Western elites it has become nearly impossible not to practise or at least profess wokeness. When seen as shorthand for Progressive identity politics, woke influence on politics, policy, culture, society, and the economy has already been enormous and, from the standpoint of conservatives, libertarians, and constitutionalists, deeply disturbing.[76]

An earlier parallel to today's ideological fervor may be found in the lead up to the War Between the States. Francis Lieber assessed that era's "rationalism in politics" as a bid to rule or ruin:

> Too frequently does tyranny creep in as popular despotism. A process, perhaps, still more remarkable, and yet frequently exhibited in history, is that by which despotism steals into power by opposition to power. It is a very common mistake of the unwary to consider opposition to power as an indication of love of liberty.[77]

The Polanyi scholar Mark Mitchell examines an ideological intersection – and moral inversion – of a Nietzschean will-to-power

---

[76] Tom Flanagan, 'Progressive Identity Politics: The New Gnosticism' *C2C Journal* (Web Article, 9 July 2021).
[77] Francis Lieber, *Manual of Political Ethics Designed Chiefly for the Use of Colleges and Students at Law* (Charles C Little and James Brown, 1838) pt I, 390.

with a secularised moral perfectionism:

> Once a society has had a deep and sustained encounter with Christianity, it is not easy to remove the Christian residue even if the dogmas of the faith are rejected. Dogmatism outlasts dogma. The idea of heavenly perfection is far more seductive for a post-Christian people than for a people that has always been pagan.[78]

The political agenda behind this 'culture of repudiation' merits public scrutiny rather than a curt dismissal. Subversive ideologies espoused by activists and echoed by intellectual elites exhibit all the characteristics of authoritarian religious cults.

> Russian bolshevism, replacing eastern Christendom by the grim religiosity of Marx, produced a caricature ... [It] forces us brutally into a parody of the monastic life amidst fellow monks and fellow nuns who hate their habit and sigh under the ferocious tyranny of their pseudo-abbot. This evil distortion of an otherwise Christian ideal is more satanic than wanton, a thoroughly pagan and diabolic opposition to Christian existence.[79]

Karl Marx's political apocalypse is a faith – a power religion – that fuses Hegelianism and Socialism.[80] This helps account for its resemblance to the ancient heresy of Gnosticism. Like Gnosticism, Marxism's doctrinal compendium is an image of Christianity: not so much a mirror as a mirage. For example, its version of original sin or the Fall of Man is not rebellion against God but the institution of private property. Salvation is a re-creation of the communist idyll but

---

[78] Mark T Mitchell, *Power and Purity: The Unholy Marriage That Spawned America's Social Justice Warriors* (Regnery Gateway, 2020) 40.

[79] Francis Start Campbell, *The Menace of the Herd or Procrustes at Large* (Bruce, 1943) 283. See Nicholas Berdyaev, *The Origins of Russian Communism* (University of Michigan Press, 1960) ch 7.

[80] Scruton (n 23) 149.

no longer in its aboriginal form.

Nearly a century ago Hans Jonas and Eric Voegelin began probing ancient Gnosticism for insights into modern philosophies and mass movements. The implications of a Gnostic perfectionism should be evident in the following passage:

> For the Gnostics, man's alienation from the world is to be deepened and brought to a head, for the extrication of the individual self which can only thus gain itself. The world (not the alienation from it) must be overcome; and a world degraded to a power system can only become overcome through power. The power of the world is overcome, on the one hand, by the power of the Savior who breaks into its closed system from without, and, on the other hand, through the power of the 'knowledge' brought by him ...[81]

This reads like a revolutionary manifesto: push the dialectic to a crisis point, then defeat the oppressors through a messianic movement. Drawing on both Jonas and Voegelin, Tom Flanagan finds in "Progressive identity politics" a common purpose that ties recent "woke" movements with the older Progressivism: destruction of the political order.[82]

VII COUNTER-HEGEMONY IN PORTLAND

In America today, social justice movements such as Antifa and Black Lives Matter ('BLM') provide many of the shock troops in the culture war that has raged for years. According to an account by the journalist Christopher Rufo:

---

[81] Hans Jonas, *The Phenomenon of Life: Toward a Philosophical Biology* (Delta, 1968) 221.
[82] Flanagan (n 76).

After George Floyd's death, Portland's radicals attacked police officers and laid siege to federal buildings. They armed themselves with rocks, bottles, shields, knives, guns, bricks, lasers, boards, explosives, gasoline, barricades, spike strips, brass knuckles, and Molotov cocktails. A year later, many downtown businesses remain closed, and insurance companies have either raised premiums or refused to issue policies because of the ongoing risk of property destruction.[83]

The rioters were granted a "free pass" from local authorities as well as the governor. This raises a rather non-academic question: If Arnold Toynbee's 'challenge and response' theory of civilization has any merit, how would he evaluate the health and status of a civilization that responds merely by shrugging off the question?

During the prolonged COVID-19 lockdowns, the ability of organisers to lead riots in open defiance of the law had a chilling effect on the citizenry by suspending ordinary life – leaving people in a state of frustrated helplessness or generalised fear.[84] As Angelo Codevilla observed of the politicisation of the pandemic:

> Like all infections, it is deadly to those weakened severely by other causes. It did not transform American life by killing people, but by the fears about it that our oligarchy packaged and purveyed. *Fortuna*, as Machiavelli reminds us, is inherently submissive to whoever bends her to his wishes. The fears and the strictures they enabled were not about health – if only because those who purveyed and imposed them did not apply them to

---

[83] Christopher F Rufo, 'The Child Soldiers of Portland', *City Journal* (Web Article, Spring 2021). See also Jamie Goldberg, 'Insurers Balk At Covering Portland Businesses', *OregonLive* (Web Article, 12 December 2021)

[84] Ibid. See Steven Alan Samson, 'Interposition: Magistrates as Shields Against Tyranny' [2020] 11 *Western Australian Jurist* 301, 38.

themselves. They were about power over others.[85]

Much of the responsibility for months of mayhem in full public view rests with public authorities and the powerful interests that defer to, defend, and even deploy these latter-day Red Guards.[86] It is difficult to penetrate the fog that surrounds events because organisations such as Antifa and BLM operate within a shadowy legal netherworld.[87] The following observations come from another journalist, Andy Ngo, whose reports from Portland Oregon have inspired repeated death threats against him:

> One of the most effective ways we've seen law enforcement agencies brought to their knees is through frivolous lawsuits bankrolled by endless donors. 'Lawfare' refers to the act of abusing the legal system to achieve goals.
>
> There exist large networks of attorneys and legal groups who bring endless lawsuits in an attempt to defund, cripple, and embarrass police.
>
> Politicians in the city are terrified of political and media for holding antifa and far-left protestors accountable. The local and national media are staunchly on the side of antifa, regardless of their violence against police and property.[88]

Ngo identifies specific donors, such as the National Lawyers Guild, which has ties to the American Communist Party. Tax-exempt

---

[85] Angelo Codevilla, 'Clarity in Trump's Wake', *American Greatness* (Web Article, 19 January 2021).
[86] On woke politics in Portland, Oregon, see Andy Ngo, *Unmasked: Inside Antifa's Plan to Destroy Democracy* (Center Street, 2021).
[87] See Stephen R Soukup, *The Dictatorship of Woke Capital: How Political Correctness Captured Big Business* (Encounter, 2021) 165; Tyler O'Neil, 'Report Shows Online Ties Linking HuffPost, the Guardian, and SPLC to Antifa', *PJ Media* (Web Article, 21 May 2019).
[88] Ngo (n 86) 59, 60-61.

247

foundations are another likely, if indirect, source of financial support.[89] Christopher Rufo focuses attention on local public schools and, by implication, parts of America's massive curriculum industry that together strive to convert schoolchildren into social justice warriors. Consider the following vignettes. Personal names are omitted.

> Portland Public Schools has institutionalized the philosophy of social justice and codified political activism into every aspect of the bureaucracy. In the district's 2019 *Racial Equity and Social Justice Plan*, the administration pledged to make 'antiracism' the district's 'North Star' and to create 'an education system that intentionally disrupts – and builds leaders to disrupt – systems of oppression.' The superintendent hired a new equity czar and announced a 'Five-Year Racial Equity Plan,' which promises a dizzying array of acronyms and academic catchphrases like 'intersectionality' and 'targeted universalism.'
>
> It's hard to overstate how entrenched the political ideology now is in the school system. A veteran elementary school teacher who described herself as a longtime liberal told me that the district's 'antiracist journey' began with good intentions a decade ago. But over time, the leadership has hardened 'antiracist' principles into dogma. Today, she and other teachers must submit to mandatory antiracism training each week.
>
> [A lead teacher] hosted an exercise resembling Orwell's Two Minutes Hate, in which minority teachers were allowed 90 seconds to berate their white colleagues. During the exercise, [she] denounced one of her white female colleagues by screaming, 'You make me feel unsafe, you make me feel unsafe' repeatedly for 90 seconds. Afterward, [she] boasted on Facebook that she had publicly humiliated a racist, despite providing no evidence of racism or misconduct. It was a pure display of racial dominance.

---

[89] See William H McIlhany II, *The Tax-Exempt Foundations* (Arlington House, 1980).

[High school] students take two semesters of critical race theory – studying white fragility, intersectionality, 'whiteness as property,' 'the permanence of racism,' 'collective organizing,' and 'being an activist,' with an eye toward training them to 'do [their] part in dismantling white supremacy.'

The next step is obvious. Children, endowed with conviction in their own moral purity, head to the front lines.[90]

VI DIVIDE AND RULE TACTICS

The toxic political environment within all levels of the American system is a continuation of what Aaron Wildavsky called 'the revolt against the masses.'[91] Contrary to Americans' historical expectation of domestic politics, the freewheeling use of subversion, disinformation, and other tools of statecraft by both public officials and private interests is designed – as it is on the international stage – to burnish the reputation of leaders, promote factional ambitions, subdue the electorate, and weaken rival bases of power.[92] Kenneth Minogue saw the same pattern at work in the hazardous court politics of Renaissance Europe:

---

[90] Rufo (n 83). Making children – whose consciences are not fully developed – complicit in such public acts of disrespect and scapegoating should strike sensible parents and citizens as a form of child abuse. See René Girard, *I See Satan Fall Like Lightning*, tr James G Williams (Orbis Books, 2001) 7-18 on scandal (Matt 18:6).

[91] Aaron Wildavsky, *The Revolt Against the Masses: And Other Essays on Politics and Public Policy* (Transaction, 2003) 29-51; see also Angelo Codevilla, 'What Is Trump to Us?', *American Greatness*.

[92] On such disinformation tactics of *glasnost* and "framing," see Ion Mihai Pacepa and Ronald J Rychlak, *Disinformation: Former Spy Chief Reveals Secret Strategies for Undermining Freedom, Attacking Religion, and Promoting Terrorism* (WND Books, 2013) 13, 44-48. On their use in statecraft, internationally and domestically, see Angelo M Codevilla, *A Student's Guide to International Relations* (ISI Books, 2010) 64-67.

Rule was a moral relationship. Kings engaged in the activity called 'policy' (which involved ruthlessness and dissembling) in relation to outside magnates, but in principle, at least, they had no need for 'policy' towards their peoples. With emerging modernity, however, it became necessary to practice 'policy' in managing their own turbulent subjects.[93]

Cultural revolutions are totalitarian in nature – discrediting or purging anyone who resists the new orthodoxy. Otto Scott's 1974 insight into France's Woke Enlightenment could be written today:

> The old regime did have one overriding problem that was unique, even unprecedented. French intellectuals, middle and upper classes had grown ashamed of their country, history, and institutions ... The men of the Enlightenment rummaged through the trashbins and graves of the past to rediscover every crime and atrocity and placed all the blame at the doorsteps of Christianity and hereditary privilege ... [They] raked and clawed mostly their own ancestors, the men who had helped clear and civilize Europe, as though the entire population was descended from criminals.[94]

The French Revolution was the seminal event of modern times. How we view the utopian, even messianic, enthusiasm of philosophes, aristocrats, and revolutionaries who favored destroying the old order – root and branch – is apt to colour our attitudes toward their latter-day counterparts.[95] The Revolution's savagery, devastation, and continuing grip on the Western imagination defies description. Coiled within its vital center was a Pandora's box filled with the incipient forms of all the ideologies, identities, and iniquities that now strut

---

[93] Minogue (n 3) 38.
[94] Otto Scott, *Robespierre: The Voice of Virtue* (Mason & Lipscomb, 1974) 6-7.
[95] See Molnar (n 43) 3-41.

across the stage.⁹⁶ Twentieth century total war had its most crucial precedent in the eighteenth.

Nevertheless, the outcry for justice grows out of real grievances which have too long been allowed to fester. 'Europe is not aging gracefully,' asserts Pascal Bruckner. 'Brooding over past crimes (slavery, imperialism, fascism, communism), Europe sees its history as a series of murders and depredations that culminated in two global conflicts.'⁹⁷ In *American Awakening*, Joshua Mitchell notes that citizens of both Europe and America are similarly:

> [H]aunted by the historical wounds their nations have authored – in America, the wound of slavery; and in Europe, the wounds of colonialism. At the moment when America and Europe lost their cultivated ignorance" of these historical wounds and the need to "make all things new" was highlighting, to what healing power could the transgressors appeal? More than half a century after the echo of slavery screamed out for attention in America and the wound of colonialism in Europe became fully visible, the answer given by identity politics is that *no healing power whatsoever* is available to them.⁹⁸

---

⁹⁶ See Steven Alan Samson, 'The Crisis of Our Age: A Retrospective Glance' (2020) (Nov-Dec) *The Market for Ideas* 26.
⁹⁷ Pascal Bruckner, 'Europe's Guilty Conscience', *City Journal* (Web Article, Summer 2010).
⁹⁸ Joshua Mitchell, *American Awakening: Identity Politics and Other Afflictions of Our Time* (Encounter, 2020) 44. A timely reminder is in order. Aeschylus's account of the taming of the Furies (*Erinyes*) into the *Eumenides* is one of the landmarks of the ancient Greek literature.

VII GREASING THE SKIDS[99]

The atavistic travesty of blaming present generations for complicity in the sins of their ancestors, class, race, or other scapegoat is an assault on the Biblical ethic of forgiveness. This politicisation of history is deliberately libelous, manipulative, and subversive. It demands open-ended confessions of complicity with crimes against humanity and endless apologies. And for what purpose – other than expressing hatred and asserting unbridled moral authority? Roger Scruton attributed such scapegoating to envy: 'In the worldview of the resentful success is not a proof of virtue but, on the contrary, a call to retribution. That explains why totalitarian ideologies invariably divide human beings into innocent and guilty groups.'[100]

Cultural revolutionaries thrive on a disregard for constitutional restraints. Frederic Bastiat's concept of legal plunder – the ability of some to use the collective force of government 'to exploit the person, liberty, and property of others'[101] – enables us to understand how businessmen as well as public officials may be extorted into accepting one-sided political bargains as the price for doing business. Non-negotiable demands are designed to disrupt ordinary politics,

---

[99] An expression from the Pacific Northwest logging industry referring to the practice of lubricating log "skids" with oil or dairy products "so that the logs would slide easily" along and down the skid road. *Oregonian* (Portland), January 3, 1890.
[100] Scruton (n 23) 151-152.
[101] Frédéric Bastiat, *The Law* (Foundation for Economic Education). See Steven Alan Samson, 'Government Regulation: From Independence to Dependency: Part One' [2013] 4 *The Western Australian Jurist* 117.

keep opponents off-balance, and elicit appeals for appeasement.[102] John Calvin recognised the moral hazard that arises when people are induced to act contrary to their conscience. It is an assault on their integrity. The imposition of such laws, taxes, and executive orders with impunity is designed to overwhelm, humiliate, or neutralise any opposition.[103] Calvin's point is illustrated by the complicity of the city fathers – 'bearing false witness' – in Queen Jezebel's unscrupulous intrigues to acquire Naboth's Vineyard (1 Kings 21). As David Chilton put it: 'Guilt produces *passivity*, and makes a man *programmed for defeat.*'[104]

To a considerable degree our lives are shaped by the manipulation of such basic motivators as guilt, pity, desire, fear, lust, jealousy, addiction, resentment, hatred, envy, and rage. The sociologist Frank Furedi cites Alvin Gouldner's claim that schools and universities provide an 'institutional basis for the *mass* production of the New Class ... The expansion of education works towards the insulation of parental cultural influence from their children.'[105]

> One of the ways in which children become culturally distanced from the values of their parents is through their 'linguistic conversion' to a form of speech that reflects the values of the

---

[102] The legalisation of abortion through lawfare and judicial activism served as a stalking horse for a wide-ranging social change agenda, implemented anonymously through the subsidization of family planning, sex education, sex change surgery, and countless other cutting-edge cultural change operations. Not only does this fit Bastiat's description of legal plunder, it also embodies the moralistic and interventionist side of Woodrow Wilson's liberal internationalism. See Steven Alan Samson, 'An Imperium of Rights: Consequences of Our Cultural Revolution' [2016] 7 *The Western Australian Jurist* 171.

[103] This arrogant style of politics is epitomised by the Rabshakeh's boasts and Sennacherib's threats in 2 Kings 18-19. See, eg, Matthew Lee, 'Biden rescinds abortion restrictions on US foreign aid', A P *News* (Web Article, 29 January 2021).

[104] David Chilton, *Productive Christians in an Age of Guilt-Manipulators* (Institute for Christian Economics, 1981). Italics in original.

[105] Frank Furedi, *First World War: No End in Sight* (Bloomsbury, 2014) 211.

new class. What Gouldner characterized as the 'culture of critical speech' of the new classes 'de-authorizes all speech grounded in traditional social authority, which authorizes itself ... as the standard of *all* 'serious' speech ... Gouldner's analysis anticipates the institutionalization of speech codes and the policing of language in the decades to follow. It also provides important insights into the vitriol that often surrounds disputes about words, the conservative reaction to what is described as political correctness and the counter-calls for the censoring of 'offensive' speech.[106]

These "campus missionaries" and opinion leaders exude intellectual disdain towards the middle and working classes,[107] yet they profess a self-contradictory 'synthesis of the anti-instrumental romantic revolt against rationalism as well as the affirmation of professional and expert authority.'[108] The aging counterculture that Theodore Roszak celebrated in the late 1960s is now a touchstone for the ruling ambitions – what Augustine called the *libido dominandi* – of the high tech, media, professional, and educational sectors that shape today's fashions and ideas.

We should ask: *cui bono*? The skids of this transformation were greased generations ago by cultural revolutionaries who renewed a long-running insurgency against Christian institutions. As H G Wells remarked of his novel, *Anticipations*: 'The book was designed to undermine ... monogamy, faith in God & respectability, all under the

---

[106] Ibid 212.
[107] John McDermott, 'Campus Missionaries: The Lying on of Culture', *Nation*, 10 March 1969; see Salena Zito and Brad Todd, *The Great Revolt; Inside the Populist Coalition Reshaping American Politics* (Crown Forum, 2018).
[108] Furedi (n 105). Propagandists do not "believe" their ideologies; they are simply instruments for mobilising people and enhancing the power of a party or state. Jacques Ellul, *Propaganda: The Formation of Men's Attitudes* (Vintage, 1965) 196-97.

guise of speculation about motor cars and electrical heating.'[109] Wells was far from alone in this ambition. By that time, politics was already degenerating into vast redistribution schemes through which wealth and power floated ever higher beyond the reach of ordinary citizens. The subsequent ruination of the working and middle classes should be a matter of grave concern rather than dismissive disdain by gentrified liberals.[110]

VIII INVERTEBRATE WEST: A SOFT TARGET

Widespread property ownership, free enterprise, general literacy, and popular suffrage are among the boons of western civilization that give individuals and families a place to stand and the footing to launch bold ventures, live their lives freely, and govern themselves. Yet the early Progressives rejected individualism and made a moralistic distinction between property rights and human rights. More than any single issue, the right to property may be the primary target of the cultural revolution.[111]

Progressive or reform liberalism has long been the ideological default setting for America's politicised intellectual class, a modern secular clerisy that helps craft public opinion and presides over the administrative state. Given the sheer diversity of the country, Woodrow Wilson 'welcomed administrative governance. The people could still

---

[109] Fred Siegel, *The Revolt Against the Masses: How Liberalism Has Undermined the Middle Class* (Encounter, 2013) 5.
[110] See Steven Alan Samson, 'Revolt of the Disdained: America's 2016 Presidential Election' [2018] 9 *The Western Australian Jurist* 33; and 'Revolt of the Disdained: Sovereignty or Servitude', *Townhall Finance* (Web Article, 27 January 2020).
[111] From the beginning of the American colonies, the state has played a role in land tenure, but the Fifth Amendment takings clause has been stretched way beyond its original purpose. See Charles Murray, *By the People: Rebuilding Liberty Without Permission* (Crown Forum, 2015) 44-48.

have their republic, but much legislative power would be shifted out of an elected body and into the hands of the right sort of people.'[112]

The machinery of the modern state enables political moralists, as Minogue called them, to reconstruct society, economy, or culture in ways that increase their influence. Edmund Burke recognised its forebears in revolutionary France:

> To them, the will, the wish, the want, the liberty, the toil, the blood of individuals is as nothing. Individuality is left out of their scheme of Government. The state is all in all. Every thing is referred to the production of force; afterwards every thing is trusted to the use of it. It is military in it's principle, in it's maxims, in it's spirit, and in all it's movements. The state has dominion and conquest for it's sole objects; dominion over minds by proselytism, over bodies by arms.[113]

The old Progressive Ascendancy, like its liberal counterpart today, disingenuously proclaimed liberty while seeking to hamstring independent institutions and close off all refuges from its ministrations. People molded by generations of often-contradictory social reform schemes – from temperance and public education to eugenics and beyond – deserve more respect. In 1913, the Rev Frederick T Gates, the head of the Rockefeller-financed General Education Board, condescendingly spoke of his 'dream' to improve residents' lives in impoverished Appalachia while keeping them in humble circumstances: 'the people yield themselves with perfect docility ... while we work our

---

[112] Philip Hamburger, *The Administrative Threat* (Encounter Books, 2007) 55. Wilson once told a British envoy: 'I am going to teach the South American republics to elect good men.' Walter A McDougall, *Promised Land, Crusader State* (Houghton Mifflin, 1997) 131.

[113] Edmund Burke, *Select Works of Edmund Burke* (Liberty Fund, 1999) vol 3, 182. For a recent illustration, see Olivier Bault, 'Polish Academic Sentenced in Germany for His Work on Homosexuality in the Church', *Visegrad Post* (Web Article, 5 August 2021).

own good will upon a grateful and responsive rural folk.'[114]

The sociologist Edward A Ross, who wrote *Social Control*, believed that society should shape and regulate the individual,[115] a task that required a new mandarin class. By 1939, the civil service was repurposed into the vanguard of a new social science-shaped administrative state.[116] Under the *Executive Reorganization Act* that year, an 'administrative presidency' was conceived as an ally of 'programmatic liberalism,'[117] which today manages policy and operations over a society of clients and dependents.[118] Any contrary political agenda earns such furious resistance that character assassination by anonymous trolls and public ambushes by colleagues are considered fair play.

Once administration is detached from ownership and effective oversight, or – as with Garrett Hardin's 'tragedy of the commons'[119] – the use of public property is detached from accountability, we suspend the rationale for the constitutional philosophy of limited government

---

[114] Frederick T Gates, *The Country School of Tomorrow* (Occasional Papers No 1, General Education Board, 1913) 6. For a substantial excerpt, see Steven Alan Samson, 'Crossed Swords: Entanglements Between Church and State in America' (University of Oregon dissertation, 1984) ch 11, n 68; Steven Alan Samson, 'Penetrating the Fog of Culture War' (2021) (Jul-Aug) *The Market for Ideas* 30. It recalls the Fabian banner: 'Remould it nearer to the heart's desire.' Lyndon Johnson later expressed his desire more crudely. See Kevin D Williamson, *The Dependency Agenda* (Encounter Books, 2012) 1.

[115] Leonard (n 69) 23; see also Thomas Sowell, *Intellectuals and Race* (Basic, 2013); Murray N Rothbard, *The Progressive Era*, ed Patrick Newman (Mises Institute, 2017).

[116] Sidney M Milkis, *The President and the Parties: The Transformation of the American Party System Since the New Deal* (Oxford University Press, 1993) 146.

[117] Ibid.

[118] See Murray (n 111) 63-78, 176-83 on 'An Extralegal State Within a State' and 'The Bankrupt Premises of the Regulatory State.'

[119] G. Hardin, 'The Tragedy of the Commons' (1968) 162 (3859) *Science* 1243.

animated by consent of the governed.[120] A panoply of sophisticated and often deceptive means of action is readily severed from the moral and constitutional ends meant to guide them. As Freud recognised, the ambiguity of our motives, including suppressed aggression and the absence of clear lines of responsibility, generates an ambivalence which can inspire a stressful, often dissociative or objectless, sense of uncertainty and even guilt.[121] A guilty conscience may be triggered and manipulated by others, as shown by P T Bauer in 'Western Guilt and Third World Poverty'[122] as well as René Girard's studies of mimetic desire, envy, rivalry, and scapegoating.[123]

These observations accord with Hans Selye's definition of stress as 'the non-specific response of the body to any demand for change.' The intensification of the pace of change has both a physically debilitating and demoralising effect.[124] When deliberately orchestrated, it serves some lower purpose, such as softening defenses or breaking down resistance. Marshall McLuhan tallied the consequences: 'Mental breakdown of varying degrees is the very common result of uprooting and inundation with new information and endless new patterns of information.'[125]

Victims of disaster, dislocation, combat, bereavement, and other traumas bear witness to the toll such intense stressors exact on body

---

[120] See James Burnham, *The Managerial Revolution* (Indiana University Press, 1960) 71-76.
[121] Sigmund Freud, *Civilization and Its Discontents*, tr James Strachey (Norton, 1961) 78-80.
[122] P T Bauer, *Equality, the Third World and Economic Delusion* (Harvard University Press, 1981) 66-85.
[123] Girard maintains that humanism, humanitarianism, and the concern for victims 'develop first on Christian soil.' Girard (n 90) 163. Rather, the whole Biblical tradition deplores the treacherous murders of Abel, Dinah's suitor, Naboth, and countless others.
[124] Hans Selye, *The Stress of Life* (McGraw-Hill, 1970).
[125] Marshall McLuhan, *Understanding Media: The Extensions of Man* (Signet, 1964) 31.

and soul alike. Viktor Frankl, a concentration camp survivor, based his 'logotherapy' on confronting the brutality of that experience and the subsequent bitterness and disillusionment which follow.[126] Similarly, the philosopher Karl Jaspers assessed the levels and layers associated with the guilt – political, moral, metaphysical, in some cases criminal – of having been the citizen of a nation-state ruled by a criminal regime.[127] Complicity in crime demoralises entire countries. An inability to resist a criminal regime often emasculates potential opposition leaders.[128] This is why acts of interposition by leaders – often in tragic defiance of political loyalties[129] – offer the prospect of a fresh start once enjoyed by the Dutch provinces and the American colonies.[130]

We live in a global village, touched by events in distant places. Our imaginative landscape has been radically reshaped within living memory. As Neil Postman put it: 'Introduce speed-of-light transmission of images and you make a cultural revolution ... Here is ideology without words, and all the more powerful for their absence.'[131] The media dominate the collective sensorium through sheer bandwidth. Postmodernists condemn conventional culture as a prison house. Satirists dismiss its mores with mockery and condescension. Deconstructionists pioneered effective strategies of

---

[126] Viktor E Frankl, *Man's Search for Meaning: An Introduction to Logotherapy* (Washington Square Press, 1963).
[127] Karl Jaspers, *The Question of German Guilt*, tr E B Ashton (Capricorn, 1961).
[128] Continued influence of the convergence theory – a gradual merger of the West and the Soviet bloc – is evident in stolen Soviet documents. See Pavel Stroilov, *Behind the Desert Storm* (Price World, 2011); Vladimir Bukovsky, *Judgment in Moscow: Soviet Crimes and Western Complicity* (Ninth of November Press, 2019), especially ch 6.
[129] René Girard, *Violence and the Sacred*, tr Patrick Gregory (Johns Hopkins, 1977) 290-97.
[130] Steven Alan Samson, 'Interposition: Magistrates as Shields Against Tyranny' [2020] 11 *Western Australian Jurist* 301.
[131] Neil Postman, *Amusing Ourselves to Death: Public Discourse in the Age of Show Business* (Penguin, 1985) 158.

cultural subversion by discrediting traditional mores.¹³² A television script writer may play up popular expectations and then, as in a sting operation, give them a novel twist. Postmodern literary tropes tend to be "subversive" and "transgressive."¹³³ Sometimes excused as "playful," they may have the serious effect of undermining language and meaning.¹³⁴ The public abuse of language presages the abuse of power.¹³⁵

The underlying purpose of such pretexts is to suspend people's sense of reality. This is especially evident when "talking heads" on television may describe an event with same catchphrases, *verbatim*. Public discussion is degenerating into verbal guerrilla warfare.¹³⁶ The resulting polarisation resembles an inverted bell curve. It is intended to exclude any middle ground.

A century ago, the publicist Edward Bernays skillfully marketed liberal and leftwing ideas while echoing the depth psychology of his uncle, Sigmund Freud.¹³⁷ In 1928, he wrote: 'The American motion picture

---

[132] Here are three illustrations: Michel Foucault: 'All my analyses are against the idea of universal necessities.' Richard Rorty: 'My sort of philosopher wants to get rid of the idea that the world or the self has an intrinsic nature.' Frank Lentricchia's objective: 'spot, confront, and work against the political; horrors of one's time.' See Stephen R C Hicks, *Explaining Postmodernism: Skepticism and Socialism from Rousseau to Foucault* (Connor Court, 2019) 2, 3.

[133] Philip Rieff calls it 'the romance of creative sacrilege' and attributes it to Friedrich Nietzsche. 'But there is another movement in modernity: that nothing is transgressive and no price need be paid. I have called this movement therapeutic.' Philip Rieff, *The Crisis of the Officer Class: The Decline of the Tragic Sensibility*, ed Alan Woolfolk (University of Virginia Press, 2007) 3-4.

[134] See, eg, Zachariah Montgomery, *Poison Drops in the Federal Senate. The School Question from a Parental and Non-Partisan Stand-Point* (Gibson Bros, 1886) 38-42 on the redefinition of words.

[135] Joseph Pieper, *Abuse of Language, Abuse of Power*, tr Lothar Kraus (Ignatius, 1992).

[136] See, eg, A D Robles, *Social Justice Pharisees: Woke Church Tactics and How to Refute Them* (Morgan James, 2021).

[137] See Edward Bernays, *Propaganda* (IG Publishing, 2005), which is a simplified, public relations version of Walter Lippmann's 'the manufacture of consent.'

is the greatest unconscious carrier of propaganda in the world today. It is a great distributor for ideas and opinions. The motion picture can standardize the ideas and habits of a nation.' This suggests America's *lingua franca* may be found in a media-generated popular culture that takes shape at the intersection of commerce, entertainment, education, and ideology.

Ion Mihai Pacepa, who rose to the top of the Communist Romanian security apparatus, defected in 1978 and later exposed the 'science of *disinformation*' which, historically, drew on earlier Czarist practices. In *Disinformation*, he cited observations by the French Marquis de Custine, who sized up the Russian Court: 'Russian despotism not only counts ideas and sentiments for nothing but remakes facts; it wages war on evidence and triumphs in the battle.'[138] Perhaps that made it a premodern version of postmodernism. As Stephen R C Hicks puts it: 'Deconstruction, Stanley Fish confesses happily, "relieves me of the obligation to be right ... and demands only that I be interesting".'[139] Cultural revolution requires rhetorical smoke screens.

Given the reductionism that converts every consideration into a material relationship, it is no wonder that disillusioned ideologues may only be left with their cynicism. The Communist playwright, Bertolt Brecht, complained of a so-called worker's paradise turning on the very people in whose name it operated:

> After the uprising of the 17th June
> The Secretary of the Writers Union
> Had leaflets distributed in the Stalinallee
> Stating that the people

---

[138] Pacepa and Rychlak (n 92) 37.
[139] Hicks (n 132) 2. Note Arte Johnson's meme – "very interesting" – on the 1960s television show, *Rowan & Martin's Laugh-In*.

> Had forfeited the confidence of the government
> And could win it back only
> By redoubled efforts. Would it not be easier
> In that case for the government
> To dissolve the people
> And elect another?[140]

Electing another people – turning citizens into subjects – is a plausible way of describing the endgame of all forms of this project. As the influence of Christianity over it diminishes, liberalism as a governing philosophy divorces itself from the sources of its attraction and becomes more unrealistic in its aims – increasingly compelled to extend its sway and remold people by coercive means.

As the scope of government continues to grow, so does the size of its appetite. In 1995 Kenneth Minogue asked: 'Can Politics Survive?'

> Political moralism … takes the independence of citizens not as a guarantee of freedom but as a barrier to the project of moralizing the world. Independent individuals disposing of their own property as they please are identified with selfishness and taken to be the cause of poverty. A socially just world is thought to require a rational distribution of the goods which pour so abundantly forth in a modern society. But states whose constitutional authority is limited to ruling by law are imperfect instruments for the immense task of rational distribution, and of the resulting necessity of rectifying the attitudes on which injustice is founded. The entity called 'the state' could, however, become adequate to this formidable task if it were to change its character …
>
> Moralizing the human condition is only possible if we can make the world correspond to some conception of social justice.

---

[140] Bertolt Brecht's "The Solution," written with reference to protests in 1953 but left unpublished. <https://www.poemhunter.com/poem/the-solution/>.

But it turns out that we can only transcend the inequalities of the past if we institute precisely the form of social order – a despotism – which Western civilization has immemorially found incompatible with its free and independent customs. The promise is justice, the price is freedom.[141]

IX PROGRESSIVISM: THE MARXISM OF THE RENT-SEEKING CLASS[142]

As the voice of America's political class, Progressives now justify advancing fluid, often contradictory, interests which enhance the power and privileges of their most well-connected clientele while effectively marginalising and even jettisoning many of the principles articulated during their salad days. Members of its intellectual wing have 'a very large, vested interest in certain beliefs, which underlie various programs from which they benefit enormously.' As Thomas Sowell points out in *Preferential Policies*, 'this is common around the world, that the elites benefit from preferential programs.'[143] Christopher Lasch's assessment of their appetite is equally harsh:

> Control has become their obsession. In their drive to insulate themselves against risk and contingency – against the unpredictable hazards that afflict human life – the thinking classes have seceded not just from the common world around them but

---

[141] Minogue (n 3) 112-113.
[142] The title was suggested by the characterisation of John C Calhoun as "The Marx of the Master Class." Richard Hofstadter, *The American Political Tradition: And the Men Who Made It* (Vintage, 1974) 86-117.
[143] Jason L Riley, *Maverick: A Biography of Thomas Sowell* (Basic, 2021) 225. See Thomas Sowell, *Preferential Policies: An International Perspective* (William Morrow, 1990) 103-115.

from reality itself.[144]

The culture wars that have convulsed America since the sixties are best understood as a form of class warfare, in which an enlightened elite (as it thinks of itself) seeks not so much to impose its values on he majority (a majority perceived as incorrigibly racist, sexist, provincial, and xenophobic), much less to persuade the majority by means of rational political debate, as to create parallel or "alternative" institutions in which it will no longer be necessary to confront the unenlightened at all.[145]

The opportunistic quality of progressive liberalism's appeal is striking. Its meliorative redistribution programs degenerate into a scramble for power, benefits, and status through elaborate political turnstile operations. This process of nest-feathering or feeding at the public trough is called "rent-seeking" by economists. Bastiat simply called it legal plunder and remarked on its tendency to become universal.[146]

It is easy to breach the West's intellectual defenses and sack its citadels when its credentialed trustees are so ready to sell the pass to the enemy.[147] Lip service paid to democratic values merely deflects attention from an oligarchic rule that is rarely acknowledged as such.[148] In *Alien Powers*, Minogue wrote: 'Ideology's encounter

---

[144] Christopher Lasch, *The Revolt of the Elites and the Betrayal of Democracy* (W W Norton, 1996) 20.
[145] Ibid. 2-21. Lasch neglects the legal and political offensives that at times threaten "rule or ruin."
[146] Bastiat (n 101).
[147] Kenneth Minogue, 'How Civilizations Fall' (2001) (April) *New Criterion*. See Jacob Neusner and Noam M M Neusner, *The Price of Excellence: Universities in Conflict during the Cold War Era* (Continuum, 1995), especially ch 4:II; David Gelernter, *America-Lite: How Imperial Academia Dismantled Our Culture (and Ushered in the Obamacrats)* (Encounter, 2012).
[148] Angelo Codevilla, *The Ruling Class: How They Corrupted America and What We Can Do About It* (Beaufort Books, 2010); Joel Kotkin, *The New Class Conflict* (Telos, 2014).

with democracy has been a tragic one, and the actual destruction of democracy in ideological states directly reflects the logic of ideology.'[149] David Guaspari observed:

> An ideologist in power has been given the task of reshaping the human condition and a corresponding claim on enormous power. That power, he argues, will not be misused because it belongs to, and is applied on behalf of, the oppressed class being liberated. While the vanguard is teaching the masses – and until they've learned their lessons, the vanguard are stewards of that power – politics has no point, thanks to what Minogue calls 'Talmon's Fork,' after the Israeli historian Jacob Leib Talmon: 'Either a democratic vote elects the enlightened to power, or it does not. If so, it is unnecessary. If not, it is pernicious.'[150]

In other hands, such "reshaping" might be criticized as patriarchy, privilege, hegemony, or racism.

In *Authority and the Liberal Tradition*, Robert Heineman advances a thesis which may be summarised: 'Contemporary American liberalism is incapable of supporting for any sustained period of time a government that acts with firmness and coherent direction.'[151] Liberalism promoted a 'tremendous expansion of government within the past several decades,' resulting in a 'government lacking in authority

---

[149] Minogue (n 68) 281. Alexis de Tocqueville noted the incompatibility of democracy and socialism.
[150] David Guaspari, 'Ideologists Amok' (2021) (June) *New Criterion* 8. In a mid-twentieth-century series of books, J L Talmon traced the history of political messianism and totalitarian democracy back to the French Revolution and the subsequent Romantic period.
[151] Robert Heineman, *Authority and the Liberal Tradition: From Hobbes to Rorty* (Transaction, 2nd ed, 1994) 1. The same has been said of France before the deluge: 'On the threshold of the Revolution France was a civilized and reasonable prosperous country but hopelessly weak in her fibers.': Molnar (n 43) 22.

and direction.'[152] Our political *means* (the sophisticated apparatus and *process* of government) outstrip the political *ends* (the *substantive* human purposes) they are supposed to serve. Many political programs are cynical, jury-rigged Procrustean beds designed to enhance power and score political points. We often meet this arrogant "can-do" mentality in modern literature, such as Mary Shelley's *Frankenstein* and C S Lewis's *That Hideous Strength*.

Liberalism favors the *expansion of government* as a political strategy but lacks a guiding purpose for doing so, giving rise to what Theodore Lowi called 'Interest-group liberalism' because the state lacks the capacity to support *any* coherent, substantive policy for a sustained period. Government oversteps its bounds because it *lacks a guiding and constraining purpose*. As public respect for authority declines, 'government must turn to *coercion* and *material inducement* to achieve its ends,'[153] perpetuating a vicious circle. In practice, programs, budgets, the electorate, and even government entities are held hostage by rent-seekers – partisan shakedown artists – until one side or another achieves its ends, whether it be greater power or more largesse.

Another implication is that *Government may not act with firmness and coherent direction* because it has been retooled to promote the *ad hoc* purposes of those who control and those who receive largess. Instead of embracing a focused and disciplined political vision, its activities are *diffuse* and chiefly concern the distribution of the spoils. Thus, the national treasury – increasingly raided to underwrite a rapidly growing national debt – becomes a political slush fund serving whatever interests are successfully able to divert its resources to their own purposes.[154]

---

[152] Heineman (n 151) 1.
[153] Ibid 1.
[154] Ibid 177.

To summarise: 'The expansion of governmental activity is a direct consequence of the inability of public officials to withstand the demands made of them' – a description of political weakness rather than strength.[155] Such weakness is made even more dangerous by the sophisticated array of means – or ends used as means – available to enforce the elite's increasingly irresponsible will. It was not settled science that brought lockdowns and riots in 2020 but a combination of political opportunism, manipulation of fear, and the public's lifelong conditioning to obey authority. The sheer stasis of the system repels any meaningful attempts at reform. Franz Kafka anticipated this plight in his parable, *The Couriers*:

> They were offered the choice between becoming kings or the couriers of kings. The way children would, they all wanted to be couriers. Therefore there are only couriers who hurry about the world, shouting to each other – since there are no kings – messages that have become meaningless. They would like to put an end to this miserable life of theirs but they dare not because of their oaths of service.[156]

X FINAL CONSIDERATIONS

The West is beset by cultural revolutions. What is on offer is akin to nirvana or nothingness: a Great Reset through global governance, a neo-Marxist cancel culture, or a Chinese-style social credit system[157] which would leave people in a state of dependency with no hope of cleaning

---

[155] An illustration of that weakness may be found in the conclusion of Grant McConnell, *Steel and the Presidency – 1962* (W W Norton, 1963).
[156] Walter Kaufmann (ed), *Existentialism from Dostoevsky to Sartre* (Meridian, 1956) 130.
[157] The Chinese Communist regime is introducing the utililitarian, soft-power "social credit" system to fine-tune its control: Thomas F Farr, 'China's Second Cultural Revolution', *First Things* (Web Article, 16 January 2021).

the slate or making a fresh start.[158]

Either by active assent or acquiescence at each stage, the old order's guardians betrayed their trust by acceding to subterfuges which battered down people's psychological defenses. Initially, the public memory began to fade with the decline of local associations and subtle reinterpretations of the common faith. Then came concentrations of power in public education and a highly centralised administrative state, together with a decline in local and family autonomy.[159] These were followed by a shrinkage of skilled labor jobs, apprenticeships, civic and community clubs, and traditional outlets for conveying the wealth of personal wisdom and experience through nurturing, teaching, and testing. Finally, people neglected to produce progeny to be their heirs. Given modernity's capacity for producing endless distraction, sins of omission may sometimes be absent-minded.

Far more worrisome is a species of cultural vandalism reminiscent of earlier bouts of revolutionary nihilism in Russia and Germany.[160] Negligence has consequences. If the West has indeed surrendered its birthright, it will take character and *courage* to repent and rebuild a depleted heritage.

---

[158] Wells envisioned a "New World Order," Rousseau a totalitarian general will, Bentham a Panopticon. Immigrants from Communist countries are struck by the resemblances between what they see in the West today and what they experienced in their home countries. See, eg, Giulio Meotti, 'If You Do Not Have Free Speech You Are Not Free': Refugees from Communism Horrified at America' *Gatestone Institute* (Web Article, 18 July 2021); Oleg Atbashian, *Shakedown Socialism* (Greenleaf Press, 2010); Daily Wire News, 'Survivor of Mao's China: Critical Race Theory "Is Racist," China Used "Wokeness" To Install Communism' Daily Wire (Web Article, 12 June 2021).

[159] See, eg, Lincoln Brown, 'A Minnesota School Board Tells Students to Keep Secrets After "Equity Audit" Survey', *PJ Media* (Web Article, 23 July 2021).

[160] For a glance at the nihilism of the New Left, see Kuehnelt-Leddihn (n 1) ch 19; on Russian nihilism, see James H Billington, *Fire in the Minds of Men: Origins of the Revolutionary Faith* (Basic Books, 1980); on the inner contradictions of the New Left thought systems, see Os Guinness, *The Dust of Death* (IVP, 1973) 140-147.

9

"Get On Your Marx, Statue Topplers!" The Links Between Marxism, Racism and Genocide

AUGUSTO ZIMMERMANN*

ABSTRACT

The New Left is commonly associated with Marxist values and ideology. Ironically, when these contemporary heirs to Karl Marx are flinging the standard slur that conservatives are "Nazis" or "Fascists", to find these dictators' (Hitler and Mussolini) real legatees they should look much closer to home. Curiously, Hitler himself was willing to concede his debt to Marx, claiming even to have 'learned a great deal from Marxism'. In fact, the modern practice of genocide was invented by committed Marxists, not the Nazis. The problem is not that the disciples of Marx have paid no attention to policies that have turned out to be genocidal, but instead that Marxism itself prepares the ideological mindset for State-sanctioned extermination of people on a massive scale. There are obvious similarities between Marxist class-warfare and Nazi race-warfare, or between destroying people because of social class and destroying people because of ethnicity. As a consequence, Marxist political regimes and their Marxist-inspired revolutionary movements killed no less than 120 million people in the 20th century alone, and they continue to do so.

---

* Head of Law, Sheridan Institute of Higher Education.

> Until its complete extermination or loss of national status, this racial trash always becomes the most fanatical bearer there is of counter-revolution, and it remains that. That is because its entire existence is nothing more than a protest against a great historical revolution ... The next world war will cause ... entire reactionary peoples to disappear from the earth. And that too is progress. – Karl Marx (1849)[1]

> The classes and the races, too weak to master the new conditions of life, must give way. They must perish in the revolutionary holocaust. – Karl Marx (1853)[2]

I FIRST CONSIDERATIONS

Across numerous Western countries left-wing protesters have vandalised statues of leading historical figures as part of the *Black Lives Matter* ('BLM') movement. These vandals have a clear ideological framework. The movement's main founder, Patrisse Khan-Cullors, created the *#BlackLivesMatter* hashtag in 2013 and has written widely about the movement. In her bestselling book 'When They Call You a Terrorist: A Black Lives Matter Memoir', she reveals her 'appreciation for the work of the US Communist Party, especially Black communists',[3] and her support for 'the great work of the Black Panther Party, the American Indian Movement, Young Lords, Brown Berets, and the great revolutionary rainbow experiments of the

---

[1] Karl Marx, 'Der Magiarische Kampf', *Neue Rheinische Zeitung*, 13 January 1849 (English translation), quoted in Malachi Martin, *The Keys of This Blood: The Struggle for World Dominion Between Pope John Paul II, Mikhail Gorbachev and the Capitalist West* (Touchstone, 1990) 235.
[2] Karl Marx, 'Forced Emigration', *New York Daily Tribune*, 22 March 1853.
[3] Patrisse Khan-Cullors, *When They Call You a Terrorist: A Black Lives Matter Memoir* (St Martin's Press, 2018) 272.

1970s'.[4] Khan-Cullors describes herself and fellow BLM co-founders as committed Marxists. In a video from 2015, she says: 'We are trained Marxists. We are super-versed on, sort of, ideological theories.'[5] As noted by Brad Polumbo, a policy analyst at the Foundation for Economic Education, 'the official Black Lives Matter organization is Marxist and anti-American in its values'.[6] It views are particularly disturbing to anyone who truly values the rule of law and the Western legal tradition of fundamental rights and freedoms.

Of course, BLM leaders claim to be fighting "systemic" racism both in America and other Western democracies. However, if these BLM activists were more seriously concerned about racism they would not be vandalising the statues of historical figures who championed equality for all. One of these statues vandalised is that of Abraham Lincoln, the celebrated US president who brought black slavery to an end at the cost of 600,000 American lives. Lincoln believed that America's founders intended everyone to be treated equally and endowed with inalienable rights to life, liberty and property. Enacted on January 1, 1863, Lincoln's Emancipation Proclamation declared that everyone who was held as a slave 'henceforward shall be free'. Situated in Boston's Park Square, the statue was intended to show the 16th President's commitment to freeing all people of colour from the scourge of slavery. It depicts Lincoln with one arm extended above a freed slave with broken shackles, symbolising that, by Lincoln's hand, the institution of slavery was broken. The inscription on the statue reads: 'A race set free and the country at peace. Lincoln rests from

---
[4] Yaron Steinbuch, 'Black Lives Matter Co-Founder Describes Herself as Trained Marxist', *New York Post* (Web Article, 25 June 2020).
[5] Brad Polumbo, 'Is Black Lives Matter Marxist? No and Yes', *Foundation for Economic Education* (Web Article, 7 July 2020).
[6] Ibid.

his labors'.⁷ Yet, the country is no longer so much at peace and a new petition, in postmodernist fashion, claims that the monument 'represents us still beneath someone else'.⁸

Similarly, BLM rioters have defaced the Robert Gould Shaw Memorial honouring the Massachusetts 54th Regiment, a monument erected in honour of the first African-American volunteer regiment that saw extensive service in the Union Army during the American Civil War. The superintendent of National Parks of Boston, Michael Creasey, explains that 'the memorial has been a beacon of hope and a rallying point for conversations about race, justice and human rights'.⁹ Another vandalised statue is dedicated to the 19th century entrepreneur and inventor Matthias Baldwin, who fought against slavery and supported black voting rights. His statue in the City Hall was defaced with paint and graffiti during recent BLM protests in Philadelphia.¹⁰ Baldwin opened a school for black children in Philadelphia and for years paid the salary of its teachers. As a machinery manufacturer, he took special delight in hiring blacks to his shops and paid them generously when that was not the norm. 'The irony of vandalizing a monument to those who died to end slavery is lost on the morons who don't know their history', complains Joe Walsh, an active member of the Friends of Matthias Baldwin Society.¹¹

---

⁷ Anthony Leonardi, 'Boston Mayor in Favor of Removing Statue of Abraham Lincoln Setting Slaves Free', *Washington Examiner* (Web Article, 15 June 2020).
⁸ Marie Fazio, 'Boston Removes Statue of Formerly Enslaved Man Kneeling Before Lincoln', *The New York Times* (Web Article, 29 December 2020).
⁹ Dan Murphy, 'Restoration Work on Shaw 54th Memorial Now Underway', *Beacon Hill Times* (Web Article, 28 May 2020).
¹⁰ Dapaul vid Mikkelson, 'Did George Floyd Protesters Deface the Statue of an Abolitionist?', *Snopes* (Web Article, 17 June 2020).
¹¹ Zachary Evans, 'Park Volunteer Outraged Over Vandalism of Philadelphia Abolitionist Statue: "He Was BLM Before There Was A Slogan"', *National Review* (Web Article, 11 June 2020).

The desecration of the beautiful statue of poet and abolitionist Jon Greenleaf Whittier provides one final example before I can proceed to the discussion about the Marxist roots of fascism, modern racism and genocide. Whittier's statue was vandalised in the very city that bears his name. The rioters wrote 'BLM' on the seated statue located in the city's Central Park. The protesters fail to understand that Whittier was a human-rights activist and a very active delegate to the first meeting of the American Anti-Slavery Movement.[12] According to Celia Caust-Ellenbogen, an archivist at the Friends History Liberty of Swarthmore College, 'Whittier edited anti-slavery newspapers, helped to establish the Liberty Party, wrote numerous poems supporting the abolitionist cause, as well as an 1833 tract in favour of immediate and unconditional emancipation of enslaved people'.[13]

II GET ON YOUR MARX, STATUE TOPPLERS!

As these BLM mobs continue to vandalise statues with impunity, they should consider targeting those of their own leftist icons.[14] Modern racism and genocide can be directly traced to that great icon of socialism and darling of the Left: Karl Marx.[15] Two centuries after his birth, he remains idolised by many left-wing activists, politicians and intellectuals, as the unveiling of a five-metre statue of him in his birthplace of Trier, Germany, in 2018 fully testifies. Another statue of Marx is found atop his tomb at Highgate Cemetery, in London. In New York, there is a white bust of Marx displayed at the Smithsonian

---

[12] Ruby Gonzales, 'Statue of Abolitionist John Greenleaf Whittier Vandalized in his Namesake City', *Whittier Daily News* (Web Article, 15 June 2020).
[13] Ibid.
[14] This part draws on Augusto Zimmermann, 'Get on Your Marx, Statue-Topplers', *Quadrant Online* (Web Article, 25 June 2020).
[15] Dinesh D'Souza, *What's So Great About Christianity?* (Regnery, 2007) 220.

Design Museum and a painting of Marx displayed at the Guggenheim Museum.

That Karl Marx viscerally abhorred people of colour is beyond dispute. Whereas Hitler later extolled the "master race" and its "right" to eliminate the so-called "weaker races", Marx believed, in his own words, that 'the races, too weak to master the new conditions of life, must give way. They must perish in the revolutionary holocaust'.[16] Thus he supported European colonisation on racial grounds and described his adversaries in dehumanising terms such as half-humans, vermin and parasites. Such people deserved elimination for retarding "the long march of history".[17]

Although ethnically a Jew, Marx often resorted to outrageous anti-Semitic tirades. He often used terms like 'dirty Jew' and 'Jewish nigger' to describe individuals he personally disliked. In 1862, for example, Marx wrote a letter to Engels to report that 'the Jewish nigger' Ferdinand Lassalle, a Prussian-German jurist and social-democratic activist, was leaving Britain to return to Germany. Marx described Lassalle as follows:

> It is now perfectly clear to me that, as the shape of his head and the growth of his hair indicates, he is descended from the Negroes who joined in Moses' flight from Egypt (unless his mother or grandmother on the father's side was crossed with a nigger). This union of Jew and German on a Negro base was bound to produce an extraordinary hybrid. The pushiness of the fellow is also nigger-like.[18]

---

[16] Ibid.
[17] Paul Johnson, *Modern Times: The World From the Twenties to the Nineties* (HarperCollins, 2001) 62.
[18] Karl Marx, 'Letter to Engels – 30 July 1862', in *Karl Marx-Friedrich Engels Werke* (East Berlin, 1956-68) vol XXX, 259, quoted in Johnson (n 16) 62.

Marx wrote to Engels, in 1861, that the Prussian Egyptologist, Karl Lepsius, had "proved" that the Jewish exodus was 'the expulsion of a Leper people from Egypt, at the hands of whom was an Egyptian priest named Moses'. Likewise, he argued that French evolutionist Pierre Trémaux, author of numerous scientific and ethnographic publications, proved that 'the common Negro type is the degenerate form of a much higher one', crowing that this appraisal was 'a very great advance over Darwin'.[19] Another example comes from his article attacking Moses Levy, the then editor of London's *Daily Telegraph*. Marx described Levy's nose as 'an elephant trunk, an antenna, a lighthouse, a telegraph'.[20]

In *On the Jewish Question*, Marx attacks Jews for 'dissolving earlier forms of solidarity and turning Europeans into this own caricature of Jews'. This book is a critique of liberalism but there one finds anti-Semitic tirades such as that 'money is the jealous god of Israel, in face of which no other god may exist'. To make "the Jew" impossible it is necessary, according to Marx, 'to abolish preconditions that produced Judaism'.[21] As stated by him, 'in emancipating itself from hucksterism and money, and thus from real and practical Judaism, our age would emancipate itself'.[22]

Marx also believed that Judaism had to disappear before capitalism could be eradicated. For socialism to become a reality, he concluded,

---

[19] Diane Paul, '"In the Interests of Civilization": Marxist Views of Race and Culture in the Nineteenth Century' (1981) 42(1) *Journal of the History of Ideas* 115, 115.
[20] Max Young, 'Karl Marx: The Racist Godfather of Leftist Racism', *1828* (Web Article, 4 September 2019)
[21] Marx (n 18) 57-58.
[22] T B Bottomore, *Karl Marx: Early Writings* (McGraw-Hill, 1963) 34-37.

it is necessary to eliminate 'the Jewish attitude to money'.²³ In other words, to make the capitalist order and its attitude to money disappear, the Jewish religion should entirely disappear. Since this theme is repeated over and over throughout Marx's political writings, it is reasonable to argue that Marxist ideology has influenced modern anti-Semitism.

Similar to Nazi Germany, Marxist ideology was applied in Soviet Russia to create entire categories of "sub-humans". In Nazi Germany, this included the physically impaired and mentally ill, followed then by the Jews. In Russia, by contrast, the main targets of mass extermination were the "enemies of the people", an abstract category that could include entire cultural, national, and ethnic groups, if they seemed (for equally ill-defined reasons) to threaten the Soviet regime. At different times the regime conducted mass arrests of Poles, Chechens, Tartars, and – on the eve of Joseph Stalin's death – Jews.²⁴ Those classified as belonging to these targeted groups were first dehumanised and then mercilessly destroyed. They were deemed *vermin, parasite,* and *infectious diseases* in order to be exterminated for the good of the community.²⁵ This Marxist regime deemed them a "pollution" and 'poisonous weeds needing to be uprooted'.²⁶ They were considered half-animals and 'something even lower than two-legged cattle'.²⁷

As further explained below, it is no wonder Marxist teachings inspired the creation in Europe of the first concentration camps.²⁸ Of course, Marx never was in a position to directly carry out large-

---

[23] Ibid.
[24] Anne Applebaum, *Gulag: A History* (Anchor Books, 2004) xxxvi.
[25] Ibid xxxvi.
[26] Ibid 102.
[27] Richard Pipes, *The Russian Revolution* (Vintage Books, 1997) 836.
[28] Ibid.

scale exterminations. However, his most successful disciples – Lenin, Stalin, Mao, Castro, etc – did practice the very kind of violence that Marx felt in his heart and which his works so strongly emanate.[29] Indeed, it is reasonable to argue that the modern practice of genocide was born out of Marx's teachings and implemented by his disciples at the cost of no less than 120 million lives in the 20th century alone.[30]

III THE OPIATE OF THE INTELLECTUALS

Since it is common practice to state that the New Left wishes to bring about "Cultural Marxism", it might be important to explain what Marxism means. Marxism provides a social-political-economic theory that interprets history through a "progressive" prism. Marx claimed to have discovered a dialectical pattern which controls history and that would eventually lead humankind towards a classless (and lawless) utopia. Indeed, Marx conceived laws as instruments of class oppression which would have to disappear when the final stage of communism was achieved. Meanwhile, as Marx put it, a socialist state should aspire to impose the 'proletarian dictatorship' consisted of a small *nomenklatura* conveniently described as 'the vanguard of the proletariat'.[31]

But Marxism is not just a scheme of social, economic and political transformation. Marxism is primarily a form of secular theology which is deeply dogmatic and contains an entire worldview based on

---

[29] Ibid 72.
[30] Ibid 71.
[31] See Yadullah Shahibzadeh, 'The Vanguard Party and the Dictatorship of the Proletariat' in Yadullah Shahibzadeh, *Marxist and Left-Wing Politics in Europe and Iran* (Palkgrave Macmillan, 2019) 27-46.

a Social Darwinian explanation of the evolution of human society. Theologically, Marxism is based on a faith that history is progressing towards a certain end, and that a small ruling elite – the "vanguard of the proletariat" – will act as a redemptive force of humanity. Marxism is endowed with prophetic dimensions and dogmatic certainties that are central parts of its message and its appeal,[32] thus working as a secular credo grounded in a certain form of ideological prophecy.

Having arrived at such a socialist prophecy of the proletariat's historic mission, Marx sought to find empirical evidence to justify it. Politics became for him a form of "secular religion" whereby history can be interpreted progressively, moving by means of an ongoing struggle between different social groups. As such, the final stage will occur when humanity transcend struggle and the eschatological consummation of global communism is achieved.[33] To realise this goal any means are justifiable, including violence and deceit, provided that these actions accelerate the advent of communism. Indeed, nothing that advances communism can ever be considered immoral or objectively wrong. As theologian Michael Green pointed out:

> Whatever the pogroms of Lenin, Trotsky, Stalin; whatever the revelations of the Gulag Archipelago and the terrifying brutality of the Soviet concentration camps; whatever the rapes of a Hungary, a Czechoslovakia, an Afghanistan, the faith of the committed Communist persists. All personal judgement is obscured in the name of faith; faith is absolutely essential if everything is not to come tumbling round his ears ...
>
> Logically, of course, there is no reason why a modern Communist

---

[32] Martyn Krygier, 'Marxism, Communism, and Narcissism' (1990) 15(4) *Law & Social Inquiry* 707, 712.

[33] David T Koyzis, *Political Visions & Illusions* (InterVarsity Press, 2003) 174.

should bother to work for a utopia in which he will never share: this is one of the [irrationalities] in Communism. But he is inspired by the vision, attracted by the prospect, stimulated by the struggle and warmed by the companionship. The millennial utopia held out by Communism ... is both a pale imitation of and unconsciously inspired by the Christian teaching of the Kingdom of God.[34]

But if Marxism can be descried as a form of secular theology, what are then the differences between Marxism and traditional religions? First of all, Marxism exercises a special appeal to the intellectual elite, whereas Christianity has always attracted the poor and the outcast. The intellectual elites feel particularly attracted to its pseudo-scientific formula, including its eschatological view of the transformation of the imperfect man into an ideal man. Marxism offers something that is particularly appealing to the subconscious mind of certain intellectuals. As noted by law professor Mary Ann Glendon and two other American legal academics,

> Marxism offers the intellectual leadership in the new world somewhere on this earth. Feudal society has been ruled by military lords, capitalist society by money-minded businessmen, but in the socialist society the intellectuals would rule in the name of the proletariat ... The Platonic fantasy of the 'philosopher king", always surviving in the intellectual's subconscious mind, would be finally realized in historical actuality.[35]

A secular religion such as Marxism is more appealing to the intellectual elites than to the ordinary citizen. Marxism provides a

---

[34] Michael Green, *I Believe in Satan's Downfall* (Hodder & Stoughton, 1988) 159–161.
[35] Mary Ann Glendon, Michael Wallace Gordon and Christopher Osakwe, *Comparative Legal Traditions* (West Publishing Co, 1985) 676.

final purpose and a sense of mission; a conviction that a person's life is worthwhile when history requires a certain intellectual "vanguard" to lead others towards a future utopia and creation of the "New Man". Other religions postpone happiness as a reward to be enjoyed in the afterlife. By contrast, Marxism promises the ultimate reward here on this earth, claiming to speak for the foreseeable future of humanity's redemption. After presenting Marxism as a form of secular religion, the late Harvard legal historian Harold Berman concluded:

> The writings of Marx and his collaborator Engels are in effect the New Testament of Communism. Lenin is the Pauline apostle to the gentiles who adopted the gospel to a new generation and a new people. Stalin is the Soviet Emperor Constantine, who make of the new religion a State Orthodoxy ... It was on the foundation of Marxian analysis of the origin, growth, and decline of societies that the Russian Revolutionaries set out to construct a new social order. Led by Lenin, these men were thoroughly grounded in Marxism and were fanatical believers in its doctrines.[36]

Whenever one focus on analogies with traditional religions, institutionalised Marxism undoubtedly has a lot in common with them. Glendon et al describe this important "religious" appeal to the intellectual elites in the following terms:

> As a world secular religion, Marxism has its dialectic which is akin to Calvinist predestination. Like other creeds, Marxism has its sacred text, its saints, as well as its holy city. If Marx is its Messiah, Lenin is its St Paul. As is true of many other world religions, Marxism too has witnessed a luxuriant proliferation of sects and subsects – the deviationists, the revisionists,

---

[36] Harold J Berman, *Justice in Russia* (Harvard University Press, 1950) 8-9.

the fundamentalists, the modernizers, and so on ... But after all these analogies have been made, what remains to be emphasized is how different Marxism is from other religious. Unlike Christianity, for instance, its appeal has always been first to the intellectuals. Christianity was resisted by the ancient philosophers, who regarded it as an aberration of the lower classes; it spread upwards. Marxism, on the contrary, has been carried out by the intellectuals to the proletarians and peasants. To intellectuals it has appealed as no other doctrine has because it integrated for them most fully discordant psychological motives. In Marxism one finds for the first time a combination of the language of science and the language of myth — a union of logic and mysticism. Scientific criticism in the 19th century has deprived intellectuals of their God and left them uncertain as to the foundation of their ethics. Scientific agnosticism was an austere self-denial in a world inherently lifeless and undramatic, a world with neither purpose nor climax. Social movements had assumed the character of a superficial altruistic anodyne ungrounded in the nature of the universe. In Marxism, however, one's ideals could be taken as expressions of an underlying historical necessity in things.[37]

There is a widespread though entirely false impression that socialism and communism are merely up-to-date secular versions of Christianity. However, as noted by Richard Pipes, 'the difference is that whereas Jesus urged his followers to give up their own possessions, the socialists and communists want to give away the possessions of others'.[38] Moreover, Jesus did not advocate for wealth redistribution and Saint Paul's well-known saying about money is often misquoted:

---

[37] Glendon, Gordon and Osakwe (n 35) 676.
[38] Richard Pipes, *Communism: A History of the Intellectual and Political Movement* (Phoenix Press, 2003) 2.

he said not that 'money is the root of all evil' but that 'the *love* of money' is – in other words, greed. Ultimately, the legacy of Marxist ideology is entirely different from Christianity's. As Professor Martyn Krygier correctly points out,

> The great world religions have endured for millennia and, if they have been involved in the infliction of pain, they have also been responsible for glorious achievements – achievements of the spirit; cultural, artistic, civilizational, architectural, monuments, both literal and metaphorical; and in certain cases, if Weber is to be believed, significant economic achievements. Institutionalized Marxism lasted 70 years [in Soviet Russia and other Eastern European nations]. In that short time it has cost millions of lives, enslaved millions of people and reduced once-civilized countries to dilapidated ruins. Its spiritual legacy is nil. Almost its only moral achievement (not small) has been the tempering of those characters that did not break or bend in hard times. The only great literature for which it was clearly responsible, and almost the only great literature produced under it, has been a literature of opposition and suffering. The less said about its monuments the better.[39]

IV MARXIST ROOTS OF NAZI-FASCISM

5 May 2018 was the 200th anniversary of Karl Marx's birth, given that Communism killed more than 120 million people in the 20th century alone,[40] we should expect the European Union oligarchs to have shown a bit more respect for the innocent victims of this complicated ideology. However, Jean-Claude Juncker, the head of the European

---

[39] Krygier (n 32) 712.
[40] This part draws on Augusto Zimmermann, 'Adolf Hitler's Debt to Karl Marx', *Quadrant Online* (Web Article, 9 May 2019).

Commission attended the celebration marking the 200th anniversary of Marx's birth in Trier, Germany, and commented that he was 'celebrating the father of Communism'. He argued that Marx was not responsible for mistakes and atrocities committed in his name after his death. Reportedly, the EU President even delivered 'an impassioned speech praising the legacy of the German philosopher'.[41]

According to French historian François Furet, Fascism grew up on the soil of Italian Marxism.[42] The Italian Fascist movement was introduced after World War I by Benito Mussolini. Raised by a Marxist mother and an Anarchist father, at the age of 29 Mussolini became 'one of the most effective and widely read socialist journalists in Europe'.[43] In 1912, he was elected leader of the Italian Socialist Party at the Congress of Reggio Emilia, proposing that Italy should be thoroughly Marxist.

Mussolini was a member of the revolutionary wing of the Socialist movement prior to supporting Italy's entry into the Great War.[44] On the eve of the First World War, Mussolini predicted: 'With the unleashing of a mighty clash of peoples, the bourgeoisie is playing its last card and calls forth on the world scene that which Marx called the sixth great power: the socialist revolution'.[45] 'Karl Marx', wrote Mussolini, 'is the father and teacher. He is the magnificent philosopher of working-class violence'.[46] Mussolini also stated: 'I wish to prepare my country

---

[41] John Stone, 'EU President Juncker Defends Karl Marx's Legacy', *The Independent* (Web Article, 5 May 2018).
[42] François Furet, *The Passing of an Illusion: The Idea of Communism in the Twentieth Century* (University of Chicago Press, 1999) 22.
[43] Johnson (n 17) 57.
[44] Furet (n 42) 22.
[45] Johnson (n 17) 37.
[46] Benito Mussolini, *Opera Omnia* (La Fenice, 1951-63) vol II, 32, 126 quoted in Johnson (n 17) 57.

and accustom it to war for the day of the greatest bloodbath of all, when the two basic hostile classes will clash in the supreme trial'.[47]

The coming of that war coupled with his determination to bring Italy into it resulted in Mussolini losing his official position within the Italian Socialist Party.[48] As a result, on 23 March 1919, he created his own Fascist Movement which promised the partial seizure of all finance capital; the control over the national economy by corporatist economic councils; the confiscation of church lands; and agrarian reform.[49] Although Lenin's economic failures in Soviet Russia turned him away from direct expropriation of industry, Mussolini's main goal was to create a socialist utopia in which a powerful State would dictate how private business should be allowed to operate.[50] As noted by Paul Johnson,

> Mussolini now wanted to use and exploit capitalism rather than destroy it. But his was to be a radical revolution nonetheless, rooted in the pre-war 'vanguard élite' Marxism and syndicalism (workers' rule) which was to remain to his death the most important single element in his politics.[51]

Mussolini pledged 'to make history, not to endure it'.[52] Lenin, another of Marx's most successful disciples, described his Bolshevik party as a highly disciplined and centralised movement. Likewise, Mussolini wanted to create a 'vanguard minority' formed by highly-trained revolutionary leaders. Through the adoption of symbolic invocations,

---

[47] Ibid.
[48] Johnson (n 17) 96.
[49] Ibid.
[50] Thomas Sowell, 'Socialist or Fascist', *The American Spectator* (Web Article, 12 June 2012).
[51] Johnson (n 17) 96.
[52] Ibid.

the fascist leaders expected to raise the consciousness of the Italian proletariat.[53] Above all, Mussolini agreed with Lenin that violence was a valid means to achieve ultimate power and complete dominance.[54]

In the 1920s another nationalist/socialist movement followed in the wake of the Italian Fascists: the *National Socialist German Workers' Party* (*National-Sozialistische Deutsche Abeiterpartei — NSDAP*). This party was established as a mass movement to bring together the ideals of nationalism and socialism. It added to that the specific element of racism and anti-Semitism in particular. Co-written in 1920 by Adolf Hitler and Anton Drexler the *NSDAP 25 Points Manifesto* were the unalterable and eternal objectives of National Socialism. Besides anti-Semitism, this manifesto promised government expropriation of land without compensation; nationalisation of all basic sectors of the national industry; the abolition of market-based lending; and the confiscation of all income unearned by work.[55] In a speech on Labour's Day on 1st May 1927, Hitler declared:

> We are socialists. We are enemies of today's capitalistic system for the exploitation of the economically weak, with its unfair salaries, with its unseemly evaluation of a human being according to wealth and property instead of responsibility and performance, and we are *determined to destroy this system under all conditions.*[56]

The combination of socialist and nationalist policies was not alien to German political culture. In its modern form the "welfare state"

---

[53] Ibid 57.
[54] Ibid 58.
[55] See Jonah Goldberg, *Liberal Fascism: The Secret History of the American Left, From Mussolini to the Politics of Change* (Three Rivers Press, 2009) 410-413.
[56] Adolf Hitler (Speech, Munich, 1st May 1927) quoted in John Toland, *Adolf Hitler* (Doubleday & Co, 1976) 306.

actually originated in 19th-century Germany and from this sort of combination.⁵⁷ The nation's statesman and militaristic Chancellor, Otto von Bismarck, pioneered what is now recognised as the modern welfare state through a series of compulsory insurance schemes enacted in the 1880s, including work accidents, health, disability, and old age.

Bismarck called these measures "State Socialism", declaring in 1882: 'Many of the measures which we have adopted to the great blessing of the country are Socialistic, and the State will have to accustom itself to a little more Socialism yet'.⁵⁸ He wanted the German workers to feel grateful to the state authorities, and therefore to him. It was the collapse of this statist model created by Bismarck in the 1930s that ushered the most oppressive of all forms of welfare state: National Socialism.⁵⁹ As Götz Aly points out,

> The National Socialist German Workers' Party was propagating two age-old dreams of the German people: national and class unity. That was the key to the Nazi popularity, from which they derived the power they needed to pursue their criminal aims. The idea of the Volkstaat – a state of and for the people – was what we would call a welfare state for Germans with the proper

---

⁵⁷ Tom G Palmer, 'Bismarck's Legacy' in Tom G. Palmer (ed), *After the Welfare State* (Jameson Books, 2012) 34.
⁵⁸ Ibid 35.
⁵⁹ 'The National Socialist welfare state, which instituted such an embracing system of patronage, dependence, and loyalty among the German population, was financed ... by means of stripping the Jews of their wealth (from their money, businesses, and homes down to their dental fillings, children's toys, and even their hair), confiscating the assets of enemies of the state, and looting the rest of Europe through requisitions and deliberate inflation of the currencies of occupied countries. It was also a pyramid scheme that required an ever-greater base of people paying into it to channel the loot upwards. Like all pyramid schemes, the Third Reich was doomed to fail'.: Palmer (n 52) 36.

racial pedigree. In one of his central pronouncements, Hitler promised 'the creation of a socially just state,' a model society that would 'continue to eradicate all social barriers'.[60]

By the time the Nazis achieved power state ownership had increased exponentially in both the war and non-war sectors of the national economy. These economic policies dramatically expanded government control over prices, labour, materials, dividends and foreign trade. They had restricted both competition and private ownership, in an attempt to redirect all segments of the economy toward a policy of "general welfare".[61]

German unionised workers' movement were strongly supportive of the Nazi regime. On 1st May 1933, Labor Day, thousands of them packed Berlin's Tempelhof district at the behest of their union bosses to provide a "gigantic demonstration" of support for Hitler and the Nazi leadership. Their beloved *Führer* spoke of the country's rebirth and of taming capitalist exploitation in order to make way for the creation of a new social and economic order.[62] As Richard Pipes points out:

> The Nazis appealed to the socialist traditions of German labor, declaring the worker 'a pillar of the community', and the 'bourgeois' – along with the traditional aristocracy – a doomed class. Hitler, who told associates that he was a 'socialist', had the party adopt the red flag and, on coming to power, declared May 1 a national holiday: Nazi Party members were ordered to

---

[60] Götz Aly, *Hitler's Beneficiaries: Plunder, Racial War, and the Nazi Welfare State* (Henry, Holt & Co, 2006) 6.
[61] Walter J Rinderle and Bernard Norling, *The Nazi Impact on a German Village* (University of Kentucky Press, 1993) 148.
[62] R C van Caenegem, *An Historical Introduction to Western Constitutional Law* (Cambridge University Press, 1995) 287.

address one another as 'comrades' (*Genossen*). His conception of the party was, like Lenin's, that of a militant organization, a *Kampfbund*, or 'Combat League' ... His ultimate aim was a society in which traditional classes would be abolished, and status earned by personal heroism. In typically radical fashion, he envisaged man re-creating himself: 'Man is becoming god ... Man is god in the making.[63]

Although Hitler condemned the incarnation of Marxism in the Soviet Union, he had no problem to describe his party as thoroughly socialist in nature. In private conversations Hitler claimed to have widely read Marxist literature, both as a young man in Munich in 1913-1914 and during his stay in Landsberg prison in 1924.[64]

He admitted that Marxism had greatly influenced his ideas. Indeed, shortly after coming to power he told his closest friends not only that had learned a great deal from Marxism but also that the whole of National Socialism was based on it. Hitler, in fact, 'often remarked that Marxists made the best Nazis because they understood that politics was a violent activity'.[65] Thus he predicted in the Spring of 1934 that:

> It is not Germany that will turn Bolshevist, but Bolshevism that will become a sort of National Socialism ... There is more that binds us to Bolshevism than separate us from it.[66]

On another occasion, Hitler confessed to his closest associates:

> I have learned a great deal from Marxism as I do not hesitate to

---

[63] Richard Pipes, *Russia under the Bolshevik Regime* (Vintage Books, 1995) 260.
[64] George Watson, *The Lost Literature of Socialism* (Lutterworth Press, 2nd ed, 1998). Watson's book details Hitler's praise of Marx and Stalin.
[65] Stephen G Fritz, 'Reflections on Antecedents of the Holocaust' (1990) 23 *The History Teacher* 162.
[66] Ibid.

admit ... The difference between [Marxists] and myself is that I have really put into practice what these peddlers and pen-pushers have timidly begun. The whole of National Socialism is based on it. Look at the workers' sports clubs, the industrial cells, the mass demonstrations, the propaganda leaflets written specially for the comprehension of the masses: all these new methods of political struggle are essentially Marxist in origin. All I had to do is take over these methods and adapt them to our purpose.[67]

There are therefore, important commonalities between Nazism and Marxism. It is patently wrong to assume that Nazism is the polar opposite of Communism, or that the Nazis were 'reactionary capitalist counter-revolutionaries'.[68] As a matter of fact, the Nazis were committed socialists who received no support from the German industrialists, even from those who later benefited from the country's rearmament. The Krupp family, for instance, financially opposed Hitler at the 1932 German presidential election. As noted by Jonah Goldberg:

> In Germany the aristocracy and business elite were generally repulsed by Hitler and the Nazis. But when Hitler demonstrated that he wasn't going away, these same elites decided it would be wise to put down some insurance money on the upstarts. This may be reprehensible, but these decisions weren't driven by anything like an ideological alliance between capitalism and Nazism. Corporations in Germany, like their counterparts today, tended to be opportunistic, not ideological ... The Nazis rose to power exploiting anti-capitalist rhetoric they indisputably believed. Even if Hitler was the nihilist cipher many portray him

---

[67] Hermann Raushning, *Hitler Speaks* (Thornton Butterworth, 1939) 134.
[68] Karl Dietrich Bracher, *The German Dictatorship: The Origins, Structure and Effects of National Socialism* (Praeger Publishing, 1970) 10.

as, it is impossible to deny the sincerity of the Nazi rank and file who saw themselves as mounting a revolutionary assault on the forces of capitalism. Moreover, Nazism also emphasized many of the themes of later New Lefts in other places and times: the primacy of race, the rejection of rationalism, an emphasis on the organic and holistic – including environmentalism, health food, and exercise – and, most of all, the need to 'transcend' notions of class.[69]

By contrast, due to ideological similarities the German Communists were happily prepared to collaborate with the Nazis against the Weimar Republic. The Nazis were assisted by the Communists when the latter refused to make common cause with the Social Democrats.[70] Working under strict orders from Moscow, German Communists regarded the Social Democrats as their main political opponents, not the Nazis. This position weakened any possible resistance against the Nazis and ultimately paved the way for their takeover from which the Communists themselves became one its first victims. In the clash between Social Democrats, Communists and Nazis, Pipes comments:

> Moscow consistently favored the Nazis over the Social Democrats, whom it called 'social Fascists' and continued to regard as its principal enemy. In line with this reasoning, it forbade the German Communists to collaborate with the Social Democrats. In the critical November 1932 elections to the Reichstag (Parliament), the Social Democrats won over 7 million votes and the Communists 6 million: their combined votes exceeded the Nazi vote by 1.5 million. In terms of parliamentary seats, they gained between them 221, against the Nazi 196.

---

[69] Goldberg (n 55) 58-59.
[70] Richard Pipes, *Communism: A History of the Intellectual and Political Movement* (Phoenix Press, London, 2003) 75.

Had they joined forces, the two left-wing parties would have defeated Hitler at the polls and prevented him from assuming the chancellorship. It thus was the tacit alliance between the Communists and the National Socialists that destroyed democracy in Germany and brought Hitler to power.[71]

Instead of joining forces with the German Social Democrats, those Communists voted together with the Nazis as a parliamentary bloc or coalition, in the Reichstag (ie, the German Parliament).[72] Their mutual support was more vividly illustrated on 12 September 1932, when Hermann Göring, a leader of the Nazi Party and one of the primary architects of the Nazi police state in Germany, with the support of the Communist MPs, was elected as President of the Reichstag. They helped him orchestrate a vote of no confidence in the von Papen government by which a Nazi-Communist coalition voted together to dismiss the cabinet.[73] As Paul Johnson points out,

> The only notice the Communists usually took of the Nazis was to fight them in the streets, which was exactly what Hitler wanted. There was something false and ritualistic about these encounters ... In the *Reichstag*, they combined to turn debates into riots. Sometimes collaboration went further ... Blinded by their absurd political analysis, the Communists actually wanted a Hitler government, believing it would be a farcical affair, the prelude to their own seizure of power.[74]

Whereas Communism embraces *International Socialism*, the Nazis aspired to a *National Socialism* that despised anything considered

---
[71] Ibid 96.
[72] Goldberg (n 55) 77.
[73] Laurence Rees, *The Dark Charisma of Adolf Hitler: Leading Millions into the Abyss* (Ebury Press, 2013) 95.
[74] Johnson (n 17) 282.

to be "supranational". Yet, the top Nazi leadership openly admired Soviet Russia. Joseph Goebbels, the Nazi Propaganda Minister, wrote: 'The good Nazi looks toward Russia, because Russia is that country most likely to take the road to socialism with us'.[75] In a 1935 article published in *Völkischer Beobachter*, Goebbels defined his ideological movement as 'a party of revolutionary socialists'.[76] The main difference between them and the Communists, wrote Goebbels, was the internationalism of the latter as compared to the alleged nationalism of the former.[77] Still, Goebbels manifested his desire to work together with the Communists against "Jewish power in the West".[78] Such a confession at a first glance appears to be rather extraordinary. However, as F A Hayek rightly notes:

> The connection between socialism and nationalism in Germany was close from the beginning. It is significant that the most important ancestors of National-Socialism – Fitche, Rodbertus, and Lassalle – are at the same time acknowledged fathers of socialism ... From 1914 onwards there arose from the ranks of Marxist socialism one teacher after another who led, not the conservatives and reactionaries, but the hardworking labourer and idealist youth into the national-socialist fold. It was only thereafter that the tide of nationalist socialism attained major importance and rapidly grew into the Hitlerian doctrine. The war hysteria of 1914, which, just because of the German defeat, was never fully cured, is the beginning of the modern development which produced National-Socialism, and it was largely with the assistance of old socialists that it rose during this period.[79]

---

[75] Fritz (n 65) 162.
[76] Max H Kele, *Nazis and Workers: National Socialist Appeals to German Labor 1919–1933* (University of North Carolina Press, 1972) 93.
[77] Ibid 92.
[78] Rees (n 73) 66.
[79] Friedrich A Hayek, *The Road to Serfdom* (Routledge, 2008) 173.

The Nazi leadership claimed to forge a socialist unity among the German *Volk*. The word *Volk* means 'people' in a sense of racial community. According to Hitler, Germany should be a nation of "one race" whereby all class distinctions would be abolished. Ethnic Germans should not be blamed for their troubles since these would be corrected in a classless society ruled by a charismatic leadership that would emerge from them and be able to gain power at the head of a national revolution.[80]

According to the late Brazilian ambassador, J O de Meira Penna, the Nazi concepts of 'lebensraum' and 'holocaust' was first developed by the young Karl Marx in his early journalistic writings. As a young journalist, wrote Meira Penna, Marx stimulated notions of German imperialism by advocating the concepts of life as a "fight for space" and of national community as "evolving organic body".[81] Marx's closest collaborator in the foundation of modern Communism, Friedrich Engels, made significant attempts to "biologise" the German sense of national identity, which is now widely condemned because of its undeniable affiliations with National Socialism.[82] Engels thought that Poland had no reason to exist and anticipated the Nazi holocaust by arguing that the Germans should exterminate the Slav populations (Russians, Czechs, Croats, etc). For example, in an article published by *Neue Rhenische Zeitung* on 14 February 1849, Engels stated:

---

[80] Rees (n 73) 31.
[81] See J O de Meira Penna, *A Ideologia do Século XX: Ensaios Sobre o Nacional Socialismo, o Marxismo, o Terceiro-Mundismo e a Ideologia Brasileira* (Editora Nórdica, 2nd ed, 1994). J O de Meira Penna (1917-2017) was a Brazilian classical liberal writer and diplomat. He was one of the exponents of Brazilian classical liberalism, the Austrian School of Economies, and an active member of the Mont Pelerin Society.
[82] Rod Burgess, 'The Concept of Nature in Geography and Marxism' (1978) 10 *Antipode* 1.

To the sentimental phrases about brotherhood which are being offered here on behalf of the most counter-revolutionary nations of Europe, we reply that hatred of Russians was and still is the primary revolutionary passion among Germans; that since the revolution hatred of Czechs and Croats has been added, and that only the most determined use of terror against these Slav peoples can we ... safeguard the revolution. We know where the enemies of the revolution are concentrated, viz in Russia and the Slav regions of Austria, and no fine phrases, no allusions to an undefined democratic future for these countries can deter us from treating our enemies as enemies. If Slav nationality leaves the revolution entirely out of account, then we know what we have to do.[83]

This racist notion derived from Marxism played a decisive role in Hitler's decision to conquer and occupy "living spaces" in the East, either by enslaving or by entirely replacing the local populations. Hitler also adhered to an economic theory advocated by Marx called the "shrinking markets" theory.[84] As a consequence, he believed that the German economy was too dependent on exports and that such dependence was a mistake. The German dictator had in mind a planned economy that would make Germany "independent" of the world economy by conquering a new *lebensraum* ('vital space') in the East. Indeed, Hitler's self-professed admiration for the Marxist economic system, as superior in his opinion to the capitalist one, is found several of his statements. In this context, addressing a small circle in August 1942, the Nazi dictator stated that Stalin was 'quite a genius', for whom 'one has to have unqualified respect', especially

---

[83] Friedrich Engels, 'Democratic Pan-Slavism', *Neue Rheinische Zeitung* (14 February 1849).
[84] Rainer Zitelmann, 'Why Hitler Wanted to Conquer New "Lebensraum" in the East', *The National Interest* (Web Article, 21 June 2021).

given his all-encompassing economic planning.[85]

Curiously, the Soviet Union under Stalin actively collaborated with Nazi Germany against Poland through the Ribbentrop-Molotov pact, which was signed in August 1939.[86] Moscow even returned to Germany all the German Communists who had sought refuge in Soviet Russia.[87] The Nazi leadership found in their Soviet counterparts 'a ready model for the one-party state'.[88] Back in those days Communist parties all over the world advocated peace with Nazi Germany at any price and actively sabotaged the war-effort when it came. At the height of the Nazi invasion of France, Maurice Thorez, head of the French Communist Party, broadcast from Moscow begging the French troops not to resist the Nazi occupation of the country.[89]

One of the factors exploited by Hitler in the elections of 1932-33 was the general fear among the Germans of a Communist takeover. One of the reasons Hitler aimed first to eliminate the socialist Left, before he went after the conservative Right, was the undeniable Nazi appeal to the same social base as well as the adoption of similar language and categories.[90] At this time Germany was ideologically split apart as popular support not only for the Nazis but also for the Communists dramatically increased.[91] By January 1932, more than six million

---

[85] Ibid.
[86] Caenegem (n 62) 279.
[87] Pipes (n 27) 76.
[88] Ibid.
[89] Johnson (n 15) 361.
[90] Goldberg (n 55) 70.
[91] Rees (n 73) 80. Rees then gives the account of Fritz Arlt, an 18-year old student in the 1930s. Influenced by an older brother, Fritz initially flirted with Communism but eventually decided to embrace National Socialism once he felt that the 'solidarity' of International Socialism across national boundaries wasn't possible because of the individual countries effectively pursuing their own national self-interests.

Germans were unemployed and when a German workman was unemployed 'there was only one thing left', said Johannes Zahn, a German economist, 'either he became a Communist or he became an SA man [ie, a Nazi Storm Trooper].'[92]

V MARXIST ROOTS OF MODERN GENOCIDE

The traditional goal of Marxism is to criticise the putative structures of "capitalist domination". In *Principles of Communism* Engels describes the idea of inalienable rights of the individual as a "fraudulent mask" used by the bourgeoisie to legitimise their social exploitation. Accordingly, all the most cherished values of western democracies, including basic legal rights, can be summarily dismissed and denounced as ideological tools for the legitimisation of an exploitive economic system.[93] Along with Engels, Marx contended that the notion of fundamental rights works as an ideological tool designed to perpetuate "bourgeois" power and to make people more selfish. What Marx had in mind was explained by George Lukacs:

> The 'freedom' of the men who are alive now is the freedom of the individuals isolated by the fact of property which both reifies and is itself reified. It is a freedom vis-à-vis the other (no less isolated) individuals. A freedom of the egoist, of the man who cuts himself off from others.[94]

Coming from this premise the western liberal tradition of inalienable rights is interpreted as a class-conditioned construct. These basic

---
[92] Ibid 80.
[93] J M Kelly, *A Short History of Western Legal Theory* (Oxford University Press, 1992) 330.
[94] Georg Lukacs, *History and Class Consciousness* (MIT Press, 1971) 315.

rights are not deemed to fixed in nature but evolving throughout the progressive stages of social warfare. In *On the Jewish Question*, Marx boldly proclaimed: 'The so-called rights of man are simply the rights of egoistic man, of man separated from other men and from the community'. Accordingly, these basic rights are no longer deemed unalienable but established on the basis of separating people; 'it is the right of such separation'.[95] If power is taken on the basis of rights, Marx wrote in *The German Ideology*, then:

> [R]ight, law, etc, are merely the symptoms of other relations upon which state power rests. The material life of individuals ... their mode of production and form of interest which eventually determine each other ... this is the real basis of the State ... The individuals who rule in these conditions, besides having to constitute their power in the form of the State, have to give their will ... a universal expression as the will of the State, as law.[96]

On this basis, can Marxists truly believe in the universality of human rights? Of course, Marx did not think so and argued that the 'narrow horizon of bourgeois right' should be entirely eliminated. He contended that no right can have a practical meaning apart from its historical context, implying that a given right only exists if it is socially recognised insofar as the ruling class creates it, accepts it, and eventually allows it to exist.[97] As noted by François Furet:

> What Marx criticized about the bourgeoisie was the very idea of the rights of man as a ... foundation of society'. Marx regarded such rights as 'a mere cover for the individualism governing

---

[95] Bottomore (n 22) 24-26.
[96] Kark Marx and Friedrich Engels, *A Critique of the German Ideology* (Progress Publishers, 1968).
[97] E A Harriman, 'Review of Enemy Property in America' (1924) 1 *The American Journal of International Law* 202.

capitalist economy. The problem was that capitalism and modern liberty were both subject to the same rule, that of freedom or plurality ... and he impugned it in the name of 'humanity's lost unity'.[98]

In addition to objecting to universal human rights, Marxism objects to objective standards of right and wrong.[99] Marx notoriously despised any such moral standards.[100] He singled out morality as invariably ideological and relative to class interests and particular modes of production.[101] In *The German Ideology* he effectively mocks such an idea as 'unscientific' and an obsolete obstacle to the advancement of revolutionary socialism. Instead, he elevated such a revolution as the only "basic good" to be achieved at all costs. To achieve it, Marx concluded, the pre-conditions of morality and circumstances of justice would have to be entirely eliminated.[102] This amounts in practice to an attack on non-relativist ethics, undermining the sense of personal responsibility and duty towards an objective moral code, which was at the centre of nineteenth-century Western civilization.[103] In Marxist ideology, writes legal philosopher Michael Freeman:

> [A]ll that 'basic laws' would do is furnish principles for the regulation of conflicting claims and thus serve to promote class compromise and delay revolutionary change. Upon the attainment of communism the concept of human rights would

---

[98] Furet (n 42) 10-11.
[99] M D A Freeman, *Lloyd's Introduction to Jurisprudence* (Sweet & Maxwell, 8th ed, 2008) 1151. Objective morality is, for instance, what one finds in Christian jurisprudence and the Western legal tradition of God-given inalienable rights of the individual.
[100] Ibid.
[101] Ibid 1150.
[102] Ibid 1152.
[103] Johnson (n 17) 11.

be redundant because the conditions of social life would no longer have need of such principles of constraint. It is also clear (particularly in the writings of Trotsky) that in the struggle to attain communism concepts like human rights could be easily pushed aside – and were.[104]

This makes it possible to speculate whether the undercurrent of violence manifested by every Communist regime might represent a projection of the Marxist foundations of lawlessness or moral relativism. The disdain of communist regimes for legality is a well-known occurrence but not a mere accident. It is certainly ideologically driven. According to Krygier, the very notion that legality can be used to restrain power was entirely 'alien to Marx's thought about what law did or could do, alien to his ideals, and alien to the activities of communists in power'.[105] As also stated by Krygier, 'the writings of Marx had nothing good to say about the rule of law; it generated no confidence that law might be part of a good society; it was imbued with values which made no space for those that the rule of law is designed to protect'.[106]

Communist regimes do not answer to higher moral standards apart from the concept of 'advancing socialism'. These regimes are controlled by a small political caste who ultimately decides who shall

---

[104] Ibid 1153.
[105] Martin Krygier, 'Introduction' in Martin Krygier (ed), *Marxism and Communism: Posthumous Reflections on Politics, Society, and Law* (Rodopi, 1994) 14.
[106] Martin Krygier, 'Marxism, Communism, and Rule of Law' in Krygier (n 106) 117.

live and who shall die for becoming "socially undesirable".[107] As such, political assassinations are justified by the dogma of a new world which is coming into being, so that everything that might assist its difficult birth can be morally justifiable.[108] In Soviet Russia, for example, the regime's primary victims were the "enemies of the people", a broad category who included not only political opponents but also ethnic groups if they seemed (for equally ill-defined reasons) to threaten the Communist regime.[109] These individuals would be arrested and executed not for what they had done but for what they were socially.[110] As Stéphane Courtois points out:

> In Communism there exists a socio-political eugenics, a form of social Darwinism. ... As master of the knowledge of the evolution of social species, Lenin decided who should disappear by virtue of having been condemned to the dustbin of history. From the moment that a decision had been made on a 'scientific' basis ... that the bourgeoisie represented a stage of humanity that had been surpassed, its liquidation as a class and the liquidation of the individuals who actually or supposedly belonged to it could be justified.[111]

---

[107] As per Editorial of the Soviet newspaper, in 1918: 'We reject the old system of morality and 'humanity' invented by the bourgeoisie ... Our morality has no precedent, and our humanity is absolute because it rests on a new ideal ... To us, everything is permitted, for we are the first to raise the sword not to oppress races and reduce them to slavery, but to liberate humanity from its shackles ... Blood? Let blood flow like water! Let blood stain forever the black pirate's flag flown by the bourgeoisie, and let our flag be blood-red forever! For only through the death of the old world can we liberate ourselves from the return of those jackals!' – Nicolas Werth, 'A State Against its People: Violence, Repression and Terror in the Soviet Union' in Stephane Courtois et al, *The Black Book of Communism: Crimes, Terror, Repression* (Harvard University Press, 1999) 102.
[108] Ibid.
[109] Applebaum (n 24) xxxvi.
[110] Ibid.
[111] Stephane Courtois, 'Conclusion: Why?' in Courtois (n 107) 752.

Marxism is the application of Darwinism to social development.[112] In Darwin's model, change in nature occurs through heredity, selection and the struggle for survival. In contrast to this model of evolutionary causation, Marxist theory envisages a mechanical reading of social progress which approaches history as a series of unique events that reveal a certain directionality.[113] Pipes explained:

> The injection of evolutionary thinking into socialist theory introduced into it the element of inevitability. According to 'scientific socialism', human actions may somewhat retard or accelerate social evolution, but they cannot alter its direction, which depends on objective factors. Thus the emotional appeal to this belief is not so much different from the religious faith in the will of God, inspiring those who hold it with an unshakable conviction that no matter how many setbacks their cause may suffer, ultimate victory is assured. It would hold especial attraction for intellectuals by promising to replace spontaneous and messy life with a rational order of which they would be the interpreters and mentors.[114]

Marxism asserts that dialectical materialism describes the unfolding succession of economic systems, each with its own contradictions creating social conflict.[115] Lenin, the founder of Soviet Russia and one of Marx's most successful disciples, defined "morality" as anything that advances class struggle; whereas immoral is anything that might hinder the inexorable historical march towards Communism.

---

[112] Paul Blackledge, 'Historial Materialism: From Social Evolution to Revolutionary Politics' in Paul Blackledge and Graeme Kirkpatrick, *Historical Materialism and Social Evolution* (Palgrave Macmillan, 2002) 16.
[113] Ibid 11.
[114] Pipes (n 27) 8.
[115] Richard Overy, *The Dictators: Hitler's Germany and Stalin's Russia* (Allen Lane, 2004) 266.

This formulation gave an unlimited confidence and opportunity for individuals like him, the so-called "vanguard of the proletariat", to advance their revolutionary struggle in line of the forms of actions which are deemed the most appropriate under the existing conditions of societal development.[116]

Leon Trotsky, another Marxist revolutionary, considered Marxism 'the application of Darwinism to human society'.[117] He explained that Marx relied on the concept of 'progress' to assume that history was invariably on his side. Since history was dogmatically interpreted in light of an evolutionist prism, when Marxists talk about "moral progress" they are simply progressing 'an amoral Darwinian theory which is held to explain the genesis of moral standards and their role as weapons in the class war'.[118] Thus wrote the late British political theorist HB Acton:

> The superiority of a moral standard consists in its replacing the standards of vanquished classes, and the superiority of a classless morality consists in its having ousted all others, just as, for Darwin, the fittest are those who succeed in surviving, not those who, in some moral sense, ought to survive ... Out of the clash of classes, they supposed, superior forms of society are developed which would never have existed at all if the clashes had been mitigated or suppressed.[119]

Under the autocratic rule of Stalin, 'evolutionary Marxism became the dominant ideology of the Soviet ruling class'.[120] Stalin, one of the

---

[116] Ibid.
[117] Ibid.
[118] HB Acton, *The Illusion of the Epoch: Marxism-Leninism as a Philosophical Creed* (Liberty Fund, 1962) 188.
[119] Ibid 188.
[120] Ibid 19.

most notorious mass-murderers in human history, thought that social changes are defined by scientific laws that, as he put it in 1952, comprise 'the reflection of objective processes which take place independently of the will of man'. In *Dialectical and Historical Materialism*, an essay he published in 1938, Stalin contended: 'Everything in nature is part of an objective material world that is both completely integrated and constantly subject to change'. In sum, he claimed that changes in society emerge dialectically, an idea first used by the German philosopher GWF Hegel to describe 'the dynamic contradictions that propel all phenomena from lower to higher forms of existence'.[121]

One of the most common characteristics of every Marxist-oriented Communist regime is the principle on which murderous policies can be rationalised and justified. When power is achieved, the repressive apparatus of the Communist State can be used to hunt people down not just for what they might have done at a personal level, but due also to their "social category". Of course, once the idea of personal guilt is eliminated, governments can more easily eliminate people on grounds of race, profession, occupation, parentage, etc. There is indeed no limit to the extent to which the "enemies of the people" principle can be applied to eliminate those who are considered undesirable by the powerful political elites. Indeed, entire groups can be classified as the "enemies" and then condemned to imprisonment and slaughter. As properly stated by Paul Johnson:

> Christianity was content with a solitary hate-figure to explain evil: Satan. But modern secular faiths needed human devils, and whole categories of them. The enemy, to be plausible, had to be an entire class or race. Marx's invention of the

---

[121] Overy (n 116) 267.

'bourgeoisie' was the most comprehensive of these hate-theories and it has continued to provide a foundation for all paranoid revolutionary movements, whether fascist-nationalist or Communist-internationalist. Modern theoretical anti-Semitism was a derivative of Marxism, involving a selection (for reasons of national, political or economic convenience) of a particular section of the bourgeoisie as the subject of attack.[122]

In Communist Russia and elsewhere the realisation of the 'New Man' implies that the authorities must be prepared to sacrifice 'the sorry specimens that populate the corrupt world'.[123] With this in mind in 1921 Lenin rationalised that the great famine of 1921-22, which led to more than 5 million people dying of starvation, would be actually a "positive" thing. Instead of lamenting that tragedy and trying to remediate the situation, instead Lenin rejoiced over it and expected that this could 'strike a mortal blow against the enemy' – the Russian Orthodox Church. In a March 1922 letter addressed to the Politburo, Lenin candidly stated:

> With the help of all those starving people who are starting to eat each other, who are dying by the millions, and whose bodies litter the roadside all over the country, it is now and only now that we can – and therefore must – confiscate all church property with all the ruthless energy that we can still muster ... We must therefore amass a treasure of hundreds of millions of gold rubles ... think how rich some of these monasteries are! ...
>
> No matter what the cost, we must have those hundreds of millions of rubles. This can be carried out only at the present moment, because our only hope is the despair engendered in the masses by the famine, which will cause them to look at us

---

[122] Johnson (n 17) 117.
[123] Ibid 68.

in a favourable light or, at the very least, with indifference. I thus can affirm categorically that this is the moment to crush the ... clergy in the most decisive manner possible, and to act without any mercy at all, with the sort of brutality that they will remember for decades ...

The more representatives from the reactionary clergy and the recalcitrant bourgeoisie we shoot, the better it will be for us. We must teach these people a lesson as quickly as possible, so that the thought of protesting again doesn't occur to them for decades to come.[124]

The other great famine of 1932–34 was not like the others that similarly devastated Russia. Rather, that famine was the result of a genocidal assault by the Communist regime on the people of the countryside. Nearly 40 million peasants were affected and at least 6 million of them died as a result of that systematically perpetuated famine. While millions were left starving to death, the regime was shipping 18 million hundredweight of grains abroad.[125] As Nicolas Werth points out:

> This famine alone, with its 6 million deaths, exacted by far the heaviest toll of Stalinist repression and constitutes an extreme and previously unknown form of violence. After having been collectivized, the kolkhoz peasants of a number of the richest agricultural regions of the country (Ukraine, North Caucasus, and Black Lands) were robbed of their entire harvests, then 'punished' for having tried to resist – passively – this plundering. This punishment managed to transform the situation from one of scarcity to one of famine.[126]

---

[124] Cited in Werth (n 108) 125.
[125] Ibid 164.
[126] Nicolas Werth, 'Strategies of Violence in Stalinist USSR' in Henry Rousso (ed), *Stalinism and Nazism: History and Memory Compared* (University of Nebraska Press, 1999) 74.

Forced to hand over everything they had, and lacking the means for buying food, millions of peasants attempted to escape to the cities just to survive. On 27 October 1932, the local authorities were ordered to ban by all means necessary the large-scale departure of peasants from Ukraine and the Northern Caucasus for the towns.[127] Desperately struggling to survive, those peasants were criminalised with a range of laws which condemned them to death by starvation. Seven decades after being emancipated, those peasants were not just re-enserfed but actually enslaved and left to die by starvation. As noted by Pipes:

> Collectivization degraded the peasant more than did pre-1861 serfdom, since as a serf he had owned (in practice, if not in theory) his crops and livestock. The new status was that of a slave labourer who received the bare minimum of subsistence.[128]

In light of the foregoing, it should not surprise that the Soviet Union was the first European nation to establish concentration camps on European soil.[129] As early as October 1923, there were more than 300 of them spread all over the country. From 1929 to 1951 at least one Russian adult male in five had passed through these concentration camps. Over that same period more than 15 million Russians were brought into forced labour, with about 1.5 million dying in prison. Six million were deported because of family ties or ethnic identity. Hitler knew about such camps and was inspired by them in order to create his own concentration camps. Hence the comment in the summer of 1940 by Hitler's closest collaborator in the "Final Solution", Heinrich Himmler, that the "physical extermination of a race" was only possible through "Bolshevik methods". Also revealingly was

---

[127] Werth (n 108) 164.
[128] Pipes (n 38) 60.
[129] Ibid.

the extent to which, from the mid-1930s' up to the state of Operation Barbarossa, 'the Gestapo and the NKVD, Stalin's successor of the Cheka collaborated and exchanged information'.[130] As noted by Kaminski:

> The leaders of Soviet communism were the inventors and creators of ... the establishments called 'concentration camps' ... [They] also created a specific method of legal reasoning, a network of concepts that implicitly incorporated a gigantic system of concentration camps, which Stalin merely organized technically and developed. Compared with the concentration camps of Trotsky and Lenin, the Stalinist ones represented merely a gigantic form of implementation ... And, of course, the Nazis found in the former as well as the latter ready-made models, which they merely had to develop. The German counterparts promptly seized upon these models.[131]

Some knowledge of Soviet laws might help us understand why the peasants formed the vast majority of prisoners in those concentration camps in the 1930s.[132] For example, a law enacted on 7th August 1932 condemned anyone who took a potato from a collective plantation (kolkhoz) to either execution or being sent to such a camp for 'theft or damage of socialist property'. That legislation also criminalised an extensive number of other minor offences. A tendency was developed throughout the 1930s and 1940s to fill those concentration camps called Gulags with millions of such prisoners. Gulag, an acronym for Main Camp Administration, was the quintessential expression of the Soviet repressive system.[133] Over time the term came to mean not

---

[130] Fritz (n 65) 173.
[131] Werth (n 108) 73.
[132] Applebaum (n 24) 47.
[133] Ibid xxix.

just those camps but the entire repressive system in all its varieties of labour camps, punishment camps, women's camps and children's camps. This was consistent with the regime's understanding that 'the class enemy had to be weeded out, destroyed and smashed, without any sign of mercy'.[134]

After all, Marx himself had explicitly advised that violence formed an essential element in the socialist revolution. That being so, Lenin never quailed before the necessity to employ Terror. He had inherited from Marx an ideological justification for the use of violence. As Lenin pointed out, in 1901: 'In principle we have never renounced terror and cannot renounce it.'[135] In a 1919 lecture at the University of Moscow, Lenin argued: 'The revolutionary dictatorship of the proletariat shall be ruled, won, and maintained by the use of violence by the proletariat against the bourgeoisie, rule that is unrestricted by any laws'.[136] According to Paul Johnson,

> Lenin always insisted that Marxism was identical to absolute truth ... Believing this, and believing himself the designated interpreter ... Lenin was bound to regard heresy with even greater ferocity than he showed toward the infidel. Hence the astonishing virulence of the abuse which he constantly hurled at the heads of his opponents within the party, attributing to them the basest possible motives and seeking to destroy them as moral beings even when only minor points of doctrine were at stake. The kind of language Lenin employed, with its metaphors of the

---

[134] Vladimir Tismaneanu, 'Communism and the Human Condition: Reflections on the Black Book of Communism' (2001) 2(2) *Human Rights Review* 126.
[135] V I Lenin, *Collected Works*(Progress Publishers, 1972) vol IV, 108 cited in Johnson (n 17) 67.
[136] *The Proletarian Revolution and the Renegade Kautsky: Selected Works*, (Progress Publishers, 1951) vol II, pt 2, 41 quoted in Martyn Krygier, 'The Rule of Law' in N J Smelser and P B Baltes (eds), *International Encyclopedia of the Social & Behavioral Sciences* (Elsevier, 2001) 13404.

jungle and the farmyard and its brutal refusal to make the smallest effort of human understanding, recalls the *odium theologicum* which poisoned Christian disputes about the Trinity in the sixth and seventh centuries, or the Eucharist in the sixteenth. And of course once verbal hatred was screwed up to this pitch, blood was bound to flow eventually ... Just as the warring theologians felt they were dealing with issues which determine whether or not countless millions of souls burned in Hell for all eternity so Lenin knew that the great watershed of civilization was near, in which the future fate of mankind would be decided by History, with himself as its prophet. It would be worth a bit of blood: indeed a lot of blood.[137]

In his celebrated *Democracy and Totalitarianism*, the late French political theorist Raymond Aron discusses ideas that inspired both Marxist regimes and Hitler's National Socialism. According to him, the notion that Nazism and Communism are polar opposites is actually a socialist fallacy that hides the fact they are actually "kindred spirits". There is indeed a remarkable convergence of ideas between these two totalitarian ideologies. Such convergence was made evident even before the German Communists joined forces with the Nazis and eventually the Soviet Union turned into a military ally of the Nazis in the outbreak of World War II. Aron's conclusion is quite simple: all the crimes, oppression and terror ever inflicted by these communist regimes are deeply inspired and directly motivated by Marxist theory.[138]

---

[137] Johnson (n 17) 56.
[138] Raymond Aron, *Democracy and Totalitarianism* (Frederick A Praeger, 1969).

VI FINAL CONSIDERATIONS

Marx believed that laws are the product of class oppression, and that legality would have to disappear with the advent of the communist utopia. In practice, the Marxist concept of 'proletarian dictatorship' turned out to be a dictatorship of a few privileged individuals over the rest of the population, especially manual labourers and peasants.[139] Marxist-oriented regimes amount to the dictatorship of a small ruling elite over all the other remaining social classes.[140] Accordingly, Marxism creates an entire justification for such political tyranny to be carried out by those who conveniently describe themselves the vanguard of the proletariat. In a society where the State machinery owns all the productive wealth, those who control it automatically become the absolute masters over everyone and everything. Or, in the words of Leon Trotsky: 'In a country where the sole employer is the state, opposition means slow starvation'.[141]

Marxism and National Socialism effectively share important assumptions drawn from Darwinism on the primary of struggle and the centrality of conflict. Both ideologies conceive the same enemies in common, particularly liberal capitalism, and both think in terms of collective guilt as well as a claim to utopianism and social transformation. Just as importantly, both claim to be "progressive". As noted by history professor Stephan Fritz, 'Hitler saw himself as did Marx, acting in accordance with the historical and scientific laws, as cold, impersonal, modern and progressive'.[142] Also according to

---

[139] Pipes (n 38) 15.
[140] Ibid 39.
[141] Leon Trotsky, 'Chapter 11: Whither the Soviet Union?' in Leon Trotsky, *The Revolution Betrayed* (1936) <https://www.marxists.org/archive/trotsky/1936/revbet/ch11.htm>.
[142] Aron (n 139) 173.

Professor Fritz, Hitler's anti-Semitism was directly rooted in Marxism. Marx developed a thesis of the rapacious Jews which appears to be saying that the Jews had poisoned European society. As he points out, 'Hitler's nightmare of the "Jewish bacillus" infecting German society and driving a class wedge between workers and employers in order to accomplish an "inner Judaization" of the German people paralleled Marx's notion of the Jewish attitude to money slowly transforming bourgeois society'.[143]

Once a Communist regime is conceived there is no limit to the extent to which Marxist principles can be used to justify tyranny and oppression. For example, entire categories of individuals can be conveniently classified as the "enemies of the people" and so to be condemned to imprisonment or slaughter on grounds of skin colour, racial origins, and even nationality. According to Paul Johnson, 'there is no essential moral difference between class-warfare and race-warfare, between destroying a class and destroying a race. Thus the modern practice of genocide was born.'[144] As mentioned, the Nazis were not the first in the business of mass deportations, concentration camps and extermination of whole groups according to objective criteria.[145] Indeed, the "class murder" of the Bolsheviks was the logical model for the late "race murder" of the Nazis. The model for the Nazis was Stalin's Gulag and Hitler simply did to the Jews what the Red Terror had done to its enemies in the 1920s and 1930s.

Above all, history shows beyond reasonable doubt that the class genocide carried out by Marxist regimes across the globe has been aided and abetted by a Darwinian theory that encourages totalitarian

---

[143] Ibid 163.
[144] Johnson (n 17) 71.
[145] Fritz (n 65) 161.

policies that turn out to be profoundly genocidal. In the past century alone, Marxist-oriented Communist regimes and Communist-inspired revolutionary movements have killed no less than 120 million people. It is not so much that self-professed Marxists have not paid enough attention to policies which have eventually turned out to be genocidal. Instead, the problem is that Marxism itself contains the ideological seed which prepares the entire mindset for the elimination of all those who are deemed socially "undesirable" and in a massive scale.

This article has also established that Marx nurtured a visceral hatred of other ethnic groups apart from the Jews. If these BLM activists really believed in equality and abhorred all forms of racial discrimination, then they would condemn the appalling racism of this great icon of the New Left, who often called one of his political adversaries a "Jewish Nigger". Arguably, those who vandalise or demand the removal of statues on racial grounds should for consistency's sake demand the removal of the bust of Marx from a place of honour in the Smithsonian Design Museum. As Allie Stuckey correctly puts it: 'If the statue-topplers were really doing so because of outrage over slavery, they would be outraged by Marx and Lenin, whose ideas led to the objectification and slaughter of millions. But they don't – they worship them'.[146]

Of course, this is all part of an ongoing assault on Western values, history and tradition. Arguably, the "useful idiots" who empower these BLM leaders by destroying the statues of people who fought against inequality are simply too ignorant and brain-washed to know what they are doing. As for the true ideologues, of course, they know

---

[146] See Bill Muehlenberg, 'The Cancel Culture: Crucify Him Again', *CultureWatch* (Web Page, 23 June 2020).

exactly what they are doing. Black lives are not important unless they are useful to advance the Marxist cause and score a few political gains. One can safely assume that these disciples of Marx are not really interested in equality but are hypocritical virtue signallers who appeal to racial issues to advance their own diabolical Marxist agenda.

General Articles

10

Natural Law, God, and Human Dignity

ROBERT P GEORGE*

ABSTRACT

What is natural law? What is the natural law theory of human dignity? What is the natural law theory of human rights? Do ideas and beliefs about God and the divine will play a role in natural law theory? What, if anything, distinguishes the "new natural law theory" from other theories or accounts of natural law? How are natural law theories similar to, and different from, other leading theories of morality, especially utilitarian and Kantian ("deontological") theories? Are natural law theories fundamentally concerned with rules or with virtues? This essay addresses all of these questions.

I INTRODUCTION: KNOWLEDGE OF NATURAL LAW

One's knowledge of natural law, like all knowledge, begins with experience, but it does not end or even tarry there. Knowing is an activity – an intellectual activity, to be sure, but an activity nonetheless. We all have the experience of knowing. But to know is not merely to experience. Knowing is a complex and dynamic activity. The role

---

* McCormick Professor of Jurisprudence, Princeton University.

of experience in the activity of knowing is to supply data on which the inquiring intellect works in the cause of achieving understanding. Insights are insights into data. They are, as Bernard Lonergan brilliantly demonstrated by inviting readers to observe and reflect on their own ordinary intellectual operations, the fruit of a dynamic and integrated process of experiencing, understanding, and judging.[1]

So what are the data supplied by experience that are at the foundation of practical judgments, that is to say, insights that constitute knowledge of natural law? They are the objects of intelligibly choice worthy possibilities – possibilities that, inasmuch as they provide reasons for acting of a certain sort (that is, more-than-merely-instrumental reasons), we grasp as opportunities.

In our experience of true friendship, for example, we grasp by what is ordinarily an effortless exercise of what Aristotle called 'practical reason' the intelligible point of having and being a friend. We understand that friendship is desirable not merely for instrumental reasons – indeed a purely instrumental friendship would be no friendship at all – but above all for its own sake. Because we grasp the intelligible point of having and being a friend, and we understand that the fundamental point of friendship is friendship itself, and certainly not goals extrinsic to friendship to which the activity of friendship is merely a means, we reasonably judge that friendship is intrinsically valuable. We know that friendship is a constitutive and irreducible aspect of human well-being and fulfillment, and that *precisely as such* friendship provides a reason for action of the sort that requires for its intelligibility as a reason no further or deeper reason or subrational motivating factor to which it is a means.

---

[1] See Bernard J F Lonergan, *Insight: A Study in Human Understanding* (Philosophical Library, 1955).

The same is true if we shift our focus to our experience of the activity of knowing itself. In our experience of wonder and curiosity, of raising questions and devising strategies for obtaining correct answers, of executing those strategies by carrying out lines of inquiry, of achieving insights, we grasp (by what is again for most people in most circumstances an effortless exercise of practical reason) the intelligible point of searching for truth and finding it. We understand that knowledge, though it may have tremendous instrumental value, is intrinsically valuable as well. To be attentive, informed, thoughtful, clear headed, careful, critical, and judicious in one's thinking and judging, is to be inherently enriched in a key dimension of human life. We reasonably judge the activity of knowing, then, to be an intrinsic (or 'basic') human good – a constitutive and irreducible aspect of our flourishing as human beings. Like friendship and a number of other types of activity, knowledge provides a reason for choice and action that requires for its intelligibility as a reason no further or deeper reason or subrational source of motivation to which it is a means.

Knowledge of natural law, then, is not innate. It does not swing free of experience or of the data provided by experience. Even when it is easily achieved, practical knowledge (ie, knowledge of natural law) is an achievement. It is the fruit of insights which, like all insights, are insights into data, data which are supplied by experience. The insight – the knowledge – that friendship or knowledge itself is intrinsically humanly fulfilling is ultimately rooted in our elementary experiences of the activities of friendship and knowing. Apart from those experiences, there would be no data on which practical reason could work to yield understanding of the *intelligible point* (and, thus, of the value) of friendship or knowledge and the judgment that these activities are intrinsic fulfillments of the human person and, as such, objects of the primary principles of practical reason and basic precepts of natural law.

Of course, not all practical knowledge is, strictly speaking, moral knowledge (that is, knowledge of moral norms or their correct applications), though all moral knowledge is practical knowledge – it is (or centrally includes) knowledge of principles for the direction and guidance of action.[2] Yet knowledge of the most fundamental practical principles directing action towards the basic human goods and away from their privations, though not strictly speaking knowledge of moral norms, is foundational to the generation and identification of such norms. That is because moral norms are principles that guide our actions in line with the primary practical principles integrally conceived. Norms of morality are specifications of the integral directiveness or prescriptivity of the various aspects of human well-being and fulfillment that together constitute the ideal of integral human flourishing. So, if the first principle of practical reason is, as Aquinas says, 'the good (*bonum*) is to be done and pursued, and the bad (*malum*) is to be avoided,'[3] then the first principle of morality is that 'one ought always to choose and otherwise will in a way that is compatible with a will towards integral human fulfillment.'[4] And just as the first principle of practical reason is specified, as Aquinas makes clear, by identifying the various irreducible aspects of human well-being and fulfillment (namely, friendship, knowledge, aesthetic

---

[2] Inasmuch as the first and most basic practical principle directing human choosing towards what is intelligibly worthwhile and away from its privations are foundational to the identification of moral knowledge, there is a sense in which knowledge of those principles is incipiently moral knowledge.

[3] St Thomas Aquinas, *Summa Theologiae*, I-II, Q 94, A 2.

[4] On the first principle of morality and its specifications, see John Finnis, Joseph M Boyle and Germain Grisez, *Nuclear Deterrence, Morality and Realism* (Clarendon Press, 1987) 281-87.

appreciation, skillful performance, religion, and so forth), so too the first principle of morality is specified by identifying the norms of conduct that are entailed by an open-hearted love of the human good (that is, the good of human persons) taken as a whole.

II NATURAL LAW AND HUMAN RIGHTS

A natural law theory is a critical reflective account of the constitutive aspects of the well-being and fulfillment of human persons and the communities they form. Such a theory will propose to identify principles of right action – moral principles – specifying the first and most general principle of morality, namely, that one should choose and act in ways that are compatible with a will towards integral human fulfillment. Among these principles are respect for rights people possess simply by virtue of their humanity – rights which, as a matter of justice, others are bound to respect, and governments are bound not only to respect but, to the extent possible, also to protect.

Natural law theorists of my ilk understand human fulfillment – the human good – as variegated. There are many irreducible dimensions of human well-being. This is not to deny that human nature is determinate. It is to affirm that our nature, though determinate, is complex. We are animals, but rational. Our integral good includes our bodily well-being, but also our intellectual, moral, and spiritual well-being. We are individuals, but friendship and sociability are constitutive aspects of our flourishing.

By reflecting on the basic goods of human nature, especially those most immediately pertaining to social and political life, natural law theorists propose to arrive at a sound understanding of principles of justice, including those principles we call human rights. In light of what I've already said about how natural law theorists understand human nature and the human good, it should be no surprise to learn that natural law theorists typically reject both strict individualism and collectivism. Individualism overlooks the intrinsic value of human sociability and tends mistakenly to view human beings atomistically. It fails to account for the <u>intrinsic</u> value of friendship and other aspects of human sociability, reducing all relationships to <u>means</u> by which the partners collaborate with a view to more fully or efficiently achieving their individual goals and objectives. Collectivism compromises the dignity of human beings by tending to instrumentalise and subordinate them and their well-being to the interests of larger social units – the community, the state, the *volk*, the fatherland, the *führer*, the future communist utopia. Individualists and collectivists both have theories of justice and human rights, but they are, as I see it, highly unsatisfactory. They are rooted in important misunderstandings of human nature and the human good. Neither can do justice to the concept of a human **person**, that is, a rational animal who is a locus of intrinsic value (and, as such, an *end-in-himself* who may never legitimately treat himself or be treated by others as a mere *means*), but whose well-being intrinsically includes relationships with others and membership in communities (beginning with the family) in which he or she has, as a matter of justice, both rights and responsibilities.

Human rights exist (or obtain) if it is the case that there are principles of practical reason directing us to act or abstain from acting in certain ways out of respect for the well-being and the dignity of persons whose legitimate interests may be affected by what we do. I certainly believe that there are such principles. They cannot be overridden by considerations of utility. At a very general level, they direct us, in Kant's phrase, to treat human beings always as ends and never as means only. When we begin to specify this general norm, we identify important negative duties, such as the duty to refrain from enslaving people. Although we need not put the matter in terms of 'rights,' it is perfectly reasonable, and I believe helpful, to speak of a <u>right</u> against being enslaved, and to speak of slavery as a violation of human <u>rights</u>. It is a right that people have, not by virtue of being members of a certain race, sex, class, or ethnic group, but simply by virtue of our humanity.[5] In that sense, it is a **human** right. But there are, in addition to negative duties and their corresponding rights, certain positive duties. And these, too, can be articulated and discussed in the language of rights, though here it is especially important that we be clear about by whom and how a given right is to be honoured.

Sometimes it is said, for example, that education or health care is a human right. It is certainly not unreasonable to speak this way; but much more needs to be said if it is to be a meaningful statement. Who is supposed to provide education or health care to whom? Why should those persons or institutions be the providers? What place should the provision of education or health care occupy on the list of social and political priorities? Is it better for education and health care to be provided by governments under socialised systems, or by private

---

[5] By the phrase 'our humanity,' I refer more precisely to the nature of humans as rational beings. The nature of human beings is a rational nature. So in virtue of our human nature, we human beings possess a profound and inherent dignity. The same would be true, however, of beings other than humans whose nature is a rational nature, if indeed there are such beings. In the case of humans, even individuals who have not yet acquired the immediately exercisable capacities for conceptual thought and other rational acts, and even those who have temporarily or permanently lost them, and, indeed, even those who do not possess them, never possessed them, and (short of a miracle) never will possess them, possess a rational nature.

providers in markets? These questions go beyond the application of moral principles. They require prudential judgment in light of the contingent circumstances people face in a given society at a given point in time. Often, there is not a single, uniquely correct answer. The answer to each question can lead to further questions; and the problems can be extremely complex, far more complex than the issue of slavery, where once a right has been identified its universality and the basic terms of its application are fairly clear. Everybody has a moral right not to be enslaved, and everybody an obligation as a matter of strict justice to refrain from enslaving others; governments have a moral obligation to respect and protect the right and, correspondingly, to enforce the obligation.[6]

What I've said so far will provide a pretty good idea of how I think we ought to go about identifying what are human rights. But in each case the argument must be made, and in many cases there are complexities to the argument. One basic human right that almost all natural law theorists would say belongs in the set is the right of an innocent person not to be directly killed or maimed. This is a right that is violated when someone makes the death or injury of another

---

[6] Having said this, I do not want to suggest a sharper difference than can be justified between positive and negative rights. Even in the case of negative rights, it is sometimes relevant to ask how a right should be honoured and who, if anyone, has particular responsibility for protecting it. Moreover, it can be the case that there is not a uniquely correct answer to questions about what place the protection of the right should occupy on the list of social priorities. Consider, for example, the right not to be subjected to assault or battery. While it is obvious that individuals have the obligation to respect this right, and equally obvious that governments have an obligation to protect persons within their jurisdiction from those who would violate it, different communities reasonably differ not only as to the means or mix of means that are used to protect persons from assault and battery, but also as to the level of resources they allocate to protect people against violations of the right. I am grateful to Allen Buchanan for this point.

person the precise object of his action. It is the right that grounds the norm against targeting non-combatants, even in justified wars, and (in my view) against elective abortion, euthanasia, the killing of hostages, and so forth. Of course, in the case of abortion, some people argue that human beings in the embryonic or fetal stages of development do not yet qualify as persons and so do not possess human rights; and in the case of euthanasia, some argue that permanently comatose or severely cognitively disabled people do not (or no longer) qualify as rights-bearers. I think that these claims are mistaken, but I won't here go into my reasons for holding that the moral status of a human being does not depend on his or her age, size, stage of development, or condition of dependency. I've presented this argument in great detail in numerous places, including my book *Embryo: A Defense of Human Life* (with Christopher Tollefsen).[7] Here I will say only that people who do not share with me the conviction that human beings in early stages of development and in cognitively disabled conditions are rights-bearers, may nevertheless agree that **whoever** qualifies as a person is protected by the norm against the direct killing of the innocent.

III NATURAL LAW AND HUMAN DIGNITY

The natural law understanding of human rights I am here sketching is connected with a particular account of human dignity. Under that account, the natural human capacities for reason and freedom are fundamental to the dignity of human beings – the dignity that is protected by human rights. The basic goods of human nature are the goods of a rational creature – a creature who, unless impaired or

---

[7] Robert P George and Christopher Tollefsen, *Embryo: A Defense of Human Life* (Witherspoon Institute Press, 2nd ed, 2011).

prevented from doing so, naturally develops and exercises capacities for deliberation, judgment, and choice. These capacities are God-like – albeit, of course, in a limited way. In fact, from the theological vantage point they constitute a certain sharing – limited, to be sure, but real – in divine power. This is what is meant, I believe, by the otherwise extraordinarily puzzling Biblical teaching that man is made in the very image and likeness of God. But whether or not one recognises Biblical authority or believes in a personal God, it is true that human beings possess a power traditionally ascribed to divinity – namely, genuine agency: the power of an agent to cause what the agent is not caused to cause. This is the power to envisage a possible reality or state of affairs that does not now exist or obtain, to grasp the intelligible point the value – of bringing it into being, and then to act by choice (and not merely by impulse or on instinct, as a brute animal might) to bring it into being. That state of affairs may be anything from the development of an intellectual skill or the attainment of an item of knowledge, to the creation or critical appreciation of a work of art, to the establishment and maintenance of a friendship. Its moral or cultural significance may be great or, far more commonly, comparatively minor. What matters for the point I am now making is that it is a product of human reason and freedom. It is the fruit of deliberation, judgment, and choice.

Of course, a further question will present itself to the mind of anyone who recognises the God-likeness of our capacities for rationality and freedom, capacities that are immaterial (and, thus, one can say spiritual) in nature. That question is whether beings capable of such powers could exist apart from a divine source and ground of their being. So one finds in the affirmation of these powers a decisive ground for the rejection of materialism, and one discerns the basis of an openness to, and even the roots of an argument for, theism. But more on that point later.

Now, what about the authority for this view of human nature, the human good, human dignity, and human rights? Natural law theorists are interested in the intelligible reasons people have for their choices and actions. We are particularly interested in reasons that can be identified without appeal to any authority apart from the authority of reason itself. This is not to deny that it is often reasonable to recognise and submit to religious or secular (eg, legal) authority in deciding what to do and not do. Indeed, natural law theorists have made important contributions to understanding why and how people can sometimes be morally bound to submit to, and be guided in their actions by, authority of various types. Think, for example, of Yves Simon's work[8] and John Finnis'.[9] But even here, the special concern of natural law theorists is with the **reasons** people have for recognising and honouring claims to authority. We do not simply appeal to authority to justify authority.

One might then ask whether human beings are in fact rational in anything more than an instrumental sense. Can we discern any intelligible reasons for human choices and actions? Everybody recognises that some ends or purposes pursued through human action are intelligible at least insofar as they provide means to other ends. For example, people work to earn money, and their doing so is perfectly rational. Money is a valuable means to a great many important ends. No one doubts its instrumental value. The question is whether some ends or purposes are intelligible as providing *more than merely instrumental* reasons for acting. Are there intrinsic, as well as instrumental, goods? Skeptics deny that there are intelligible ends or purposes that make possible rationally *motivated* action. Natural law theorists, by contrast,

---

[8] See Yves R Simon, *A General Theory of Authority* (University of Notre Dame Press, 1962).
[9] See John Finnis, *Natural Law and Natural Rights* (Oxford University Press, 2nd ed, 2011) 59–127.

hold that friendship, knowledge, critical aesthetic appreciation, and certain other ends or purposes are intrinsically valuable. They are intelligibly "choice worthy," not simply as means to other ends, but as ends-in-themselves. They cannot be reduced to, nor can their intelligible appeal be accounted for exclusively in terms of, emotion, feeling, desire, or other subrational motivating factors. These basic human goods are constitutive aspects of the well-being and fulfillment of human persons and the communities they form, and they thereby provide the foundations of moral judgments, including our judgments pertaining to justice and human rights.

Of course, there are plenty of people today who embrace philosophical or ideological doctrines that deny the human capacities I maintain are at the core of human dignity. They adopt a purely instrumental and essentially non-cognitivist view of practical reason (eg, Hume's view that reason is nothing more than 'the slave of the passions')[10] and argue that the human experience of deliberation, judgment, and choice is illusory. The ends people pursue, they insist, are ultimately given by non-rational motivating factors, such as feeling, emotion, or desire. 'The thoughts are to the desires,' Hobbes has taught them to suppose, 'as scouts and spies, to range abroad and find the way to the thing desired.'[11] Truly rationally motivated action is impossible for creatures like us. There are no more-than-merely-instrumental reasons for action – no basic human goods. Now, if proponents of this non-cognitivist and subjectivist view of human action are right, then it seems to me that the entire business of ethics is a charade, and human dignity is a myth. But I don't think they are right. Indeed, I don't think

---

[10] David Hume, *A Treatise of Human Nature* (Clarendon Press, 1888) bk II, pt III, § III, 415.

[11] Thomas Hobbes, *Leviathan* (Hackett Publishing Company, 1994) 41.

that they can give any account of the norms of rationality to which they must appeal in making the case against reason and freedom that is consistent with the denial that people are capable of more-than-merely-instrumental rationality and true freedom of choice. I do not deny that emotion figures in human action – obviously it does, and on many occasions it (or other subrational factors) does the main work of motivation. But I maintain that people can have, and often do have, basic reasons for their actions – reasons provided by ends they understand as humanly fulfilling *and desire precisely as such*. These ends, too, figure in motivation.[12]

IV HUMAN IMPERFECTION AND MORAL FAILING

Now, if I and other natural law theorists are correct in affirming that human reason can identify human rights as genuine grounds of obligation to others, how can we explain or understand widespread failures to recognise and respect human rights and other moral principles? As human beings, we are rational animals; but we are imperfectly rational. We are prone to making intellectual and moral mistakes and capable of behaving grossly unreasonably – especially when deflected by powerful emotions that run contrary to the demands of reasonableness. Christians have a name for this: sin. And another name: fallenness. We suffer weakness of will and darkness of intellect. Even when following our consciences, as we are morally bound to do, we can go wrong. A conscientious judgment may nevertheless be

---

[12] I offer a detailed critique of Humean skepticism, and a defense of my own view of the relationship of reason to feeling, emotion, and the like, in Robert P George, *In Defense of Natural Law* (Oxford University Press, 1999) ch 1. See also, John Finnis, *Reason in Action* (Oxford University Press, 2011) ch 1 ('Practical Reason's Foundations').

erroneous. Of course, sometimes people fail to recognise and respect human rights because they have self-interested motives for doing so. In most cases of exploitation, for example, the fundamental failing is moral, not intellectual. In some cases, though, intellectual and moral failures are closely connected. Selfishness, prejudice, partisanship, vanity, avarice, lust, ill-will, and other moral delinquencies can, in ways that are sometimes quite subtle, impede sound ethical judgments, including judgments pertaining to human rights. Whole cultures or subcultures can be infected with moral failings that blind large numbers of people to truths about justice and human rights; and ideologies hostile to these truths will almost always be both causes and effects of these failings. Consider, for example, the case of slavery in the antebellum American south. The ideology of white supremacy was both a cause of many people's blindness to the wickedness of slavery, and an effect of the exploitation and degradation of its victims.

V NATURAL LAW AND GOD

Let us turn now to the question of God and religious faith in natural law theory. Most, but not all, natural law theorists are theists. They believe that the moral order, like every other order in human experience, is what it is because God creates and sustains it as such. In accounting for the intelligibility of the created order, they infer the existence of a free and creative intelligence – a personal God. Indeed, they typically argue that God's creative free choice provides the only ultimately satisfactory account of the existence of the intelligibilities humans grasp in every domain of inquiry.[13]

Natural law theorists do not deny that God can reveal moral truths

---

[13] See, eg, John Finnis, *Religion and Public Reasons* (Oxford University Press, 2011), especially ch 1 ('Darwin, Dewey, Religion, and the Public Domain').

and most believe that God has chosen to reveal many such truths. However, natural law theorists also affirm that many moral truths, including some that are revealed, can also be grasped by ethical reflection apart from revelation. They assert, with St Paul, that there is a law 'written on the hearts' even of the Gentiles who did not know the law of Moses – a law the knowledge of which is sufficient for moral accountability. So the basic norms against murder and theft, for example, though revealed in the Decalogue, are knowable even apart from God's special revelation.[14] The natural law can be known by us, and we can conform our conduct to its terms, by virtue of our natural human capacities for deliberation, judgment, and choice. The absence of a divine source of the natural law would be a puzzling thing, just as the absence of a divine source of any and every other intelligible order in human experience would be a puzzling thing. An atheist's puzzlement might well cause him to re-consider the idea that there is no divine source of the order we perceive and understand in the universe. It is far less likely, I think, to cause someone to conclude that our perception is illusory or that our understanding is a sham, though that is certainly logically possible.

The question then arises: Can natural law – assuming that there truly are principles of natural law – provide some measure of common moral and even political ground for people who do not agree on the existence or the nature of God and the role of God in human affairs? In my view, anybody who acknowledges the human capacities for reason and freedom has good grounds for affirming human dignity and basic human rights. These grounds remain in place whether or not one adverts to the question: "Is there a divine source of the moral order

---

[14] See Aquinas (n 3) I–II, Q 91, art 2, Q 100, art 1.

whose tenets we discern in inquiry regarding natural law and natural rights?" I happen to think that the answer to this question is "yes," and that we should be open to the possibility that God has revealed himself in ways that reinforce and supplement what can be known by unaided reason. But we do not need agreement on the answer, so long as we agree about the truths that give rise to the question, namely, that human beings, possessing the God-like (literally <u>awesome</u>) powers of reason and freedom, are bearers of a profound dignity that is protected by certain basic rights.

So, if there is a set of moral norms, including norms of justice and human rights, that can be known by rational inquiry, understanding, and judgment even apart from any special revelation, then these norms of natural law can provide the basis for a common understanding of human rights – an understanding that can be shared even in the absence of religious agreement. Of course, we should not expect consensus. There are moral skeptics who deny that there are moral truths. There are religious fideists who hold that moral truths cannot be known apart from God's special revelation. And even among those who believe in natural law, there will be differences of opinion about its content and implications for certain issues. So it is, I believe, our permanent condition to discuss and debate these issues, both as a matter of abstract philosophy and as a matter of practical politics.

VI CHALLENGES TO NATURAL LAW PHILOSOPHY

It is sometimes regarded as an embarrassment to natural law thinking that some great ancient and medieval figures in the natural law tradition failed to recognise – and indeed have even denied – human rights that are affirmed by contemporary natural law theorists, and even regarded as fundamental. Consider, for example, the basic human right to religious liberty. This right was not widely acknowledged in the past, and was even denied by some prominent natural law theorists. As Professor Finnis has observed, they wrongly believed that a wide conception of liberty in matters of faith presupposed religious relativism or indifferentism, or entailed that religious vows were immoral or non-binding, or the comprehensive subservience of ecclesial communities to the state.[15] It is interesting that when the Catholic Church put itself on record firmly in support of the right to religious freedom in the document *Dignitatis Humanae* of the Second Vatican Council, it presented both a natural law argument and an argument from specifically theological sources. The natural law argument for religious liberty is founded on the obligation of each person to pursue the truth about religious matters and to live in conformity with his conscientious judgments.[16] This obligation is, in turn, rooted in the proposition that religion – considered as conscientious truth-seeking regarding the ultimate sources of meaning and value – is a crucial dimension of human well-being and fulfillment. It is among the basic human goods that provide rational motivation for our choosing. The right to religious liberty follows from the dignity of man as a conscientious truth-seeker.

This right, and other human rights, are denied and attacked today from various quarters, and in many parts of the world are routinely violated. The ideological justification for their denial and violation can be religious or secular. In some parts of the world, religious freedom and other basic human rights are denied in the name of theological truth.

---

[15] See John Finnis, *Moral Absolutes: Tradition, Revision, and Truth* (The Catholic University of American Press, 1991) 26 and n 50.

[16] Second Vatican Council, *Declaration on Religious Liberty: Dignitatis Humanae* (1965) § 2–3, reprinted in Vatican Council II, *The Conciliar and Post Conciliar Documents* (Austin Flannery, OP ed, rev ed, 1988) 800-801.

In other parts of the world, the threats are from secularist ideologies. Where secularist ideologies are liberal in form, it is often claims to an overarching right to autonomy (or a corrupted version of the true right to have one's equal dignity respected) that are asserted to justify choices, actions, and policies that natural law theorists believe are unjust and undermine the common good. If the natural law view of these matters is correct, then it is moral failings conspiring with intellectual errors that sustain ideologies that compromise human rights. In a certain sense, the failings are at opposite poles. Yet, from a natural law vantage point partisans of the competing ideologies make valid criticisms of each other. Militant religious fundamentalists, for example, harshly condemn the decadent features of cultures in which the "me-generation" ideology of "if it feels good, do it" flourishes. On the other side, ideological liberals denounce the subjugation of women and the oppression of religious dissenters where religious fundamentalism holds sway.

As natural law theorists see it, threats to human dignity and human rights exist because all of us, as human beings, are imperfectly reasonable and imperfectly moral. To put it in Christian terms, we are fallen creatures, sinners. At the same time, hope exists because we really do possess the capacities for reasonableness and virtue; truth – including moral truth – is accessible to us and has its own splendor and powerful appeal. We will never, in this vale of tears, grasp the truth completely or in a way that is entirely free from errors. Nor will we fully live up to the moral truths we grasp. But just as we made progress by abolishing the evil of slavery, by ending legally sanctioned racial segregation in the United States and elsewhere, by recognising the right to religious freedom, and by turning away from the eugenics policies once favored by so many respectable people, natural law theorists hope that we can make progress, and reverse declines, in other areas.

Of course, people who reject the natural law understanding of human dignity and human rights will differ from natural law theorists on questions of what constitutes progress and decline. From certain religious fundamentalist points of view, the type of religious freedom defended by natural law theorists will be regarded as licensing heresy and religious irresponsibility. Natural law ideas will be seen as just a rhetorically toned down form of western liberal secularism. By contrast, from the perspective of certain secularist ideologies, natural law ideas about abortion, sexuality, and other hot-button moral issues will be regarded as intolerant and oppressive – a philosophically gussied-up form of religious fundamentalism. In the end, though, natural law ideas – like the ideas proposed by any school of thought, be it religious or secularist – will have to stand or fall on their merits. Anyone who wonders whether they are sound or unsound will have to consider the arguments offered in their support and the counterarguments advanced by their critics.

VII THE "NEW" NATURAL LAW THEORY

As I observed earlier, there are competing accounts of natural law and natural rights among people who are or have been regarded, or who regard themselves, as natural law theorists. I have in various writings associated myself with what is sometimes called, the 'new natural law theory' of Germain Grisez and John Finnis. But whether there is anything much that is really new in our approach is questionable. The core of what Grisez, Finnis, and I say at the level of fundamental moral theory is present, at least implicitly, in the writings of Aristotle, Thomas Aquinas, and other ancient, medieval, and early modern thinkers. Some commentators have insisted that what we say is fundamentally new (and, from the point of view of our critics within the natural law camp, wrongheaded) because we are resolute about respecting the distinction between description and prescription and avoiding the fallacy (as we see it) of proposing to derive normative judgments from *purely* factual premises *describing* human nature. An example of the fallacy is the putative inference of the value of knowledge from the fact that human beings are naturally curious and desire to know. But here we are being faithful to the methodological insights and strictures of Aquinas. Contrary to what is sometimes supposed, he recognised that what would later come to be called 'the naturalistic fallacy' is indeed a fallacy, and was far stricter about avoiding it even than was David Hume, who is sometimes credited with "discovering" it.[17]

If, standing on the shoulders of Aristotle and Aquinas, we have been able to contribute something significant to the tradition of natural law theorising, it is founded on Professor Grisez's work showing how what he calls 'modes of responsibility' follow as implications of the integral directiveness of the most basic principles of practical reason – principles that direct human action towards basic human goods and away from their privations. The modes of responsibility are intermediate in their generality between the first and most general principle of morality ("always choose in ways that are compatible with a will towards integral human fulfillment") and fully specified moral norms that govern particular choices. The modes include the Golden Rule of fairness and the Pauline Principle that acts that are in themselves evil (*mala in se*) may not be done, even for the sake of good consequences. They begin to specify what it means to act (or to fail to act) in ways that are compatible with a will oriented positively (or, at least, not negatively) towards the well-being of all human beings in

---

[17] See Finns (n 9) 33-48.

all the respects in which human beings can flourish – integral human fulfillment.

Our account of the modes of responsibility helps to make clear the ways that natural law theories are both like and unlike utilitarian (and other consequentialist) approaches to morality, on the one hand, and Kantian (or "deontological") approaches on the other. Like utilitarian approaches, and unlike Kantian ones, natural law theories are fundamentally concerned with human well-being and fulfillment and, indeed, identifying principles directing our choosing towards basic human goods, and away from their privations, as the starting points of ethical reflection. Unlike utilitarian approaches, however, they understand the basic forms of human good (as they figure in options for morally significant choosing) as incommensurable in ways that render senseless the utilitarian strategy of choosing the option that overall and in the long run promises the net best proportion of benefit to harm (however 'benefit' and 'harm' may be understood and defined). Natural law theorists share with Kantians the rejection of aggregative accounts of morality that regard the achievement of sufficiently good consequences or the avoidance of sufficiently bad ones as justifying choices that would be excluded by application of moral principles in ordinary circumstances. Unlike Kantians, however, they do not believe that moral norms can be identified and justified apart from a consideration of the integral directiveness of the principles of practical reason directing human choosing towards what is humanly fulfilling and away from what is contrary to human well-being. Natural law theorists do not believe in purely "deontological" moral norms. Practical reasoning is reasoning about both the 'right' and the 'good,' and the two are connected. The content of the human good shapes moral norms inasmuch as such norms are entailments of the basic aspects of human well-being and fulfillment considered integrally.

Such a view presupposes, of course, the possibility of free choice – that is, choosing which is the pure product neither of external forces nor internal but subrational motivating factors, such as sheer desire. So a complete theory of natural law will include an account of principles of practical reason, including moral norms, as principles for the rational guidance of free choices, and a defense of free choice as a genuine possibility. This entails the rejection of strict rationalism, according to which all phenomena are viewed as caused. It understands human beings – some human beings, at least sometimes – as capable of causing realities that they bring into existence <u>for reasons by free choices</u>. On the natural law account of human action, freedom and reason are mutually entailed. If people were not really free to choose among options – free in the sense that nothing but the choosing itself settles what option gets chosen – truly rationally motivated action would not be possible. Conversely, if rationally motivated action were not possible, the experience we have of freely choosing would be illusory.[18]

Another feature of the natural law account of human action that is stressed by those of us who are regarded as "new" natural law theorists is the set of distinctions between various modes of voluntariness. We understand morality as fundamentally a matter of rectitude in willing. In sound moral judgments and upright choices and actions, the will of the agent is oriented positively towards the human good integrally conceived. In choosing and acting, one is not, of course, pursuing every human good – that is not possible – but one is pursuing

---

[18] In defense of freedom of choice (or freedom of the will) as described here, see Joseph M Boyle, Jr, Germain Grisez and Olaf Tollefsen, *Free Choice: A Self-Referential Argument* (University of Notre Dame Press, 1976).

at least one basic human good well, and if one is choosing and acting in a morally upright way one is respecting the others. Yet, is it not obvious that many upright choices – choices of good ends sought by morally good means – have some bad consequences? For example, do we not know with moral certainty that by constructing a system of highways on which drivers of automobiles are authorised to drive at a speed of, say, 65 miles per hour we are permitting a circumstance to exist in which several thousand people each year will be killed in driving accidents? Indeed, we do. But according to the natural law understanding of human action, there is a real and sometimes morally critical distinction between intending harm to a basic human good (and thus to a person, since human goods are not mere abstractions, but are aspects of the well-being of flesh-and-blood human beings) and accepting foreseen harm as a *side-effect* of an otherwise morally justified choice. One can intend harm in two different ways: as an end-in-itself or as a means to some other end. One intends harm as an end when, for example, one seeks to injure or kill someone out of hatred, anger, or some similarly powerful emotion. One intends harm as a means when, for example, one seeks to kill a person in order to recover on the victim's life insurance policy. The key thing to see is that intending death (whether as end or means) is distinct from accepting death as a side-effect (even if the side effect is clearly foreseen, as we foresee, for example, the deaths of motorists and passengers on the highways in ordinary accidents).[19]

---

[19] Although the distinction between intending, on the one hand, and accepting bad side effects, on the other, is often pertinent to moral evaluation on a natural law account, one should not suppose that it is impossible to violate moral norms in accepting side effects. On the contrary, one may behave *unjustly*, for example, in accepting bad side effects, even where one has not run afoul of the norm against intending, say, the death or injury of an innocent human being. See, eg, George (n 12) 106.

VIII CONCLUSION: NATURAL LAW AND MORAL VIRTUE

Let me conclude with one more proposition stressed by natural law theorists, namely the fact (or in any event what we believe to be the fact) that by our choices and actions we not only alter states of affairs in the world external to us, but also at the same time determine and constitute ourselves – for better or worse – as persons with a certain character.[20] Recognition of this self-shaping or "intransitive" quality of morally significant choosing leads to a focus on virtues as habits born of upright choosing that orient and dispose us to further upright choosing – especially in the face of temptations to behave immorally. People sometimes ask: Is natural law about rules or virtues? The answer from the point of view of the "new natural law" theory is that it is about *both*. A complete theory of natural law identifies norms for distinguishing right from wrong as well as habits or traits of character whose cultivation disposes people to choose in conformity with the norms and thus compatibly with a what we might call, borrowing a phrase from Kant, a good will, viz, a will towards integral human fulfillment.

---

[20] See, eg, Aristotle, *Nicomachean Ethics*, 1113b5–13.

11

Psychological Harm and the Prohibition of 'Conversion Therapy'

ANDREW S KULIKOVSKY*

ABSTRACT

Prohibition of 'conversion therapy' relating to homosexual and transgender people is being considered by Australian jurisdictions, with some (Queensland and ACT) already having passed legislation. What constitutes 'conversion therapy' is broadly defined and those in favour of prohibition claim that it is not only ineffective but extremely harmful. This paper examines these claims, their underlying assumptions, and the applicable body of scientific literature regarding 'conversion therapy' and concludes that the assumptions and claims of harm behind the call for prohibition are without foundation. Moreover, the disconnect between such claims and the lived experience of particular individuals and the community has led prohibition ideologues and legislators to become increasingly intolerant and authoritarian.

---

* PhD candidatate, Charles Stuart University.

I INTRODUCTION

Many recent legislative programs and corporate policies have been concerned with eliminating or reducing 'harm' – from drug injecting rooms, to child protection responses, to anti-bullying campaigns. That a person may be needlessly harmed – either physically or psychologically – is viewed as entirely unacceptable. Therefore, if harm can be substantially reduced or avoided altogether, government intervention through legislation and law enforcement agencies is warranted and justified.

But what exactly does 'harm' entail? What is the meaning and scope of the term? What behaviour may be regarded as harmful? What legal tests are involved? Breaching 'anti-harm' laws could have serious consequences, so defining what behaviour is and is not harmful is paramount. Legislative provisions and other enforceable policies must be clear in order to provide legal certainty.

This paper will examine how claims of 'harm' by various advocates have been used to influence legislators and the general public regarding the prohibition of so-called 'conversion therapy' (or 'reparative therapy') – the attempt to convert a person from homosexuality to heterosexuality, or to dissuade a person who expresses a gender identity different from their biological sex.

There is a popular, politically correct view that to do anything other than affirm non-traditional sexual identities and relationships will cause serious psychological harm to those involved, to the point where they may even resort to taking their own lives.

But are such claims justified? And what impact will the prohibition of these allegedly 'harmful' debates and activities have on child protection measures, parental rights, and religious teaching?

Note that the following discussion uses the term 'homosexual' to refer to gay, lesbian, and bisexual orientations, and 'transgender' refers to someone who identifies as a gender different from their birth sex.

II DATA COLLECTION AND IDEOLOGICAL BIAS

Assessing the truth claims of those advocating for particular positions on controversial and politically charged issues is fraught with danger. Advocates for a particular position will cite research and studies that support their views, and either conveniently ignore contradictory research or dismiss it out of hand as flawed and invalid. Objectivity in social science research often gives way to ideological bias. As Sarewitz has pointed out:

> Alarming cracks are starting to penetrate deep into the scientific edifice. They threaten the status of science and its value to society. And they cannot be blamed on the usual suspects – inadequate funding, misconduct, political interference, an illiterate public. Their cause is bias, and the threat they pose goes to the heart of research.[1]

Many – if not most – studies on sexual orientation and transgenderism suffer from serious methodological flaws, the most common being the use of volunteers who are ideologically and politically motivated to provide responses favourable to their own agenda. Moreover, the sample sizes are often very small.

In addition, there are instances where researchers, editors and publishers

---

[1] D Sarewitz, 'Beware the Creeping Cracks of Bias' (2012) 485 *Nature* 149.

have been hounded and bullied into withdrawing, disavowing, or minimising the significance of otherwise sound research merely because it goes against the prevailing politically correct opinion. For example, Hindawi Limited, the publisher of *Depression Research and Treatment*, felt the need to 'express concern' about a paper they published by D Paul Sullins titled 'Invisible Victims: Delayed Onset Depression among Adults with Same-Sex Parents' after several readers raised concerns about this article, despite the fact that the proper review process was followed and the journal editor and peer reviewers believed the article worthy of publication.[2]

Similarly, psychiatrist Robert Spitzer published a paper in 2003 in the *Archives of Sexual Behavior* reporting that homosexuals and lesbians had found 'conversion therapy' beneficial, and some had experienced a transformation from a predominantly homosexual orientation to a predominantly heterosexual orientation.[3] However, after publication Spitzer received an 'outpouring of hatred' from LGBT activists who had once viewed him as a hero. Having spoken with Spitzer, Dutch psychologist Gerard van den Aardweg reported that he had 'nearly broken down emotionally after terrible personal attacks from militant

---

[2] See 'Expression of Concern on "Invisible Victims: Delayed Onset Depression among Adults with Same-Sex Parents"' [2017] *Depression Research and Treatment* 4981984:1, 1. Note that Sullins had already published a thorough refutation of the criticisms raised against his research: D P Sullins, 'Response to: Comment on 'Invisible Victims: Delayed Onset Depression among Adults with Same-Sex Parents" [2016] *Depression Research and Treatment* 68343618:1-3.

[3] Robert L Spitzer, 'Can Some Gay Men and Lesbians Change Their Sexual Orientation? 200 Participants Reporting a Change from Homosexual to Heterosexual Orientation' (2003) 32 *Archives of Sexual Behavior* 403. Spitzer was instrumental in pushing for the American Psychiatric Association to remove homosexuality as a mental disorder from their *Diagnostic and Statistical Manual of Mental Disorders*.

gays and their supporters.'[4] After nearly a decade of abuse, at the age of 80 and suffering from Parkinson's Disease, Spitzer capitulated to the pressure and publicly apologized 'for making unproven claims of the efficacy of reparative therapy.' Spitzer asked the editor of the journal to retract the article, but the editor, Ken Zucker, refused to do so, telling Spitzer 'You didn't falsify the data. You didn't commit egregious statistical errors in analyzing the data. You didn't make up the data' and that a mere change in how the author interprets their own data is not grounds for retraction.[5]

It is important to note that Spitzer has never said that his observations and impressions about the reported changes in his subjects were false, or that they had lied to him. Indeed, his article examined this hypothesis, but Spitzer was convinced his subjects were reliable and telling the truth. Therefore, Spitzer's disavowment of his study does not change his results, and his 'apology' has no bearing on their validity.

There has also been cases of *ad hominem* and slanderous attacks on the credibility of some researchers. For example, a PhD dissertation by Toby Canning cited a 2001 paper by Stacey and Biblarz claiming that Paul Cameron, an opponent of same-sex parenting, 'was not only denounced by the American Sociological Association, but was also expelled from the American Psychological Association for willfully misrepresenting research on the punitive effects of gay male parenting on children' and referred to the psychological community's

---

[4] Interview with Gerard van den Aardweg, 'Frail and aged, a giant apologizes', *MercatorNet* (Web Article, 31 May 2012).
[5] Alice Dreger, 'How to Ex an "Ex-Gay" Study', *Psychology Today* (Web Article, 12 April 2012).

condemnation of his 'unethical practices.'⁶ However, none of these claims are true and when Cameron challenged Canning and the dissertation assessment committee members on the accuracy of that statement, a correction was inserted into the dissertation copy stating:

> Paul Cameron was not expelled from the American Psychological Association or the American Sociological [sic], nor is there any evidence that he 'willfully misrepresented research'. Toby Canning and his dissertation committee (Malcolm Gray, Bob Jacobs, Cyd Strickland, and Thomas Vail) sincerely regret these inaccuracies. We acknowledge that Dr Cameron's extensive research on homosexuality and homosexual parents (eg, 38 articles listed on PubMed) appears in peer-reviewed journals.⁷

In light of the above, this paper will treat the results of any research that is based on self-selected subjects and self-reporting without any controls or validation as methodologically flawed and inherently unreliable due to a high degree of probability of being subject to bias.

III PROHIBITION OF 'CONVERSION THERAPY'

A *What constitutes 'conversion therapy'?*

The common perception of such therapies is that of coercive surgical, hormonal, pharmacological, behavioural, or psychoanalytic treatments aimed at forcibly altering the sexual desires of patients. This approach has rightly been condemned by both psychiatrists and

---

⁶ Walter R Schumm, 'Sarantakos's research on same-sex parenting in Australia and New Zealand: Importance, substance, and corroboration with research from the United States' (2015) 4 *Comprehensive Psychology* 1, 23 n 8.

⁷ As cited in Ibid n 8.

religious groups, and the overwhelming consensus is that the approach is ineffective, harmful, and unethical.[8] Indeed, the prevalence of this approach has been exaggerated, and it is not clear to what extent such practices were employed, and whether they were employed at all in Australia.[9] In addition, the perception that religious 'conversion therapy' involves the exorcism of demons or some medieval ritual is without foundation.[10]

'Conversion therapies' developed and employed by the 'ex-gay movement' and adopted by religious groups were based on popular self-help practices, behavioural and psychoanalytic practices derived from clinical psychotherapy, and spiritual activities. Typical methods included 'Alcoholics Anonymous'-style accountability groups, individual and group counselling, and psychoanalytical activities and counselling aimed at discovering possible reasons or causes of a person's orientation/identification. These counselling and support group activities are usually augmented with spiritual activities (prayer, scripture reading, and fasting) aimed at examining and discovering possible spiritual reasons or causes of a person's orientation/identification, as well as addressing those reasons or causes on a spiritual level (spiritual healing and deliverance).[11]

From an evangelical Christian perspective, change in sexual orientation is possible, and feelings of desire to identify as a gender other than one's biological sex can be substantially diminished, if not virtually eliminated. In this sense, 'conversion therapy' is a means to facilitate

---
[8] Timothy W Jones, et al, 'Preventing Harm, Promoting Justice: Responding to LGBT Conversion Therapy in Australia' (Report, Human Rights Law Centre, La Trobe University, 2018) 3.
[9] Ibid 72-73.
[10] Ibid 13.
[11] Ibid.

such changes. It is a program of therapy involving three parties: (1) a person seeking change; (2) a person helping and facilitating change (pastor, counsellor, psychologist, or psychiatrist); and (3) the Holy Spirit. This is not a clinical or mechanical procedure that can be applied to any person, but must be tailored to each individual's specific history, circumstances, and needs, and the success or effectiveness of the therapy will depend on the skill of the provider, the willingness and commitment of the person seeking treatment, and, possibly, supernatural intervention. Moreover, the treatment's success or effectiveness does not necessarily need to result in 100% conversion from homosexuality or feelings of being trapped in the wrong body – especially in the short to medium term. As with any therapy, 'conversion therapy' is a process, and may take many years. Yet, any treatment that leads to a reduction in such desires and feelings may be regarded as effective.

Nevertheless, legislative definitions of what constitutes 'conversion therapy' are broad and vague. The Queensland legislation defines it as 'treatments and practices that attempt to change or suppress a person's sexual orientation or gender identity.'[12]

The Australian Capital Territory ('ACT') legislation defines 'conversion practice' as any 'treatment or other practice the purpose, or purported purpose, of which is to change a person's sexuality or gender identity.'[13]

The Victorian Government's legislation[14] defines it as 'a practice or conduct directed toward a person' – regardless of the person's consent

---

[12] Explanatory Notes, Health Legislation Amendment Bill 2019 (Qld) 4.
[13] *Sexuality and Gender Identity Conversion Practices Act 2020* (ACT) s 7.
[14] *Change or Suppression (Conversion) Practices Prohibition Act 2021* (Vic).

– 'on the basis of the person's sexual orientation or gender identity' and 'for the purpose of (i) changing or suppressing their sexual orientation or gender identity; or (ii) inducing the person to change or suppress, their sexual orientation or gender identity of the person.' (s 5(1)). The Act's definition of 'practice' (s 5(3)) includes healthcare practices, religious practices, and referrals to others to perform any such practices. The definition of religious practice includes (but is not limited to) 'a prayer based practice, a deliverance practice or an exorcism.' Moreover, the Explanatory Notes state that the intention is 'to capture a broad range of conduct, including, informal practices, such as conversations with a community leader that encourage change or suppression of sexual orientation or gender identity.'[15]

All the current legislation includes a subsection identifying practices that are *not* considered 'conversion therapies': (a) assisting a person undergoing gender transition; (b) assisting a person considering a gender transition; (c) assisting a person to express their gender identity; (d) providing acceptance, support or understanding; or (e) facilitating a person's coping skills, social support or identity exploration and development.[16]

In any case, these definitions cover a wide range of seemingly innocuous practices performed by a variety of people and groups including not only healthcare providers but parents, teachers, counsellors, and priests/pastors, religious schools, and religious institutions.

---

[15] Explanatory Notes, Change or Suppression (Conversion) Practices Prohibition Bill 2020 (Vic) 5.

[16] Health Legislation Amendment Bill 2020 (Qld) s 28(2); *Sexuality and Gender Identity Conversion Practices Act 2020* (ACT) s 7(2); *Change or Suppression (Conversion) Practices Prohibition Act 2021* (Vic) s 5(2). Note that the Victorian legislation includes an additional condition that the conduct must be 'supportive of or affirms a person's gender identity or sexual orientation' but does not specify which gender identity or sexual orientation must be supported where an individual is confused or unsure about their identity or orientation.

B *Claims*

Transgender advocate, Dr Michelle Telfer, has argued that psychological practices that attempt to realign a person's gender identity with "their sex assigned at birth" (ie conversion or reparative therapies) 'lack efficacy, are considered unethical and may cause lasting damage to a child or adolescent's social and emotional health and wellbeing.'[17]

A joint report by the Human Rights Law Centre and La Trobe University in 2018 ('HLRC-La Trobe Report') noted the lack of scholarly research on religious 'conversion therapy' in Australia and that international research 'is largely confined to psychological studies on the effectiveness of various treatments.'[18] The researchers interviewed a small group of homosexual and transgender people who had undergone some form of religious conversion activity. Participants claimed that

> [I]t was not just the trauma associated with particular therapies or the cumulative effects of being subject to such therapies over many years that caused lasting harm. It was also the ways in which conversion therapy messaging was embedded in all aspects of the culture and day-to-day practices of their faith communities.[19]

The report relays the participants' accounts of how they were treated by their faith communities, and the alleged psychological harm they experienced as a result. It goes on to criticise the churches' 'welcoming but not affirming' approach as 'insidious' and condemns the traditional

---

[17] Michelle Telfer et al, *Australian Standards of Care and Treatment Guidelines for Trans and Gender Diverse Children and Adolescents, Version 1.2* (The Royal Children's Hospital, Melbourne, 2020) 5.
[18] Jones et al (n 8) 7.
[19] Ibid 29.

Christian view that homosexual practices are sinful[20] and accuses churches of 'disguising its anti-LGBT ideology and reorientation efforts in the language of spiritual healing, mental health and religious liberty.'[21]

The HLRC-La Trobe Report recommends Australian governments ban 'conversion therapies.' In response, Victorian Premier Daniel Andrews announced that his government would introduce legislation to ban homosexual 'conversion therapy' – 'an evil practice … bigoted quackery…practices from the dark ages...' Andrews went on to describe it as 'a most personal form of torture, a cruel practice that perpetuates the idea that LGBTI people are in some way broken.'[22] The Victorian Government's aim is to eliminate so far as possible any change or suppression practice, to protect and promote the rights described in the Victorian Charter of Human Rights and Responsibilities, and to ensure each person – regardless of sexual orientation and gender identity – feels welcome and valued.[23]

The Queensland government has already passed legislation (*Health Legislation Amendment Bill 2019* (Qld)) 'prohibiting conversion therapy … to protect the Queensland LGBTIQ community from the harm caused by conversion therapy' because:

> There is no evidence of any benefits from conversion therapy, nor that sexual orientation or gender identity can be changed through therapeutic or other interventions. To the contrary, clinical and social science research has produced overwhelming

---

[20] Ibid 17.
[21] Ibid 4.
[22] Daniel Andrews, 'Statement On Conversion Therapy' (Media Release, 3 February 2019).
[23] *Change or Suppression (Conversion) Practices Prohibition Act 2021* (Vic) s 3(1).

evidence that conversion therapy is psychologically harmful and correlated with higher rates of suicidality, self-harm and other adverse health outcomes. Many professional and expert bodies, including the Australian Psychological Association, Australian Medical Association and World Health Organization, formally oppose the use of conversion therapy and acknowledge that these practices are harmful and unethical.[24]

The Bill's Explanatory Notes defines 'gender identity' as 'a broad term that encompasses a person's internal and individual experience of gender, including the person's personal sense of the body and how they express their gender to themselves and others,'[25] and argues that the ban is justified because 'conversion therapies' amount to a form of 'torture and cruel, inhuman or degrading treatment' as stated in the *Human Rights Act 2019* (Qld) and the *International Covenant on Civil and Political Rights*.[26]

Indeed, the Australian Labor Party's national policy platform declared that the Party accepts the scientific evidence that any attempt to change a person's sexual orientation or gender identity is 'both false and harmful.' The ALP policy included a plan to not just ban all types of so-called 'conversion therapies' but also to prohibit mere 'claims' that sexual orientation or gender identity can change. Moreover, their policy treats 'conversion therapies' as 'serious psychological abuse' and a form of 'domestic violence' if conversion attempts occur within the family – presumably by parents.[27]

---

[24] Explanatory Notes, Health Legislation Amendment Bill 2019 (Qld) 4.
[25] Ibid 8.
[26] Ibid 9.
[27] Australian Labor Party, *A Smart, Modern, Fair Australia* (2018) 193. As a result of a campaign by the Australian Christian Lobby, the ALP have now backed away from these policies.

C What constitutes harm?

In *On Liberty*, John Stuart Mill famously declared that 'the only purpose for which power can be rightfully exercised over any member of a civil community, against his will, is to prevent harm to others.'[28] According to the *Oxford English Dictionary*, 'harm' primarily refers to the inflicting of physical injury, but psychologists have rightly pointed out that harm also extends to emotional or psychological injury. The common law has always imposed prohibitions and penalties on physical abuse, but legislators have, for some time now, rightly sought to impose similar prohibitions and penalties for psychological and emotional abuse.

The *Oxford English Dictionary* definition reflects the common *outcome-based* definition of harm, ie an action must have objectively negative consequences for it to be harmful. However, Holtug has noted the problem of scope when determining if some action is harmful.[29] For example, if some people find homosexuality offensive, does this mean they are psychologically harmed, and thus legalisation of homosexuality should not be permitted as it results in harm? To view mere disagreements and objections to one's moral convictions as being harmful seems absurd, and Holtug's point is that 'not all negative effects on people are to be considered harms in the relevant sense.'[30]

Therefore, harm has commonly been construed in moral terms ie it must involve an actual wrongdoing. This means that abusing someone

---

[28] John Stuart Mill, *The Basic Writings of John Stuart Mill* (Random House, 2002) 11.
[29] Nils Holtug, 'The Harm Principle' (2002) 5 *Ethical Theory and Moral Practice* 357, 364.
[30] Ibid 364.

physically or psychologically amounts to actual harm, whereas being offended by homosexual acts, or by the publication of Salman Rushdie's *The Satanic Verses* does not because no one was actually wronged.[31] Of course, this raises the question of which acts (or omissions) constitute moral wrongs? In the absence of a universally agreed moral theory, we will have to be content with a definition comprising the violation of another's legal or human rights.

Although there is no contention regarding physical abuse as wrong and thus an actual harm, psychological abuse is a different story. According to the American Psychiatric Association's *Diagnostic and Statistical Manual of Mental Disorders* ('DSM-5'), psychological abuse involves:

> [V]erbal or symbolic acts with the potential to cause psychological harm (eg, berating or humiliating the person; interrogating the person; restricting the person's ability to come and go freely; obstructing the person's access to assistance; threatening the person; harming or threatening to harm people or things that the person cares about; restricting the person's access to or use of economic resources; isolating the person from family, friends, or social support resources; stalking the person; trying to make the person think that he or she is crazy).[32]

Regarding the psychological abuse of children, DSM-5 states:

> Child psychological abuse is nonaccidental verbal or symbolic acts by a child's parent or caregiver that result, or have reasonable potential to result, in significant psychological harm to the

---

[31] Ibid 387.
[32] American Psychiatric Association, *Diagnostic and Statistical Manual of Mental Disorders* (American Psychiatric Association Publishing, 5th ed, 2013) 722 ('DSM-5').

child ... Examples of psychological abuse of a child include berating, disparaging, or humiliating the child; threatening the child ... coercing the child to inflict pain on himself or herself; and disciplining the child excessively (ie, at an extremely high frequency or duration, even if not at a level of physical abuse) through physical or nonphysical means.[33]

Australian jurisdictions have echoed the above definitions in their respective child protection legislation.[34] It is important to note that the legislation of most jurisdictions explicitly or implicitly recognise that mere exposure of a child or young person to physical or psychological abuse directed at another person is also a potential cause of psychological harm.

Yet, in relation to 'conversion therapy' or public discussion and criticism of homosexuality and transgenderism, the standard for what constitutes 'harm' is much lower. To fail to affirm an individual's gender identity or sexual preference is tantamount to psychological abuse. Merely questioning someone's life choices may cause psychological distress, and praying for someone who has unwanted sexual feelings and desires is no different to coercive clinical treatment with drugs or electric shocks.

Unfortunately, as shown below, there has been a growing tendency for policy makers to adopt what Holtug calls a 'top-down' approach where some acts are characterised *a priori* as harmful – despite the absence

---

[33] Ibid 719.
[34] See *Children and Young People Act 2008* (ACT) s 342; *Children and Young Persons (Care and Protection) Act 1998* (NSW) s 71(1); *Care and Protection of Children Act 2007* (NT) s 15; *Child Protection Act 1999* (Qld) s 9; *Children and Young People (Safety) Act 2017* (SA) s 17; *Children, Young Persons and Their Families Act 1997* (Tas) s 3(1); *Children, Youth and Families Act 2005* (Vic) s 162(1); *Children and Community Services Act 2004* (WA) s 28.

of any wrongdoing – and this justifies government intervention to prevent or limit such acts.[35]

Various politicians, activists, and media personalities have simply asserted that public debates and discussions around policy issues concerning homosexuality, transgenderism and gender identity will expose those struggling with their sexuality or sexual identity to emotional and psychological distress, and thus, cause them psychological harm.[36] Similarly, employing 'conversion therapy' is viewed as forcing a person to deny their true identity and thus hinder their emotional and psychological development.[37] But are such claims justified?

D Can sexual orientation and 'gender identity' change?

Ironically, the critical factor behind the acceptance of homosexuality by the wider community as a valid and normative sexual expression and the recognition of homosexual rights in legislation has been the claim that homosexuals "are born that way" ie same-sex attraction is part of their genetic make-up, and therefore cannot be changed. Indeed, this point played a central role in US Supreme Court case of *Obergefell v Hodges* which sought to strike down all state laws defining marriage as 'the union of one man and one woman.' Kennedy J declared: 'Only in more recent years have psychiatrists and others recognized that sexual orientation is both a normal expression of human sexuality and immutable.'[38]

---

[35] Nils Holtug (n 29) 377-378.
[36] Telfer et al (n 17) 5.
[37] Andrews (n 22)
[38] *Obergefell et al v Hodges, Director, Ohio Department of Health et al*, 576 US 8 (Kennedy J) (2015).

However, Kennedy J's assertion has no scientific foundation. According to the American Psychiatric Association's *Handbook*, '[W]e are far from identifying potential genes that may explain not just male homosexuality but also female homosexuality.'[39] Nor is some same-sex sexuality biologically determined and some not: 'The inconvenient reality ... is that social behaviors are always jointly determined' by nature, nurture, and opportunity.[40]

Yet all current legislation banning 'conversion therapy' presupposes that an individual's sexual orientation cannot be changed and that one's chosen or preferred gender identity is not a disorder or disease, and therefore does not need fixing.[41]

In any case, opponents of 'conversion therapy' have created a strawman by asserting that therapists and counsellors claim they can guarantee their clients a change from 100% homosexual to 100% heterosexual. This assertion completely misrepresents 'conversion therapy' in two ways: (1) no therapist or counsellor for any condition can 'guarantee' that every client will achieve success, and no practitioner of 'conversion therapy' would make such a claim; (2) conversion with respect to sexual orientation can refer to any degree of change in sexual attraction, sexual behaviour or sexual self-identification. Therefore, if a client experiences any significant reduction in homosexual attractions or behaviours, or increase in heterosexual attractions, as a result of 'conversion therapy,' then that therapy can be considered

---

[39] Deborah L Tolman and Lisa M Diamond (eds), *APA Handbook on Sexuality and Psychology* (American Psychological Association, 2014) vol 1, 579 (*'APA Handbook on Sexuality and Psychology'*).
[40] Ibid vol 1, 256-257.
[41] Explanatory Notes, Health Legislation Amendment Bill 2019 (Qld) 4-5; *Sexuality and Gender Identity Conversion Practices Act 2020* (ACT) s 6; and *Change or Suppression (Conversion) Practices Prohibition Act 2021* (Vic) s 3.

effective, and many clients would consider it successful, even if some occasional same-sex attractions remain. As with other conditions (eg depression), an effective therapy will not necessarily eliminate all symptoms entirely all the time.

The principal evidence of 'harm' caused by 'conversion therapy' is the personal testimonies of individuals who claim to have undertaken it, and then subsequently experienced depression or suicidal thoughts. But such anecdotal evidence (even if true) does not constitute scientific proof that 'conversion therapy' is harmful. Correlation is not causation, so in order to prove that 'conversion therapy' is harmful, an objective study would need to demonstrate the following:

1. The number of clients reporting harm exceeds the number reporting benefits;
2. Negative mental and physical health indicators of those who have undergone 'conversion therapy' exceed those who have undergone alternative 'gay-affirming' therapy;
3. Negative mental and physical health indicators of those who have undergone 'conversion therapy' exceed those with same-sex attractions who have had no therapy at all; and
4. Negative mental and physical health indicators of those who have undergone 'conversion therapy' exceed those who have had therapy or counselling for other conditions.

Yet there is simply no scientific evidence to prove each of these points. On the contrary, there are several studies that show the opposite. A study of 125 religious men by Santero et al found that 68% reported a reduction in same-sex attraction and behaviour, ranging from 'some' to 'much' as well as an increase in attraction to women. On the whole, the participants found their therapy helpful. Only one reported extreme negative effects.[42] About one in seven (14%) claimed that their orientation had changed from exclusively homosexual to exclusively heterosexual. As the authors point out, many men with religious convictions may think that a 14% chance of success is well worth taking.[43] While some homosexuals may not want to change, men with religious convictions are more likely to desire it, and given that any therapy should be tailored to the individual, banning 'conversion therapy' would result in some people being denied the treatment they desire and the help they wish.

Several other studies have also shown that sexual orientation can change. Savin-Williams and Ream have shown that for adolescents, all orientations apart from heterosexuality had a lower likelihood of stability over time. In fact, people who at first reported exclusively heterosexual attractions and behaviour tended to remain very stable in their sexuality, but those who first reported same-sex attractions or behaviour were much more likely to change to heterosexuality rather than bisexuality. In other words, conversion from homosexual behaviour to exclusively heterosexual behaviour was more common than conversion from heterosexuality to any homosexual behaviour.[44]

---

[42] Paul L Santero et al, 'Effects of Therapy on Religious Men Who Have Unwanted Same-Sex Attraction' (2018) 20 *The Linacre Quarterly* 1, 11. Note that this study was recently retracted due to 'unresolved statistical differences.' A statistical review of the paper found that the Chi-Square test results were invalid because the test requires groups that are similar but the paper did not identify whether the subjects were treated in the same way, for the same period of time and by similarly qualified therapists. The authors' rightly responded that the only uniformity required was whether the subjects were involved in 'conversion therapy.' Other factors are irrelevant in determining whether subjects experienced benefits or harms. This suggests the retraction was motivated by factors other than "statistical differences."

[43] Ibid 11-12.

[44] Ritch C Savin-Williams and Geoffrey L Ream, 'Prevalence and Stability of Sexual Orientation Components During Adolescence and Young Adulthood' (2007) 36 *Archives of Sexual Behavior* 385, 389.

Moreover, Savin-Williams and Ream provided some indication of how extraordinarily rare exclusive homosexuality among adolescents actually is: 'Same- and both-sex behavior was (sic) collapsed into one category because exclusively same-sex behavior was so rare in all three waves (usually <1%).'[45] The authors also noted that 'if having romantic attraction to both sexes counted as same-sex oriented, then the prevalence rate was nine times higher than if the criterion was exclusive same-sex attraction.'[46]

The *Growing Up Today Study* ('GUTS') longitudinal cohort study of male and female adolescents living throughout the United States, showed:

> Of the 7.5% of men and 8.7% of women who chose a nonheterosexual descriptor at ages 18 to 21, 43% of the men and 46% of the women chose a different category by age 23. Among the same- sex-attracted youth who changed, 57% of the men's changes and 62% of the women's changes involved switching to *Completely heterosexual.*[47]

A study of approximately 1,000 children born in Dunedin, New Zealand in 1972 and 1973 concluded: 'Much same-sex attraction is non-exclusive and unstable. The large size of this unstable group ... is consistent with a large role for the social environment ... Overall these findings argue against any single explanation for homosexual attraction.'[48]

Moreover, Diamond and Rosky noted in their summary of the Dunedin data:

---

[45] Ibid 389.
[46] Ibid 392.
[47] Lisa M Diamond and Clifford J Rosky, 'Scrutinizing Immutability: Research on Sexual Orientation and US Legal Advocacy for Sexual Minorities' (2016) 53 *Journal of Sex Research* 363, 372 (emphasis in original).
[48] Nigel Dickson et al, 'Same-sex Attraction in a Birth Cohort: Prevalence and Persistence in Early Adulthood' (2003) 56 *Social Science & Medicine* 1607, 1614.

[R]ates of change do not appear to decline as respondents get older. Rates of change in attractions among same-sex-attracted men ranged from 26% to 45%, and rates of change in same-sex-attracted women ranged from 55% to 60%. Among the same-sex-attracted men reporting change, between 67% and 100% of the changes were toward heterosexuality, and this also was true for 83% to 91% of the same-sex-attracted women undergoing changes.[49]

Mock's and Eibach's analysis of the National Survey of Midlife Development in the United States found:

> Overall, 55 (2.15%) participants reported a different sexual orientation identity ... Among women, 1.36% with a heterosexual identity changed, 63.3% with a homosexual identity changed, and 64.71% with a bisexual identity changed. Among men, 0.78% with a heterosexual identity changed, 9.52% with a homosexual identity changed, and 47.06% with a bisexual identity changed ... for both men and women heterosexuality was significantly more stable than homosexuality or bisexuality.[50]

Jones and Yarhouse conducted 'a quasi-experimental longitudinal study spanning 6-7 years' tracking a sample of 61 subjects engaged in 'religiously mediated' 'conversion' efforts. They found that 53% of the final sample reported either conversion (23%) or chastity (30%). Only 25% reported failure (confused or identifying as homosexual).[51] Similar results were found by Karten and Wade.[52]

---

[49] Diamond and Rosky (n 47) 373.
[50] Steven E Mock and Richard P Eibach, 'Stability and Change in Sexual Orientation Identity Over a 10-Year Period in Adulthood' (2012) 41 *Archives of Sexual Behavior* 641, 645-646.
[51] Stanton L Jones and Mark A Yarhouse, 'A Longitudinal Study of Attempted Religiously Mediated Sexual Orientation Change' (2011) 37 *Journal of Sex and Marital Therapy* 404, 422.
[52] Elan Y Karten and Jay C Wade, 'Sexual Orientation Change Efforts in Men: A Client Perspective' (2010) 18 *The Journal of Men's Studies* 84, 84-102.

In addition, Spitzer's comprehensive study of 200 individuals (143 males, 57 females) who had experienced 'reparative therapy' (ie 'conversion' therapy) and had reported some change in orientation from homosexual to heterosexual after at least five years. He found that 11% of males and 37% of females reported complete change from homosexuality to heterosexuality.[53] In addition, '26% of the males and 49% of the females reported being bothered "not at all" by unwanted homosexual feelings,' and 'only 1 male and no female reported being "markedly" or "extremely" bothered by unwanted homosexual feelings.'[54] Moreover, 29% of males and 63% of females had only very low values on measures of homosexual orientation after experiencing 'conversion therapy', and 66% of males and 44% of females 'satisfied the criteria for Good Heterosexual Functioning.' Most importantly, Spitzer found that depression was not a side effect of the experienced 'therapy' and participants 'often reported that they were "markedly" or "extremely" depressed [before 'conversion therapy'] (males 43%, females 47%), but rarely that depressed [after 'conversion therapy'] (males 1%, females 4%).'[55] Therefore, Spitzer concluded:

> [S]ome gay men and lesbians, following reparative therapy, report that they have made major changes from a predominantly homosexual orientation to a predominantly heterosexual orientation. The changes following reparative therapy were not limited to sexual behavior and sexual orientation self-identity. The changes encompassed sexual attraction, arousal, fantasy, yearning, and being bothered by homosexual feelings. The changes encompassed the core aspects of sexual orientation. Even participants who only made a limited change nevertheless

---

[53] Spitzer (n 3) 403.
[54] Ibid.
[55] Ibid 410-412.

regarded the therapy as extremely beneficial.[56]

One of the largest studies of 'conversion' therapy results involved surveying 882 (689 men, 193 women) "dissatisfied homosexually oriented people."[57] The researchers found that over 67% of the participants indicated they were exclusively homosexual or almost entirely homosexual at one time in their lives, but only 12.8% indicated that they now considered themselves homosexual. Before treatment, only 2.2% considered themselves as exclusively or almost entirely heterosexual, whereas after treatment more than 34% did so. Of the 318 participants who viewed themselves as exclusively homosexual, 56 (17.6%) reported that they now consider themselves as exclusively heterosexual; 53 (16.7%) now view themselves as almost entirely heterosexual; and 35 (11.1%) now view themselves as more heterosexual than homosexual.[58] Moreover, only 7.1% of participants "reported that they were doing worse on three or more [out of 17] of the psychological, interpersonal, and spiritual well-being items after treatment."[59]

---

[56] Ibid 413. Spitzer acknowledged that self-reporting opens a theoretical possibility that the reports could be biased or inaccurate. However, he concluded that 'the participants' self-reports in this study are by-and-large credible and that probably few, if any, elaborated self-deceptive narratives or lied.': at 412-413. Hershberger agreed with this conclusion (Scott L Hershberger, 'Guttman Scalability Confirms the Effectiveness of Reparative Therapy' in Jack Drescher and Kenneth J Zucker (eds) *Ex-Gay Research: Analyzing the Spitzer Study and Its Relation to Science, Religion, Politics, and Culture* (Harrington Park Press, 2006) 137-140): 'Because participants were self-selecting, generalizations regarding the effectiveness of "conversion" therapy for any particular individual are not possible. Nevertheless, Spitzer's study demonstrates that change is *possible* for some.'

[57] Joseph Nicolosi et al, 'Retrospective Self-Reports of Changes in Homosexual Orientation: A Consumer Survey of Conversion Therapy Clients' (2000) 86 *Psychological Reports* 1071, 1076.

[58] Ibid 1078.

[59] Ibid 1080-1081.

Contra the accepted view that sexual orientation is immutable, the aforementioned studies show there is ample evidence that substantial change – if not complete change – is indeed possible, particularly if one desires change. Moreover, homosexual activists appear duplicitous in encouraging people to change their orientation from heterosexual to homosexual, yet balk at the possibility of change in the other direction.

In any case, if sexual orientation was immutable, where does that leave transgenderism? As already noted, there is no scientific evidence that sexual orientation is genetically determined and all attempts to find a 'gay' gene have failed. Yet a person's sex or 'gender' is genetically encoded into every cell of their body! Those who view sexual orientation as immutable but accept the legitimacy of transgenderism appear to suffer from a clear case of cognitive dissonance. Moreover, the entire proposition is a loaded question. Using the term 'gender identity' instead of 'sex' presupposes the possibility of non-binary and fluid options. However, this is ultimately a denial of reality, as Morabito explains: 'This puts us on the path to banning recognition of the reality that every single human being exists through the union of one male and one female. There are no exceptions to this reality. You exist as the union of the two opposites through whom you were created.'[60]

APA's DSM-5 indicates that 70-98% of gender dysphoric boys and 50-88% of gender dysphoric girls eventually accept their chromosomal sex.[61] The *APA Handbook* states that 'it is critically important for clinicians not to assume that any experience of same-sex desire or behavior is a sign of latent homosexuality and instead to allow

---

[60] Stella Morabito, 'A De-Sexed Society is a De-Humanized Society' (25 May 2016) *Public Discourse*.
[61] DSM-5 (n 32) 455.

individuals to determine for themselves the role of same-sex sexuality in their lives and identity.'[62] The origin of transgender identity is 'most likely the result of a complex interaction between biological and environmental factors ... Research on the influence of family of origin dynamics has found some support for separation anxiety among gender-nonconforming boys and psychopathology among mothers.'[63]

Contra Telfer's demand for affirmative responses, the *APA Handbook* states:

> Premature labeling of gender identity should be avoided. Early social transition (ie, change of gender role, such as registering a birth-assigned boy in school as a girl) should be approached with caution to avoid foreclosing this stage of (trans)gender identity development ... the stress associated with possible reversal of this decision has been shown to be substantial...[64]

Moreover, the *APA Handbook* warns that the full acceptance approach 'runs the risk of neglecting individual problems the child might be experiencing and may involve an early gender role transition that might be challenging to reverse if cross-gender feelings do not persist.'[65]

E *Counter-claims*

It must be noted that the HLRC-La Trobe Report has fundamental methodological flaws. Participants were recruited by solicitation through social media, LGBT media reportage of the project, and through various LGBT, queer and ex-gay survivor networks, and the

---

[62] *APA Handbook on Sexuality and Psychology* 257.
[63] Ibid vol 1, 743.
[64] Ibid vol 1, 744.
[65] Ibid vol 1, 750.

selections were claimed to be broadly representative of religious and LGBT demographics in Australia.[66] Less than fifty people responded to the researchers' invitation, and *only 15* of these people were interviewed![67] Apart from the tiny sample size, studies that rely on self-selecting participants who report their own unverified experiences are nearly always subject to self-justification and self-presentation bias, or, as some researchers call it, 'social desirability bias': a desire to support a particular social agenda by painting their ideological opponents in the worst possible light. Suffice to say the 'findings' in this study are practically worthless.

A 2009 survey report by the American Psychological Association stated: 'We found that there was some evidence to indicate that individuals experienced harm from [conversion therapy].'[68] However, much of the research fails to distinguish between individual and group responses. A therapy that caused 'harm' to 10% of subjects may be considered unacceptable by a group standard, but beneficial for the other 90% of subjects. Similarly, a therapy that helped only 10% of subjects would be considered ineffective by a group standard but possibly life-changing for those individuals that were helped.

Nevertheless, the Australian Psychological Society's position statement asserted that '[t]here is no clinical evidence demonstrating that approaches that claim to change a person's sexual orientation are

---

[66] Jones et al (n 8) 8. Participants were aged 18 to 59 years, from six states and one territory, with experiences of conversion therapy dating from the 1980s to the present. Nine participants identified as homosexual male, two as lesbian female, two as transgender, one as bisexual female and one as non-binary. Thirteen participants were from Christian backgrounds, one from a Jewish background and one from a Buddhist background.

[67] Ibid.

[68] American Psychological Association, *Report of the Task Force on Appropriate Therapeutic Responses to Sexual Orientation* (2009) 3.

effective' and 'the "failure" of such approaches can further contribute to negative mental health outcomes.'[69] But, as is often the case with ideologically charged issues, researchers have chosen to ignore the positive results of many conversion therapy studies over several decades. For example, the study on the effect of conversion therapy on religious men by Santero et al concluded that it is 'neither ineffective, nor harmful' and noted that social pressures did not predominate as the reason for seeking treatment.[70] Indeed, they conclude that 'The concept of the immutability of sexual attraction must be rejected.'[71]

The notion that universal acceptance of homosexuality would eliminate or greatly reduce psychological harm is highly dubious. A large study from the Netherlands – known for its broad and longstanding acceptance and celebration of homosexuality – found homosexual youths are four times as likely to suffer major depression, three times as likely to suffer anxiety disorder, five times as likely to smoke, six times more likely to suffer multiple disorders, six times more likely to have attempted suicide, and four times as likely to have succeeded at suicide.[72] Thus, it appears far more likely that homosexuality itself is a major risk factor for mental health disorders rather than being caused or exacerbated by social hostility and stigma.

---

[69] Australian Psychological Society Task Force, *APS Position Statement on the Use of Psychological Practices that attempt to change Sexual Orientation* (American Psychological Association, August 2015).
[70] Santero et al (n 42) 14-15.
[71] Ibid 12.
[72] Theo G M Sandfort et al, 'Same-Sex Sexual Behaviour and Psychiatric Disorders: Findings from the Netherlands Mental Health Survey and Incidence' (2001) 58 *Archives of General Psychiatry* 85-91. See also R Garofalo et al, 'Sexual Orientation and Risk of Suicide Attempts Among a Representative Sample of Youth' (1999) 153 *Archives of Pediatric and Adolescent Medicine* 487, 487-493.

In addition, the general positive effect that religion has on an individual's mental and physical health must also be considered. Seybold and Hill note that it has been widely held that religion has a predominantly negative influence on health, but recent research indicates the impact of religion and spirituality on physical and mental health 'is largely beneficial.'[73] Indeed, Townsend et al examined the effects of religion on patients by reviewing clinical trials that assessed the relationship between religion and a measurable heath outcome. They found that religious activities appeared to benefit blood pressure, immune function, depression, and mortality.[74]

IV LEGAL IMPLICATIONS

A *Health service providers*

Queensland has already enacted legislation prohibiting health service providers from performing 'conversion therapy' on a homosexual or transgender person.[75] The definition of a health service provider is broad, comprising any individual or entity that provides a service that is, or purports to be, for maintaining or improving a person's health or wellbeing. It includes unregistered health practitioners such as counsellors, naturopaths and social workers.[76] The offence will apply regardless of whether the service is paid for or provided for free, and regardless of the location where the service is provided. The Bill's

---

[73] Kevin S Seybold and Peter C Hill, 'The Role of Religion and Spirituality in Mental and Physical Health' (2001) 10 *Current Directions in Psychological Science* 21, 21.
[74] Mark Townsend et al, 'Systematic review of clinical trials examining the effects of religion on health' (2002) 95 *Southern Medical Journal* 1429, 1429.
[75] *Public Health Act 2005* (Qld) ss 213E-213I.
[76] *Health Practitioner Regulation National Law Act 2009* (Qld) s 5.

Explanatory Notes state:

> It would be a violation of the trust that the community places in health service providers to allow these practices to be carried out in the health care system. Prohibiting conversion therapy by health service providers also sends the message that these practices are opposed by the Queensland Government and that being a LGBTIQ person is not a disorder that requires treatment.[77]

The *Explanatory Notes* continue:

> A term of imprisonment is necessary to send the message that conversion therapy is not condoned by the Queensland Government and to ensure the offence is a strong deterrent... This may result in registration consequences for the practitioner, which is a further disincentive for health practitioners to engage in conversion therapy...A higher penalty acknowledges that vulnerable people, including children, people without legal capacity or people with an impairment that may limit their understanding of the treatment, are especially susceptible to these unproven and unethical practices.[78]

The ACT has enacted similar legislation but the prohibition is not limited to health service providers.[79] It defines 'conversion practice' as any 'treatment or other practice the purpose, or purported purpose, of which is to change a person's sexuality or gender identity.'[80] Indeed, anyone who performs a sexuality or gender identity conversion practice on a child or person with an impairment faces criminal sanctions regardless of whether consent has been given.[81]

---

[77] Explanatory Notes, Health Legislation Amendment Bill 2019 (Qld) 9.
[78] Ibid 14.
[79] *Sexuality and Gender Identity Conversion Practices Act 2020* (ACT).
[80] Ibid s 7.
[81] Ibid s 8.

The Victorian legislation imposes substantial criminal penalties (including lengthy prison terms) on *anyone* engaging in a 'change or suppression practice,' regardless of whether consent was given. Therefore, the prohibition covers all registered and unregistered health service providers. Moreover, the legislation applies to health service providers outside of Victoria if there is a substantial link with Victoria (eg the individual receiving the 'conversion therapy' is a resident of Victoria). In addition, there are fines for anyone advertising a 'change or suppression practice.'

Note that the HLRC-La Trobe Report also contained the following non-legislative recommendations that may have consequential legal implications if implemented:

1. Strengthening health professionals' Codes of Conduct to ensure conversion therapy is specifically prohibited and enforcement action is available;

2. Forcing professional bodies representing health practitioners, counselling psychologists, social workers and Christian counsellors to inform public of the risks, make members aware of the ethical issues, deliver training on the potential harms of conversion therapy, monitor impacts of conversion therapy, and to collaborate with other professions to bring an end to conversion therapy; and

3. Provision of training regarding the potential risks and harms of conversion therapy as part of mental health and other health professionals' curriculum and continuing professional development.

These recommendations and legislative provisions not only discourage but effectively prohibit practitioners from exploring any underlying conditions and causes of patients' distress. Practitioners are effectively forced to put their professional stamp of approval on a predetermined diagnosis that is more than likely wrong, and will only exacerbate their patients' suffering.

Yet, there is the potential for a defendant practitioner to argue that their treatment does not constitute 'conversion therapy' based on the legislative exclusions noted above (section IIIA). If a person was born male, lived as a female, but now expressed a desire to transition back to being male, then a practitioner – according to one interpretation of the legislation – may 'assist' that person to transition back to their birth identity, or to express their birth identity. In addition, the practitioner may provide acceptance, support, and understanding, or facilitate the person's coping skills, and their identity exploration and development.

If a person living as a homosexual felt uneasy or uncomfortable about their sexual identity and expression, and wanted to explore the possibility of a heterosexual identity, then a practitioner – again, according to one interpretation of the legislation – may provide acceptance, support, and understanding for this person's feelings and desires, and facilitate the 'exploration and development' of their sexual identity, and connect the person to a community of people who will provide social support during their exploration.

B *Parental rights*

What about parents who want to affirm the biological sex of a child who is confused about their identity, or just enjoys doing activities typically done by the opposite sex? Existing and recommended legislation puts parents in real danger of serious legal sanctions.

ACT legislators also amended the *Human Rights Commission Act 2005* (ACT) to allow complaints from anyone to the Human Rights

Commission regarding 'conversion practices'.[82] In addition, the Act will potentially criminalise parents, guardians, teachers and pastors who provide moral, ethical and religious care and formation for children. Furthermore, it imposes criminal sanctions on anyone who performs a sexuality or gender identity conversion practice on a 'protected person' – a child or a person with an impairment regardless of consent.[83]

Thus, if a 5-year old biological girl tells her parents that she wants to be a boy, criminal proceedings could be brought against her parents if they continue to treat her as a girl or if they counsel her against taking any action to change her appearance.

Like the ACT legislation, the Victorian prohibition applies to all including parents. Victoria's Education Department already allows school principals to facilitate a student's transition while at school without parental knowledge or consent. If a parent finds out and attempts to stop the school from interfering with, or manipulating their child's state of mind, this would be considered a 'suppression practice', and expose the parent to possible criminal sanctions and/or child protection interventions. Indeed, the Australian Labor Party's national policy platform included provisions to categorise parents and other family members who do not affirm a child's sexual orientation or gender identity as perpetrators of domestic violence![84]

In addition, the HLRC-La Trobe Report made the following regulatory recommendations that may have consequential legal implications:[85]

1. Classifying and rating 'ex-gay' and 'ex-trans' publications

---

[82] *Human Rights Commission Act 2005* (ACT) s 53ZA.
[83] *Sexuality and Gender Identity Conversion Practices Act 2020* (ACT) s 8.
[84] Australian Labor Party (n 27) 193.
[85] Jones et al (n 8) 67-71.

(television, books, online content) to reflect their negative impact on the psychological health of individuals; and

2. State Government agencies to explicitly identify conversion practices as unlawful and falling within the definition of reportable conduct prompting responses by child protection services, justice agencies and family violence support services.

So if 'ex-gay' and 'ex-trans' publications are given a legally enforceable classification similar to R18+, parents providing such material to their children may not only be participating in a 'conversion' practice, but breaching the Classification Regulations as well. Moreover, such parents could be reported by teachers to child protection services, and be subject to Government intervention.

C Churches and religious institutions

The ACT legislation includes a clarification note stating that 'a mere expression of a religious tenet or belief' would not constitute a sexual preference or gender identity conversion therapy.[86] However, the Victorian legislation contains no such clarification. Therefore, the blanket prohibition in Victoria exposes all religious institutions and their leaders and members to possible criminal sanctions for merely proclaiming or expressing a view that does not affirm homosexual relationships or the possibility of changing one's gender.

In any case, in both jurisdictions, religious leaders and religious institutions who instruct, proclaim, or appeal to those experiencing feelings of having a divergent sexual identity, or having homosexual desires, not to act on those feelings and desires, may be liable for

---

[86] *Sexuality and Gender Identity Conversion Practices Act 2020* (ACT) s 7(2).

engaging in 'conversion therapy.' Thus, a Pastor, Priest, or Christian counsellor who counsels a member of their congregation regarding unwanted same-sex attraction is at risk of exposure to a conversion therapy complaint to the ACT Human Rights Commission[87] or the Victorian Equal Opportunity Commission[88] regardless of whether the person being counselled sought counselling of their own volition. The same applies to a teacher in a Christian school.

Note that, in the ACT, contested complaints will be decided by the ACT Administrative Tribunal ('ACAT') and if financial compensation is deemed appropriate, there is no limit to the amount that may be ordered.[89]

Once again, the HLRC-La Trobe Report also makes the following non-legislative recommendations that may have consequential legal implications:[90]

1. Insertion of specific clauses into funding agreements with schools and providers of school chaplaincy programs to prohibit conversion practices by school chaplains and/or any referrals or support to gain access to conversion practices;

2. Mandatory training for school chaplains that addresses the potential harm caused by conversion therapy to same-sex attracted and gender questioning young people;

3. State Government agencies to explicitly identify conversion practices as unlawful and falling within the definition of reportable conduct prompting responses by child protection services, justice agencies and family violence support services;

---

[87] *Human Rights Commission Act 2005* (ACT) s 42(1)(ec).
[88] *Change or Suppression (Conversion) Practices Prohibition Act 2021* (Vic) s 24.
[89] *Human Rights Commission Act 2005* (ACT) s 53ZF.
[90] Jones et al (n 8) 67-71.

4. Rolling out of education and training within religious organisations and faith communities to ensure religious ministers are fully aware of their responsibilities to report unlawful conversion activities;

5. Classifying and rating 'ex-gay' and 'ex-trans' publications (television, books, online content) to reflect their negative impact on the psychological health of individuals.

These recommendations not only prohibit religious leaders and religious institutions from doing anything but affirming an individual's gender identity or sexual preference, they also regulate the way religious leaders and institutions must behave, and restrict the kind of information that may be provided to, or accessed by, people within their sphere of influence. Moreover, religious leaders will be legally obligated to report to authorities anyone who violates or resists the mandate to affirm an individual's gender identity or sexual preference resulting in government intervention that may result in the destruction of that person's reputation and/or career, the breaking up of their family, or even criminal prosecution.

These recommendations would make it extremely difficult for religious institutions to articulate orthodox teaching regarding sexual identity and preference, or to offer the most basic and unobtrusive pastoral care including prayer and counselling. Indeed, they would make it extremely difficult to preach the Christian gospel!

V CONCLUSIONS

Legislative restrictions and bans on 'conversion therapy' are based on faulty assumptions and assertions that are not supported by scientific evidence. As shown above, studies that purported to indicate that 'gender' is *not* an innate, fixed property of human beings, and that a person might be 'a man trapped in a woman's body' or 'a woman trapped in a man's body' have been shown to be seriously, methodologically flawed, or unreplicable. Yet such studies are still accepted and propagated as settled scientific fact.

Moreover, it appears that 'conversion therapy' is perfectly acceptable when applied in one direction but not in the other. There is no problem with counselling an individual to adopt a gender identify different to their biological sex, or to encourage an individual to act on homosexual desires, even if that person is reluctant to do so. In other words, 'conversion therapy' is fine if practiced by homosexual or transgender activists, but reprehensible and harmful if practiced by religious conservatives.

In addition, there is an ideological and politically correct view that traditional Christian moral teaching is inherently harmful because it critiques and rejects non-traditional intimate relationships and non-binary gender identity, and asserts that people can and do change their sexual orientation. But this overlooks the causes of real harm, which are often suppressed or dismissed out of hand because they do not fit the prevailing social narrative.

But what about those who freely and voluntarily seek counselling or help to eliminate their gender confusion or homosexual desire? Nicholas Cummings, a former President of the American Psychological Association, contends that counselling should be available for people experiencing unwanted same-sex attraction on the principle of patient choice.[91]

---

[91] Nicholas A Cummings, 'Sexual reorientation therapy not unethical', *USA Today*, (Web Article, 30 July 2013).

Nevertheless, the sexual revolution has changed gears. Rather than just campaigning for sexual freedom, ideologues are now obsessed with coercively eliminating any and all disapproval of another's choices and actions. They employ state power to enforce a worldview that contradicts reality itself and the lived experience of the community. Indeed, the transgender agenda has become more aggressive and pervasive in redefining human relationships to marginalise and de-normalise traditional marriage and family. This has resulted in legislators and government functionaries becoming more intolerant of those who object to, or push back against, the homosexual and transgender social agenda. Policy makers have become increasingly insulated from voters' concerns, and are bullied into enacting the ideologues' agenda despite the intractable realities of human beings and human society.[92] As Kersten put it, the 'transgender crusade ... is inherently authoritarian ... because it has to be. Nature and common sense oppose it ... [therefore c]ritics who persist in drawing attention to reality must be discredited or silenced.'[93]

---

[92] Paul Adams, 'Gender Ideology and the Truth of Marriage: The Challenge for Christian Social Workers' (2017) 44 *Social Work & Christianity* 143, 155–156.
[93] Katherine Kersten, 'Transgender Conformity' *First Things* (Web Article, December 2016)

12

A Cross-Cultural Analysis of Women, Religion and the Law

LAURIE STEWART*

ABSTRACT

Protecting women from violence and discrimination is a hot topic. The feminist movement claims to address these issues in its fight for women's rights. However, without knowing the true source for women's rights – or human rights – communities will fail to accurately diagnose the problem and to effectively provide a solution. This article compares four major worldviews and their impact on laws regarding the treatment of women in order to convince the reader that Christianity offers the best treatment of women. Part I defines women's rights in the context of defining human rights. Part II compares laws pertaining to women's rights through the lens of the following major competing worldviews, Islam (specifically Saudi Arabia), Atheist (China), Hindu (India), and Christian (United States). Part III demonstrates that all non-Christian worldviews create extreme problems for so-called women's rights, and that biblical Christianity is the only worldview that offers the best hope for recognising the value, dignity, worth and equality of women. Moreover, this article concludes that this is an important topic for apologetics in providing a defence against the argument Christianity oppresses women; rather, Christianity has the best answers for ending violence and discrimination against women.

---

* Adjunct Professor, Trinity Law School. This chapter is a condensed version of her Master's Thesis.

INTRODUCTION

> Not until the half of our population represented by women and girls can live free from fear, violence and everyday insecurity, can we truly say we live in a fair and equal world.
> —UN Secretary-General Antonio Guterres.[1]

Eradicating discrimination and violence against women is an increasingly familiar global topic. Turn on the news any day and discover another report of a woman (or women) suffering from sexual harassment, assault, domestic violence, sex trafficking, rape, or murder. Other examples of discrimination and violence against women include forced marriages, child brides, female genital mutilation, honor killings, dowry deaths, acid attacks, and forced abortions.[2] The World Health Organisation estimates 1 in 3 women worldwide have experienced physical or sexual violence.[3] Discrimination and violence against women is a common international problem.

Mistreatment of women is not new. It has a long history. What appears to be new is the relentless, almost simultaneous, global cry of women to eliminate discrimination and violence against them. In 2006, the #MeToo grass-roots movement was born and went viral, giving a voice to victims of sexual violence.[4] Better treatment of women is a cross-cultural interest – shared by liberals and conservatives, religious

---

[1] United Nations, 'International Day for the Elimination of Violence against Women - 25 November', *United Nations: UN Women*, Note: The terms 'woman' and 'women' in this paper, will be used generically to describe the female human being of all ages with XX chromosomes. This paper will not discuss 'gender' as a social construct or as deconstructed.

[2] Office of the High Commissioner for Humans Rights, *Women's Rights are Human Rights*, HR/PUB/14/2 (2014) 27-28 ('*Women's Rights are Human Rights*').

[3] World Health Organisation, Violence Against Women Prevalence Estimates 2018 (Report, 2018) xvi

[4] 'About: History and Vision', *MeToo* (Web Page).

and irreligious, Easterners and Westerners, developed and developing countries, rich and poor, people of all color, ages and abilities.

The unfair treatment of women can be corrected in the legal arena through laws. Legal discrimination against women can occur directly and indirectly. Directly, it can occur through *de jure* discrimination (direct discriminatory provisions), when a law or policy restricts, prefers or distinguishes between certain groups – eg, prohibiting women from driving, voting or inheriting property.[5] Indirectly, discrimination can also occur through *de facto* discrimination (discriminatory impact), when a law or policy which appears to be gender neutral yields a harmful effect on women – eg, aid programs which benefits the "head of household" may not benefit women equally since men are more often considered the head of a household.[6]

What causes the problem of discrimination and other mistreatment of women? Is it based on "systems of power" as some feminists would argue?[7] Laws may be able to provide protection, remedies, and guidance – but which laws? What provides the proper foundation for the most effective laws to end discrimination and violence against women? Which foundational set of principles provides the best hope for women gaining better treatment, and recognition of their inherent dignity and worth? Is there a religious worldview that offers good news for women or do all religions oppress women (as some atheists claim)?[8]

---

[5] *Women's Rights are Human Rights* (n 2) 30-31.
[6] Ibid.
[7] Margaret L Anderson and Patricia Hill Collins (eds), *Race, Class & Gender: An Anthology* (Cengage Learning, 9th ed, 2016) 2. Note: While current feminist ideology cannot fully be understood without discussing feminist critical theory (ie systems of power and oppression), that is beyond the scope of this paper.
[8] Karen L Garst (ed), *Women v Religion: The Case Against Faith – and for Freedom* (Pitchstone Publishing, 2018) 70-71.

Protecting women from violence and discrimination is an obvious growing concern. The current feminist approach addresses women's rights as human rights.[9] While this makes perfect sense (even if feminist ideology does not make perfect sense), without knowing the source of women's rights – or human rights – communities will fail to accurately diagnose the problem and effectively provide a lasting solution. In a world of competing ideas, options must carefully examined before forming conclusions regarding the best approach to eliminating discrimination and violence against women.

This article analyses four major religious worldviews and compares their impact on laws regarding the treatment of women to demonstrate that *biblical Christianity* and its influence on laws offers the best hope for ending invidious discrimination and violence against women – even if *Christians* have not always treated women fairly, with dignity and respect.[10]

This article takes a juridical approach to this epistemological question – which religious worldview offers the best hope for women? Decisions about law can only be made once facts have been established.[11] As attorney, theologian, and Christian apologist John

---

[9] 'Unity Principles', *Women's March* (Web Page, 2021). Women's rights are human rights and human rights are women's rights.
[10] A worldview analysis is simply the study of religions and ideologies; the study of religion can apply to different disciplines like the law, and is necessarily cross-cultural. Ninian Smart, *Worldviews: Crosscultural Explorations of Human Beliefs* (Prentice Hall, 3rd ed, 2000) 2, 4. Some intersectional feminists may dismiss this article as sourced by a woman's "privilege of whiteness." However, this article attempts to address specific issues experienced by women, as viewed from a multi-cultural, multi-racial, and multi-religious perspective, and cites to a variety of reputable sources.
[11] John Warwick Montgomery, *Defending the Gospel in Legal Style: Essays on Legal Apologetics & the Justification of Classical Christian Faith* (Wipf & Stock, 2017) 55. Note: A "juridical approach" is a method by which courts interpret law, ie to administer justice per the law. Epistemology is the investigation of what distinguishes justified belief from opinion.

Warwick Montgomery describes it, '[L]awyers and legal scholars must employ the most effective techniques possible in arriving at factual conclusions on which life or death may depend and these must be sufficiently persuasive to convince the 'triars [sic] of fact' (juries and judges) to arrive at just verdicts.'[12]

Part I defines women's rights in the context of defining human rights. Part II compares laws pertaining to discrimination and violence against women, through the lens of Islam (specifically, Saudi Arabia), Hinduism (India), Atheism[13] (China), and Christianity (United States). Finally, Part III demonstrates that all non-Christian worldviews create problems for women's rights, and biblical Christianity is the worldview which offers the best hope for recognising the equal value and dignity of all women.

Admittedly, historical and contemporary Christianity are replete with examples of *Christians* articulating unfavorable views toward women and even mistreating them, *in the name of Christianity*. Regardless of their error, this does not negate the truth – Jesus Christ offers the best hope for women. Christianity offers the best hope for ending invidious discrimination and violence against women, not because of Christians (maybe even despite them), but because of Jesus Christ.

---

[12] Ibid.
[13] This article treats atheism as a religious worldview. The US Supreme Court has stated that religion should not be defined narrowly. *McCreary County, Ky v ACLU*, 545 US 844 (2005). The Seventh Circuit Court explained that the Supreme Court adopted a broad definition of 'religion' that includes theistic, non-theistic and atheistic beliefs. *Kaufman v McCaughtry*, 419 F 3d 678, 682 (7th Cir, 2005). Thus, atheism will be treated as a religious worldview for this analysis.

I GLOBAL CALL FOR WOMEN'S RIGHTS AS HUMAN RIGHTS

Men, their rights, and nothing more; women, their rights, and nothing less. —Susan B Anthony[14]

'Women's rights are human rights' is a phrase often used by feminists who may have some valid points in their advocacy for better treatment of women. However, the phrase is not exclusively used by feminists.[15] Assuming women's rights are human rights, the threshold question ought to be: "What are human rights and where do they come from?"

To answer this question, another question must first be answered, "What does it mean to be human?" In the United States, one does not have to guess at a definition because it is defined under federal law. 'Human being' is defined as someone who is a member of the species *homo sapiens*.[16] This view is also supported by the United Nations ('UN's') *Universal Declaration of Human Rights* ('UDHR'), which indicates that 'humans' are all members of the human family.[17] While this may seem obvious, there are some who would question this definition.[18] This article begins with the premise that women are members of the species *homo sapiens*, members of the human family

---

[14] Elizabeth Cady Stanton and Parker Pillsbury (eds), *The Revolution* (New York, 11 February 1869) 81.
[15] The United Nations promotes this idea in their e-book, *Women's Rights are Human Rights* (n 2) 27-28.
[16] 1 US Code § 8(a): 'In determining the meaning of any Act of Congress, or of any ruling, regulation, or interpretation of the various administrative bureaus and agencies of the United States, the words "person", "human being", "child", and "individual", shall include every infant member of the species homo sapiens who is born alive at any stage of development.' Note, although I hold the position that an unborn child is a human being, that topic is beyond the scope of this paper.
[17] *Universal Declaration of Human Rights*, Preamble.
[18] David Livingstone Smith, 'What Does it Mean to be Human?: We Can't Turn to Science for an Answer', *Psychology Today* (Web Article, 16 May 2012) Note: Arguments about what it means to be human go beyond the scope of this paper.

– that is, women are human beings.

After understanding what it means to be 'human,' the next question is 'what are human rights and where do they come from?' The traditional view of human rights is that they are: (1) based on a higher law; (2) inherent (humans are born with rights); and (3) universal (these rights apply to all humans).[19] This was expressed in 1776 in the *United States Declaration of Independence*, which reveals all three elements of the traditional view. In part, it states, 'We hold these truths to be self-evident, that *all* men [universality] are *created* equal [inherency], that they are *endowed by their Creator* [higher law] with certain *unalienable Rights* [human rights], that among these are Life, Liberty and the pursuit of Happiness.'[20] In this historical context, 'all men' is generally understood to be a reference to all 'humanity.'[21]

On a global scale, in 1948, inherency and universality were clearly communicated in the UDHR Preamble: 'Whereas recognition of the *inherent* [inherency] dignity and of the equal and inalienable rights of *all* members of the human family [universality] is the foundation of freedom, justice, and peace in the world.'[22] It is also conveyed in Article 1 of the UDHR, '*All* human beings are *born* free and equal in dignity and rights.'[23] The UDHR clearly affirms the admonition

---

[19] See generally, John Warwick Montgomery, *The Law Above the Law* (NRP Books, 2015); UDHR.
[20] *United States Declaration of Independence* (emphasis added).
[21] Note: Although some people question whether 'all men' meant all of humanity, in its historical context, it is generally understood that 'all men' was another way of saying 'humanity.' (This was the view taken by, for example, Elizabeth Cady Stanton, Abraham Lincoln, and Martin Luther King:. see Library of Congress, 'Creating the Declaration of Independence' (Web Page).
[22] UDHR Preamble (emphasis added).
[23] UDHR art 1 (emphasis added).

for equal rights for all.[24] In fact, equal rights for everyone is a basic principle guiding the UN.[25]

If equal rights are inherent in everyone, they are necessarily inherent for all women. In order to address this specific application to women, the UN created the Commission on the Status of Women ('CSW') to prepare international standards to focus on clearly communicating the equal rights of women and define the guarantees of non-discrimination for women.[26] CSW's efforts resulted in several declarations and conventions that protect and promote human rights, aimed specifically at women.[27] For example, in 1979, the UN adopted the *Convention on the Elimination of All Forms of Discrimination against Women* ('CEDAW').[28] It gathered world-wide endorsement. Currently, 189 countries are parties to the CEDAW treaty – only a handful of countries have not ratified it.[29] Despite near global community support for CEDAW, violence against women remains an insidious problem worldwide.[30]

As a result of the troubling persistence of violence against women, in 1993, the UN adopted the *Declaration on the Elimination of Violence*

---

[24] UDHR art 1: 'All human beings are born free and equal in dignity and rights. They are endowed with reason and conscience and should act towards one another in a spirit of brotherhood.'
[25] United Nations, 'Member States' (Web Page). The UN has almost 200 member states from around the world.
[26] UN Women, 'A Brief History of the Commission on the Status of Women' (Web Page).
[27] Ibid.
[28] Ibid.
[29] *Convention on the Elimination of All Forms of Discrimination against Women*. The United States is one of those few countries who has signed it (in 1980), but not ratified it.
[30] United Nations, 'International Day for the Elimination of Violence against Women 25 November', (Web Page).

Against Women ('DEVAW').[31] DEVAW defines violence against women as 'any act of gender-based violence that results in, or is likely to result in, physical, sexual or psychological harm or suffering to women, including threats of such acts, coercion or arbitrary deprivation of liberty, whether occurring in public or in private life.'[32] In adopting DEVAW, the UN recognised a compelling need to advance women's rights with regard to 'equality, security, liberty, integrity and dignity of all human beings.'[33]

Unfortunately, in 2003, CSW experienced a considerable disappointment after spending two weeks drafting 'Agreed Conclusions', which addressed the elimination of all forms of violence against women.[34] One women's news article explained:

> The document on ending violence against women and girls would have been used by advocates to strengthen legislation to end domestic violence and sexual exploitation and trafficking of women. It would also have been used to educate governments on how to promote and protect women's human rights. Consensus on the conclusions came to an end when Iran, Egypt, Pakistan, Sudan and the US raised objections. The Iranian delegation objected to a specific paragraph that said governments must not use religion or custom as an excuse for violence against women. But the failure to pass this text was about more than cultural differences.[35]

---

[31] Ibid.
[32] *Declaration on the Elimination of Violence Against Women*, GA Res 48/104, UN Doc A/RES/48/104 (20 December 1993).
[33] UN Women, 'International Day for the Elimination of Violence against Women' (Web Page, 14 November 2019).
[34] Emily Freeburg, 'UN Pact Sinks on Issue of Violence Against Women', *Women's E-News* (Web Article, 24 April 2003).
[35] Ibid. The Security Council met at the same time as CSW met. When the Security Council experienced a breakdown over Iraq, governments became preoccupied and angry about loss of power at the Security Council. Many United Nations conflicts are grounded in differences in religion and custom.

UN efforts present an attempt to advance human rights for women. It is creating an awareness of the incessant problem of discrimination and violence against women. Nevertheless, the problem persists. It is not enough to declare the need to eliminate invidious discrimination and violence against women. It is important to know the source of human rights for women. This leads to the third point – there is a higher law.

Human rights must have a source to give meaning to the standard. That source must be objective and unchanging for the standard to last from generation to generation. Do women's rights, by way of human rights, result from man-made law or from a law that is higher than man-made law? If rights are only made possible because of man-made governing documents or cultural traditions, what gives women the right to complain about domestic violence, forced marriage, abortions, or any kind of unjust treatment resulting from laws or customs? Are there ultimate truths about human beings and human values, an objective universal moral code? Is there a higher law, ie God's law?

II MAJOR RELIGIOUS WORLDVIEWS AND THEIR IMPACT ON LAWS REGARDING THE TREATMENT OF WOMEN

> Whereas recognition of the inherent dignity of the equal and inalienable rights of the human family is the foundation for freedom, justice and peace in the world.
>
> —Preamble, *Universal Declaration of Human Rights*

'What is the ultimate source of women's rights as human rights?' Are they purely positive law (ie man-made), or is there a higher law (ie God's law)? If there is no God, the ultimate source of these rights would be man-made law. On the other hand, if there is an ultimate source of law above man – ie God – which god? Most importantly, which ultimate source offers the best hope for ending discrimination and violence against women?

This section compares laws pertaining to women's rights through the lens of four major competing religious worldviews: Islam (specifically, Saudi Arabia), Hinduism (India), Atheism (China), and Christianity (United States). Each worldview begins with a brief background of the country, its primary religion, and the source of its laws. Then each country's laws are examined as they pertain to women in discrimination in family matters and violations of bodily integrity.[36] Discrimination in the family covers topics such as marriage, divorce, and adultery. Violations of bodily integrity includes topics such as violence against women, domestic violence, rape, sexual harassment, and female genital mutilation ('FGM'). This article cites directly to the country's specific law when possible. Upholding the rule of law is a critical factor in the fight for women's rights.

A Islam: Women and the Laws of Saudi Arabia

The Prophet said: 'I was shown the Hell-fire and that the majority of its dwellers were women who were ungrateful.' It was asked, 'Do they disbelieve in Allah?' (or are they ungrateful to Allah?) He replied, 'They are ungrateful to their husbands and are ungrateful for the favors and the good (charitable deeds) done to them. If you have always been good (benevolent) to one of them and then she sees something in you (not of her liking), she will say, "I have

---

[36] Due to the limited scope of this article, discussion about women's civil liberties, financial and health resources, discrimination, reproductive and abortion issues are excluded.

never received any good from you.'"

—Sahih Bukhari (2:28)[37]

Saudi women are considered the most controlled group of women in the world.[38] When Muslims from all over the world visit Saudi Arabia's two Holy cities Mecca and Medina, they expect a spiritual experience.[39] Therefore, Saudi Arabia is pressured to encourage spirituality and not distract Muslims on a pilgrimage.[40] Saudi women must serve as role models for non-Saudi Muslim women who might visit.[41] Compared to other Muslim countries, Saudi Arabia is more fundamentalist, following a strict belief in the literal interpretation of religious texts.[42]

1 *Background*

Saudi Arabia is an Arab Islamic country – its official religion is Islam.[43] Islam was born in the early 7th century AD in two Muslim Holy cities in Saudi Arabia (Mecca and Medina) through their Prophet Muhammed.[44] 'Islam' means the submission of one's will to Allah, but it is not merely a religious ideology.[45] Its precepts direct the legal,

---

[37] Sahih Bukhari (2:28), Sahih Bukhari (Web Page).
[38] Amnah Abahussain, 'The Rising Tide of Change: Saudi Arabian Women in Dispute Resolution' (2018) 73(2) *Dispute Resolution Journal* 94.
[39] Ibid.
[40] Ibid.
[41] Ibid.
[42] Ibid.
[43] *Basic Law of Governance 1992* (Saudi Arabia) art 1 (*'Basic Law of Governance'*).
[44] Mona Almunajjed, *Women in Saudi Arabia Today* (New York, 1997) 1; Abahussain (n 38) 92.
[45] Almunajjed (n 44) 9.

economic and social teachings of Islam, and impact the entire way of life.[46]

The primary source of law in Saudi Arabia is Sharia (from the Arabic verb *sharaa*, meaning 'to legislate'), which is considered divine in nature.[47] There are four primary sources for Sharia: (1) the Quran (Islamic holy book, the revealed message of Allah to the Prophet Muhammad); (2) the Hadith or *sunnah* (teachings or actions of the Prophet Muhammad); (3) Qiyas (analytic comparisons of Hadiths and Quran); and (4) Al Ijma (religious scholars' consensus on Islamic issues).[48] Saudi Arabia's interpretation of Sharia law may be viewed as the "purest" interpretation, coinciding with the teachings of the early Prophet of Islam.[49]

The Quran is not just a book about the Islamic religion, but a book about how good Muslims should live.[50] Yet, this Muslim Holy book has been understood to place women in subservient roles, forcing them to endure discrimination.[51] The following surahs (chapters) from the Quran[52] are a few examples:

- Men shall take full care of women with the bounties which God has bestowed more abundantly on the former than on the latter, and with what they may spend out of their possessions. And the righteous women are the truly devote ones, who guard the intimacy which God has (ordained to be) guarded. And as for

---
[46] Ibid.
[47] *Basic Law of Governance*, arts 7, 8, 23, 26, 46, 48, 55.
[48] Almunajjed (n 44) 9; Abahussain (n 38) 91.
[49] Mackenzie Glaze, 'Historical Determinism and Women's Rights in Sharia Law' (2018) 50 *Case Western Reserve. Journal of International Law* 349, 362-363.
[50] Abahussain (n 38) 92.
[51] Ibid.
[52] Muhammad Asad, *The Message of the Quran* (The Book Foundation, 2003).

those women whose ill-will you have reasons to fear, admonish them (first); then leave them alone in bed; then beat them; and if thereupon they pay you heed, do not seek to harm them. Behold, God is indeed most high, great! (Surah 4:34)

- And call upon two of your men to act as witnesses; and if two men are not available, then a man and two women from among such as are acceptable to you as witnesses, so that if one of them should make a mistake, the other could remind her ... (Surah 2:282)

- [B]ut, in accordance with justice, the rights of the wives (with regard to their husbands) are equal to the (husbands') rights with regard to them, although men have precedence over them (in this respect) ... (Surah 2:228)

- And if you have reason to fear that you might not act equitably towards orphans, then marry from among (other) women such as are lawful to you – (even) two, or three, or four ... (Surah 4:3)

- Prophet! Behold, we have made lawful to thee thy wives unto whom thou hast paid their dowers, as well as those whom they right hand has come to possess from among the captives of war whom God has bestowed upon thee ... (Surah 33:50)

These examples reveal that the Quran approves of the following: (1) Muslim husbands may beat their wives; (2) a woman's testimony is half as valuable as a man's; (3) husbands have authority over wives; (4) men may marry up to four wives (women have one husband); and (5) men may take sex slaves. Since Muslims respect the Quran, these interpretations have not been heavily criticised by them, leaving women to suffer.[53] The Hadiths pick up on these themes and provide

---

[53] Abahussain (n 38) 92-93.

further evidence of approving of Islam's low view of women and approval of mistreatment.[54]

In addition to Sharia, legislation is another source of law in Saudi Arabia.[55] Royal Orders are made by the King and adopted through legislation.[56] However, Sharia law is supreme over man-made statutes because it is understood to be 'the word of God to whom all humans are subordinate.'[57] Sharia law always trumps man-made legislation.[58]

Sharia Courts have jurisdiction over family, property, and criminal matters.[59] Judges must be male and Muslim.[60] Secular laws adopted by legislation may supplement, but not replace Sharia law.[61] All regulations must be in accordance with Sharia law.[62] It is important to note, decisions of Sharia Courts are not considered legally binding precedent for subsequent cases to follow.[63] In other words, the application of Sharia law in one case does not affect the outcome of another case.[64] It is not difficult to imagine inconsistent application of

---

[54] 'What Does Islam Teach About a Woman's Worth?', *What Makes Islam So Different?* (Web Page). For example: Sahih Bukhari (2:28) and Sahih Bukhari (54:464) (Women comprise most of Hell's occupants. This is important because the only women in heaven mentioned explicitly by Muhammad are the virgins who serve the sexual desires of men.); Kanz al-'ummal (22:10) (suggests that 99% of women go to Hell); Sahih Bukhari (62:58) (A woman presents herself in marriage to Muhammad, but he does not find her attractive, so he "donates" her on the spot to another man.); Abu Dawud (2155) (Women are compared to slaves and camels with regard to the "evil" in them.)
[55] Abahussain (n 38) 93.
[56] Ibid.
[57] Ibid.
[58] Ibid.
[59] Ibid. Sharia Courts have followed the Hanbali School of Islamic jurisprudence since 1928.
[60] Ibid 103.
[61] Ibid 93.
[62] Ibid.
[63] Ibid 94.
[64] Ibid.

the laws if there is no binding precedent.

As for Human Rights in Saudi Arabia, they are specifically defined by Sharia law.[65] Because Sharia controls, assertive women have been viewed as rebels.[66] Eleanor Abdella Doumato, Middle East Women's Studies scholar, professor and author, sums it up this way:

> The Basic Law of the Kingdom of Saudi Arabia does not guarantee gender equality. To the contrary, gender inequality is built into Saudi Arabia's governmental and social structures, and it integral to the country's state-supported interpretation of Islam, which is derived from a literal reading of the Koran and Sunna. In issuing religious opinions, state-funded *ulema* (religious scholars) generally avoid consideration of judicial precedent and evolving social contexts, so that their official posture resists pressure for change, especially when it comes to controlling women's behavior.[67]

This background gives context for the next section which will discuss Saudi laws as they pertain to women in following focused areas: (1) discrimination in the family and (2) violations of bodily integrity.

2 Family Matters

In Saudi Arabia, law regarding family and marriage is derived from the Quran.[68] Judges make decisions about family matters based on their own interpretation of Sharia law.[69]

---

[65] *Basic Law of Governance* art 26, ('the State shall protect human rights in accordance with Islamic sharia.')
[66] Abahussain (n 38) 103.
[67] Eleanor Abdella Doumato, 'Saudi Arabia' in Sanja Kelly and Julia Breslin (eds), *Women's Rights in the Middle East and North Africa: Progress Amid Resistance* (Freedom House, 2010) 1.
[68] Doumato (n 67) 1.
[69] Ibid.

(a) Marriage/Child marriage

Sharia favors men when it comes to marriage.[70] A marriage contract is usually executed by the groom and guardian of the bride (not by the bride), and must specify if the bride (not the groom) is a virgin, widow or divorcee.[71] Men are allowed up to four wives at a time, provided the wives can be supported and treated equally.[72] Males are guardians over women and girls.[73]

There is no legal definition for the minimum age to marry in Saudi Arabia. Child marriage is common because there are no laws against it.[74] One of the wives of the Prophet Muhammed, Aisha, was six years old when they became engaged, and nine years old when the marriage was consummated.[75] It is legal to marry a girl even one-hour old.[76]

In 2011, two sisters (ages 8 and 10) were reported to be marrying men in their 60s.[77] The 10-year old would be her husband's fourth wife.[78] The girls were getting married because their father was struggling financially and needed the money that their dowries would provide.[79] Girls this age can be worth as much as $40,000 each.[80] Women and girls are like a commodity where the price is negotiated to transfer them from one male guardian to another.

---

[70] Ibid 8.
[71] Ibid 8-9.
[72] Ibid 2; *The Message of the Quran,* Surah 4:3.
[73] 'Why is No One Protecting Saudi Arabia's Child Brides?', *Girls Not Brides* (Web Page, 8 November 2011).
[74] Ibid.
[75] See Aisha's account in Sahih Al-Bukhari, vol 5, bk 58, Hadith 234.
[76] *Girls Not Brides* (n 73).
[77] Ibid.
[78] Ibid.
[79] Ibid.
[80] Ibid.

Child marriage would not exist without tacit support and approval from the country's leadership.[81] The Saudi monarchy itself has a long history of marrying very young girls.[82]

(b) Divorce

When it comes to divorce, Saudi Arabia has strict laws and favor men over women.[83] Saudi men have unilateral power and can divorce women without legal grounds or a judge.[84] On the other hand, a woman cannot divorce her husband without the consent of both her husband and a court.[85] Divorce can send a woman into poverty, because before the divorce is final, the woman must surrender all money and assets that were given to her during her marriage to her husband.[86] If a woman is fortunate enough to gain custody of her children, she will retain custody only until the children are nine years old, then custody goes to the husband.[87] Throughout the entire divorce process, the husband remains his wife's legal guardian.[88] For women who do divorce, there is a strong negative social perception and religious stigma towards them.[89]

(c) Adultery

The traditional punishment for adultery is stoning to death and is still practiced today.[90] Saudi judges are free to interpret Sharia Law as

---

[81] Ibid.
[82] Ibid.
[83] Although this article examines the differences between women's right to divorce among the various countries, this is not to suggest that it argues the merits of divorce.
[84] Glaze (n 49) 349, 352.
[85] Ibid 352.
[86] Ibid.
[87] Ibid.
[88] Ibid 353.
[89] Ibid 352.
[90] Ibid 356.

applied to adultery as they wish, eg fines, detention, imprisonment, flogging, and the death penalty.[91]

Saudi punishment for adultery is not equally applied to men and women. Women face stricter laws when charged with adultery. In 2015, a married Saudi woman was sentenced to death by stoning after admitting to adultery, while the man with whom she had sex received a punishment of 100 lashes.[92] In addition, rape victims are often charged with adultery, because Islamic law favors men in nearly every social and legal setting.[93]

3 Violations of Bodily Integrity

(a) Violence Against Women

Saudi Arabia does not have any specific laws addressing violence against women, even though there are numerous reports that violence against women is rampant in Saudi Arabia.[94] In fact, human rights activists are jailed for denouncing it.[95]

(b) Domestic Violence

The Saudi government has not clearly defined domestic violence.[96]

---

[91] Ibid.
[92] Ibid 357. See Sophie Jane Evans, 'Saudi Arabia Sentences Maid to Death by Stoning for Adultery-But the Man She Slept With Will Escape With 100 Lashes', *Daily Mail* (Web Article, 28 November 2015), (discussing how women who commit adultery are more likely than males to receive a harsher sentencing).
[93] Glaze (n 49) 357.
[94] Adam Coogle, 'Saudi Arabia to Women: "Don't Speak Up, We Know What's Best For You"', *Human Rights Watch* (Web Article, 26 June 2013).
[95] Ibid.
[96] US State Department, *Saudi Arabia 2018 Human Rights Report* (Report, 2018) 43-44.

Yet, there is a general law against abuse.[97] In 2015, Saudi Arabia's Justice Ministry reported that the courts saw 8,016 violence cases in a one-year period.[98] The ministry recounted that 57.5% of the cases involving violence between spouses were purportedly resolved "amicably."[99]

Male guardianship contributes significantly to domestic abuse. Women are considered legal minors under the control of their *mahram* (closest male relative) and subject to legal restrictions regarding their personal behavior that do not apply to men.[100] Under this system, adult women must obtain permission from a male guardian – usually a husband, father, brother, or son – to do many things, such as travel abroad, obtain a passport, marry, or be discharged from prison.[101] Saudi Arabia's male guardianship system has continued despite government assurances to end it.[102]

If a woman wants to file a legal complaint for domestic abuse, she must bring her guardian with her to court to file the report.[103] In other words, to bring a case for domestic abuse against her husband, she must bring her husband to court with her to file her case.

Saudi women's rights advocates have been critical of domestic

---

[97] See *Consideration of reports submitted by States Parties under article 18 of the Convention: Combined third and fourth periodic reports of the States parties due in 2013: Saudi Arabia*, UN Doc CEDAW/C/SAU/3-4 (23 August 2016) 8-9.
[98] '8,016 cases of abuse recorded in one year', *Arab News* (Web Article,16 December 2015).
[99] Ibid.
[100] Doumato (n 67) 3.
[101] Kenneth Roth, "World Report 2019: Saudi Arabia Events of 2018," *Human Rights Watch*, (Web Page).
[102] Ibid.
[103] Organisation for Economic Co-operation and Development, *Social Institutions & Gender Index: Saudi Arabia* (2019).

violence investigations because some investigators require permission from the male head of household to enter the home – the very man who may have committed the violence.[104] Furthermore, there are reports of domestic violence investigators encouraging victims and perpetrators to reconcile to keep the families intact, rather than prosecute the cases.[105] Police and judges have been known to return women directly to their abusers, as many were their legal guardians.[106]

(c) Rape

Saudi Arabia does not have a penal code and there is no written law which specifically criminalises rape.[107] People are subject to arbitrary arrest and detention; the convicted are punished in accordance with Sharia as interpreted by individual judges.[108]

Sometimes the rape *victim* is punished. In 2006, a Saudi judge sentenced a woman who was the victim of gang rape, to 90 lashes, along with her rapists.[109] When she appealed, her sentenced increased to six months in prison and 200 lashes.[110] In 2007, King Abdullah pardoned the woman from the punishment.[111]

(d) Female genital mutilation

Female genital mutilation includes all procedures that involve partial or total removal of the external female genitalia, or other injury to the female genitalia for non-medical reasons. In 2016, the US State

---

[104] US State Department (n 96) 43.
[105] Ibid.
[106] Ibid.
[107] Doumato (n 67) 5.
[108] Ibid.
[109] Ibid 13.
[110] Ibid.
[111] Ibid.

Department reported that FGM is not a common practice in Saudi Arabia.[112] However, this is incorrect. A study conducted in 2016 and 2017 at King Abdulaziz University Hospital, in Jeddah, Saudi Arabia ('Jeddah study'), explained that it was presumed that FGM was not common because Sharia prohibits the practice.[113] When the Jeddah study initiated a survey of 963 women over an eight-month period regarding their FGM status and attitudes toward the practice, the results showed that FGM is prevalent in Jeddah, among both immigrant and Saudi women.[114] The actual prevalence, however, was unknown.[115]

4 *Extraction*

The stereotypical Saudi woman is subservient and controlled by the men.[116] However, the Kingdom has slowly allowed women to enjoy some freedom.[117] Regardless, Saudi Arabia is still an Islamic country, based on Sharia. Saudi women suffer child marriages, polygamous marriages, and unequal divorce, adultery and rape laws. The Islamic worldview cannot offer a coherent, compatible and consistent set of laws to protect women from discrimination and violence. Although the Islamic worldview offers a "higher law" approach to human rights – and therefore women's rights – Islamic laws do not present hope for eliminating discrimination and violence against women.

---

[112] Abdulrahim A Rouzi et al, 'Survey on female genital mutilation/cutting in Jeddah, Saudi Arabia' (2019) 9(5) *BMJ Open* e024684:1-6, 1.
[113] Ibid.
[114] Ibid.
[115] Ibid.
[116] Abahussain (n 38) 91-92.
[117] Ibid 91. In 2015, Saudi women could vote for the first time. In 2018, the ban on Saudi women driving was lifted.

B *Hinduism: Women and the Laws of India*

A woman must be dependent upon her father in childhood, upon her husband in youth, and upon her sons in her old age; she should never be free. — Manu[118]

India is pluralistic in its laws and religion, and has a history of devaluing women. Since the 1970s, Indian reformers have advocated for equalising laws for men and women.[119] The Hindu Nationalist movement pushed equality activists to accept a plural civil code in the name of Legal Pluralism.[120] Yet, while Hindu leaders criticised discrimination practices among Muslims, they ignored similar prevalent practices among Hindus and in Hindu law.[121]

1 *Background*

Hinduism was birthed in India.[122] It is the world's third largest religion, after Christianity and Islam.[123] Hinduism is not confined to one particular doctrine – it embraces several theological perspectives, including monotheism, polytheism and pantheism, absorbing views from other religions.[124] Hinduism is cultural, assimilating many traditions of its ancestors, not just a single teaching.[125] It is so diverse,

---

[118] Flavia Agnes, 'Law and Gender Equality: The Politics of Women's Rights in India' in Flavia Agenst, Sudhir Chandra and Monmayee Basu (eds), *Women & Law in India* (Oxford University Press, 2004) 11.
[119] Carolyn E Holmes, 'Conventions, Courts, and Communities: Gender Equity, CEDAW and Religious Personal Law in India' (2019) 57(7) *Journal of Asian and African Studies* 965, 969.
[120] Ibid.
[121] Ibid.
[122] Steven J Rosen, 'Hinduism' in Lee Worth Bailey (ed), *Introduction to the World's Major Religions* (Greenwood Press, 2006) vol 6, xvi.
[123] Ibid.
[124] Ibid.
[125] Ibid.

it has been called a living encyclopedia of religions.[126] India's contemporary legal system deliberately subsumes Buddhism, Jainism, and Sikhism under the Hindu label.[127] In spite of the diversity, the Hindu tradition with the most followers today is Vaishnavism, a religion centered on the worship of Vishnu, 'the all-pervasive Lord.'[128]

While there is no precise definition of the word 'Hindu' through statutes or judicial pronouncements, in 1966 the India Supreme Court attempted to define it, explaining: 'Acceptance of the Vedas with reverence, recognition of the fact that the means of ways to salvation are diverse and realisation of the truth that number of gods to be worshipped is large is the distinguishing features of Hindu religion.'[129]

In reality, any simple definition of the Hindu religion proves inadequate.[130] A person who practices or professes Hinduism is clearly a Hindu.[131] However, a Hindu who no longer practices or professes faith in Hindu religion or philosophy may still be considered a Hindu.[132] A Hindu who starts practicing or professing a non-Hindu religion may also still be considered a Hindu.[133] Even atheists do not cease to be a Hindu.[134] On the other hand, if a Hindu formally converts to another faith, he may finally cease to be recognised as a Hindu.[135] Today a Hindu community governed by Hindu laws is somewhat a fiction – it

---

[126] Ibid.
[127] Ibid xvii-xiii.
[128] Ibid xvi.
[129] *Shastri Yagnapurushadasji v Muldas Vaishya*, AIR 1966 SC 1119; (1967) 69 BOMLR 1, cited by Aapka Consultant, 'Definition of a Hindu' (Web Page, 2 January 2018).
[130] Agnes (n 118) 25.
[131] Ibid.
[132] Ibid.
[133] Ibid.
[134] Ibid.
[135] Ibid.

is not a religious entity or a social reality.[136] It is a cacophony of beliefs and practices.

According to Indian lawyer Flavia Agnes, plurality of laws and customs were the characteristics of ancient Indian communities.[137] During the pre-colonial era in India, there was no distinction between religion, law and morality, that is, *dharma*.[138] Three sources of dharma are *shruti* (the divine revelations, primarily the *Vedas*), *smriti* (the memorised word – the *dharmasutras* and the *dharmashastras*) and *sadachara* (good custom).[139] The Vedas were treated as the "fountainhead" of Hindu law by jurists, but they did not contain positive law (man-made law).[140] Codified laws governing Hindu marriage and family derive their roots from the smritis and *nibandhas* (commentaries and digests).[141]

India is well known known for its Hindu caste system, which is based in religion.[142] It has been in existence for about 3,000 years.[143] It can be described as a social hierarchy of groups of people based on work and dharma.[144] There are four primary groups: Brahmins, Kshatriyas, Vaishyas and Shudras.[145] Brahmins are the purest and highest caste, whereas the Shudras are the lowest caste; Dalits are considered even

---

[136] Ibid 26.
[137] Ibid 12.
[138] Ibid.
[139] Ibid.
[140] Ibid.
[141] Ibid.
[142] Ahmed Usman, 'A Comparison of Hindu and Muslim Caste System in Sub-continent' (2017) 32(1) *A Research Journal of South Asian Studies* 91, 92.
[143] 'What is India's Caste System?', *BBC News* (Web Article, 19 June 2019).
[144] Usman (n 142) 91.
[145] What is India's Caste System? (n 143): 'The main castes were ... divided into about 3,000 castes and 25,000 sub-castes, each based on their specific occupation.'

lower, outside of the caste system.[146] Although the Indian constitution prohibits caste discrimination, it remains prevalent.[147]

According to Monmayee Basu, Associate Professor of History at the University of Delhi, the condition of Hindu women in India began to deteriorate after Muslim conquerors settled India:

> By and large women lost their opportunities and freedom, and became increasingly dependent on men ... Worse still, undesirable social customs crept in, which gradually reduced the Indian woman to a state of perpetual bondage. When raids and warfare became a common occurrence, the fear of insecurity which affected unmarried young women was, perhaps largely responsible for the emergence of the system of *early marriage*. This most probably led to the beginning of the cruel and reprehensible *dowry* system which has prevailed for centuries and persists even today. The fear of insecurity was, to a great extent, responsible for the growth and continuance of the system of *sati*. The emergence of the *purdah* system and seclusion of women was another byproduct of such fear. The effect of these disabilities was awesome. Gradually, the belief grew in India society that women were destined to a status inferior to men. At the beginning of the nineteenth century, the position of Indian women had reach the 'lowest depth of degradation.'[148]

This background gives context for the next section which will discuss India's laws as they pertain to women regarding: (1) discrimination in the family and (2) violations of bodily integrity.

---

[146] Ibid 91-92.
[147] US State Department, *India 2018 Human Rights Report* (Report, 2018) 46.
[148] Monmayee Basu, 'Hindu Women and Marriage Law: From Sacrament to Contract' in Monmayee Basu (ed) *Women & Law in India* (Oxford University Press, 2001) 2-3 (emphasis added).

2 Family Matters

India's pluralistic legal system is reflected in the Indian Constitution, where personal laws to vary according to religion: the Hindu population is governed by the *Hindu Marriage Act 1955*[149]; the *Muslim population is governed by the Muslim Personal Law Sharia Application Act 1937*;[150] and Muslim Women's *Protection of Rights on Divorce Act 1986*;[151] the Christian population is governed by the *Indian Christian Marriage Act 1872*;[152] and the Zoroastrian population is governed by the *Parsi Marriage and Divorce Act 1936*.[153] This article focuses on Indian laws governing Hindus.

(a) Marriage/Child marriage

In the late nineteen century, child marriage (known as *gouridan*), was common in Hindu society.[154] The *Age of Consent Act 1861* raised the minimum age for a girl to marry from ten to twelve years old.[155] Due to Hindu custom, many people continued to support child marriage, even into the twentieth century.[156] Child marriage was finally prohibited under the *Prohibition of Child Marriage Act 2006*.[157] Currently, there are no legal exceptions to the minimum age for marriage for women (18) and men (21).[158] However, while there has been a decline in child marriages reported, they remain pervasive in India.[159]

---

[149] *The Hindu Marriage Act* 1955 (India).
[150] *The Muslim Personal Law (Shariat) Application Act 1937* (India).
[151] *The Muslim Women (Protection of Rights on Divorce) Act 1986* (India).
[152] *The Indian Christian Marriage Act 1872* (India).
[153] *The Parsi Marriage and Divorce Act 1936* (India).
[154] Basu (n 148) 4.
[155] Ibid.
[156] Ibid 52-53.
[157] *The Prohibition of Child Marriage Act 2006* (India).
[158] Organisation for Economic Co-operation and Development, *Social Institutions & Gender Index: India* (2019) 2.
[159] Ibid.

Typically, after her marriage, the young girl went to her husband's house and found a miserable life.[160] Under complete control of her husband's family, she had no freedom.[161] The mother-in-law was usually the supreme authority and the young wife was required to obey her.[162] Young housewives were prohibited from stepping out of the house.[163] *Purdah* was the common practice of shutting away women, forcing them into a secluded life.[164]

While Hindu widows were often treated like a slave in the family, conditions for the child widow were even worse – she was neglected and mistreated from her very childhood and was destined to suffer.[165] Upper caste child widows were not permitted to remarry.[166] Many widows were compelled to burn themselves on the funeral pyres of their husbands (a practice known as *sati* or *suttee*).[167] So long as her husband was alive, the wife had an acceptable status in society – but as soon as he died, she became doomed to a life of forced labor.[168] Therefore, the widow preferred to die with her husband.[169] Eventually the practice of *sati* was prohibited and made a criminal offense in 1829.[170]

The *Hindu Widow Remarriage Act 1856* was enacted to encourage widows to remarry.[171] However, it was not as successful as intended;

---

[160] Basu (n 148) 4.
[161] Ibid.
[162] Ibid.
[163] Ibid 8.
[164] Ibid.
[165] Ibid 6.
[166] Ibid 7.
[167] Ibid 67.
[168] Ibid 68.
[169] Ibid.
[170] Ibid 67.
[171] Ibid 69.

90% of the prostitutes were widows.[172] In response, the *Special Marriage Act 1872* was enacted to popularise widow remarriage.[173] Not as successful as hoped, Social reformers realised that without education, the problems of the Hindu widows could never be solved.[174]

After India became independent in 1947, Hindu law was codified and women were granted substantial rights. Unfortunately, the problem of widows remained unsolved and widow-remarriage rarely took place.[175] Finally, in the mid-twentieth century, women had access to education and advanced studies, opening opportunities to earn money through employment.[176] The same was true for Hindu widows.[177] Education and employment brought women a measure of freedom from a life of bondage.

The dowry system was another problem that existed in Hindu society during the second half of the nineteenth century. As a rule, dowry had to be paid at the time of the girl's marriage.[178] Dowry was not a gift made by the bride's parents to their daughter as her separate property; it was a gift to the bride's in-laws.[179] While dowry took different forms in different communities, the custom was almost universal.[180] A daughter was a burden in a Hindu family since she had to be married at the right age and within the accepted caste framework.[181]

During the mid-twentieth century and later, the dowry system became

---

[172] Ibid 7.
[173] Ibid 75.
[174] Ibid.
[175] Ibid 76.
[176] Ibid 78.
[177] Ibid 76.
[178] Ibid 7.
[179] Ibid 86.
[180] Ibid 88.
[181] Ibid 7.

an outrage of enormous magnitude – it became known as the groom's price, to procure more money in the marriage market.[182] In other words, fathers of brides were force to pay more to marry off their daughters. Hence, daughters became an even greater burden to their families.

The Dowry Prohibition Act 1961 outlawed dowry in India.[183] Even so, the US State Department reports that dowry continues to be widely practiced and often contributes to violence against young brides, sometimes resulting in death.[184] Dowry deaths – like bride burning – is a tragic method of punishing women for insufficient dowries or creating an opportunity for the husband to remarry and receive another dowry.[185] In 2013, the Indian government announced the appointment of dedicated, full-time Dowry Prohibition Officers to enforce the Act and train law enforcement agencies on issues of dowry related harassment and dowry deaths.[186] However, in 2016, authorities reportedly arrested 20,545 persons for dowry deaths.[187] Someday dowry may disappear, but this goal seems remote when bride burning cases consistently appear in the news.[188]

---

[182] Ibid 88.
[183] *The Dowry Prohibition Act 1961* (India).
[184] US State Department (n 147) 38.
[185] See 'Bride Burning: What is it, where does it happen and how to end it', *Rights Universal* (Web Article, 15 April 2017). Bride burning occurs when a wife is soaked with a flammable liquid and set on fire. Women rarely survive. Those who do survive are severely and permanently scarred. This extremely violent act is performed by the husband or his family because the bride's family has refused to pay an additional dowry. Bride burning, also known as a dowry death, primarily occurs in India and Pakistan. It is estimated that 8,000 women die from bride burning each year.
[186] Planning Commission (Government of India), *Twelfth Five Year Plan 2012-2017* (Sage Publications India, 2013) vol III, 172.
[187] US State Department (n 147) 38.
[188] Basu (n 148) 96.

(b) Divorce

The right to divorce in India depends on the laws under which one marries, civil or religious.[189] According to the *Special Marriage Act 1954*,[190] and *Hindu Marriage Act 1955*,[191] either the husband or wife may petition for a divorce.[192] Hindu men and women have equal right to a divorce.

(c) Adultery

Until 2018, adultery was a crime under s 497 of the *Indian Penal Code 1860* (*'Indian Penal Code'*), which defined it from the man's perspective:

> Whoever has sexual intercourse with a person who is and whom he knows or has reason to believe to be the wife of another man, without the consent or connivance of that man, such sexual intercourse not amounting to the offence of rape, is guilty of the offence of adultery, and shall be punished with imprisonment of either description for a term which may extend to five years or with fine or with both. In such case the wife shall not be punishable as an abettor.[193]

In September 2018, the Supreme Court of India, unanimously struck down s 497 as unconstitutional.[194]

---

[189] *SIGI: India* (n 158) 3.
[190] *The Special Marriage Act 1954* (India).
[191] *The Hindu Marriage Act 1955* (India).
[192] *SIGI: India* (n 158) 3.
[193] *The Indian Penal Code 1860* (India) s 497 (*'Indian Penal Code'*).
[194] 'Explainer: What Is Adultery Law And Section 497 Of IPC', *Outlook India* (Web Article, 27 September 2018).

3 Violation of Bodily Integrity

(a) Violence Against Women

Women in India face many obstacles to their safety and protection from physical, sexual and psychological violence. Rape, domestic violence, dowry-related deaths, honor killings and sexual harassment pose serious threats to women's physical integrity in Indian society.[195] Women from lower castes and tribes (eg Dalit women) are especially vulnerable to sexual violence due to caste-based discrimination.[196]

India does not have an overarching law covering violence against women.[197] Instead, violence against women is covered by sections of the *Indian Penal Code*,[198] the *Protection of Women from Domestic Violence Act 2005*[199] (*'Domestic Violence Act'*) and the *Protection of Children from Sexual Offences Act 2012*.[200]

Acid attacks continue to take place, despite amendments to *Indian Penal Code* in 2013 which increased penalties for acid-throwing from five to seven years.[201] Victims of acid attacks are often women who challenge norms, eg opposing a marriage proposal.[202] The Delhi government announced it would cover 100% medical expenses for victims of acid attacks in private hospitals in its territory.[203] The

---

[195] Women's International League for Peace & Freedom, *Caught Between Arms: The State of Women's Rights in India, Shadow Report to CEDAW 58th Session* (Report, 2014).
[196] Report of the Special Rapporteur on Violence Against Women, Its Causes and Consequences, Rashida Manjoo, UN Doc A/HRC/26/38 (28 May 2014).
[197] *SIGI: India* (n 158) 4.
[198] *Indian Penal Code*.
[199] *The Protection of Women from Domestic Violence Act 2005*.
[200] *The Protection of Children from Sexual Offences Act 2012* (India).
[201] *Indian Penal Code* s 326B.
[202] *SIGI: India* (n 158) 6.
[203] US State Department (n 147) 36.

Supreme Court of India has also approved assistance to acid attack victims, up to 800,000 rupees ($11,500) for acid attack injuries.[204]

(b) Domestic Violence

Domestic Violence is against the law in India under the *Domestic Violence Act*[205] and the *Indian Penal Code*.[206] Domestic violence includes physical, psychological, sexual and economic abuse.[207] The punishment is up to three years in prison.[208] The *Protection of Women from Domestic Violence Act* sets forth measures to prevent and reduce domestic violence, including free legal aid for women and access to free services of official service providers.[209] Domestic violence in India continues to be a problem.

(c) Rape

The *Indian Penal Code* criminalises rape, which is punishable by imprisonment up to ten years and up to twenty years for gang rape.[210] Rape is the lack of consent to sexual intercourse and does not require evidence of force or resistance, but it does require penetration.[211] Gang rape of minors is rampant.[212] The punishment for raping a girl under the age of 16 is between twenty years and life.[213] The punishment for raping a girl under the age of 12 is life imprisonment or the death

---

[204] Ibid.
[205] *The Protection of Women from Domestic Violence Act 2005* (India).
[206] *Indian Penal Code* s 498A.
[207] *The Protection of Women from Domestic Violence Act 2005* (India).
[208] US State Department (n 147) 37.
[209] *The Protection of Women from Domestic Violence Act 2004* (India).
[210] US State Department (n 147) 36.
[211] *Indian Penal Code* s 376 A-D.
[212] US State Department (n 147) 37.
[213] Ibid 36.

penalty.²¹⁴ Marital rape is illegal when the wife is under 18 years old.²¹⁵

Rape is the country's fastest-growing crime in India, likely due in part to the increased willingness of victims to report their rapes, albeit a large number of rape cases remain unreported.²¹⁶ Even so, law enforcement and legal recourse for rape victims remain largely inadequate.²¹⁷ Police have been known to attempt to reconcile rape victims and their attackers, even encouraging the rape victims to marry their attackers.²¹⁸ Inadequate victim support, protection of witnesses, and health care guidelines for victims leads to lack of convictions.²¹⁹ Low conviction rates is considered one of the main reasons sexual violence against women continues.²²⁰

(d) Female genital mutilation

India has no law specifically addressing FGM, despite the common practice.²²¹ Human rights groups and non-governmental organisations report that between 70 and 90 percent of the *Dawoodi Bohras* practiced FGM, a population of approximately one million.²²² The government continues to investigate the issue and strategise how to respond.²²³

(e) Forced abortion/sex selection

The government of India has promoted female sterilisation as a form of

---

[214] Ibid.
[215] Ibid.
[216] Ibid.
[217] Ibid.
[218] Ibid.
[219] Ibid.
[220] Ibid.
[221] *SIGI: India* (n 158) 5.
[222] US State Department (n 147) 37-38.
[223] Ibid.

"family planning" for decades.[224] Reports of coerced and involuntary sterilisation are not uncommon.[225] As of 2018, several states still had policies penalising families with more than two children.[226] Women continue to be forced or choose to abort a girl child in India (gender-selective abortion) despite the passage of the *Pre-Conception and Pre-Natal Diagnostic Techniques (Prohibition of Sex Selection) Act 1994*.[227] However, almost all states have implemented "girl child promotion" to counter sex selection based on son preference.[228]

4 *Extraction*

India's pluralistic religion and laws have not adequately protected women from unjust discrimination and violence. Indeed, Hinduism has lent itself to the diminished value of women as evidenced by child marriages, *purdah*, *sati*, rape, dowry deaths, acid attacks, son preference, etc. While women are making progress through education and reform, this progress cannot be supported by Hinduism which ranks people in value pursuant to a hierarchical caste system. Thus, the Hindu religious worldview does not appear to offer much hope for ending discrimination and violence against women.

C *Atheism: Women and the Laws of China*

Vocal feminism and atheism now are moral obligations: anything less makes us complicit in the dehumanization, commoditization, and sexual exploitation of women. To protect

---

[224] Ibid 39.
[225] Ibid.
[226] Ibid 40.
[227] *SIGI: India* (n 158) 6.
[228] US State Department (n 147) 40.

the defenseless and progress toward humanism, women must abandon religion. —Lauri Weissman[229]

Some women think all religion is bad for women, that it stands in the way of advancing women's rights as human rights and better treatment of women. Madhavi Sunder, Professor of Law at Georgetown University, insists that securing human rights requires deconstructing religion.[230] Atheist feminist Karen L Garst goes further, declaring that religion is anti-women and the last cultural barrier to gender equality, due to the historical subjugation and degradation of women.[231] If all this is true, then one would expect to see the best example of human rights protections and gender equality (not to mention the end of the discrimination and violence against women) in an atheistic state. This section will examine laws from China, the most atheistic country in the world, to show this it does not offer the best hope for women.

1 *Background*

In 2019, a WIN/Gallup International poll revealed that China is the least religious country in the world.[232] Less than 10% of residents of China stated that they feel religious and over 60% are 'convinced atheists.'[233] Although China's constitution guarantees religious freedom, the reality is that any religious organisation without official

---

[229] Lauri Weissman, 'Half Human: How Jewish Law Justifies the Exclusion and Exploitation of Women' in Karen L Garst (ed), *Women v Religion: The Case Against Faith – and for Freedom* (Pitchstone Publishing, 2018) 71.
[230] Madhavi Sunder, 'Piercing the Veil' (2003) 112 *Yale Law Journal* 1399, 1404.
[231] Karen Garst, 'Introduction', in Garst, (n 229) 13.
[232] 'Least Religious Countries Population', *World Population Review* (Web Page, 16 August 2019); see also 'Religion Prevails in the World', *Gallup International* (Web Article, 10 April 2017).
[233] Ibid.

approval faces state persecution.[234] China is officially an atheist state.[235]

In addition to being the most atheist country in the world, according to the US State Department, the People's Republic of China ('PRC') is an authoritarian state in which the Chinese Communist Party ('CCP') is the supreme authority.[236] CCP members hold almost all the top government and security positions.[237] Atheism is the basic doctrine for the CCP.[238] Therefore, atheist propaganda is necessary to exterminate religion.[239] Although the CCP acknowledges the presence of religion and people practicing religion in China, it affirms that religion will eventually fade away and atheist propaganda should be carried out relentlessly.[240] It is important to keep this communist propaganda agenda in mind when examining purported equality laws in China.

This background gives context for the next section which will discuss China's laws as they pertain to women regarding: (1) discrimination in the family and (2) violations of bodily integrity.

2 *Family Matters*

Chinese law espouses equality, expressly giving husbands and wives

---

[234] 'China Population 2019', *World Population Review*, (Web Page, 11 July 2019).
[235] China does not survey its people on their religion. Therefore, the religious demographics may not be accurate.
[236] US State Department, *China (includes Tibet, Hong Kong, and Macau) 2018 Human Rights Report* (Report, 2018) 1.
[237] Ibid.
[238] Fenggang Yang, 'Between Secularist Ideology and Desecularizing Reality: The Birth and Growth of Religious Research in Communist China' (2004) 65(2) *Sociology of Religion* 101, 103.
[239] Ibid.
[240] Ibid 105.

equal status in the family.²⁴¹ Women even have the same legal rights as men to be recognised as head of household.²⁴² Marital property is partial community property and both spouses must agree how to manage the property.²⁴³ Both mother and father have equal rights and responsibilities to their children, during and after marriage.²⁴⁴ The same applies to children born out of wedlock.²⁴⁵

Regardless of the Chinese government's purported efforts to promote equality of men and women, the reality is that general stereotypes exist – women take care of working inside the home, men take care of working outside of the home.²⁴⁶ Further, despite equality laws, discrimination and violence against women remains a problem.

(a) Marriage/Child Marriage

Under Chinese law, the consent of both husband and wife is required for marriage.²⁴⁷ Protections exist for a spouse (wife) who is coerced into marriage.²⁴⁸ Regardless of marriage equality laws, Chinese birth limitations and cultural preference for sons created a culture where men outnumber women, leaving large numbers of single men, especially in rural areas.²⁴⁹ According to the US State Department, this has increased demand for foreign women as brides for Chinese men and triggered an increase in human trafficking and forced marriages.²⁵⁰These women

---

[241] Organisation for Economic Co-operation and Development, *Social Institutions & Gender Index: China* (2019) 2.
[242] Ibid 2.
[243] *Marriage Law of the People's Republic of China* arts 17, 19.
[244] *Marriage Law of the People's Republic of China* arts 17, 19.
[245] Ibid art 25.
[246] *SIGI: China* (n 241) 2-3.
[247] *Marriage Law of the People's Republic of China* art 5.
[248] Ibid art 11.
[249] US State Department, *2017 Trafficking in Persons Report: China* (Report, 2017).
[250] *SIGI: China* (n 241) 2-3.

may be kidnapped or sold by relatives and transported to China.[251]

In China, the legal age to get married is not the same for men and women – 22 years old for men, and 20 for women.[252] Parents or guardians are prohibited from allowing or forcing minors into marriages, or arranging such marriages.[253] This is likely the consequence of the increase in human trafficking and young foreign brides.

As for statistics regarding child marriage in China, there is a lack of data.[254]

(b) Divorce

Men and women have the same divorce rights under Chinese Marriage Law. Additionally, Chinese law offers protection for pregnant women – husbands may not apply for divorce within one year of his wife giving birth, or with 6 months after the termination of her pregnancy.[255] Women are not subject to the same restriction.[256]

Despite equal divorce rights, women suffer from the social stigma of divorce more than men because traditional Chinese standards are more liberal for men when it comes to family.[257] Therefore, women – especially rural women – are likely to suffer economic hardship because their husbands were the only source of financial income.[258] Equal opportunity for divorce does not yield equal consequences.

---

[251] Tahirih Justice Center: Forced Marriage Initiative, 'Forced Marriage Overseas: China' (Web Page).
[252] *Marriage Law of the People's Republic of China* art 6.
[253] *SIGI: China* (n 241) 2.
[254] Ibid. Although UNICEF is an organisation which collects data on child marriage for East Asia, there is a lack of data on child marriage in China in the UNICEF database.
[255] Ibid.
[256] *SIGI: China* (n 241) 3.
[257] Ibid.
[258] Ibid.

3 Violations of Bodily Integrity

Human trafficking is the most common type of violence against women in China.[259] Women and children are the primary victims of kidnapping, physical and sexual assault, and sale.[260] The women's slave trade has affected hundreds and thousands of families in rural areas and in the cities.[261] No official statistics exist regarding how many women and children have been kidnapped and sold in the black market.[262]

(a) Violence Against Women

The Chinese Constitution prohibits the mistreatment of women, children, and the elderly.[263] However, the law that was designed to protect women who were victimised by domestic violence or trafficking lacks teeth to provide civil or criminal remedies to punish the perpetrators.[264] In other words, it is a law with no remedy. When it comes to sexual violence, the criminal law does not address it, although it does prohibit rape.[265]

(b) Domestic Violence

For a long time, domestic violence was considered a private matter in China.[266] Finally, in 2016, China's first domestic violence law went into effect.[267] Domestic violence is defined as physical and psychological

---

[259] *SIGI: China* (n 241) 4.
[260] Ibid.
[261] Ibid.
[262] Ibid.
[263] Chinese Constitution art 49.
[264] *SIGI: China* (n 241) 4.
[265] Ibid 5.
[266] Ibid 4.
[267] Ibid.

abuse of family members and cohabitating non-family members.[268] Due to the new law, more women have reported domestic violence. Despite this progress, the US State Department opines that the law has been inconsistently implemented due to lack of awareness of the law.[269] Thus, victims of domestic violence often remain reluctant to report the abuse to authorities or go to court due to the prevailing sentiment that these are largely private matters.[270]

(c) Rape

Rape is against the law in China and defined as a female victim's lack of consent – punishable by a maximum of 10 years in prison.[271] According to a US State Department human rights report on China, some convicted rapists in China were executed.[272] The law does provide enhanced remedies for aggravated forms of rape and sexual violence.[273] As for China's law regarding statutory rape, it prohibits consensual sexual contact with a person under the age of 14.[274] Punishment is even more severe if the younger party was under 14 and acting as a prostitute.[275] There is no separate law for spousal rape, but a wife can file a complaint for the rape.[276]

Unfortunately, victims of rape are still likely to be blamed in Chinese culture. A study conducted by the University of Pennsylvania in 2016 found that Chinese culture considers rape at least partly a

---

[268] Ibid.
[269] US State Department (n 236) 49-50.
[270] *SIGI: China* (n 241) 5.
[271] Ibid 5.
[272] US State Department (n 236) 49.
[273] *SIGI: China* (n 241) 5.
[274] Ibid.
[275] Ibid.
[276] Ibid.

woman's fault.[277] The topic is taboo and shameful, hindering women's willingness to report it.[278]

(d) Female genital mutilation

There is no evidence that female genital mutilation is common in China.[279]

(e) Forced abortion/sex selection

In 2018, the U.S. State Department reported coerced abortions and sterilisations in China, although exact statistics were not available.[280] The Chinese government restricts the parents' rights to choose how many children they have.[281] On 1 January 2016, the birth limit imposed on its citizens was raised from one to two children per married couple – finally ending the 1979 "one-child policy."[282] Nevertheless, Chinese law requires a woman with an unauthorised pregnancy to abort the baby or pay a fee, which can be ten times a person's annual disposable income.[283]

Due to the birth limitation policy and traditional preference for sons over daughters, sex-selective abortions, and the abandonment and neglect of baby girls continues to be a problem.[284]

4 *Extraction*

Like women in Saudi Arabia and India, Chinese women are not treated

---

[277] Ibid.
[278] Ibid.
[279] *SIGI: China* (n 241) 6.
[280] US State Department (n 236) 52.
[281] Ibid.
[282] *SIGI: China* (n 241) 7.
[283] US State Department (n 236) 53.
[284] Ibid 56.

as valuable as Chinese men. Although the law purports equality between men and women, women still suffer unjust discrimination and violence as evident in son-preference, forced abortions (usually girl babies), and human trafficking. Propaganda serves to advance Chinese communism and atheism. Therefore, laws purporting freedom and equality for women must be met with some skepticism. Without a transcendent source for law, China's man-made laws are subjective, arbitrary and subject to change on a whim by those in power. In a country where communism is the highest goal, the reality is, genuine freedom for women is a pipedream.

D *Christianity: Women and the Laws of the United States*

> There is neither Jew nor Gentile, neither slave nor free, nor is there male and female, for you are all one in Christ Jesus.
>
> —Galatians 3:28

From its founding, the law of the United States were influenced by biblical Christianity. Although not perfect, the history of the advancement of women's rights in the US is long and complex.[285] While unjust discrimination and violence against women still exist in the US, women have more freedom in the US than the other countries discussed in this article.

---

[285] Anne M Boylan, *Women's Rights in the United States: A History in Documents* (Oxford University Press, 2016) 3. Often the advancement of women's rights in the US is examined through the different waves of feminism. In general, the first wave of the feminist movement culminated with the 19th Amendment to the *United States Constitution*, giving women the right to vote. The second wave of the feminist movement emerged in the 1960's, with the advancement of the Equal Rights Amendments (which did not pass). Subsequent feminist waves have not been so clearly distinguished: at 8. An examination of the different waves of feminism is beyond the scope of this paper.

1 Background

In the early American colonies, women were under the authority of a husband or father.[286] European settlers from England, France, Spain, or Holland, brought their traditions of the written law with them.[287] The British Northern American colonies established its legal system based on the British Common Law.[288] French, Spanish and Dutch colonies established their legal systems based on Roman Law.[289] The notion of individual rights evolved slowly and ignited at the time of the American Revolution.[290]

For early European settlers, a woman's economic and legal rights depended on her marital status.[291] In the British colonies, under English Common Law, single women (*feme sole*) could stand "alone" or "solo" before the law, while a married woman (*feme covert*, ie covered by her husband) had no right apart from her husband.[292]

The French, Spanish and Dutch colonies treated these matters differently, in the Roman law tradition.[293] Married women kept the property they brought into the marriage, co-owned property acquired during marriage, and sometimes owned part of their late husband's personal property.[294] This legal principle is known as *community property*[295] and is applied in many states in the US today.

---

[286] Ibid 3.
[287] Ibid.
[288] Ibid.
[289] Ibid.
[290] Ibid.
[291] Ibid 17.
[292] Ibid.
[293] Ibid 22.
[294] Ibid.
[295] Ibid.

Historical documents reveal that American women struggled for better treatment and more rights from the early colonies and the American Revolution.[296] An example is a letter Abigail Adams wrote to her husband, John Adams, who became the second President of the United States in 1797. Abigail Adams wrote:

> I long to hear that you have declared an independancy—and by the way in the new Code of Laws which I suppose it will be necessary for you to make I desire you would Remember the Ladies, & be more generous & favourable to them than your ancestors. Do not put such unlimited power into the hands of the Husbands. Remember all Men would be tyrants if they could. If perticuliar care and attention is not paid to the Laidies we are determined to foment a Rebellion, and will not hold ourselves bound by any Laws in which we have no voice, or Representation.
>
> That your Sex are Naturally Tyrannical is a Truth so thoroughly established as to admit of no dispute, but such of you as wish to be happy willingly give up the harsh title of Master for the more tender & endearing one of Friend. Why then, not put it out of the power of the vicious & the Lawless to use us with cruelty & indignity with impunity. Men of Sense in all Ages abhor those customs which treat us only as the vassals of your Sex. Regard us then as Beings placed by providence under your protection & in imitation of the Supreem Being make use of that power only for our happiness.[297]

Nearly all citizens of early colonial America were Christians – the

---

[296] See generally ibid.
[297] Ibid 48 (spelling in original).

overwhelming majority were Protestants.²⁹⁸ Values and customs of Protestant Christianity permeated civil and political life. From the early colonists and until the mid 1900's, the Christian religion saturated American public life.²⁹⁹ All three branches of government – legislature, judicial, executive – affirmed and endorsed America as a religious, even Christian, nation.

As for the legislature, it declared that religion was necessary for good government. In 1789, the First Congress of the United States passed the *Northwest Ordinance*, which provided: 'Religion, morality, and knowledge, being necessary to good government and the happiness of mankind, schools and the means of education shall forever be encouraged.'³⁰⁰ On the same day, James Madison also introduced proposed amendments which became the *Bill of Rights*, including the first amendment for religious freedom.³⁰¹

As for the judiciary, as early as 1799, the United States Supreme Court declared Christianity the established American religion: 'By our form of government, the Christian religion is the established religion; and all sects and denominations of Christians are placed upon the same equal footing, and are equally entitled to protection in their religious liberty.'³⁰²

---

[298] Stephen B Epstein, 'Rethinking the Constitutionality of Ceremonial Deism' (1996) 96 *Columbia Law Review* 2083, 2099.
[299] Leonard W Levy, *The Establishment Clause* (2ⁿᵈ ed., University of North Carolina Press, 1994) xiv.
[300] *SIGI: China* (n 241) 3.
[300] *An Act to provide for the Government of the Territory of the River Ohio*, Journals of the Continental Congress: 1774-1789, vol 32 (13 July 1787) 340, recodified at 1 Stat 50, 51 na (7 August 1789); *Wallace v Jaffree*, 472 US 38, 100 (1985) (Rehnquist J dissenting).
[301] *Wallace v Jaffree* 472 US 38, 100.
[302] See *Runkel v Winemiller*, 4 H & McH 429, 442 (1799) (held that a mandamus was proper to restore a pastor to his pulpit after he had been wrongfully dispossessed by part of his congregation).

As for the executive branch, President George Washington publicly prayed at his inaugural address in 1796, offering 'fervent supplications to that Almighty Being who rules over the universe, who presides in the councils of nations, and whose providential aids can supply every human defect.'[303] Since that first inaugural prayer, formal prayers offered by Christian ministers have been associated with presidential inaugurations.[304]

America's grounding in Christianity paved the way for women to petition for rights. After obtaining the right to vote, other laws were enacted to advance women as equal in value and dignity.[305]

This background gives context for the next section which will discuss the United States laws as they pertain to women regarding: (1) discrimination in the family and (2) violations of bodily integrity.

---

[303] President George Washington, 'Washington's Farewell Address' (17 September 1796), reprinted in James D Richardson (ed) *A Compilation of the Messages and Papers of the Presidents* (United States Government Printing Office, 1896) vol 1, 213-34; see also Epstein (n 298) 2109.
[304] Epstein (n 298) 2106.
[305] In 1920, American women were given the right to vote with the ratification of the 19th Amendment to the *United States Constitution*. In 1961, the President's Commission on the Status of Women ('PCSW') was established by President John F Kennedy, chaired by Eleanor Roosevelt to expose sex discrimination. In 1963, the *Equal Pay Act* was signed. In 1964, Title VII was signed into law to prohibit employment discrimination based on race or sex. In 1972, the Equal Rights Amendment ('ERA') was passed by Congress and sent to the states for ratification (it failed by ratified by the states). Boylan, *Women's Rights in the United States* (n 285) 141, 203-203, 207-208, 241-246.

2 Family Matters

(a) Marriage/child marriage

In the US, marriage is generally governed by the laws of each State.[306] Most states established the minimum age for marriage without parental consent at 18, and with parental consent at 16.[307] Every state has exceptions to the minimum age when there is parental consent or judicial approval.[308] A few states have passed laws prohibiting forced marriage.[309] This may help prevent the parental-consent exception from being misused by immigrant parents who coerce their children into early arranged marriages.[310]

In 2011, a survey of immigrant families was conducted regarding forced marriages in the US Over 3,000 cases were reported, with victim's families originating from 56 different countries, including: India, Pakistan, Bangladesh, Mexico, the Philippines, Yemen, Afghanistan, and Somalia.[311] Almost half of the reporting victims recounted actual physical violence from their forced marriage.[312] Over a quarter of these reported death threats.[313]

---

[306] Occasionally the federal government does create law regarding marriage, eg, in *Obergefell v Hodges* 2584 SCt (2015), 135 the US Supreme Court ruled that same-sex couples had the right to marry pursuant to both the Due Process Clause and the Equal Protection Clause of the Fourteenth Amendment to the *United States Constitution*

[307] *Report of the working group on the issue of discrimination against women in law and practice on its mission to the United States of America*, UN Doc A/HRC/32/44/add.2 (4 August 2016).

[308] Tahirih Justice Center: Forced Marriage Initiative, *Understanding State Statutes on Minimum Marriage Age and Exceptions* (1 July 2019) 1.

[309] Tahirih Justice Center, *Forced Marriage in Immigrant Communities in the United States: 2011 National Survey Results* (Report, 2011) 1, n 4.

[310] Ibid.

[311] Ibid 2, 8.

[312] Ibid 9.

[313] Ibid.

Polygamy is illegal in every state in the United States.[314] Regardless of the illegality, it is still practiced in the US based on certain religious beliefs, especially among Fundamentalist Mormons and Muslims.[315]

(b) Divorce

Women and men have equal rights to initiate divorce in the United States.[316] Divorce laws are a matter of state law, not federal law.[317] Since at least the 1940's, women are more likely to initiate divorce than men, initiating about 2/3 of the divorces.[318] A recent Stanford study explained this phenomenon by a power differential between the spouses and difference in perceived relationship quality.[319] A woman who experiences a controlling husband or an unhappy marriage may initiate a divorce as a way out of a disappointing marriage.

(c) Adultery

US adultery laws extend before the founding.[320] Most early states criminalised adultery.[321] In more recent years, many states have decriminalised adultery.[322] In 2015, twenty states still had adultery on

---

[314] Casey E Faucon, 'Marriage Outlaws: Regulating Polygamy in America' (2014) 22 *Duke Journal of Gender Law & Policy* 1, 1-2.
[315] Ibid 2.
[316] Organisation for Economic Co-operation and Development, *Social Institutions & Gender Index: United States* (2019) 3.
[317] Ibid 3.
[318] Michael J Rosenfeld, 'Who Wants the Breakup?: Gender and Breakup in Heterosexual Couples' (June 2017) 3.
[319] Ibid 21.
[320] Alyssa Miller, 'Punishing Passion: A Comparative Analysis of Adultery Laws in the United States of America and Taiwan and their Effects on Women' (2018) 41 *Fordham International Law Journal* 425, 428.
[321] Ibid.
[322] Ibid 429-32.

the books as a crime, but rarely is it prosecuted.[323] Regardless of the decline in the number of criminal statutes prohibiting adultery, adultery may be relevant in the legal system, eg as an injury in family law matters.[324] According to a 2013 Gallup poll, adultery was still viewed as immoral (over 91%).[325] Regardless, moral opposition to adultery has not been successful at deterring it.

3 Violations of Bodily Integrity

According to a 2018 Center for Disease Control ('CDC') report, 43.6% of women in the US (nearly 52.2 million) have experienced some form of sexual violence in their lifetime.[326] Approximately 1 in 6 women (an estimated 19.2 million) have experienced sexual coercion.[327] More than a third of women (approximately 44.3 million) have reported unwanted sexual contact.[328] Over half of female stalking victims were stalked before the age of 25, including 21.2% who reported being stalked before the age of 18.[329]

(a) Violence Against Women

The *Violence Against Women Act of 1994* ('VAWA') is a United States federal law.[330] VAWA established the Office on Violence Against

---

[323] Ibid 434. (States include Alabama, Arizona, Florida, Georgia, Idaho, Illinois, Kansas, Maryland, Massachusetts, Michigan, Minnesota, Mississippi, New York, North Carolina, Oklahoma, Rhode Island, South Carolina, Utah, Virginia and Wisconsin).
[324] Ibid 430-31.
[325] Ibid 435.
[326] Center for Disease Control, *National Intimate Partner and Sexual Violence Survey: 2015 Data Brief-Updated Release* (Report, November 2018) 2.
[327] Ibid.
[328] Ibid.
[329] Ibid 6.
[330] Title IV, § 40001-40703 of the *Violent Crime Control and Law Enforcement Act*, HR 3355, signed as Pub L No 103–322 by President Bill Clinton on September 13, 1994 (codified in part at 42 USC §§ 13701-14040).

Women ('OVW') within the Department of Justice ('DOJ').[331] OVW administers assistance to communities across the country that are developing policies aimed at ending domestic violence, dating violence, sexual assault, and stalking.[332] As of 2019, VAWA was expired.[333]

(b) Domestic Violence

According to a 2015 CDC's National Intimate Partner and Sexual Violence Survey, over one in three women (43.6 million) experienced sexual violence, physical violence, and/or stalking by an intimate partner during their lifetime.[334] Most women were under 25 when they first experienced such victimisation (71% or nearly 31 million), 25.8% were under 18.[335]

Domestic laws vary from state to state, including the definition of domestic abuse, when mandatory reporting is required and police arrest policies.[336] Most states have adopted *preferred* arrest policies that require police to either arrest one or both parties at the scene, or justify why an arrest is not made.[337] Some states have *mandatory* arrest policies requiring that an officer make an arrest if the domestic violence meets certain criteria.[338]

(c) Rape

---

[331] US Department of Justice Office on Violence Against Women, 'About the Office' (Web Page, 25 January 2021).
[332] Ibid.
[333] Madison Hartman, 'Employment-Based Legal and Policy Solutions for Female Victims of Intimate Partner Violence' (2019) 31 *Health Lawyer* 17, 25.
[334] National Intimate Partner and Sexual Violence Survey (n 327) 7.
[335] Ibid 10.
[336] 'State Domestic Violence Laws', *FindLaw* (Web Page, 23 November 2018).
[337] Ibid.
[338] Ibid.

Sexual assault is a significant problem in the United States. It is defined by the DOJ as 'any nonconsensual sexual act proscribed by Federal, tribal, or State law, including when the victim lacks capacity to consent.'[339] Anyone can experience sexual violence, but most victims are female; the person responsible for the violence is typically male and usually someone known to the victim.[340]

According to a 2018 CDC report, 1 in 5 women experienced rape or attempted rape during her lifetime.[341] Approximately 81.3% of female victims reported the age of their first rape or attempted rape was before the age 25.[342] Those under the age of 18 was 43%.[343] And those between 11 and 17 was 30.5%.[344]

(d) Female genital mutilation

Female genital mutilation, or cutting the labia majora, labia minor, or clitoris of a girl under the age of 18, is a federal crime in the US and punishable for up to 5 years in prison.[345] In 1996, the US Congress passed the law and at least 23 states have passed FGM laws.[346] In 2013, the law was updated to make it illegal for a person to knowingly send a family member to another country for FGM.[347]

---

[339] US Department of Justice Office on Violence Against Women, 'What is Sexual Assault?' (Web Page).
[340] Centers for Disease Control and Prevention, 'Sexual Violence' (Web Page, 5 February 2021).
[341] National Intimate Partner and Sexual Violence Survey (n 327) 2.
[342] Ibid 4.
[343] Ibid.
[344] Ibid.
[345] 18 USCS § 116.
[346] Mark Mather and Charlotte Feldman-Jacobs, 'Women and Girls at Risk of Female Genital Mutilation/Cutting in the United States', *Population Reference Bureau* (Web Page, 5 February 5, 2016).
[347] Ibid.

A CDC report published in 2016, revealed that approximately 513,000 women and girls in the US were at risk for FGM in 2012.[348] This was three times higher than an earlier estimate based on 1990 data; the risk for girls under the age of 18 was four times as high.[349] The increase was entirely the result of fast growth in the number of US immigrants from FGM practicing countries.[350] They did not estimate the number of women and girls who actually suffered the procedure.[351] FGM violates several human rights principles and is associated with a wide variety of physical, sexual, and psychological/emotional complications, both immediate and long term.[352]

4 *Extraction*

Comparatively speaking, laws in the US offer women greater protection from invidious discrimination and violence, than Saudi Arabia, India or China. Child marriages and FGM are due to an influx of immigrants bringing their cultural traditions. While discrimination and violence against women exists, the legal remedies in the US offer better protection and enforcement than in the other three countries. Biblical Christian principles undergird the foundation of the American system of government and laws. This is key to understanding why the US offers more protection for women against discrimination and violence. The final section of this article demonstrates how the biblical Christian worldview offers the best hope for women to end invidious discrimination and violence.

---

[348] Howard Goldberg et al, 'Female Genital Mutilation/Cutting in the United States: Updated Estimates of Women and Girls at Risk, 2012' (2016) 131(2) *Public Health Reports* 340, 340.
[349] Ibid.
[350] Ibid.
[351] Ibid 341.
[352] Ibid 2.

III THE BEST HOPE FOR WOMEN

> Lord, to whom shall we go? You have the words of eternal life. We have come to believe and to know that you are the Holy One of God. —John 6:68-69

The idea of dignity, value and equality for women did not develop in a vacuum. This idea has been nurtured because the ancient problem of invidious discrimination and violence against women has persisted. This article identified the problem of discrimination and violence against women. Part I discussed women's rights in the context of human rights. Part II explored various laws as they relate to women from four different countries, representing four different religious worldviews: Saudi Arabia (Islam), India (Hinduism), China (Atheism), US (Christian). The treatment of women, as viewed through the lens of the laws, varied significantly between the countries. While none of them may seem perfect in the treatment of women, one country stood out as superior than the others in its efforts to achieve better treatment for women. This Part will highlight the results of that comparative religious worldview analysis as viewed through the lens of the law.

UDHR Article 2 announces: '*Everyone* is entitled to all the rights and freedoms set forth in this Declaration, without distinction of any kind, such as race, colour, sex, language, religion, political or other opinion, national or social origin, property, birth or other status.'[353] Since everyone necessarily includes women, what is the source for this instinct for universality?

This instinct for the universality of human rights cannot come from Islam. Islam was born in Saudi Arabia. An examination of Saudi laws

---

[353] UDHR art 2 (emphasis added).

as they pertain to women, family, discrimination and violence against women, expose that Islam does not give the equal treatment of women, but rather treat women as inferior and subservient. Islamic law is based on the Quran and Sharia. It is higher law, as revealed from Allah to the Muslims' Prophet Muhammad. The problem is that Sharia favors men and devalues women. Women must have male guardians, who dictate what they can do. Women are treated unequally in marriage, divorce, child custody, inheritance, adultery, and rape. Men may beat their wives and have sex slaves. None of these are examples of inherent human rights for everyone, certainly not for women.

This instinct for the universality of human rights cannot come from Hinduism. Hinduism is a pluralistic belief system and the basis for India's laws. It has made a theology out of the caste system. Upper castes have more rights than lower castes. Indians prefer sons over daughters. Hinduism has contributed to the inferior value of women as evidenced by child marriages, *purdah*, *sati*, rape, bride-burning, acid attacks, female genital mutilation, etc. There is no evidence of inherent human rights for everyone in a Hindu religious worldview. Thus, it does not offer hope for ending discrimination and violence against women.

This instinct for the universality of human rights cannot come from an atheist worldview like China. An atheistic worldview is anti-supernatural, and therefore, materialistic. It cannot look to a higher law – God's law – as a source for human rights. Without an objective, transcendent basis for equality laws, they must be purely man-made, which are subjective, arbitrary, and subject to change on a whim by those in power. A naturalistic, materialistic worldview values the strong more than the weak (ponder Charles Darwin's "survival of the fittest"). Therefore, an atheistic worldview must devalue those lacking capacity, competency, or agency. It must devalue the weak, poor, old, uneducated, unborn, disabled, ill and infirm. Like India, China has son-preference – it favors boys over girls. Due to birth limitations, China also has forced abortion (usually baby girls). In addition, China also has a growing human trafficking problem. Despite China's purported equality laws, the reality is that women are viewed as inferior and less valuable than men. China does not demonstrate inherent human rights for all. Therefore, it cannot offer hope to end discrimination and violence against women.

Admittedly, there are Muslims, Hindus, and atheists who strongly believe and advocate for the equality of all human beings. This is a common global moral understanding. And rightly so. But the irony is that their worldviews, when followed consistently, do not support their advocacy for human rights.

Human rights is the common language of morality in our time. However, human rights are impossible without the transcendent basis for human rights that Christianity offers. The United States was highly influenced by biblical Christian principles at its founding. Its laws, and the progression of laws protecting women from discrimination and violence, demonstrate a view of women that is superior than other worldviews (even if not perfect). In addition, the United States demonstrates a more consistent enforcement of its laws. The Christian worldview is the only worldview that grounds human rights in a sustainable, coherent, and consistent way. An article in *Christianity Today* magazine stated it this way:

> It is in Christianity and, more specifically, in the Bible that we find the source of universal human rights. All humans are created

in the image of God – this is the abolitionists' argument for the dissolution of slavery. All women are created in the image of God – this is the argument of women's rights advocates for equal pay and voting rights. Children are created in the image of God – this is the argument against child labor. For pro-life advocates, this truth extends even into the womb, as they argue that every fetus is a human being, an image bearer in utero, and therefore is deserving of freedom and life.[354]

The consistent message of Christian Scripture is that human beings are inherently and universally valuable not because of rationality, agency, capability or anything else, but because human beings are created in the image of God, and He loves them. Though this lesson is simple, it is deeply profound.

The Christian worldview identifies the ultimate source of the human rights problem and a lasting solution. As described in Genesis chapters 1 and 2, while in paradise, God created man and woman in His image.[355] Human beings are his image bearers. As such, human beings should reflect the nature of God. God is love, and he commanded human beings to love him and each other.[356] This is the essence of human rights, treating one another with love because human beings are his image bearers.

But then came the fall. Sin infected all humanity.

Understanding this creates a context for the real problem underlying human rights violations, and underlying discrimination and violence

---

[354] Lauren Green McAffee and Michael McAffee, 'The Bible's Impact on Human Rights: The ideas of human dignity and respect for all didn't develop in a vacuum', *Christianity Today* (Web Page, 29 June 2019).
[355] Genesis 1:27.
[356] 1 John 4:8; Matthew 22:36-39.

against women. These problems are not external – they are internal. The problem is the human heart, due to the sin nature.

Human efforts alone cannot solve the problem of the human heart, our sin nature. The forces of evil are strong. Human beings need the help of one who is stronger. In the gospel of Luke, Jesus tells a story: 'When a strong man, fully armed, guards his own house, his possessions are safe. But when someone stronger attacks and overpowers him, he takes away the armor in which the man trusted and divides up his plunder.'[357] In this parable, Satan is the strong man, guarding his evil dominion, over people's naturally evil hearts. However, Jesus is the 'someone stronger,' more powerful than Satan, attacking and overpowering him, taking away his defense and possessions. In other words, Jesus can destroy the evil dominion in hearts. His death on the cross provided the way for humanity to be saved from the penalty, power, and eventually the presence of sin. Jesus is the only way to take a wicked heart and make it new.[358]

Jesus's death and resurrection provide a way for a new heart, a new life, a life of freedom, freedom from the bondage of the sin nature and evil heart, for those who believe and follow him. After all, Jesus declared: 'I am the way, the truth and the life. No one comes to the

---

[357] Luke 11:21-11.
[358] Ezekiel 11:19 ('And I will give them one heart, and a new spirit I will put within them. I will remove the heart of stone from their flesh and give them a heart of flesh.'); Jer. 36:26 ('And I will give you a new heart, and a new spirit I will put within you. And I will remove the heart of stone from your flesh and give you a heart of flesh.'); Jer 31:33 ('For this is the covenant that I will make with the house of Israel after those days, declares the LORD: I will put my law within them, and I will write it on their hearts. And I will be their God, and they shall be my people.'); Heb 8:10 ('For this is the covenant that I will make with the house of Israel after those days, declares the Lord: I will put my laws into their minds, and write them on their hearts, and I will be their God, and they shall be my people.').

Father but through me.'[359] Apart from Jesus we can do nothing.[360] Only through a transformed life in Jesus are human beings able to truly love others. This is the only lasting way to stop invidious discrimination and violence against women.

All human beings have inherent dignity, value and worth because God created us in His image. As image-bearers, women are enormously valuable. As such, women should be treated with equal dignity, value and worth. All people should advocate for laws that reflect this.

IV CONCLUSION

The problem of discrimination and violence against women is undeniable and exists in all countries and all cultures. Laws of Saudi Arabia, India, China and the United States are designed to remedy the inequality toward women. However, in practice, only the laws of the United States deliver the protections women deserve and elevate the status of women to equal men. This article has presented evidence to support the primary reason for why American laws and practices are superior for women, namely that they are derived from a transcendent God and are rooted in biblical Christianity, the dominant worldview of America. Biblical Christianity reveals both the root of the problem (sin in the human heart) and the solution (a new heart through faith in Jesus). From Scripture, we see that women's rights are human rights, such as when Jesus affirmed the humanity of the Samaritan women at the well by caring for her soul and offering her 'living water' (John 4:1-42), and the Apostle Paul stating that 'in Christ there is neither

---

[359] John 14:6.
[360] John 15:5.

male nor female' (Galatians 3:28).

The evidence presented demonstrates that laws shaped by a Christian worldview are much better for women than laws shaped by Islam, Hinduism or atheism. Biblical Christianity, therefore, has the best answers for ending invidious discrimination and violence toward women. This evidence further serves to defeat the challenge that somehow Christianity suppresses women. Thus, for purposes of Christian Apologetics, we can point to both the laws and the application of the laws of America that affect women, and the biblical foundation behind those laws, as a demonstration of the superiority of the Christian worldview. In Christ, women are free. And if the Son makes you free, you will be free indeed (John 8:36).

BOOK REVIEW

HEART OF WOKENESS: A REVIEW OF *CYNICAL THEORIES* AND *COUNTER WOKECRAFT*

JOSHUA FORRESTER*

Helen Pluckrose and James Lindsay, *Cynical Theories: How Universities Made Everything about Race, Gender, and Identity – and Why This Harms Everybody* (Swift Press, 2020)

Charles Pincourt and James Lindsay, *Counter Wokecraft: A Field Manual for Combatting the Woke in the University and Beyond* (Independently published, 2021)

James Lindsay is a grizzled veteran of the culture wars. But he was not always so. According to Lindsay, reading 'Glaciers, gender, and science: A feminist glaciology framework for global environmental change research'[1] sent him to a very dark place mentally.[2] He didn't come out of his room for three days.[3] Helen Pluckrose (herself a now-grizzled culture war veteran), recalls needing 'to talk him down'[4] (presumably from a ledge, and hopefully only a figurative one).

---

[1] Mark Carey, M Jackson, Alessandro Antonello and Jaclyn Rushing, 'Glaciers, gender, and science: A feminist glaciology framework for global environmental change research' (2016) 40(6) *Progress in Human Geography* 770.
[2] Jordan B Peterson, 'Interview with the grievance studies hoaxers' (YouTube, 11 January 2019) 01:02:11-01:02:57.
[3] Ibid.
[4] Ibid 01:02:58-01:03:08.

---

* Lecturer, Sheridan Institute of Higher Education.

Such is the cost of engaging with what Roger Scruton describes as the 'nonsense machine'.[5] However, both Pluckrose and Lindsay endured, and have made significant contributions to the fight against wokeness.[6] Pluckrose edited *Areo Magazine* from 2018 to 2021,[7] and founded Counterweight,[8] an organisation that supports 'individuals who are subject to mistreatment and abuse for questioning ideology'.[9] Lindsay founded *New Discourses*, a website that provides resources to understand 'Critical Social Justice'[10] (which could be considered the formal name for wokeness). Pluckrose and Lindsay's most notable contribution to the culture wars was their work, along with Peter Boghossian, comprising the 'grievance studies affair'. Here, Pluckrose, Lindsay and Boghossian submitted a number of articles to what they termed 'grievance studies' journals. The articles contained obvious errors, but used what would be described today as woke language. Out of the 20 articles they wrote, 7 were accepted for publication and, of these, 4 were published.[11]

Another notable contribution of Pluckrose and Lindsay is *Cynical Theories: How Activist Scholarship Made Everything about Race, Gender, and Identity – and Why This Harms Everyone* ('*Cynical*

---

[5] Roger Scruton, *Fools, Frauds and Firebrands: Thinkers of the New Left* (Bloomsbury Continuum, 2015) 191-196.
[6] In this review, the term 'wokeness' is intended to encompass variants like 'wokeism'/'wokism', 'woke ideology' and, indeed, 'Wokeshevism'. I use this term for the sake of consistency with this review's title. (Yes, 'Heart of Wokeness' is a nod to Joseph Conrad, and ties in the quote by Elon Musk that is found later in this review.)
[7] Helen Pluckrose, 'Editorial Announcement', *Areo Magazine* (Web Page, 6 April 2021).
[8] 'About Us', *Counterweight* (Web Page).
[9] 'Counterweight Mission and Values', *Counterweight* (Web Page).
[10] 'About', *New Discourses* (Web Page).
[11] James A Lindsay, Peter Boghossian and Helen Pluckrose, 'Academic Grievance Studies and the Corruption of Scholarship', *Areo Magazine* (Web Article, 2 October 2018).

Theories').[12] Lindsay has also collaborated with Charles Pincourt, to write *Counter Wokecraft: A Field Manual for Combatting the Woke in the University and Beyond* (*'Counter Wokecraft'*).[13] (It should be noted that 'Charles Pincourt' is a pen name. He works as a professor at a university in North America.[14] Given the treatment of other academics who have infringed woke sensibilities, Pincourt's prudence regarding his identity is wise.) Both books are timely and necessary, and I recommend them to readers interested in understanding and defeating wokeness.

Each book covers the 'weaponisation' of postmodern theories and their wide deployment in public discourse. How this happened must be understood. In my academic experience, I have seen complex theories once confined to academia converted into tweet-sized packages to bamboozle and browbeat[15] opposition in broader society. Bamboozling uses esoteric terms to confuse opponents while making those using them appear informed, sophisticated, or both. Browbeating uses 'loaded language' ('istophobe' terms,[16] and the like) to shut down

---

[12] Helen Pluckrose and James Lindsay, *Cynical Theories: How Universities Made Everything about Race, Gender, and Identity – and Why This Harms Everybody* (Swift Press, 2020).
[13] Charles Pincourt and James Lindsay, *Counter Wokecraft: A Field Manual for Combatting the Woke in the University and Beyond* (Independently published, 2021).
[14] 'Welcome to the Woke Dissident Blog', *Woke Dissident Blog* (Web Page, 3 May 2022).
[15] I am not alone in thinking 'browbeat' is an appropriate term; Pluckrose and Lindsay use it themselves: Pluckrose and Lindsay (n 12) 131.
[16] Terms like 'racist', 'sexist', 'homophobe', 'Islamophobe', and 'transphobe'.

arguments, portraying opponents as bigoted, ignorant, or both.[17]

Coining an important new term, Pluckrose and Lindsay describe *applied postmodernism*: the use of postmodern theories to serve activism.[18] After providing a brief history of postmodern thought,[19] they distill postmodern theories into those principles and themes that activists now use routinely. The two principles are the *postmodern knowledge principle* and the *postmodern political principle*.[20] The *postmodern knowledge principle* is a '[r]adical skepticism about whether objective knowledge or truth is obtainable and a commitment to cultural constructivism.'[21] Postmodern theorists may concede that there is an objective reality.[22] However, knowledge and truth are cultural constructs.[23] These constructs are products of dominant discourses within a culture: those with sociopolitical power determine what is 'knowledge' and what is 'true'.[24] Hence, any claims about truth are limited by one's culture, and reflect prevailing socioeconomic power in any event.[25]

The postmodern knowledge principle leads to *postmodern political principle*, which is 'a belief that society is formed of systems of power

---

[17] Scruton (n 5) 9 observes:
>Newspeak occurs whenever the primary purpose of language – which is to describe reality – is replaced by the rival purpose of asserting power over it. ... Newspeak sentences sound like assertions, but their underlying logic is that of the spell. They conjure the triumph of words over things, the futility of rational argument, and also the danger of resistance.

[18] Pluckrose and Lindsay (n 12) 24, ch 2.
[19] Ibid 21-30.
[20] Ibid 31.
[21] Ibid 31, 32-35.
[22] Ibid 32-34.
[23] Ibid.
[24] Ibid.
[25] Ibid 34.

and hierarchies, which decide what can be known and how'.[26] Dominant discourses permeate society; all within it perpetuate them 'through routine interactions, expectations, social conditioning, and culturally constructed discourses that express a particular understanding of the world.'[27] Consequently, the system privileges some and oppresses others.[28] Further, while this result may not have been intended by anyone in the system, all within it will have done their part to bring it about.[29]

The four themes are *the blurring of boundaries, the power of language, cultural relativism*, and *the loss of the individual and the universal.*[30] *The blurring of boundaries* challenges categories so to 'deny [them] any objective validity and disrupt the systems of power that might exist across them.'[31] Hence, boundaries are blurred between categories such as objective and subjective, truth and belief, science and the arts, natural and artificial, high and low culture, man and animal, man and machine, and health and sickness.[32] They are also blurred between categories of gender and sexuality.[33] *The power of language* involves two ideas. First, that language has 'enormous power to control society and how we think and thus is inherently dangerous'.[34] Second, that language is 'an unreliable way of producing and transmitting knowledge'.[35] *Cultural relativism* rejects the idea that cultures

---

[26] Ibid 31, 35-39.
[27] Ibid 36.
[28] Ibid 36-37.
[29] Ibid.
[30] Ibid 31.
[31] Ibid 39.
[32] Ibid.
[33] Ibid.
[34] Ibid 39-40.
[35] Ibid 40.

can meaningfully critique one another.[36] Each culture has its own discourses that shape the knowledge of its members, and will bias any critique of another culture.[37] *The loss of the individual and universal* involves rejecting individual autonomy, as individuals are products 'of powerful discourses and culturally constructed knowledge'.[38] Further, universals concerning human nature and human rights are rejected as 'at best naïve' or, '[a]t worst... an attempt to enforce dominant discourses on everybody'.[39] Pluckrose and Lindsay note:

> The postmodern view largely rejects both the smallest unit of society – the individual – and the largest – humanity – and instead focuses on small, local groups as the producers of knowledge, values, and discourses. Therefore, postmodernism focuses on sets of people who are understood to be positioned in the same way – by race, sex, or class, for example – and have the same experiences and perceptions due to this positioning.[40]

Indeed, a key concept in applied postmodernism is *positionality*. This is 'the idea that one's position in society, as determined by group identity, dictates how one understands the world and will be understood in it'.[41] Further, a person's identity may be comprised of not one 'self' but multiple 'selves', each one occupying a particular position and subject to its own privileges and oppressions.[42] Thus, any one person has intersecting privileges and oppressions, and the applied postmodernist concept of *intersectionality* explores this dynamic.[43] Pluckrose and Lindsay note that '[t]he number of axes of social

---

[36] Ibid 41.
[37] Ibid.
[38] Ibid 42.
[39] Ibid.
[40] Ibid.
[41] Ibid 118.
[42] Ibid 118.
[43] Ibid 125-128.

division under intersectionality can be almost infinite', however – and importantly – 'they cannot be reduced to the *individual*'.[44] Pluckrose and Lindsay continue:

> People often joke that the individual is the logical endpoint of an intersectional approach that divides people into smaller and smaller groups – but this misunderstands the fundamental reliance on group identity. Even if a person were a unique mix of marginalized identities, thus intersectionally a unique individual, she would be understood through each and all of those group identities ... She would not be understood as an individual.[45]

This aspect of applied postmodernism should not be overlooked. Indeed, in *Counter Wokecraft*, Pincourt and Lindsay add an additional principle to the postmodern knowledge principle and the postmodern political principle, which they call the *subject principle*:

> The subject principle is that individuals are primarily defined by their group identity (white, female, black, European, cisgendered, etc). That is to say that they are subjected to their group identity in society - which is why I call this the subject principle (this is how the post-structuralists aka the (high-) postmodernists often referred to individuals, ie as subjects). This implies that people are oppressors or oppressed according to what group/groups they are identified with. Similarly, it implies that how people behave is primarily a function of group identity, and (taken together with the political principle) that their behavior supports and helps perpetuate the oppressive systems around them unconsciously. White people for example, simply can't help but behave in ways that perpetuate their oppression over non-white people in society. Importantly, it also implies black

---

[44] Ibid 127 (emphasis in original).
[45] Ibid 127-128.

people behave in such a way that perpetuates their oppression, although from a different perspective, and that is one reason they behave differently than white people.

A corollary of this principle is that since individual behavior is defined by one's identity, individuals are responsible or accountable for actions associated with any identity to which they are associated. As such, the oppressive acts of one member of a group is the oppressive act of all members of that group. Finally, this accountability is valid across time. The oppressive act of a member of a group at one time can be attributed to a group identity (and its members) at another time.[46]

Taking up Lindsay and Pincourt's observation, the subject principle opens the door to what I term *unwarranted collective guilt*. What do I mean by this? Here, I distinguish between *warranted* and *unwarranted* collective guilt. Warranted collective guilt is finding members of a group liable when they have acted together to commit a wrong. For example, criminal laws concerning parties to offences and conspiracies are a way of finding warranted collective guilt.[47] Unwarranted collective guilt is attributing guilt to members of a group when the link between the wrongdoing and those members is tenuous or non-existent. Finding someone liable for wrongs they did not do is profoundly unjust. This includes finding them liable for the present or past actions of others.

But let's return to my overview of *Cynical Theories*. Pluckrose and Lindsay describe the influence of applied postmodernism with respect to certain academic fields, namely postcolonial theory,[48] queer

---

[46] Pincourt and Lindsay (n 13) 5-6.
[47] See, eg, *Criminal Code* (WA) chs II, LVIII.
[48] Pluckrose and Lindsay (n 12) ch 3.

theory,[49] critical race theory and intersectionality,[50] feminisms and gender studies,[51] and disability and fat studies.[52] They then describe the concept of *reified postmodernism*. Here, radical doubt about the human capacity to know reality won't do, at least not to activists.[53] Rather, there has to be *some* reality to ground their approach.[54] The reality is that of oppression,[55] and of socially constructed categories.[56] Pluckrose and Lindsay then cover the spread of applied and reified postmodernism from universities into broader culture.[57]

Both *Cynical Theories* and *Counter Wokecraft* provide ideas regarding how wokeness can be defeated. When it comes fighting wokeness in particular organisations, Pincourt and Lindsay argue for early intervention if possible.[58] Those seeking to combat it must know woke terminology and, when they see it being used, to take it seriously.[59] (Pincourt and Lindsay note that such language is used as entry points from which wokeness spreads in an organisation.)[60] Further, they argue for identifying and thwarting the appointment and advancement of the woke in organisations, and for identifying, protecting, and promoting anti-woke allies.[61]

For their part, and speaking more generally, Pluckrose and Lindsay argue for secularism, which rests on the principle that 'no matter

---

[49] Ibid ch 4.
[50] Ibid ch 5.
[51] Ibid ch 6.
[52] Ibid ch 7.
[53] Ibid 46-48.
[54] Ibid 51-52, 182-183.
[55] Ibid.
[56] Ibid 57-58, 182-183, 186.
[57] Ibid ch 9.
[58] Pincourt and Lindsay (n 13) 49, 51.
[59] Ibid 49-54.
[60] Ibid 23, 34-37.
[61] Ibid 57.

how certain you may be that you are in possession of the truth, you have no right to impose your belief on society as a whole'.[62] With this principle is 'the inalienable right to reject the moral injunctions and prescriptions of any particular ideology *without blame*'.[63] They observe that '[n]o one is subject to the *oughts* of any particular moral group, no matter how strong the conviction of its members'.[64] But '[t]he postmodernist project, especially following the applied turn – and even more so after its reification – is overwhelmingly prescriptive, rather than descriptive'.[65] So:

> [W]e must oppose the institutionalization of its belief system. Because the Social Justice movement is not officially a religion and because genuine social justice aims are in keeping with antidiscrimination legislation, it has been allowed to bypass the barriers to imposing one's belief system on others. As liberals, we must object to this imposition and defend people's rights to disbelieve in Social Justice, without incurring any form of punishment.[66]

Pluckrose and Lindsay also argue for defeating wokeness in the marketplace of ideas.[67] They observe that liberalism has an impressive track record of dealing with issues.[68] Here, they note the role of empathy:

> Humans are capable of great empathy and of horrifying

---
[62] Pluckrose and Lindsay (n 12) 263.
[63] Ibid (emphasis in original).
[64] Ibid (emphasis in original).
[65] Ibid.
[66] Ibid 264. Pluckrose and Lindsay distinguish between social justice and 'Social Justice'. The former term is concerned with addressing social inequalities: at 13. The latter term 'refers to a very specific doctrinal interpretation of the meaning of "social justice" and means of achieving it while prescribing a strict, identifiable orthodoxy around the term': at 14.
[67] Ibid 264-265.
[68] Ibid 246-248.

callousness and violence. We have evolved this way because it has been in our interest to both cooperate within our own groups and compete with others. Our empathy is therefore largely limited to those whom we see as members of our own tribe and our callous disregard and violence is reserved for those seen as competitors and traitors. By seeking to expand our circle of empathy ever wider, liberal humanism has achieved unprecedented human equality. It did so by exploiting the better part of our nature – our empathy and sense of fairness. By seeking to divide humans into marginalized identity groups and their oppressors, Social Justice risks fuelling our worst tendencies – our tribalism and vengefulness. This cannot work out well for women, or for minority groups, or for society as a whole.[69]

Pluckrose and Lindsay note the example of Martin Luther King who '[appealed] to white Americans' pride in their country as the Land of Opportunity and their sense of fairness, and making common cause with them in their hopes for the next generation. He called upon their empathy and stressed their shared humanity.'[70] They note that King would have met with less success had he adopted Robin DiAngelo's approach, '[asking] white Americans to be "a little less white, which means a little less oppressive, oblivious, defensive, ignorant, and arrogant"'.[71]

Here, it is useful to use DiAngelo's works to illustrate some of what Pluckrose and Lindsay (and Pincourt and Lindsay) have been saying. DiAngelo is an academic who facilitates workplace training on racism. She has written two influential works. The first is her article 'White Fragility'.[72] The second is her book *White Fragility: Why It's So Hard*

---

[69] Ibid 258 (citations omitted).
[70] Ibid (citations omitted).
[71] Ibid (citations omitted).
[72] Robin DiAngelo, 'White Fragility' (2011) 3(3) *International Journal of Critical Pedagogy* 54 ('White Fragility').

*for White People to Talk About Racism.*⁷³ (I will refer to the article as 'White Fragility', and the book as *White Fragility*. Hence, please note the format.) I will first comment about certain arguments that DiAngelo makes. I will then comment about empathy.

DiAngelo makes a number of arguments in both works. Examining all of them is beyond the scope of this review. My comments are directed to DiAngelo's approach to positionality, the individual, and the universal.

In 'White Fragility', DiAngelo's gives the following definition of racism:

> [Racism encompasses] economic, political, social, and cultural structures, actions, and beliefs that systematize and perpetuate an unequal distribution of privileges, resources and power between white people and people of color. This unequal distribution benefits whites and disadvantages people of color as a group.⁷⁴

In *White Fragility*, DiAngelo explores the definition of racism in more detail.⁷⁵ She argues:

> When a racial group's collective prejudice is backed by the power of legal authority and institutional control, it is transformed into racism, a far-reaching system that functions independently from the intentions and self-images of individual actors. J Kēhaulani Kauanui, professor of American studies and anthropology at Wesleyan University, explains, 'Racism is a structure, not an

---

[73] Robin DiAngelo, *White Fragility: Why It's So Hard for White People to Talk About Racism* (Allen Lane, 2019) ('*White Fragility*'). Pluckrose and Lindsay also summarise and critique *White Fragility*: see Pluckrose and Lindsay (n 12) 205-207.
[74] DiAngelo, 'White Fragility' (n 72) 56 (citations omitted).
[75] DiAngelo, *White Fragility* (n 73) 19-24.

event.'[76]

She continues:

> [R]acism – like sexism and other forms of oppression – occurs when a racial group's prejudice is backed by legal authority and institutional control. This authority and control transforms individual prejudices into a far-reaching system that no longer depends on the good intentions of individual actors; it becomes the default of society and is reproduced automatically. Racism is a system.[77]

Thus, DiAngelo identifies the structures and systems in which individuals are positioned.

DiAngelo is dismissive of individualism generally and individuals in particular. In *White Fragility*, she states:

> Individualism is a story line that creates, communicates, reproduces, and reinforces the concept that each of us is a unique individual and that our group memberships, such as race, class, or gender, are irrelevant to our opportunities. Individualism claims that there are no intrinsic barriers to individual success and that failure is not a consequence of social structures but comes from individual character. According to the ideology of individualism, race is irrelevant. Of course, we do occupy distinct race, gender, class, and other positions that profoundly shape our life chances in ways that are not natural, voluntary, or random; opportunity is not equally distributed across race, class,

---

[76] Ibid 20 (citations omitted). It should be noted that DiAngelo defines prejudice at 19 as 'pre-judment about another person based on the social groups to which that person belongs', which 'consists of thoughts and feelings, including stereotypes, attitudes, and generalizations that are based on little or no experience and then are projected onto everyone from that group'.
[77] Ibid 21.

and gender.[78]

In 'White Fragility', DiAngelo says the following with respect to individualism and white people:

> [Whites] are ... taught to value the individual and to see themselves as individuals rather than as part of a racially socialized group. Individualism erases history and hides the ways in which wealth has been distributed and accumulated over generations to benefit whites today. It allows whites to view themselves as unique and original, outside of socialization and unaffected by the relentless racial messages in the culture. Individualism also allows whites to distance themselves from the actions of their racial group and demand to be granted the benefit of the doubt, as individuals, in all cases.[79]

Indeed, to DiAngelo, it is 'narcissism' when whites 'respond defensively when linked to other whites as a group or "accused" of collectively benefitting from racism, because as individuals, each white person is "different" from any other white person and expects to be seen as such'.[80]

In a statement that recalls what has been said above concerning positionality and the subject principle, DiAngelo states:

> We bring our racial histories with us, and contrary to the ideology of individualism, we represent our groups and those who have come before us. Our identities are not unique or inherent but constructed or produced through social processes. What's more, we don't see through clear or objective eyes – we see through racial lenses. On some level, race is always at play, even in its

---

[78] Ibid 10.
[79] DiAngelo, 'White Fragility' (n 72) 59.
[80] Ibid 60.

supposed absence.[81]

As to universalism, it:

> [F]unctions similarly to the discourse of individualism but instead of declaring that we all need to see each other as individuals (everyone is different), the person declares that we all need to see each other as human beings (everyone is the same). Of course we are all humans, and I do not critique universalism in general, but when applied to racism, universalism functions to deny the significance of race and the advantages of being white. Further, universalism assumes that whites and people of color have the same realities, the same experiences in the same contexts (ie, I feel comfortable in this majority white classroom, so you must too), the same responses from others, and assumes the same doors are open to all.[82]

I make two remarks here. The first is that DiAngelo largely disregards the value of individuals. In *No Offence Intended: Why 18C is Wrong*, Lorraine Finlay, Augusto Zimmermann and I note the uniqueness of the human species[83] and of each human in it. We cite[84] the following observations by Patrick Lee and Robert P George concerning the intrinsic worth of humans:

> What distinguishes human beings from other animals, what makes human beings persons rather than things, is their rational nature. Human beings are rational creatures by virtue of possessing natural capacities for conceptual thought, deliberation and free

---

[81] DiAngelo, *White Fragility* (n 73) 85-86.
[82] DiAngelo, 'White Fragility' (n 72) 59.
[83] Joshua Forrester, Lorraine Finlay and Augusto Zimmermann, *No Offence Intended: Why 18C is Wrong* (Connor Court, 2016) 67-68, 137 ('*No Offence Intended*').
[84] Ibid 67. Please note that the excerpts I am about to quote do not have the emphasis that we placed on certain words in *No Offence Intended*.

choice, that is, the natural capacity to shape their own lives.[85]

And further:

> The capacity for conceptual thought in human beings radically distinguishes them from other animals known to us. The capacity is at the root of most of the other distinguishing features of human beings. Thus, syntactical language, art, architecture, variety in social groupings and in other customs, burying the dead, making tools, religion, fear of death... wearing clothes, true courting of the opposite sex, free choice, and morality – all of these and more, stem from the ability to reason and understand.[86]

We further note that every human is an individual unique in time and space.[87] Indeed, '[a] person's uniqueness in time and space is perhaps the one thing that they can claim against everyone and everything else.'[88] Hence, each human life has worth: when a human dies, something unique is lost.

My second remark concerns the role of humans individually and collectively in generating the type of systems and structures DiAngelo refers to, namely social constructs.[89] My departure point here is a thought experiment. In *White Fragility*, DiAngelo contends that there are far-reaching systems that function independently of individual intentions and that are reproduced automatically. However, suppose every individual in a system was removed. What would happen to it?

---

[85] Patrick Lee and Robert P George 'The Nature and Basis of Human Dignity' (2008) 21(2) *Ratio Juris* 173, 174.
[86] Ibid 184-185 (citations omitted).
[87] Forrester, Finlay and Zimmermann (n 83) 68, 138, 144.
[88] Ibid 138.
[89] DiAngelo does not appear to be referring to physical and biological systems that exist independently of human consciousness.

The answer is clear: the system would cease to exist.[90] This suggests that individuals play a critical role in creating and maintaining a system. The same can be said for the economic, political, social, and cultural structures, actions and beliefs that DiAngelo notes in 'White Fragility'. If all individuals within the structures are removed, then the structures cease to exist. If there are no individuals, then there are no beliefs, and no actions.

So individuals are important to systems and structures, but how? To answer this, I will refer to some of the work of John Searle. Searle is an analytic philosopher who has written in the fields of the philosophy of mind, the philosophy of language, and the philosophy of society. Searle's work is extensive, and a detailed examination of it is beyond the scope of this review. All I can do is provide enough detail to show the problems in DiAngelo's approach.

To Searle, human consciousness has *intentionality*, which is:

> [T]hat capacity of the mind by which it is directed at, or about, objects and states of affairs in the world, typically independent of itself. So if I believe that it is raining, fear a rise in interest rates, want to go to the movies, or prefer cabernet sauvignon to pinot noir, I am in each case in an intentional state. Intentional states are always *about* or *refer to* something. Intending, in the ordinary sense in which I intend to go to the movies, is just one type of intentional state among many others such as belief,

---

[90] It could be contended that individuals from other systems could 'revive' a system that ceased to exist. But that only underlines the importance of individuals in creating and maintaining systems. It could also be contended that other systems could revive the system that ceased to exist (rather than the individuals in those systems). However, if all individuals were removed from the other systems, then those systems would cease to exist.

desire, hope, and fear.[91]

Searle notes that intentionality is a biological phenomenon generated in the brain, as shown by hunger and thirst, desires involving bodily needs.[92] Damage to the brain can affect whether or not someone feels these desires.[93] Further, there is not only individual intentionality but collective intentionality:[94] 'wherever you have people sharing their thoughts and feelings ... you have collective intentionality'.[95] Hence, there are collective beliefs, desires, hopes, fears, and intentions.[96] That said, collective intentionality only exists in the brains of individuals – it cannot exist anywhere else.[97]

Searle distinguishes between intrinsic intentionality and derived intentionality.[98] Intrinsic intentionality is an intentional state that someone has 'regardless of what anyone else thinks about it'.[99] Derived intentionality is that 'derived from agents who have intrinsic intentionality'.[100] Importantly, Searle notes that '[a]ll linguistic

---

[91] John R Searle, *Making the Social World: The Structure of Human Civilization* (Oxford University Press, 2010) 25 (emphasis in original) (*'Making the Social World'*). It should be noted that DiAngelo uses 'intentionality' in *White Fragility* and 'White Fragility': see DiAngelo, *White Fragility* (n 73) 153; DiAngelo, 'White Fragility' (n 72) 58, 62. However, she uses 'intentionality' in the sense of 'purpose' and not 'directedness'.

[92] John R Searle, *Mind, Language and Society: Philosophy in the Real World* (Basic Books, 1999) 95 (*'Mind, Language and Society'*).

[93] Ibid.

[94] Searle, *Making the Social World* (n 91) 43; see also Searle, *Mind, Language and Society* (n 92) 118-120, John R Searle, *The Construction of Social Reality* (Free Press, 1995) 23-26 (*'The Construction of Social Reality'*).

[95] Searle, *Mind, Language and Society* (n 92) 120.

[96] Ibid 118.

[97] Searle, *Making the Social World* (n 91) 44.

[98] Searle also distinguishes intrinsic and derived intentionality from ascriptive intentionality, which is using intentional states metaphorically: see Searle, *Mind, Language and Society* (n 92) 93. My focus in this review is on intrinsic and derived intentionality.

[99] Ibid 93.

[100] Ibid.

meaning is derived intentionality'.[101] To illustrate, Searle contrasts the statement 'I am very hungry right now' with 'In French, "J'ai grand faim en ce moment" means I am very hungry right now'.[102] The former statement describes someone's intrinsic intentional state: the person is hungry, regardless of what anyone else thinks.[103] The latter statement 'is derived from the intrinsic intentionality of French speakers'.[104] He continues:

> That very sentence might have been used by the French to mean something else, or it might have meant nothing at all, and in that sense its meaning is not intrinsic to the sentence but is derived from agents who have intrinsic intentionality.[105]

To Searle, collective intentionality is the basis, ultimately, for

---

[101] Ibid.
[102] Ibid.
[103] Ibid.
[104] Ibid.
[105] Ibid.

language and social constructs.[106] However, and to repeat, collective intentionality depends on individual minds.

Here, I add observations by Daniel Kahneman and Steven Pinker. Once again, intentionality concerns what a mind is *directed at*. It is important, therefore, to discern what a mind was (or minds were) directed at when determining meaning. However, human minds have a limited capacity for attention. Daniel Kahneman observes that '[t]he often-used phrase "pay attention" is apt: you dispose of a limited budget of attention that you can allocate to activities, and if you try to go beyond your budget, you will fail'.[107]

This 'limited budget' should be kept in mind when discerning

---

[106] See Searle, *Making the Social World* (n 91) chs 3-5. DiAngelo draws on the work of Pierre Bourdieu and his concept of *habitus*, which 'is the result of socialization, the repetitive practices of actors and their interactions with each other and with the rest of the social environment. Because it is repetitive, our socialization produces and reproduces thoughts, perceptions, expressions and actions.': DiAngelo, *White Fragility* (n 73) 101; see also DiAngelo, 'White Fragility' (n 72) 57-58. However, as Searle observes in Searle, *Making the Social World* (n 91) 62 (citations omitted):

> All of the philosophers of politics and society that I know of take language for granted. They all assume that we are language-speaking animals and then they are off and running with an account of society, social facts, ideal types, political obligation, the social contract, communicative action, validity claims, discursive formations, the habitus, bio-power, and all the rest of it. It may seem odd that I claim that Habermas, Bourdieu, and Foucault take language for granted because they all have a great deal to say about it and they recognize its importance for their philosophical/sociological researches. But the problem with all of them is that they do not tell us what language is. They take it for granted that we already know what language is and go on from there.

Searle's account of intentionality's role in language and social constructs arguably provides a more complete analysis than Bourdieu's concept of *habitus*. (That said, Searle notes similarities between Bourdieu's concept of *habitus* and his own concept of the 'Background': see Searle, *The Construction of Social Reality* (n 94) 132.)

[107] Daniel Kahneman, *Thinking, Fast and Slow* (Farrar, Straus and Giroux, 1st paperback edition, 2013) 23 ('*Thinking, Fast and Slow*').

intentionality in both its intrinsic and derived forms. Attention will ordinarily be directed at denoting or describing the object or state of affairs in the world. Attention will *not* ordinarily be directed at deceiving or dominating (or both) while denoting or describing, as this takes extra effort. Such things happen, to be sure, but it is unwise to assume that they happen all or even most of the time. Here, there is much to commend a *graceful* approach. I use 'graceful' in two senses: first, skillful discernment using depth, breadth, and rigour; second, applying the principle of charity (which I detail later). Such an approach helps sort those who mean well from those who don't.

So, to illustrate with Searle's example, an individual's attention is directed at their hunger. The attention of French speakers is directed at describing the state of hunger. In neither case is attention directed at hunger *and* oppressing someone. Further, it is *not* profound or sophisticated to think that this is what is actually happening. Rather, it's paranoid. And silly.[108]

Pinker's observations concern how children can create complex languages. Pinker notes two examples. The first example concerns pidgin languages, that arise '[w]hen speakers of different languages have to communicate to carry out practical tasks but do not have the opportunity to learn one another's languages'.[109] Hence, pidgin is a 'makeshift jargon' comprised of 'choppy strings of words ... highly variable in order and with little in the way of grammar'.[110] However,

---

[108] It could be argued that individuals and groups are motivated by unconscious bias. Further, that systems and structures have a racist impact regardless of intentions. My focus is on the role of individuals in generating systems and structures. However, I address unconscious bias in (n 122). I address impact later in this review, including in (n 138).

[109] Steven Pinker, *The Language Instinct: How the Mind Creates Language* (Penguin, 1995) 20. Pinker draws on examples from the Atlantic slave trade and indentured servitude in the South Pacific.

[110] Ibid.

when children are exposed to pidgin, they create complex grammars that smooth it out.[111] The resulting language, termed a creole, has grammatical features like 'auxiliaries, prepositions, case markers and relative pronouns'.[112]

Pinker's second example concerns sign languages. In Nicaragua, prior to the introduction of schools for the deaf, the deaf were isolated from one another.[113] After schools for the deaf were introduced and gathered the deaf together, the deaf developed, in effect, a pidgin sign language.[114] However, deaf children who learned this sign language from around the age of four began to creolise it.[115] In another case, deaf parents taught sign language to their profoundly deaf son.[116] The son learned sign language from no other source.[117] The parents did not learn sign language until they were fifteen or sixteen years old, and signed badly.[118] The son, however, smoothed out the clunkiness in his parents' sign language.[119] Pinker observes that this 'is an example of creolization by a single living child'.[120] (It's almost as if an individual is creating a system…)[121]

There is something else worth noting in these examples. When creating language, the children's attention appears directed at improving the language so that it better describes things. It does not appear that the

---

[111] Ibid 21.
[112] Ibid.
[113] Ibid 24.
[114] Ibid.
[115] Ibid.
[116] Ibid 27.
[117] Ibid.
[118] Ibid 26.
[119] Ibid 27.
[120] Ibid.
[121] This is a case of creating systems that smooth out an existing system. Still, it's intriguing evidence.

children's attention is directed at creating or maintaining systems of oppression.[122]

So, individuals are important to systems and structures, as are individual and collective intentionality. Further, when individuals or groups create or use a system or structure, it is important to consider *what* their attention is directed at. True, the attention of an individual or a group may be directed at judging or treating others unfavorably on (for example) racial grounds. They may also do this while claiming that this is not what they doing. However, in many cases this is not what is happening. When considering intentionality in individuals, groups, systems, and structures, discernment is key.

---

[122] In *Thinking, Fast and Slow*, Kahneman notes that, if someone is talented, less energy is required to exercise a skill: Kahneman (n 107) 35. Kahneman says that the mind has two systems: System 1 and System 2. '*System 1* operates automatically and quickly, with little or no effort and no sense of voluntary control'; '*System 2* allocates attention to the effortful mental activities that demand it, including complex computations. The operations of System 2 are often associated with the subjective experience of agency, choice, and concentration': at 20-21 (emphasis in original). It could be argued that the children are exercising a System 1 talent for language creation, and using spare energy to implicitly (or unconsciously) oppress others. I make three points in brief reply. First, and once again, language is derived intentionality, and the children's intentional state appears directed at making their language work better. Second, the science of implicit (or unconscious) bias has significant issues with reliability and validity: see Olivia Goldhill, 'The world is relying on a flawed psychological test to fight racism', *Quartz* (Web Article, 3 December 2017). Third, attributing such unconscious motives to the children evidences hostile interpretation. There are issues with hostile interpretation for the reasons I give later in this review.

It could also be argued that making any kind of distinction in language engages in discrimination and exclusion, and is therefore oppressive. However, this is a non sequitur. Yes, it is a matter of fact that language *discriminates* by distinguishing between words, and it *excludes* properties from the definitions of words. However, it does *not* follow that this is a bad thing. If language did not do these things, it could not work. (Indeed, it would not be possible for language to distinguish good from evil, right from wrong, and freedom from oppression.) Further, arguing that 'discrimination' and 'exclusion' are necessarily bad things commits a fallacy of ambiguity between the factual and normative senses of these terms.

Here, it is worth noting the role that conventions play in discerning intentionality in general and intent in particular. Searle notes that conventions are socially recognised, repeatable devices that speakers can use regularly to convey a message.[123] Here, I add that there are what I term conventions of certainty, creativity, and possibility. What do I mean by these terms? *Conventions of certainty* are used to discern, clarify, confirm, and verify. *Conventions of creativity* are used to create new terms or expand existing ones.[124] *Conventions of possibility* are used to deal with chance.[125]

Conventions of certainty can be employed to clarify where there is confusion. We can discern such things as fact from fiction, spiritual from secular, tangible from intangible, objective from subjective, and part from whole.[126] To illustrate this I will use an example that Searle uses concerning the 'argument from conceptual relativity':[127]

> Here is how it goes. All of our concepts are made by us as human beings. There is nothing inevitable about the concepts we have for describing reality. ... For example, relative to one conceptual scheme, if I am asked 'How many objects are in this room?' I may count the various items of furniture in this room. But relative to another conceptual scheme, that does not distinguish between the elements of a set of furniture but just treats the furniture set as one entity, there will be a different answer to the question 'How many objects are there in the room?' As an answer in the first conceptual scheme, we can say that there are

---

[123] Searle, *Making the Social World* (n 91) 75-76.
[124] These conventions also concern applying existing, expanded or new terms to create fiction.
[125] Such conventions deal with the chance that something will happen, is happening, or has happened.
[126] This list is not intended to be exhaustive.
[127] Searle, *Mind, Language and Society* (n 92) 22.

seven objects in the room. Within the second scheme, there is one object. So how many are there really?[128]

Searle continues:

> There really are seven objects in the room as counted by one system of counting, and there really is only one object, as counted by another system of counting. But the real world doesn't care about which system of counting we use; each gives us an alternative and true description of the one world, using a different system of counting.[129]

Note how the conventions of certainty are being used. Through them, we can *distinguish* different systems of counting. We understand that each system *groups* and *splits* a different way. We can discern how *human-created concepts* relate to *objective, tangible* objects in *physical reality*.[130]

My point here is that, by using such conventions, it is possible for to be clear about general and specific matters. As to general matters, recall that intentionality is about what the mind is directed at. Through conventions of clarity, it is possible to discern whether minds in a group are directed at the same thing. It is possible to discern whether views differ or are shared. Individuals can discern these things with other individuals, and groups with other groups. Ultimately, it is possible to discern general (if not universal) views about objects and

---

[128] Ibid 22-23. Searle is making this argument in reply to the claim that, because we have different conceptual schemes, we cannot know reality.
[129] Ibid 23.
[130] If need be, we could also, for example, discern whether or not the situation described was fictional or the objects had spiritual significance.

states of affairs in the world.[131] Indeed, discerning such views appears to be routine. To recall Searle's example from earlier, we can arrive at general (if not universal) views about hunger. We can also arrive at such views about, for example, thirst, water, rain, soil, sky, sun, and stars. We have our differences, to be sure, and let's talk about them. But we have a lot in common, not least our shared experiences of a beautiful world and a wonderful universe. Let's talk about them too.

As to specific matters, we can discern what an individual intended to say. Misspeaking is hardly a rare occurrence. Conventions of clarity can confirm the meaning of what was said. They can clarify what the mind was directed at when speaking. Here, empathy plays a role, and this brings me to my next comment about DiAngelo's works.

One thing that has struck me about the works of wokeness is that their approach is often *graceless*. The graceless approach is the converse of the graceful one I outlined earlier. Like I did with 'graceful', I am using 'graceless' in two senses. The first sense is 'lacking skill', such as failing to apply any or all of perspective, insight, or rigour sufficiently. The second sense is 'lacking charity', that is, failing to apply the principle of charity. What is the principle of charity? As The Ethics Centre explains:

> The basic idea behind the principle of charity is thinking well of people. Those we're debating are intelligent and unlikely to be advancing stupid or illogical ideas. When a charitable listener hears something that doesn't make sense to them, they will try

---

[131] In passages from *White Fragility* and 'White Fragility' quoted earlier in this review, DiAngelo notes the effects of socialisation, and also that people see through racial lenses. Through conventions of certainty, it is possible to identify how people are socialised and how their various "lenses" work. It is also through such conventions that people can overcome the limitations that their socialisation and lenses impose. Once again, shared views are possible.

to work out what was really meant.[132]

So, '[f]or a discussion to be successful, we need to do our best to understand what a person means rather than what they explicitly say.'[133] The Ethics Centre notes the advantages of this approach:

> First, we show respect to our opponents as thinkers and as people. We don't assume we're smarter than them at the outset. Instead, we use arguments as an opportunity to learn.
>
> Second, we give ourselves the chance to hone important ethical skills. We exercise imagination and empathy to understand someone else's view before going on the attack.[134]

Pincourt and Lindsay summarise the principle of charity as follows: '[c]harity ... involves making an effort to understand what people are trying to argue while providing people the benefit of the doubt if they do so imperfectly'.[135] However, they observe:

> A common Woke technique is to abandon any pretense of charity of interpretation, which is often done by problematizing what people say independent of what they intended to say.
>
> This is justified from the [Critical Social Justice] perspective because it is assumed that people unconsciously speak to and perpetuate oppressive power structures to which they are subject. As such, even what they may have 'meant' to say is meaningless in contrast to the uncovering of the oppressive meaning that they cannot help but express.[136]

---

[132] 'Ethics Explainer: The Principle of Charity', *The Ethics Centre* (Web Article, 10 March 2017).
[133] Ibid.
[134] Ibid.
[135] Pincourt and Lindsay (n 13) 29.
[136] Ibid.

Not for nothing did Pluckrose and Lindsay title their book *Cynical Theories*: hostile interpretation is routine in the works of wokeness.[137] Pluckrose and Lindsay note the influence the Jacques Derrida. To Derrida 'the speaker's meaning has no more authority than the hearer's interpretation and thus intention cannot outweigh impact. ... [S]ince discourses are believed to create and maintain oppression, they have to be carefully monitored and deconstructed.'[138]

But why is hostile interpretation routine? I venture three reasons. First, hostility is confused with insight. A speaker cannot *possibly* mean well; rather, something dark and dangerous must drive them, and this must be exposed! Now, a speaker may be driven by fear, anger, hate,

---

[137] Pluckrose and Lindsay (n 12) 14-16, 36-37, 39-41, 131-132, 166, 239.

[138] Ibid 40. It is perhaps unsurprising that John Searle and Jacques Derrida clashed, but the Searle-Derrida debate is beyond the scope of this review. That aside, I make three brief points concerning focusing on impact and not intentions. First, there are issues with assessing statements (or actions) by the subjective impact it makes on the hearer. Such impacts can vary widely from hearer to hearer. Further, it is too easy for someone to contrive some sort of negative impact.

Second, focusing on impact often overlooks *what* is being impacted. In *No Offence Intended*, Finlay, Zimmermann and I developed the 'body/idea distinction': Forrester, Finlay and Zimmermann (n 83) 136-145, which I have developed into the 'capacity/product distinction': see Joshua Forrester, 'Rights and the Rectification of Names' (Conference Paper, NCC National Conference, 24 February 2021). As I say in the latter work at 7 (emphasis in original):'[t]here is a qualitative difference between harming a body with the *capacity* for thoughts and feelings on the one hand and, on the other, harming the *products* of those capacities, namely the thoughts and feelings themselves.' Thoughts and feelings have an intangible quality that in fact can make them very resilient: at 8. This should be considered when assessing the impact of statements about a person's (or group's) beliefs and/or practices, as beliefs and practices are ultimately sourced in thoughts and feelings.

Third, there are issues with considering impact in the context of "oppressive systems". Using DiAngelo's definition of racist systems as an example, such systems distribute privileges, resources and power unequally between whites and people of colour: see DiAngelo, 'White Fragility' (n 72) 56. Putting aside the difficulties with concepts like 'distribute', 'privilege', and 'power', labeling unequal outcomes as racist is simplistic. Such outcomes are causally complex (for a detailed exploration see Thomas Sowell, *Discrimination and Disparities* (Basic Books, 1st rev ed, 2019). Further, treating the system and all who are in it as racist is tyrannical, as it justifies "anti-racist" measures that are pervasive and drastic.

disgust, or the like. However, great care should be exercised when discerning this.[139] For example, concern should not be confused with fear, frustration with anger, dislike with hate, or unease with disgust.

The second reason is related to the first: intellectual pretention. That is, hostile interpretation is thought to be intellectually sophisticated. One *surely* must be thought clever when one shows how even innocuous statements perpetuate vast systems of oppression! If anyone disagrees, you can have them choke on a big serve of jargon salad. Perhaps this is the appeal of applied postmodernism and other woke theories: they *look* intellectually sophisticated. However, woke theories are by people who are not as smart as they think they are, for people who are not as smart as they think they are.[140] There are real issues with woke arguments concerning systems and structures. As I argued earlier, individual and collective intentionality have roles to play in systems and structures, and should be part of any analysis.

The third reason is that hostile interpretation is a power play. That is, it allows power to be wielded against the speaker. Whatever the speaker says can be disregarded, or used as the basis for state and/or societal censure. Ultimately, there is a chilling effect: if what someone says will be misconstrued and even punished, then what is the point of speaking?

But the lack of empathy goes beyond just hostile interpretation. *White Fragility* provides a stark illustration of this. DiAngelo recounts the following situation:

---

[139] Ironically, it is often easiest to discern in the works of wokeness. (Actually, it's not that ironic; Lindsay has coined 'The Iron Law of Woke Projection' for good reason: James Lindsay, 'What the Iron Law of Woke Projection Tells Us About Marxists', *New Discourses* (Web Page, 22 February 2022).)

[140] It should not surprise that this is something that can also be said of postmodernism and Marxism.

A cogent example of white fragility occurred during a workplace anti-racism training I co-facilitated with an inter-racial team. One of the white participants left the session and went back to her desk, upset at receiving (what appeared to the training team as) sensitive and diplomatic feedback on how some of her statements had impacted several of the people of color in the room. At break, several other white participants approached me and my fellow trainers and reported that they had talked to the woman at her desk, and that she was very upset that her statements had been challenged. (Of course, 'challenged' was not how she phrased her concern. It was framed as her being 'falsely accused' of having a racist impact.) Her friends wanted to alert us to the fact that she was in poor health and 'might be having a heart-attack.' Upon questioning from us, they meant this literally. These coworkers were sincere in their fear that the young woman might actually die as a result of the feedback. Of course when news of the women's potentially fatal condition reached the rest of the participant group, all attention was immediately focused back onto her and away from engagement with the impact she had had on the people of color.[141]

This is a remarkable passage, and I don't think DiAngelo realises just how bad it makes her look.[142] On DiAngelo's own account, a woman who is in poor health appears to be having a heart attack at a training that DiAngelo is co-facilitating. The woman's coworkers genuinely fear for her life. DiAngelo appears to do nothing to help a woman suffering a serious, potentially fatal, health emergency.[143] Rather,

---

[141] DiAngelo, *White Fragility* (n 73) 111.
[142] It should be noted that DiAngelo also mentions this example in 'White Fragility': DiAngelo, 'White Fragility' (n 72) 64-65.
[143] My focus is on DiAngelo's response as someone present at the workplace training seminar. There is also the matter that DiAngelo is co-facilitating this training seminar and thus is in a leadership position. Someone in her position would be expected to lead a response in a health emergency.

DiAngelo's concern is that the woman is a *distraction*, drawing attention away from the people of color.[144]

This is not a sound emotional response. Indeed, it would not have been out of place among gulag guards.[145] I daresay that this is the result of viewing people in terms of how they fit into a system. They are not viewed as individuals unique in time and space whose death is a permanent loss, but as interchangeable and replaceable cogs.

Then there is the matter of DiAngelo's towering condescension. This is evident early in *White Fragility* when DiAngelo says of white people that 'our opinions are uninformed',[146] 'we don't understand socialization',[147] and 'we have a simplistic understanding of racism'.[148] In 'White Fragility', DiAngelo asserts that whites 'have not had to build the cognitive or affective skills or develop the stamina that would allow for constructive engagement across racial divides'.[149] Further, they 'receive little or no authentic information about racism and are thus unprepared to think about it critically or with complexity'.[150] For the reasons I gave earlier, not thinking critically or with complexity is a criticism that more aptly applies to DiAngelo's approach. Being

---

[144] It could be argued that my interpretation of this passage from DiAngelo is uncharitable. To avoid doubt, I applied the principle of charity. This is an emergency situation, and it would be understandable if DiAngelo was shocked into inaction. But DiAngelo does not say this. Rather, she had enough presence of mind to think that the woman's health emergency was a distraction.

[145] Interestingly, DiAngelo observes that emotions are political, being 'shaped by our biases, beliefs and cultural frameworks': DiAngelo, *White Fragility* (n 73) 132. Even if this premise is granted, DiAngelo's response to this situation says nothing good about her own biases, beliefs and cultural frameworks.

[146] Ibid 7. Please note that the quote is a heading (as are the next two quotes). I have altered the format from the all caps and bold text in which they are formatted in *White Fragility*.

[147] Ibid 9.

[148] Ibid 13.

[149] DiAngelo, 'White Fragility' (n 72) 57.

[150] Ibid 58.

mired in identity politics, DiAngelo's perspective is limited. In fact, those whom DiAngelo criticises for considering the individual and the universal have a deeper and broader perspective than DiAngelo's.

Indeed, when I re-read *White Fragility*, I read certain examples[151] DiAngelo provides as scenes from a comedy like *The Office*. That is, DiAngelo is a clueless, Michael Scott-like character[152] who presents workplace training seminars in which she makes poor arguments and unfair accusations. She then gives laughably oblivious reasons for why people are upset. Reading the examples this way is hilarious. However, the laughter dies when reading DiAngelo's reaction to the worker apparently suffering a heart attack. Here, the fictional comparison is less Michael Scott and more *Harry Potter's* Dolores Umbridge.

As Matt Taibbi remarks, 'DiAngelo isn't the first person to make a buck pushing tricked-up pseudo-intellectual horseshit as corporate wisdom, but she might be the first to do it selling Hitlerian race theory.'[153] Indeed. If Leni Riefenstahl were around today she might have filmed a documentary praising *White Fragility's* increasing influence in academia, media, business, education, the arts, and elsewhere. Given the intellectual and emotional shortcomings in DiAngelo's approach,

---

[151] Such as the examples in DiAngelo, *White Fragility* (n 73) ch 9.
[152] Just to cover my bases, you can also read DiAngelo as a David Brent-like character from the British version of *The Office*. It is certainly arguable that David Brent is the better comparison.
[153] Matt Taibbi, 'On "White Fragility"', *TK News by Matt Taibbi* (Web Article, 29 June 2020).

perhaps it could have been called *Triumph of the Dull*.[154]

While we can joke, the fact remains that *White Fragility's* influence *has* grown, and is but a part of the growing influence of wokeness generally. Recall that DiAngelo's work includes facilitating workplace training on racism. She is far from alone. Every day, people like DiAngelo are presenting work like DiAngelo's.[155] This is a cause for deep concern because, as Elon Musk observes, '[a]t its heart, wokeness is divisive, exclusionary, and hateful. It basically gives mean people ... a shield to be mean and cruel, armoured in false virtue.'[156]

Wokeness must be fought wherever it is spread.[157] The fight won't be easy, but it is necessary. It will take place in workplaces, classrooms, boardrooms, bureaucracies, and in all forms of media, arts, and entertainment. *Cynical Theories* is an important contribution to

---

[154] This variation of *Triumph of the Will* has been used previously: see, eg, Brian Winston, 'Triumph of the dull' (2001) 11(9) *Sight and Sound* 60; Paul Krugman, 'Triumph of the dull', *New York Times* (Blog Post, 27 February 2009); Binoy Kampmark, 'The Archibald in the Yarra', *Scoop Independent News* (Web Article, 4 August 2011); 'Film Review: Zero Dark Thirty – Triumph of the dull', *Phuket News* (Web Article, 7 February 2013). However, this does not mean that it cannot be used where appropriate...

[155] Christopher F Rufo has written a number of articles concerning the use of Critical Race Theory and related theories in business and education. This is a selection of them: Christopher F Rufo, 'Walmart v Whiteness', *City Journal* (Web Article, 14 October 2021); Christopher F Rufo, 'Don't Be Evil', *City Journal* (Web Article, 8 September 2021); Christopher F Rufo, 'Intersectional AmEx', *City Journal* (Web Article, 11 August 2021); Christopher F Rufo, 'The Woke Defence Contractor', *City Journal* (Web Article, 6 July 2021); Christopher F Rufo, 'The Woke-Industrial Complex', *City Journal* (Web Article, 26 May 2021); Christopher F Rufo, 'The Wokest Place on Earth', *City Journal* (Web Article, 7 May 2021); Christopher F Rufo, 'Subversive Education', *City Journal* (Web Article, 17 March 2021); Christopher F Rufo, 'Failure Factory', *City Journal* (Web Article, 23 February 2021); Christopher F Rufo, 'Woke Elementary', *City Journal* (Web Article, 13 January 2021).

[156] The Babylon Bee, 'Full Interview: Elon Musk Sits Down with The Babylon Bee' (YouTube, 22 December 2021) 00:14:28-00:14:50.

[157] It should be clear from the context, but to avoid all doubt: I am not advocating physical violence. The fight is a philosophical one, not a physical one.

understanding wokeness. *Counter Wokecraft* builds on this, and offers tactical tips. Counterweight and *New Discourses* provide resources and support. But all of this is only a start. More philosophical weapons need to be developed and deployed. More organisations need to join the fray. Pluckrose, Lindsay, and Pincourt are out there fighting the culture war. Let's go join them.

www.ingramcontent.com/pod-product-compliance
Lightning Source LLC
Chambersburg PA
CBHW070803300426
44111CB00014B/2415